**Labour law: management decisions and workers' rights**

# Labour law

*management decisions*
*and workers' rights*

Third Edition

**Steven D Anderman** BA, LLB, MSc
Birkett Long Professor of Law, University of Essex

**Butterworths**
London, Edinburgh, Dublin
1998

| | |
|---|---|
| United Kingdom | Butterworths, a Division of Reed Elsevier (UK) Ltd, Halsbury House, 35 Chancery Lane, LONDON WC2A 1EL and 4 Hill Street, EDINBURGH EH2 3JZ |
| Australia | Butterworths, a Division of Reed International Books Australia Pty Ltd, CHATSWOOD, New South Wales |
| Canada | Butterworths Canada Ltd, MARKHAM, Ontario |
| Hong Kong | Butterworths Asia (Hong Kong), HONG KONG |
| India | Butterworths Asia, NEW DELHI |
| Ireland | Butterworth (Ireland) Ltd, DUBLIN |
| Malaysia | Malayan Law Journal Sdn Bhd, KUALA LUMPUR |
| New Zealand | Butterworths of New Zealand Ltd, WELLINGTON |
| Singapore | Butterworths Asia, SINGAPORE |
| South Africa | Butterworths Publishers (Pty) Ltd, DURBAN |
| USA | Lexis Law Publishing, CHARLOTTESVILLE, Virginia |



A CIP Catalogue record for this book is available from the British Library.

First Edition 1992
Second Edition 1993

ISBN 0 406 90189 9

Printed and bound in Great Britain by William Clowes Limited, Beccles and London

# Preface to the third edition

The third edition of this book takes the same fundamental approach to the subject of Labour Law as a form of regulation of managerial decisions as previous editions (see Preface to the first edition). It incorporates changes in the statutory framework introduced by the Employment Rights Act 1996, as well as major developments in the case law since the Second Edition. All chapters have required updating, but the most significant changes have occurred in the chapters on Discrimination (Chapter 13), Equal Pay (Chapter 14), Takeovers and Transfers (Chapter 11) and Legal Support for Trade Unions, Collective Bargaining and Employee Representation (Chapter 16), reflecting major changes in the interpretation of European Union Law. A new chapter on Maternity Rights (Chapter 8) has been added to clarify the relationship between the implemented Pregnancy Directive and the pre-existing employment protections relating to maternity leave and pay. There have also been important developments in the case law in the field of Contracts of Employment, where greater weight has been given to the enforcement of the terms of collective agreements through the mode of incorporation (Chapter 5) and in the field of Redundancy (Chapter 10), where British judges have shown a new predisposition to interpret statute law more purposively rather than assume automatically that the contractual considerations govern the interpretation of statutory terms. Just as the third edition was in its final stages, the Labour Government's White Paper, *Fairness at Work*, was published. A summary of its contents is included in the Appendix.

*Steven D Anderman*
University of Essex
August 1998

# Preface to the first edition

This book examines the subject of labour law from a new perspective. Instead of viewing labour legislation solely as a source of 'rights' for workers – implying minimum standards – it suggests that labour law can more accurately be studied as a form of regulation of managerial decisions.

In this new perspective the emphasis is placed on the way legislative rules, whatever their form, operate to strike a balance between workers' rights and another value – the value of managerial autonomy to make decisions. This is useful to highlight the way legislation as drafted often invites a regulatory line to be drawn by industrial tribunals or judges, which is not necessarily in accord with the values of Parliament. It is also a useful perspective for those who respond to labour law as a set of legal rules which must be translated by employers or trade unions into internal organisational rules.

Finally, by studying the subject from this angle, it is possible to learn more about the structure of labour law as a whole. Labour legislation is only one layer of regulation in a field in which other forms of regulation of managerial decisions abound – for example market regulation, job regulation by collective bargaining, common law regulation and regulation by European Community law. To understand how UK labour legislation functions it is necessary to see more precisely how it shares the field and interacts with these other forms of regulation. This book, therefore, sets the scene by including a section on UK legislation and new European Community legal order. It then divides the remaining chapters into three parts:

I The contractual foundations of the employment relationship;
II Individual employment legislation; and
III Collective labour legislation.

Intended for students who either wish an introduction to the subject or a second text with a particular perspective in which to place the material found in traditional textbooks, the book will also be useful for legal advisers – in whatever capacity – as well as managers and trade union officials.

While suggesting a new perspective from which to view the subject of labour law, I would like to acknowledge my indebtedness to all who have helped to establish the well travelled routes of the subject. I should also like to thank those who helped more specifically in the formulation of my ideas in the preparation for this book, in particular the late Sir Otto Kahn Freund, Professor Bob Hepple, Professor Lord Wedderburn, Dr Mark Freedland, Paul Davies, Mickey Rubenstein, David Lewis, Graham Moffat, Professor Hugh Collins, Erika Szyszczak, Bob Simpson, Gillian Morris, Pat Leighton, Professor John Wood, Professor Sheldon Leader, Peter Stone and Nick Bernard.

I would also like to thank Kathy Prior and Jane Smith for their help in the preparation of the discs for publishing.

Finally, I dedicate this book to my wife, Gunilla, and son Benjamin, for whom this book represents a period during which other activities of equal importance have been sacrificed.

*Steven D Anderman*
University of Essex
1 December 1991

# Contents

## CHAPTER 3

### THE TERMS OF EMPLOYMENT CONTRACTS: IMPLIED TERMS 37



## CHAPTER 4

### THE TERMS OF EMPLOYMENT CONTRACTS: EXPRESS TERMS 58



## CHAPTER 5

### COLLECTIVE AGREEMENTS AND CONTRACTS OF EMPLOYMENT 79



## CHAPTER 6

### WRONGFUL DISMISSAL: REMEDIES AND CONSEQUENCES FOR STATUTORY CLAIMS 96

## PART II

## INDIVIDUAL EMPLOYMENT LEGISLATION

CHAPTER 11

**REORGANISATION IN THE CONTEXT OF TAKEOVERS AND TRANSFERS 199**



CHAPTER 12

**MANAGEMENT REORGANISATIONS AND WORKERS' RIGHTS: A SUMMARY OF THE CURRENT POSITION 209**



CHAPTER 13

**SEX DISCRIMINATION 222**



CHAPTER 14

**EQUAL PAY 258**



PART III

**COLLECTIVE LABOUR LEGISLATION**

**INTRODUCTION 283**

CHAPTER 15

## RIGHTS OF ASSOCIATION 289



CHAPTER 16

## LEGAL SUPPORT FOR TRADE UNIONS AND COLLECTIVE BARGAINING AND EMPLOYEE REPRESENTATION 314



CHAPTER 17

## MANAGEMENT DECISIONS AND INDUSTRIAL ACTION 336

APPENDIX

**FAIRNESS AT WORK (CM 3968) 385**

# Table of statutes

# List of cases

**D**

## N

**Y**



**Z**

Decisions of the European Court of Justice are listed below numerically. These decisions are also included in the preceding alphabetical list.

CHAPTER 1

# Introduction

The enormous increase in labour legislation in the past four decades has thrust labour law into the role of widely regulating business decisions. Employment protection legislation, whether individual or trade union based, regulates these decisions directly by creating legal obligations for employers. Other labour legislation, focused upon trade unions and industrial action, operates more indirectly, by influencing the capacity of trade unions to engage in joint regulation with management through collective bargaining.

There is a tendency to portray these legislative provisions as conferring 'rights' upon workers, as if they provide minimum standards of protection to the right holder. In the case of individual employment legislation we commonly say, for example, that an individual employee has a 'right' not to be unfairly dismissed or discriminated against on grounds of sex or a 'right' to equal pay. Even collective labour legislation, though in form highly regulative of trade unions, is viewed as conferring upon trade unions a 'right to strike', a 'right to be informed and consulted' and for trade union members there is a 'right to trade union membership and activity'.

While the rhetoric of rights may be useful to the politician, for the lawyer, and those affected by the law, it misleads rather more than it instructs. It is probably more accurate to view labour legislation as a form of legal regulation of business activity which, like other elements of labour law, explicitly or implicitly strike a balance between the interests of management autonomy and the interests of workers' protection. For the statutory duties placed upon employers are rarely absolute. Most, if not all, incorporate some variant of a 'rule of reason' test. The phrases 'reasonably practicable', 'reasonable in the circumstances', 'justification', 'shall not unreasonably refuse', recur with sufficient regularity to ensure that the general legislative standard of protection of workers will be balanced with another value – the unfettered discretion of employers to take decisions in the course of their business activity.

The second value is rarely articulated as clearly as the first in the legislation; the legislator does no more than hint at it by the inclusion of the reasonableness qualification. There is rarely any clear indication of a legislative priority as to how the balance should be struck. As a consequence, considerable discretion is often left to the fact finder, whether tribunal or judge, to find the proper balance between the competing interests. Even where there is a Code of Practice to be taken into account in deciding cases, the actual priority in applying the reasonableness criterion is rarely spelt out.

To obtain an accurate picture of the way legislation actually regulates employers, therefore, one must closely examine the way the discretionary elements in the statutory standards have been interpreted to impinge upon management decisions. Have they been interpreted to create 'pressure points' for a change of practice on the part of management? To what extent have they instead been interpreted to create 'safety valves', allowing managers to preserve the essentials of the status quo prior to the legislation?

The intention of this book is to examine the subject of labour law, in large measure, by emphasising the way labour legislative rights regulate managerial decisions. One object of the exercise is to highlight the fact that the form in which legislation is drafted, allows a regulatory line to be drawn by interpretation by tribunals and judges which is not necessarily in accord with legislative values and intentions.

There is, however, a second reason for using this perspective. We can by its use learn more about the way legislation fits into the wider structure of labour law. Labour legislation in the UK, whatever its appearance, does not impose a code of mandatory rights and duties in a vacuum. The reality is that it is only one layer of regulation inserted into a field in which other forms of regulation of managerial decisions abound: managerial self-regulation, market regulation, job regulation by collective bargaining, common law regulation and Community law. To understand how UK labour legislation functions it is necessary to see more precisely how it shares the field and interacts with these other forms of regulation.

## MANAGERIAL INITIATIVES AND LABOUR LAW

A good starting point for a regulatory perspective is to recognise quite explicitly that many of the managerial decisions that labour law attempts to regulate are those which are part of a series implementing earlier investment decisions by management to commit capital resources to a particular type of business operation.[1] In implementing such investment

1 Cf discussion of the relationship between strategic management decisions and personnel decisions in Purcell 'The Impact of Corporate Strategy on Human Resource Management' in Storey *New Perspectives in Human Resource Management* (1991).

decisions managers exercise an initiative choosing the location of the operation, the size of the workforce and the mix of labour to be used, the occupational structure and the hours of work. This initiative extends to subsequent decisions to open and close plants, increase and decrease, organise and reorganise workforces. By making such choices, management decisions in the aggregate help to determine the overall labour market structure. At a company or establishment level, decisions in respect of recognition or derecognition, and management 'strategies' towards trade unions and collective bargaining influence collective labour relations by shaping the institutional arrangements.[2] They also affect individual employment. Management, personnel and human relations approaches influence the structure of rules in individual firms in the form of employee handbooks, work rules, procedures, job descriptions, etc.

These rules include an element of self-regulation by employers. However, they also ensure that, even where there is collective bargaining, and protective labour legislation, workers experience employment as entering into a managerial system of rules governing their daily relations and their rights vis-à-vis their employer.[3]

This is not meant to diminish the importance of trade unions and workers as key actors in the drama of employment and labour relations, nor to underestimate the potential for collective bargaining to provide a countervailing source of social power to, and indeed a mechanism for participation in, management decisions. Nor is it to underestimate the potential of legislation to regulate employers' decisions. It is simply to establish the point that management initiatives *as a matter of fact* set the stage upon which the drama unfolds and provide much of its initial direction.

## MARKET REGULATION

As a matter of further fact, these investment-implementing initiatives of management are regulated by the competitive forces of the particular product and services markets in which their firms are located. These markets impose a discipline upon managers, punishing poor choices by ultimate business failure.[4] However, they also leave some room within

2 See Part III Introduction.

3 See Collins, H 'Market Power, Bureaucratic Power and the Contract of Employment' (1986) 15 ILJ 1 at 4.

4 The market also arguably exerts pressures upon management through the market for corporate control. See eg Bradley 'Corporate Control: Markets and Rules' [1990] MLR 170.

which managers may make choices, for managerial decisions on labour market issues may take some time before they affect the competitive position of a firm on the product market. Market forces therefore create some space for trade unions and legislation to influence managerial choices. At the same time, however, such influence must be exercised within the parameters of market forces in the sense that in so far as they affect a company's competitive position, mistakes at this level are eventually punished.

## COLLECTIVE BARGAINING AND THE REGULATION OF MANAGEMENT DECISIONS

Although collective agreements are not directly legally binding between employers and trade unions,[5] collective bargaining is underpinned by the potential threat of employees to strike and cause economic damage to the firm, and therefore it operates as an important social constraint upon managerial discretion providing a basis to reverse or modify managerial decisions. If managerial initiatives are not to be forced through they must be 'sold' to employees and their representatives. However, while collective bargaining is a system of conflict resolution which results in joint trade union/management regulation, its scope in fact has generally been confined to the lower levels of managerial decision making – wages, hours and other terms – rarely if ever reaching into investment and financial decisions. Moreover, it does not act solely as a counterweight to managerial authority but helps to reinforce it both explicitly, by the way collective agreements are drafted and procedures are designed, and implicitly, by the assumptions of the parties about managerial prerogative as a quid pro quo for workers' rights.[6]

## LABOUR LAW AND THE REGULATION OF MANAGEMENT DECISIONS

The common law and labour legislation both regulate management decisions, though their characteristics as regulatory processes differ markedly.

5 See discussion, Ch 5.
6 See Ch 5; see too Storey *Managerial Prerogative and the Question of Control* (1983) Ch 6; Storey *The Challenge to Management Control* (1980) Ch 2.

## Common law and management decisions

The contract of employment at common law creates reciprocal rights and duties for both employer and employee. In addition to the express terms of the contract, there are standard fundamental obligations imposed on employees to obey lawful orders to co-operate and to faithfully serve employers in exchange for employers' obligations, among others, to pay agreed remuneration, to provide safe work and not to undermine the trust and confidence in the relationship.

These terms give a strong legal foundation for managerial authority and the exercise of managerial discretion, retaining certain of the features of an earlier period when the contract of employment far more unambiguously underpinned the authority of the employer.[7] Moreover, the drafting power of the employer can be used with effect to shape the express terms of the contract in ways which are conducive to reserving managerial discretion.

From a regulatory point of view, however, these common law implied terms, together with the express terms of the employment contract and terms incorporated from collective agreements also provide a set of legal constraints upon managerial decisions in the form of an action for breach of contract or wrongful dismissal, whenever a term of the contract, whether express (Ch 4) or implied (Ch 3), is broken by the employer.

By viewing the contract of employment in terms of its role as a regulator of employer decisions, one's interest is drawn to a particular set of questions. To what extent does the contract on balance confer legal powers of unilateral decision-making upon management? What precisely are the legal constraints upon the exercise of that discretionary authority? How effective are they in influencing managerial decisions?

## Labour legislation and management decisions

Labour legislation, as we have seen, cannot be regarded as a straightforward imposition of a code of mandatory rights and duties upon individuals and organisations. For the new layers of statutory regulation only partially displace and modify the pre-existing systems of managerial discretion, contractual regulation and collective bargaining.

Many of the individual employment protection statutes have conditions of eligibility which preclude certain forms of 'atypical' contractual relationships, individuals without a minimum period of continuous service or hours of work per week. Since employers may choose the form of contract to offer employees, they are in a position to influence the extent to which statutory protection is applicable. Other statutory provision, eg

7 See Davies and Freedland *Labour Law: Texts and Materials* (2nd edn) p 311.

unfair dismissal, redundancy payment, etc, have been drafted in a form which allows the terms of the individual contracts to determine the actual standard of statutory protection. In the event a measure of deregulation may be built into the legislation.

Second, as mentioned before, employment protection laws, whether employee or trade union based, contain a definition of employers' obligations which incorporates a 'reasonableness' test. The precise form may vary but built into the fabric of almost all regulatory legislation are discretionary elements in which the balance struck between workers' rights and autonomy for organisational decisions will significantly affect the actual standard established by the statutory right. In the event, to obtain an accurate picture of the way the legislation actually regulates employers, the legislation must be analysed with a particular emphasis on the way in which the legal duty has been drafted and interpreted to impinge upon managerial discretion. What patterns can be discerned in the interpretation of legislation in respect of the balance struck between the two competing values of worker protections and managerial autonomy?

Finally, as mentioned, the law of industrial action, while directed at trade union organisations and trade union members, can be viewed as part of the statutory framework for business decisions. For it operates to control the form and the scope of industrial action and thereby influences the capacity of trade unions to use collective bargaining to place constraints upon management decisions. In the event, the legal rules regulating industrial action, whether statutory or judicial, can usefully be studied in the perspective of regulating managerial decisions.

In the course of studying the way in which statute law and judicial interpretation in the UK create 'pressure points' and 'safety valves' for managerial discretion, we have a ready-made basis of comparison with EC law. Today, given the membership of the UK in the EC and the development of its social policy by legislation and judicial interpretation since 1972, it is no longer possible to study UK labour law without an understanding of EC labour law on its own terms and its relationship with UK labour law. We have long tended to think of UK and EC law as two separate systems. Within certain spheres of labour law, however, it is increasingly clear that this is no longer the case; a measure of integration has taken place. In the process, we also have a basis for comparison of regulatory styles and techniques. For there are distinct differences in the approach to the regulation of business decisions in the EC and the UK. The social market and social democratic consensus in the EC, as well as the civil law tradition, have led to different methods of legal regulation. To what extent does EC law, by comparison with UK law, provide a mode of regulation which strikes a different balance between the values of management autonomy and worker protection? To what extent is this reflected in legislative standards? To what extent is it noticeable in the techniques of judicial interpretation of legislative standards? Throughout the book comparisons will be made on these points.

The study will be divided into three main parts. In Part I we shall look at the contractual foundations of the employment relationship. In Parts II and III we shall look at the legislation: Part II concentrating on individual employment legislation and Part III considering collective labour legislation. Before this is done, however, it is necessary to set the scene by looking at the relationship between UK labour legislation and the new European Community legal order.

CHAPTER 2

# Setting the scene: UK labour legislation and the new EC legal order

## A UK LABOUR LEGISLATION

The regulatory legislation in the UK of the past three decades, in marked contrast to earlier legislation,[1] takes the form of general labour standards, applicable in principle if not in practice to a wide group of workers. One important reason for this has been that much of this legislation was, in fact, prompted by obligations incurred by Britain as part of its membership in international organisations, such as the International Labour Organisation (ILO), the Council of Europe and the European Community, which have been committed each in its own way to developing general legal minimum standards of protection.[2]

The motives of these organisations for this legislation were mixed. There was clearly a concern to provide acceptable minimum standards of legal protection for workers but this was prompted by economic as well as social considerations. These organisations were particularly concerned to reduce disparate labour costs as an element influencing competition between countries.

For example, the Conventions and Recommendations of the ILO have been motivated in large measure by the concern of employers and trade unions in the higher wage, higher labour standard countries to reduce distortions to commercial competition between countries stemming from the lower pay and conditions of work in the lower labour cost countries. In the European Community (EC), there has been a strong impetus to

1 Prior to the 1960s, regulatory legislation concentrated upon a narrow range of issues applying to specific targeted groups of workers who were not adequately protected by collective bargaining: the Factory Acts, Truck Acts and Wages Act. See eg Deakin and Wilkinson *Labour Law, Social Security and Economic Equality* IER p 35.

2 See eg Davies and Freedland *Labour Legislation and Public Policy* (Clarenden Press, Oxford, 1993).

harmonise working conditions within the European Union as a whole, partly to ensure that all member states are competing equally on an economic front and partly to ensure social cohesion and harmony as the member states move ever closer to a common market.

Within Britain, furthermore, employment protections were introduced not simply to help to create general standards but more specifically as a method of spreading enlightened managerial policies and hence improving managerial efficiency. Redundancy payments, unfair dismissals, disclosure of information, and the time off provisions, each in their own way have been designed to affect managerial practice as well as provide employees with protective rights. In recognition of this point a series of Codes of Practice accompany the legislation which spell out in considerable detail the nature of employers' statutory duties.

Although the sources of protective labour legislation have not been solely trade union based and have had their roots in wide public concerns of both a social and an economic nature, much of the employment protection legislation of the 1970s has been viewed as linked with the Social Contract between the Labour government and the TUC during that period. For the 'labour standards' legislation was enacted in conjunction with provisions which gave trade unions rights of association and legal support for recognition,[3] and ensured that rates of pay and other terms and conditions established by collective bargaining in any industry or district could be extended to other groups of workers.[4]

Moreover, the collective rights to consultation, whether based on EC directives, such as the collective redundancy provisions,[5] or based on domestic policy, such as the Health and Safety at Work etc Act 1974,[6] were given to recognised trade unions rather than employee representatives more generally. Furthermore, the employment rights protections were accompanied by a set of trade union immunities that created a wide right to strike: trade unions themselves were not liable in tort and industrial action taken in contemplation or furtherance of a trade dispute was lawful even if it involved secondary action, ie action against an employer uninvolved in the primary dispute. Finally, the Social Contract also involved a form of co-operation between government and trade unions which was meant to help to manage the economy by a form of central co-ordination of wage levels established by collective bargaining.

When the Conservative government assumed power in 1979, it was determined to break with the Social Contract legislative policy of the Labour government of 1974–1979, as well as the legislative policies of

3 Employment Protection Act 1975, s 11.
4 Employment Protection Act 1975, Sch 11.
5 Now TULR(C)A 1992, ss 188–98.
6 See eg s 5.

previous Conservative governments. It had decided that policies based on attempts to achieve a consensus with trade unions on incomes restraint in conjunction with macroeconomic measures to maintain employment levels had been discredited by the performance of the British economy. It felt that the strategic way forward in terms of overall economic management was to allow market forces and economic competition to have a greater influence upon the British economy. This, it was thought, would improve business efficiency and Britain's economic competitiveness internationally, and hence maintain or even improve standards of living. This new market ideology entailed a radically new view of labour legislation as well as trade unions.

Labour legislative policy, influenced by the writings of Hayek,[7] was based on the view that both employment legislation and trade unions were restraints impeding the workings of the labour market.

The employment protection laws enacted in the 1960s and 1970s were viewed as obstacles to the effective working of markets in general and of the labour market in particular.[8] The statutory trade union rights propped up collective bargaining resulting in 'trade union rates' instead of market rates. The individual employment protection legislation burdened industry by making excessive administrative demands on small and medium-sized firms which acted as a disincentive to their growth and employment creation. The legislative prescription that followed from this diagnosis was to 'deregulate' business activity by lifting the burden of employment legislation and decollectivise employment relations.[9]

Trade unions were viewed as labour monopolies, often propped up by the coercive measures of the closed shop.[10] Viewed in this perspective, trade unions interfered with the working of the labour market, producing higher labour costs and higher unemployment than that which would result from a 'free' market. This perspective gave little weight to the role of trade unions as a collective counterweight to managerial power on behalf of employees with inadequate bargaining power as individuals. The labour legislation which gave trade unions a wide right to strike underpinning collective bargaining was regarded as conferring excessive privileges rather than essential rights.

The changed view of the legitimacy of trade unions as bargaining representatives on behalf of employees was accompanied by a

7 See Wedderburn 'Freedom of Association and Philosophies of Labour Law' (1989) ILJ 1 at p 7.

8 See Chancellor of the Exchequer's Budget Statement, March 1985 HC Official Report, 19 March 1985 Col 792.

9 See eg Department of Employment *Building Business, not Barriers: Lifting the Burden* (1986) London.

10 See Wedderburn 'Freedom of Association and Philosophies of Labour Law' (1989) ILJ 1 at p 7.

determination to reduce the role of trade unions as political representatives at national level. Informal and formal discussions between trade union leaders and ministers were virtually ended. The extensive membership of trade unions in governmental and quasi-administrative bodies such as the National Economic Development Organisation in Health and Safety Commission, the Manpower Services Commission (now the Training Commission) and the Advisory, Conciliation and Arbitration Service, etc, which had been built up by succeeding governments was to be reduced if not altogether eliminated. Resort to incomes policies, whether statutory or voluntary, was unthinkable, although the state could operate a co-ordinated wages and salary policy in the public sector by virtue of being an employer. Finally, the legislative support for the political funds, which provided links between the trade unions and the Labour party, was to be re-examined.

## (i) The Conservative government's attempt to reduce trade union power

This diagnosis of the position of trade unions led to a fundamental change in the legislative framework to reduce the power of trade unions on three fronts: in their relationship with employers; in their relationships with individual employees, whether members or non-members; and in their relationship to the Labour Party.

The programme of trade union legislation introduced by the Conservative government involved six major stages: the Employment Acts of 1980 and 1982, the Trade Union Act 1984, the Employment Acts of 1989 and 1990 and the Trade Union Reform and Employment Rights Act 1993.[11] These enactments, together with other legislative developments,[12] introduced five major changes to the legal framework for industrial relations: first, the trade union immunities for industrial action have been considerably narrowed; second, trade unions have been made legally responsible for industrial action; third, the process of preparing lawful, official industrial action has been regulated by a requirement for strike ballots and notification; fourth, special measures have been introduced to make unofficial strikers legally vulnerable; and fifth, individuals have been given protection of their right to refuse to join trade unions (Ch 14) and

11 These six acts are now, for the most part, consolidated into the Trade Union and Labour Relations (Consolidation) Act 1992.

12 For example the Wages Act 1986 (now Part II of the Employment Rights Act 1996), the Sex Discrimination Act 1986, the Employment Act 1989 etc.

trade union members have been given statutory rights against trade union organisations (Ch 16).

These will be examined in Part III of this book.

## (ii) The programme of 'deregulation'

The Conservative government was also committed to a policy of 'deregulation' of individual employment and decollectivisation of employment relations.[13]

### *(a) The 'deregulation' of collective bargaining legislation: 'decollectivisation'*

The Conservative Government's programme of decollectivisation dismantled the legal supports for collective bargaining: both the legislation providing for compulsory recognition of trade unions by employers and the statutory supports for collective bargaining which directly affected wage rates. In 1979 a statutory order abolished the statutory recognition procedure introduced by the Employment Protection Act 1975 (see Ch 15). Subsequently, a series of provisions were enacted, which while not designed solely or primarily with the recognition issue in mind nevertheless changed the legal framework from one which was positively encouraging to one which is distinctly unfriendly to recognition attempts by groups of employees. The trade union immunities were progressively narrowed to make unlawful the use of sympathetic or secondary action to support recognition and industrial action against an employer to obtain or maintain 'union-only' or 'recognition' clauses in commercial contracts.[14] Moreover, employers were given an ever-widening immunity to dismiss their work-force for engaging in industrial action (see Ch 16). Finally, in 1993, the protection of individual union membership was reduced in cases where employers used financial incentives to persuade employees to abandon collective bargaining and accept personal contracts (see Ch 14).

The second target of the deregulation programme were the legal measures which more directly propped up wage levels and extended 'union wage rates'. First, the statutory procedure which allowed recognised trade unions unilaterally to refer an employer to arbitration by the Central Arbitration Committee to determine whether he had been providing pay or other terms and conditions of employment which fell below the minimum rates established by collective bargaining, was repealed. Then,

13 See Budget Statement by N Lawson, March 1985 HC Official Report, 19 March 1985 col 792.

14 The Labour Government plans to retain these elements of the legal framework while reforming others: see 'Fairness at Work' (1998, Cm 3968), Appendix below.

in 1983, the government rescinded the Fair Wages Resolution which required employers renewing public contracts to match prevailing rates established by collective bargaining. Later, it dismantled the Wages Council's machinery which provided statutory minimum wages for employees in specific low paid sectors.[15] Firstly, in 1986, it excluded all workers under 21.[16] Then in 1993 it repealed all Wages Council protection for the 2.8 million low paid part of the workforce, most women, many part-time, many non-unionised.[17]

Finally, the government introduced legislative 'guidelines' for management conduct, a new type of essentially permissive legislation designed to stave off a regulatory framework of mandatory legislation on consultation and information. In the Employment Act 1982, s 1 required that the boards of directors of public limited companies with more than 250 workers include in their annual reports to shareholders a statement of the action 'taken during the year to provide employees with information and to consult them or their representatives'.

The government attempted, moreover, to export its deregulatory approach to the European Community. Almost all new directives proposed by the European Commission for legislation in its Social Action programme were discouraged by Britain in informal discussion and vetoed in the Council of Ministers. The British government argued that Codes of Practice within guidelines to management in the form of codes rather than mandatory legislation should be the standard means of implementing social policy in the EC and that social legislation would raise costs for industry leading to unemployment.[18]

### *(b) The deregulation of individual employee rights*

The deregulation of individual employment protections was designed to ensure that employment relations reverted 'to the basic principle that terms and conditions of employment are matters to be determined by the employer, and by the employee concerned, where appropriate through their own representatives, in the light of their own individual circumstances', in effect to restore the contract of employment as the framework for employment relations.[19] This, it was thought, would lift the burden of potential legislation upon employers, particularly small employers, and

15 Department of Employment *Wages Councils Consultative Document* December 1988.
16 Wages Act 1986, s 12(3).
17 Trade Union Reform and Employment Rights Act 1993 s 35.
18 See eg Department of Employment and Department of Trade and Industry Joint Consultative Document on Draft Directive for Information Procedures, November 1983.
19 Department of Employment 'Building Businesses, Not Barriers' (1986) London, para 22.

create a climate which was favourable to enterprise.[20] Despite empirical evidence to the contrary,[1] the government was convinced that employment protections such as unfair dismissal, maternity leave, guarantee payments and sex discrimination legislation were creating a web of legal regulation for small businessmen that was so burdensome as to discourage them from employing more people. Hence one focus of deregulation was to restrict the scope of such legislation by extending the qualifying periods or by reducing the extent of benefit. The service qualification for redundancy payment, unfair dismissal, the higher level of maternity payment and the right to a written statement of the reasons for dismissal was extended to two years.[2] The burden of proof placed on the employer to prove 'reasonableness' in unfair dismissals cases was removed and a more neutral evidentiary test was established.[3] The substantive test of reasonableness was modified so that the size and administrative resources of the employer had to be explicitly taken into account.[4] A waiver of rights to unfair dismissal could be inserted in fixed term contracts of one year or more (the former minimum period of fixed term contracts for waiver was two years) and exceptions were introduced for the formerly 'irreducible minimum' basic award.[5] Pre-hearing assessments were introduced with the purpose of weeding out unmeritorious claims and in some cases imposing a deposit of £150 for an employee to pay as a condition to bring a claim of unfair dismissal. There were restrictions introduced to the entitlement to statutory guarantee pay and firms of five or fewer employees were given complete exclusion from employees having a right to return to work after maternity leave. Moreover, all employees claiming the right to return to work after maternity leave had to meet a new formal notification requirement.[6] The Truck Acts' protection on payment of wages was repealed and replaced by a less restrictive form of protection – the Wages Act 1986.[7] The Factories Act's restrictions on women's hours of work were repealed. Even the Health and Safety at Work etc Act was modified to allow firms with less than 20 employees to dispense with the publication of their safety policies and their written statements to employees setting out disciplinary procedures.[8] Finally, accompanying the deregulation of

20 Ibid.
1 See eg Daniel 'The Impact of Employment Laws' (1978).
2 See eg ERA s 98.
3 Now ERA s 98(4).
4 Ibid.
5 ERA ss 197 and 122 respectively.
6 ERA s 80.
7 Now Part I of the Employment Rights Act 1996.
8 SI 1975/1584.

employment legislation was a comprehensive reduction in the scope of social security legislation.[9]

### *The constraints upon deregulation*

In contrast to their freedom to reformulate the legislative framework for trade unions and industrial action the Conservative government's attempts to implement a fully-fledged policy of 'deregulation' were subject to three major constraints.

In the first place, despite its rhetoric of deregulation, the government had to make some concession to the expectation of the electorate to have individual legal rights at work. Thus the government gave an assurance in the 1986 White Paper that 'there is no intention to dismantle the whole framework of employment protection in current legislation'.[10] And in the debate on the Employment Act 1989 a government spokesman stated that the intentions of the amendments to the EPCA was to strike 'an appropriate balance' between safeguarding employees' rights and enabling employers to improve their competitiveness and create new job opportunities.[11] In the event the government left many of the individual employment protections in place but restricted in their application, resulting in an inequality of treatment to employees depending upon their length of continuous employment, hours of work, etc (see Ch 7).

A second constraint on the policy of deregulation consisted of the new developments at common law accompanying the reduction and removal of legislative restrictions on employers. Employees, whether or not they qualify for statutory protections, can now enforce a wider range of rights against employers in the ordinary courts under their contracts of employment. The common law rules now place upon employers a general duty not to destroy the trust and confidence of the employment relationship[12] (see Ch 3). Moreover, the ordinary courts will now entertain common law actions by employees to enforce their rights under grievance and disciplinary procedures where these have been incorporated into their employment contracts[13] (see Ch 6). Finally, in several recent cases, employees have successfully brought claims for breach of contract against

9 Deakin and Wilkinson *Labour Law, Social Security and Economic Inequality* IER (1989) p 3; see also Deakin and Wilkinson *The Economics of Employment Rights* (1991) IER.

10 *Building Businesses . . . Not Barriers* para 7.2.

11 Lord Trefgarne, Hansard HL Debates col 523 (14 July 1989).

12 See eg *Woods v W M Car Services (Peterborough) Ltd* [1981] ICR 666, [1981] IRLR 347.

13 *Gunton v Richmond-upon-Thames London Borough Council* [1981] Ch 448, [1980] ICR 755; *Irani v Southampton and South West Hampshire Health Authority* [1985] ICR 590, [1985] IRLR 203; *Dietman v Brent London Borough Council* [1988] ICR 842, [1988] IRLR 299, CA.

employers based on terms incorporated from collective agreements into their employment contracts[14] (see Ch 5). The common law now provides an expanded second tier regulatory framework for the exercise of managerial discretion which applies even in the absence of legislation.

A third, and probably more substantial, constraint upon the British government's freedom to deregulate protective legislation was its membership in the European Community. Membership in the EC means that, in general, UK law is subordinate to the provisions of the Treaty of Rome, the Single European Act as well as the regulations and directives made under the Treaty. We can see dramatic evidence of this in the amendments considerably strengthening health and safety protections, maternity rights, transfer of undertakings and redundancy consultation legislation, contained in TURER 1993[15], which were compelled by community law. Membership also means in particular that the UK is subject to the strong impetus to harmonise working conditions and hence 'labour costs' within the European Community, one which is built into the very fabric of Title III of the Treaty of Rome, 'Social Policy', and influences the decisions of the European Court of Justice in interpreting those provisions.[16]

To understand labour law in the UK, therefore, it is essential to obtain a clear understanding of the way the social policy in the European Community impinges upon UK labour law. This in turn requires a basic knowledge of the logic of the 'new legal order' created by European Community law.

## B UK LAW AND THE NEW EUROPEAN COMMUNITY LEGAL ORDER

With the accession of the UK to the Treaty of Rome in 1972 it was initially necessary to incorporate Community law into national law by means of a further enactment. For the UK subscribes to a 'dualist' doctrine of international law, according to which the national and international systems are separate systems independent of each other and the rules of international law can be applied domestically only after their translation into national rules.

14 See eg *Rigby v Ferodo Ltd* [1988] ICR 29, [1987] IRLR 516, HL.
15 See Chs 8, 11 (transfer of undertakings), 13 (maternity rights and sex discrimination) and 16 (collective redundancies).
16 The Labour government has now proposed a series of changes in a white paper 'Fairness at Work'. These proposals are summarised in the Appendix.

The European Communities Act 1972 which incorporated the Treaty into UK law was, however, no ordinary dualist enactment. In s 2(1) it provides that

> 'all such rights, powers, liabilities, obligations and restrictions *from time to time* created or arising by or under the Treaties, and all such remedies and procedures from time to time provided for by or under the Treaties, as in accordance with the Treaties are without further enactment to be given legal effect or used in the United Kingdom *shall be recognised and available in law, and be enforced, allowed and followed accordingly* . . .' (emphasis added)

The effect of this enactment was to commit UK law to a body of Community law as it evolves. Instead of two separate systems, we had now entered a new legal order, in 'which the States have limited their sovereign rights, albeit within limited fields'.[17] One reassurance to the UK government at the time perhaps was the requirement in the Treaty of Rome for unanimity in the Council of Ministers for most new legislation, particularly labour legislation. Another was the Luxembourg Accord.

However, the commitment to Community law went beyond the legislative level. It also applied to the case law developed by the Court of Justice interpreting the legislation. To understand the way EC labour law has had an impact upon UK labour law therefore it is necessary to look at two developments:

(a) the development of Community legislation under the Treaty by the Council of Ministers; and
(b) the development of legal rules in the case law referred to the European Court of Justice.

## (a) The development of Community legislation under the Treaty by the Council of Ministers

When the Conservative government signed the Treaty of Rome in 1972 there was little in the Treaty itself to suggest the extent of the Community's commitment to an active social policy. In Title III, 'Social Policy', the Treaty committed itself in general terms to 'harmonisation' of labour standards but Article 119 – 'equal pay for equal work' – was its only substantive provision. Article 117, repeating the preamble to the Treaty, provided that member states agree upon the need to promote improved working conditions and an improved standard of living for workers, so as to make possible their harmonisation while the improvement is being

17 *Algemene Transport-en Expeditie Onderneming van Gend and Loos NV v Nederlandse administratie der belastingen*: 26/62 [1963] ECR 1, ECJ.

maintained. Article 118 required the Commission to promote close co-operation between states in the social field, particularly in matters relating to employment law, working conditions, vocational training, social security, prevention of occupational accidents and diseases, the right of association and collective bargaining.

Although neither of these articles provided a secure legal base upon which to expand social policy, they were accompanied by Article 100 which empowered the Council of Ministers to issue directives by unanimous vote on a proposal by the Commission for the approximation or harmonisation of the laws, regulations or administrative action of the member states which could directly affect the establishment of the Common Market.

Moreover, Article 235 provided another legal base for social policy measures in cases where there was a need for Community action to attain one of the objectives of the Treaty in the course of the operation of the Common Market and where the Treaty of Rome did not otherwise provide the necessary powers.

It was possible to read into the absence of substantive commitment in the original treaty an acceptance of a free market approach to social policy in which the improvement of standards of living would occur as an automatic consequence of the functioning of a 'Common Market'.[18] It was equally possible, however, that there was a concern to achieve harmonisation but an unpreparedness to spell out the precise mode of social regulation at that time.[19]

Certainly by 1972 there was little doubt that a coalition of member states had arrived at the view that there was a need to establish a social market dimension to the Community. At the Paris summit meeting in October 1972 a final communiqué was issued which made the point:

> 'The Heads of State or Heads of Government emphasised that they attached as much importance to rigorous action in the social field as to the achievement of the Economic and Monetary Union. They thought it essential to ensure the increasing involvement of labour and management in the economic and social decisions of the Community . . .'

This led to the Social Action Programme of 1974–1976,[20] which resulted in a series of directives in the period 1974–1979, based either on Article 100 or Article 235, by a unanimous vote of the Council of Ministers. The main legislative measures which emerged from this programme were fewer

18 See eg Szyszczak 'L'espace Sociale Europée Reality Dreams or Nightmares' [1990] *German Yearbook of International Law* 284.

19 Cf Collins, D *The European Social Policy of the First Phase* (1975) London.

20 The Commission's draft proposals for a social action programme were passed in a resolution of the Council of Ministers on 21 January 1974.

in number and less ambitious than the original set of Commission proposals. They fell into two categories:

(i) the Equal Treatment Directives:

Equal Pay Directive
75/117/EEC
Equal Treatment Directive
76/107/EEC
State Social Security Directive
79/7/EEC

and

(ii) the directives concerned with information, consultation and the protection of employment rights when undertakings are restructured:

Directive on Collective Redundancies
75/129/EEC
Directive on Acquired Rights
77/187/EEC
Directive on Insolvency
80/987/EEC.

With the change in UK government in 1979, any opportunity for further development of new social legislation was lost. The Conservative government, taking the view that the way to achieve a social dimension in Europe was to limit the regulation of business so as to provide new jobs, blocked almost all new proposals for social legislation.[1] Only health and safety at work measures and the Directive on Equal Treatment in Occupational Social Security 86/378/EEC[2] and Equal Treatment for the Self-Employed 86/613/EEC[3] were allowed through.

During this period, however, the UK government signed the Single European Act which provided amendments to the Treaty with the aim of achieving a common internal market by the end of 1992. The Single European Act introduced changes to Title III of the EEC Treaty by adding Article 100A which allows qualified majority voting within the Council of Ministers for the adoption of 'measures necessary for the establishment and the functioning of the internal market'. However, at the UK's insistence, Article 100A, Part 2 specifically excluded qualified majority voting in cases where provisions relate to 'the rights and interests of employed persons'.

1 Among the measures blocked were the proposals for Directives for part-time work, temporary work and a recommendation on the reduction and reorganisation of working time.
2 OJ L 255/86.
3 OJ L 359/56.

The SEA also added Articles 118A and B to Title III.[4] Article 118A requires member states to pay particular attention to encouraging improvements, especially in the working environment, as regards the health and safety of workers, and empowers the Council to adopt directives by a qualified majority. It was on this somewhat unsteady legal foundation that the implementation of the European Charter of Fundamental Social Rights had to proceed. In 1992, the Treaty of European Union (Maastricht) introduced further amendments to Articles 117-122 which were initially contained in a separate Social Policy Agreement and a Protocol to the Treaty, the 'Social Chapter', and which, initially, did not bind the UK. With Labour's accession to power in 1997, however, and its acceptance of the Social Chapter, the Chapter was incorporated into the Treaty drafted at the Amsterdam ICG of 1998. Yet the issue of the appropriate legal base for EC directives and regulations remains.[5]

The Social Policy Agreement extends the areas in which directives can be enacted by a qualified majority (and codecision) to include: (i) health and safety; working conditions; information and consultation; equality measures; and integration of persons (Art 2(2)). It continues to require unanimity (and consultation) for: social security and social welfare; representation and collective defence of workers; conditions of employment for non-EU nationals; financing job promotion and creation (Art 2(3)). It also has introduced the possibility for the Social Partners to implement Community directives based on Art 2(4).[5A]

The Commission's Action Programme for Directives is carefully concentrated on the fields of health and safety at work, atypical employment, working hours, protection of young workers, freedom of movement, disabled workers, pregnant women workers, and workers' rights to consultation and participation. It has refrained from any new proposals in the field of minimum wages, freedom of association, the right to bargain collectively and the right to strike. In these areas the Commission, in accordance with the principle of 'subsidiarity', and following Article 6 of the Social Policy Agreement, has decided that it is 'the responsibility of the member states in accordance with national practices, notably through legislative measures or collective agreements, to guarantee the fundamental social rights in the Charter and to implement the social measures indispensable to the smooth operation of the internal market...' In other words there is little weight to be placed upon

4 See eg Council Directive 88/642/EEC, 1988 OC L376/74 amending Council Directive 80/1107/EEC.

5 See Barnard (1997) ILJ 275.

5A See eg Barnard *EC Employment Law* (Wiley, 1996), p 71.

Community-wide support for trade union rights as such. The Community consensus does not extend that far.

Initially, the Commission was able to implement only health and safety measures based on Article 118A: The Framework Directive 89/391, Safety of Temporary Workers 91/383 and Maternity and Safety 92/85 and non-binding Recommendations and Codes of Practice, eg on sexual harassment.[6] Yet it could also stretch the concept of health and safety to provide the legal base for the Pregnant Workers Directive (92/85/EC); a Directive on Health and Safety for Atypical Workers (91/383/EEC); the Working Time Directive (3/104/EC); and the Young Workers Directive (94/33/EC).[7] After Maastricht, the Commission's agenda could be widened to include other features of its Social Action Plan to implement the Social Charter: Parental Leave Directive (COM (83) 686); revisions to the Transfer of Undertakings Directive and the Collective Redundancies Directive and a European Works Councils Directive (94/95/EC) based on Article 2(2); and the Part-time Work Directive based on consultation with the Social Partners.[8]

Finally, alongside the Social Charter is a series of planned enactments which seek to encourage workers' participation in managerial decisions, lodged more in company law than in labour law.[9]

In so far as Community legislation has been enacted, there are limits to the extent to which any member state has the freedom to avoid its obligations under existing EC legislation. For under Article 169, if the Commission considers that a member state has failed to fulfil an obligation under Community law it may bring infringement proceedings against the state before the Court of Justice and obtain a declaration obliging the member state to terminate that violation.[10] Moreover, the UK is subject to the interpretation given to EC law by the Court of Justice, particularly in response to references from the courts of member states under Article 177.

6 See James *The European Community* (1993) IER.

7 See eg Fitzpatrick (1997) ILJ 115. See too the Notification of Terms of Employment Directive.

8 See eg Fitzpatrick 'Community Social Law after Maastricht' (1992) ILJ 199. See too Posted Workers Directive (96/C220/01) and the Burden of Proof Directive.

9 See Hall (1991) ILJ 147.

10 Article 117 EEC Treaty. The main bases for infringement are as follows: expiry of the time limit for implementation; a failure to provide provisions of a nature which ensure effective application of the directive within the legal order; and a failure to provide implementing measures which are sufficiently precise, clear and transparent and not in conflict with directly effective provisions of Community law.

## (b) The development of the 'new legal order' in the case law referred to the European Court of Justice

Starting in the early 1960s it became clear that the European Court of Justice was prepared to use such references to take an active role in developing Community law as a 'new legal order' independent of the legislation of member states.[11] The European Court of Justice first developed the doctrine of 'supremacy' to ensure that member states whose Constitutions subscribed to a 'dualist' approach to international law[12] would not be able to argue that Community law was a separate system requiring enactment into national law before being binding on individuals and organisations.

### *(i) Supremacy*

In *Costa v ENEL*[13] the Court held that:

> 'the transfer by the States from their domestic legal system to the Community of the rights and obligations arising under the Treaty carries with it a permanent limitation of their sovereign rights (within limited fields) against which a subsequent legislative act incompatible with the concept of the Community cannot prevail.'

The Court's position as developed in the case law was that if Community law did not enjoy supremacy over national law it would be impossible to develop Community law with any degree of uniformity.[14] In the Court's view the very legal basis of Community law could be undermined if the validity of a Community measure or its effect within the member state could be called into question by a national law or even a national right based upon a constitutional provision.[15]

### *(ii) Direct effect*

Closely linked with the doctrine of supremacy was the doctrine of direct effect, ie the idea that Community law could apply not only to member states but also direct to the individuals and organisations within them.

In *Van Gend and Loos*[16] the Court of Justice held that the subjects of the new Community legal order comprised 'not only member states but

11 See eg *Van Gend and Loos*: 26/62 [1963] ECR 1.
12 UK, Germany, Italy, Denmark and Ireland.
13 6/64: [1964] ECR 585 at 594.
14 *Amministrazione delle Finanze dello Stato v Simmenthal SpA*: 106/77 [1978] ECR 629.
15 *Internationale Handelsgesellschaft mbh v Einfuhr-und Vorratsstelle für Getreide und Futtermittel*: 11/70 [1970] ECR 1125.
16 26/62: [1963] ECR 1.

also their nationals'. Independently of the legislation of member states, Community law is not only intended to confer obligations on individuals but also is intended to confer upon them rights. These rights arise not only where they are expressly granted in the Treaty, but also by reason of obligations which the Treaty imposes in a clearly defined way upon individuals.

In other words, the Court's view was that individuals can derive rights from obligations imposed upon other subjects within Community law.[17] However, there were certain preconditions for Community provisions to be directly applicable to individuals. They must be 'unconditional'[18] and 'sufficiently precise'. For example, Article 119 states that each member state shall during the first stage ensure and subsequently maintain the application of the principle of equal pay for equal work. In so far as a particular term or condition of employment, such as redundancy payment or occupational pension is concerned,[19] the Court is able to use the criteria of equal work and equal pay alone to establish discrimination based on difference of sex, the provision of Article 119 will apply directly to the situation.

Where a Community law has direct effect, the doctrines of supremacy and direct effect combine to provide that a litigant may rely upon Community law before a national court in order to persuade that court to depart from any national legislation including provisions resulting from collective agreements.[20] The national court must apply the provisions of Community law in full, misapplying where necessary any contrary provision of national legislation without waiting for the removal of that provision by legislative means or by any other constitutional process.

From an early stage moreover, it was made plain by the Court that in such a situation:

> 'every national court must in a case within its jurisdiction protect rights which [Community law] confers on individuals and must accordingly set aside any provision of national law which may conflict with it, whether prior or subsequent to the Community rule.'[1]

17 Ibid at 27.

18 Ie not dependent upon a further judgment of a Community or member state institution. Cf Timmermans, C, 'Directives: their effects within the national systems' CML Rev 1979, p.539.

19 *Barber v Guardian Royal Exchange Assurance Group* [1983] ICR 521, [1983] IRLR 240.

20 *Kowalska v Freie und Hansestadt Hamburg*: C-33/89 [1990] ECR I-2591, [1990] IRLR 447; *Nimz v Freie und Hansestadt Hamburg*: C-184/89 [1991] ECR I-297, [1991] IRLR 222.

1 *Amministrazione delle Finanze dello Stato v Simmenthal SpA*: 106/77 [1978] ECR 629 at 644.

### *(iii) Vertical and horizontal direct effect*

Unlike provisions of the Treaty, directives can have direct effect only as against the member state itself and its relations with individuals. This rather limited form of direct effect, often called vertical direct effect, presupposes that the provisions of the directive are unconditional and sufficiently precise and that either the state has failed to implement the directive within the prescribed period or it has failed to implement it correctly. For in such a case the member state may not as against individuals plead its own failure to perform the obligations which the directive entailed.[2]

Treaty provisions are also able to confer rights upon private individuals as well as impose obligations upon them, even when the provision is not addressed specifically to individuals. In such cases Treaty provisions are said to have 'horizontal direct effect', ie a private individual, say an employee, may invoke a Treaty provision against another private individual, say an employer. This is true, for example, of Article 119.[3]

In 1986, however, the ECJ decided in *Marshall's*[4] case that directives, unlike provisions of the Treaty, were not meant to have horizontal direct effect. As the Court put it:

> '. . . according to Article 189 of the EEC Treaty the binding nature of a directive, which constitutes the basis for the possibility of relying on the directive before a national court, exists only in relation to each member state to which it is addressed. It follows that a directive may not of itself impose obligations on an individual and that a provision of a directive must not be relied upon as against such a person.'[5]

### *(iv) Public authority*

The distinction drawn by *Marshall*'s case meant that different groups of employees would have different rights depending upon whether their employer was a private person or 'public authority'. It therefore threw into bold relief the issue of how exactly 'the state' would be defined. In *Marshall* the state was defined as extending to any capacity in which it is acting, whether employer or public authority.[6] In *Foster v British Gas plc*,[7]

2 On the other hand, where further Community or national measures are required to apply a provision it will not be directly applicable. See discussion in *Defrenne v Sabena*: 43/75 [1981] 1 All ER 122n, [1976] ICR 547.

3 See also Articles 48, 85 and 86.

4 *Marshall v Southampton and South West Area Health Authority (Teaching)*: 152/84 [1986] QB 401, [1986] ECR 723.

5 Ibid at 749.

6 *Marshall v Southampton and South West Area Health Authority (Teaching)*: 152/84 [1986] QB 401, [1986] ECR 723.

7 C-188/89: [1991] ICR 84, [1990] IRLR 353, ECJ.

the Court of Justice, after making the point that it was the appropriate forum to decide the categories of persons against whom the provisions of a directive could be relied, stated that the provisions of the directive could be relied upon against 'a body, whatever its legal form, which has been made responsible, pursuant to a measure adopted by the state, for providing a public service under the control of the state and has for that purpose special powers beyond those which result from the normal rules applicable in relations between individuals'. In effect, the category of 'public authority' for the purpose of EC law could extend to a newly privatised industry in certain circumstances.[8]

### *(v) 'Indirect effect'*

At the same time, the distinction drawn in *Marshall*'s case has begun to be eroded by another doctrine of the Court of Justice, giving indirect effect to directives.

The doctrine of 'indirect effect' maintains that national courts, as authorities of the member states, are themselves bound to interpret national laws adopted to implement a directive so as to ensure that a directive is fully effective. As the Court has stated in *Von Colson and Kamann* as well as other cases:[9]

> 'In applying national law and particularly those provisions of national law specially introduced to give effect to a Directive, the national court is bound to interpret its national law in the light of the text and of the aim of the Directive to reach the result envisaged by Article 189(3) of the Treaty.'

In effect, the Court views national courts as 'agents' of Community law bound to ensure that even though member states are free to choose how to implement Community directives, they must meet their Community law obligation to adopt all measures necessary to ensure that the directive concerned is fully effective in pursuing its objectives.[10] In such a case, quite independently of direct effect, a national court must interpret national law

8 The UK had argued that because of the anomaly there should be no direct effect, vertical or horizontal. The Court rejected the argument by pointing out that the unfairness could be avoided if the member state correctly implemented the directive. See eg Howells, 1991 MLR 456.

9 14/83 [1984] ECR 1891, [1986] 2 CMLR 430; *Harz v Deutsche Tradax GmbH*: 79/83 [1984] ECR 1921, [1986] 2 CMLR 430; *Murphy v Bord Telecom Eireann*: 157/86 [1988] ECR 673, [1988] 1 CMLR 879; *Officier van Justite v Kolpinghuis Nijmegen BV*: 80/86 [1987] ECR 3969, [1989] 2 CMLR 18.

10 See discussion in Preschal and Burrows *Gender Discrimination Law of the European Community* (1990) p 35. Docksey and Fitzpatrick [1991] ILJ 113 at 117–120.

in conformity with Community law in so far as it is given discretion under national law to do so.[11]

UK courts have for some time subscribed to the view that they should interpret national law in accordance with Community law if at all possible. As the House of Lords stated in *Garland v British Rail Engineering Ltd*:[12]

> 'It is a principle of construction of United Kingdom statutes, now too well established to call for citation of authority, that the words of the statute passed after the Treaty has been signed and dealing with the subject matter of the international obligation of the United Kingdom, are to be construed, if they are reasonably capable of bearing such a meaning, as intended to carry out the obligation, and not to be inconsistent with it. A fortiori is this the case where the Treaty obligation arises under one of the Community treaties to which section 2 of the European Communities Act 1972 applies as long as they are reasonably capable of bearing such a meeting.'

Indeed in both *Pickstone v Freemans plc*[13] and *Litster v Forth Dry Dock and Engineering Co Ltd*[14] the House of Lords was prepared to accept Lord Templeman's words that:

> '. . . the courts of the United Kingdom are under a duty to follow the practice of the European Court by giving a purposive construction to directives and regulations issued for the purpose of complying with directives.'[15]

However, the House of Lords has also taken the position in *Duke v GEC Reliance Ltd*[16] that national law had to be interpreted by national courts looking at the language of the legislation considered in the light of the circumstances at the time the statute was enacted. In *Duke* the House of Lords decided that since the Sex Discrimination Act 1975 was enacted before the Equal Treatment Directive, and was not intended to give effect to it, it was not possible under UK law to give an interpretation to it which gave effect to Community law.

In *Marleasing SA v La Comercial Internacional de Alimentacion SA*, however, the ECJ held that:

> '. . . in applying national law, whether the national law pre-dates or post-dates the Directive, the national court interpreting the national law is obliged

11 This obligation extended to other forms of national law and is not limited to statutes enacted specifically to implement a directive. See *Johnston v Chief Constable of the Royal Ulster Constabulary*: 222/84 [1987] QB 129, [1986] ECR 1651; *Officier van Justite v Kolpinghuis Nijmegen BV*: 80/86 [1987] ECR 3969, [1989] 2 CMLR 18.

12 [1983] 2 AC 751, [1982] IRLR 257.

13 [1989] AC 66, [1988] 2 All ER 803.

14 [1990] 1 AC 546, [1989] 1 All ER 1134.

15 Ibid at 1139.

16 [1988] ICR 339, [1988] IRLR 118, HL; see too *Finnegan v Clowney Youth Training Programme Ltd* [1990] ICR 462, [1990] IRLR 299, HL, considering Northern Ireland order enacted after the directive but based on the SDA 1975.

> to do everything possible in view of the wording and objectives of the Directive to achieve the result laid down by it and thereby comply with Article 189(3) of the Treaty.'[17]

The decisions from *Von Colson* to *Marleasing* called into question the view of the House of Lords in *Duke* that it could not construe a national act purposively because the national law was adopted subsequently.

In *Webb v Emo Air Cargo UK Ltd*[18] the House of Lords accepted that 'it is for a United Kingdom court to construe domestic legislation in any field covered by a Community Directive so as to accord with the interpretation of the Directive as laid down by the European Court. ... whether the domestic legislation came after or, as in this case, preceded the Directive'. However, the Law Lords added two caveats: (1) 'if that could be done without distorting the meaning of the domestic legislation' (citing *Duke*); and (2) '...only if it is possible to do so. That means that the domestic law must be open to an interpretation consistent with the directive whether or not it is also open to an interpretation inconsistent with it.' (citing *Marleasing*).

The second, at least, is an issue of national law.

Moreover, the requirement that national courts do everything possible to achieve a reconciliation cannot mean that courts should interpret national provisions *contra legem*. Furthermore, as the ECJ held in *Kolpinghuis*,[19] a directive cannot, independently of implementing legislation, create or aggravate the criminal liability of one who had breached its provisions because the duty of national courts to interpret law in the light of the directive was limited by the general principles of law and in particular the principles of legal certainty and non-retroactivity.

Along with developments in *Marleasing* the ECJ began to develop a new approach to remedies for breach of a directive. After more than a decade of limiting EC law to substantive law and leaving remedies to the member states, the court dramatically redefined the relationship in a series of cases.[20] Thus in *Factortame*[1] the ECJ made it clear that where the sole obstacle to the enforcement of an EC regulation (Community Law) by interim relief was a rule of national law, that national law must be set aside.

17 *Marleasing SA v La Comercial Internacional de Alimentacion SA* C-106/89 [1990] ECR I-4135, [1992] 1 CMLR 305.

18 [1993] IRLR 27 at 32.

19 *Officier van Justite v Kolpinghuis Nijmegen BV*: 80/86 [1987] ECR 3969.

20 *Marleasing SA v La Comercial Internacional de Alimentacion SA*: C-106/89 [1990] ECR I-4135. See, eg, Maltby 'Marleasing: What is all the fuss about?' [1993] LQR 301.

1 *R v Secretary of State for Transport, ex p Factortame (No 2)* [1990] ECR I-2433.

Then, in *Francovich v Italy*[2] it held that a state could be liable in damages for a failure properly to implement a directive.[3]

In later case law,[4] the conditions of liability were modified, culminating in *Dillenkofer*[5] in which the ECJ set out three conditions which had to be satisfied before a member state had liability for a failure to implement a directive.

1. The obligation infringed must be intended to confer rights upon individuals. If a directive, the contents of the rights must be discernible from the provisions of the directive;
2. The breach must be 'sufficiently serious';
3. There must be a direct causal link between the breach of the obligation and the damage sustained.

This defined the liability of the member state for a complete failure to implement a directive.[6] In the case of a failure to implement a directive correctly, the member state has the defence of acting in good faith in incorrectly interpreting an ambiguous clause, which presupposes that the incorrectness of the interpretation was not obvious from the Court's case law or the terms of the directive.[7]

Applying the three conditions set out in the *Dillenkofer* judgment, the most obvious failure of the British government to implement a directive in good time in recent years was the Working Time Directive (93/104/EEC) which was supposed to be implemented in November 1996 and was still not implemented by the time this book went to press in July 1998. This failure would appear to qualify individuals to pursue claims against the state.[8]

Consequently, while the doctrine of indirect effect of directives, evolving from *Von Colson* to *Marleasing* to *Francovich* and *Dillenkofer* cannot completely erode the distinction between vertical and horizontal direct effect, it does constitute a significant outflanking manoeuvre.

2 C-6/90: [1992] IRLR 84, ECJ. Ross *Beyond Francovich* [1993] MLR 55.

3 See also *Emmott v Minister for Social Welfare and A-G* [1991] IRLR 387, ECJ, for the time limits in cases against the state for failure properly to implement a directive.

4 See eg *Factortame III and Brasserie de Pêcheur* [1996] ECR I-1029; *British Telecommunications* [1996] ECR I-1631, [1996] IRLR 300; *Dillenkofer v Federal Government of Germany* [1996] ECR I-4845, [1997] IRLR 60.

5 Ibid.

6 In *Dillenkofer*, the point was also made that a failure to implement was always a sufficiently serious breach and could enjoy no extra period of grace.

7 See eg *British Telecommunications* [1996] ECR I-1631.

8 See discussion in Hervey (1997) ILJ 74

In summary, given the judicial developments of supremacy, direct effect and indirect effect in Community law, it is quite clear that the capacity of a member state to act independently in pursuing a particular labour legislative policy is subject to certain limits. Although the member state may have the voting capacity at the Council of Ministers to ensure that no new social legislation is enacted, it cannot stop the steady expansion of Community social law as it is interpreted by Community and national courts.

Finally, as mentioned, the advent of a Labour government has led to a new chapter in EU Social Law both literally and figuratively. The UK is now formally signed up to the 'Social Chapter', and the Agreement on Social Policy in the Maastrict Treaty and has agreed to the new draft Amsterdam Treaty which contains an amended chapter on social policy which incorporates the 'Social Chapter', the agreement on social policy and revisions to Articles 117-121.[9] This chapter will be included in the EC Treaty, once it is agreed by all 15 members[10] and should provide the basis for a more extensive programme of social legislation.

9 See Section II of the Treaty, 'The Union and the Citizen.'

10 See Barnard 'The United Kingdom, the Social Chapter and the Amsterdam Treaty' (1997) ILJ 275.

PART I

# The contractual foundations of the employment relationship

# Introduction

The contract of employment is a central element in the structure of British labour law. It is a legal concept that one is forced to turn to repeatedly when resolving labour law problems. It was always to be expected that this common law legal relationship would operate as a residual factor in labour law, providing rules to regulate situations left unregulated by statute law. However, despite the enormous growth of statute law the employment contract remains prominent and pervasive. Moreover, although in Britain the employment relationship often takes place in the context of collective bargaining by trade union representatives, with at least 50% of the workforce, even if not trade union members, having their terms and conditions of work determined by collective agreements, the contract of employment is the dominant legal construct.

There are at least four reasons for the central role of the individual contract of employment in UK labour law. First, the statutory system has never been used to provide an alternative legal structure of a collective nature. Thus, collective agreements have not been made legally enforceable between trade unions and employers, a process which has occurred in the USA, Sweden, Germany and France.[1] In the UK the terms of collective agreements attain legal force only when they are incorporated into the terms and conditions of individual employment contracts or when they are built into statutory rights. Moreover, thus far we have not shown interest in a statutory works council model such as that in Germany which might have been used as a central legal structure governing managerial powers over employees.[2] For the British lawyer dealing with the legal rights and obligations of employers and employees today, therefore, 'the collectivity

1 Schmidt and Neal 'Collective Agreements and Collective Bargaining' *International Encyclopaedia of Comparative Law* Vol XV, Ch 12. Wedderburn, 'Inderogability, Collective Agreements and Community Law' [1992] ILJ 245.

2 *International Encyclopaedia for Labour Law and Industrial Relations* 'West Germany'.

of the workplace continues to be dissolved into a series of individual contractual relationships'.[3]

Second, much employment protection legislation has been drafted in reliance on contractual definitions. Indeed, the very statutory employment protections such as unfair dismissal, redundancy, etc, which have been enacted specifically to set limits to the employer's discretion within the purely contractual relationship have been drafted in such a way as to rely heavily upon common law contractual concepts in defining important elements of the statutory rights.[4] In the event they have invited the judiciary to draw upon common law values and assumptions in interpreting the statutory language, despite the different values projected by the legislation.

Third, the law of industrial action, which is based upon a process of giving statutory immunities against common law economic torts, continues to be influenced by whether or not a breach of the employment contract has occurred.

Fourth, in recent years, partly as a result of the weaknesses of existing statutory rights and remedies and partly owing to the 'deregulation' policy of the Conservative Government in the 1980s and 1990s, the contract of employment has been used more extensively as a freestanding source of rights and obligations in employment law.[5]

In the event, a thorough understanding of the characteristics of the contract of employment is a virtual precondition to an understanding of the subject of labour law.

## THE CHARACTERISTICS OF THE CONTRACT OF EMPLOYMENT

At common law, the contract of employment is often depicted as a particular application of the general rule of contract, based on the general assumptions of freedom of contract.

The hiring stage is viewed by courts as an agreement characterised by offer and acceptance by employer and employee, the consideration provided by the mutual exchange of promises: the employer to pay wages or salary, the employee to perform work. The important terms of the contract are in theory agreed between the parties and again in theory any

3 O Kahn Freund 'Legal Framework' in Flanders and Clegg (eds) *The System of Industrial Relations in Great Britain* (1954) p 45.

4 For example, 'dismissal' as an element of unfair dismissal or redundancy is defined as termination of the contract of employment. See Chs 8 and 9.

5 This trend could accelerate now that tribunal jurisdiction has been extended to hear claims of breach of contract on termination of the employment (see Industrial Tribunals Extension of Jurisdiction Orders) 1994, SI 1994 No 1623 (England and Wales), SI 1994 No 1624 (Scotland).

changes or variations in such terms must also be mutually agreed. Finally, at common law termination is also regarded as consisting of a mutual right of equal parties to the contract with each having the right freely to terminate the contract for any reason whatever as long as proper notice is given.

To picture the employment relationship as exclusively or predominantly 'contractual', however, can be somewhat misleading. There is undoubtedly a contractual dimension to the employment relationship particularly at the hiring stage when the contract is formed. The employee often knowingly chooses to work with an employer and the employer often engages the employee after a selection procedure, however rudimentary. Furthermore, the employee generally knows certain terms of the employment contract - pay and other forms of remuneration, the hours of work, the type of work to be performed, the place where the work will take place, etc.

The image of contract fades, however, when one looks more closely at the way the terms and conditions of the employment contract are established. The second tenet of freedom of contract is that the parties are free to establish the terms of their contractual relationships, the terms upon which they intend to be bound. However, to a large extent the reciprocal rights and obligations in the contract of employment are pre-established for most employees.

For most employees, apart from the rare individual with bargaining power comparable to that of the employer, the express terms of the employment contract are drafted by the employer, and, although modified by collective agreements in certain respects, are presented to the employee on a take it or leave it basis. Moreover, along with the express terms of the contract there is a virtual code of standard terms, implied into all employment contracts by the judiciary. Consequently, for most employees, once the initial contractual decision is made to go to work for a particular firm, employment is experienced as entering a private managerial system in which most legal rights and obligations of the ongoing working relationship are already established.[6]

A number of commentators have drawn attention to these developments and have suggested that they make the employment relationship more a status relationship than a contractual one.[7]

However, as interesting as the phenomenon of a return from contract to status may be,[8] it is at least as important to observe what impact the rules which are pre-determined for the employee and employer actually have upon the employment relationship. To what extent do these rules of

6 Collins, H, 'Market Power, Bureaucratic Power and the Contract of Employment' [1986] ILJ 1.

7 See, eg, Napier 'The Contract of Employment' in Lewis (ed) *Labour Law in Britain*.

8 This refers to the irony that the employment contract originally derived from the master–servant status relationship of the 19th century.

contract provide legal authority for managerial discretion? To what extent do they place constraints upon the exercise of managerial authority? To understand the way in which these rules of the employment relationship operate it is useful to start by studying the way in which the terms and conditions of the contract of employment are established, both by managerial drafting and by judicial implication.

CHAPTER 3

# The terms of employment contracts: implied terms

To understand the legal view of the employment relationship it is useful to begin with the terms judicially implied into the contract of employment. In principle, the parties to the employment contract are free to reach mutual agreement on whatever terms they choose. If, however, the contract is silent on a particular issue, the courts may imply a term either as a matter of law or fact. In theory, they are supposed to use a test which is grounded upon the unexpressed intentions of the parties. In the case of contracts of employment, however, they have tended to use the device of the implied term to press a wide variety of employment relationships into a similar mould. This has long been true of the terms implied in law, which are essentially standard terms which courts impose upon all employment contracts. In recent years this view has also begun to influence judicial decisions in respect of implied terms of fact.

At common law, it is assumed that employers and employees have certain fundamental reciprocal duties in their contractual relationship. On the one hand all employees owe to their employer a duty to work in accordance with lawful orders, to co-operate with their employer, to serve the employer faithfully and honestly and to exercise skill and care in the performance of work.

In turn, employers have an obligation to pay wages for work performed or for which the employee is ready to perform, to take reasonable care for the safety of the employee, to provide work and to provide safe work, to act in good faith towards the employee and not to act in such a way as to undermine the trust and confidence of the employment relationship.

A breach of any of these fundamental terms by the employer is often a serious breach of contract or repudiation and can give rise to an action for wrongful dismissal or breach of contract. Moreover, a contractual repudiation by the employer may also be treated by the employee as a constructive dismissal, ie as the basis for a complaint of unfair dismissal or redundancy.[1]

A breach of contract by the employee is often dealt with by the self-help, disciplinary measures of the employer, such as suspension of pay, or dismissal. Only rarely will the employer bring an action for damages[2] or an injunction.[3] However, employers do require assistance from the courts in the form of injunctions to enforce a ban on confidential information, working in competition and passing on trade secrets both during and after employment.

## THE EMPLOYEE'S IMPLIED OBLIGATIONS

### (a) The duty of obedience

The central obligation of the employee, implied into all contracts of employment, is to work in accordance with the lawful contractual orders of the employer. The duty of obedience has its origins in the more coercive conditions of the nineteenth-century Master-Servant Acts, yet it has been carefully preserved in the modern contractual relationship as an implied fundamental term.[4] Breach of this duty constitutes a repudiation of the contract and the employee can be subject to summary dismissal without prior warning or notice of termination. In cases of partial performance, under certain conditions, the employer can withhold pay.[5]

The common law power of instant dismissal is a reserve power underpinning managerial authority. After all attempts at request and persuasion have failed, managers have the power to insist that the employee must accept the policies formulated by management as well as the particular role specified for the employee in implementing such policies, subject only to the limits of the express and implied terms of the contract and legislation. That is why Davies and Freedland[6] rightly conclude that:

> 'This implied term has the effect of lodging managerial prerogative firmly in the centre of the structure of the contract of employment.'

1 The jurisdiction of industrial tribunals has been extended by ministerial order to claims for damages for breach of employment contracts brought on termination of employment or in addition to other types of tribunal claim. See Industrial Tribunals Extension of Jurisdiction orders 1994, SI 1994 No 1623 (England and Wales), SI 1994 No 1624 (Scotland).

2 *National Coal Board v Galley* [1958] 1 All ER 91, [1958] 1 WLR 16.

3 See discussion under the duty of fidelity in this chapter and working in competition, Ch 4.

4 Napier 'The Contract of Employment' in *Lewis* p 329; see also Selsnick 1969, *Law, Society and Industrial Justice*, p 136.

5 For a detailed look at this issue, see Ch 16.

6 P Davies and M Freedland *Labour Law - Text and Materials* (2nd edn, 1984) p 311.

That said, the duty of obedience as a prop to managerial prerogative has undoubtedly been ameliorated in its modern form by three developments. In the first place a change in managerial practice has resulted in a more reasoned approach to the management of discipline[7] and the widespread use of disciplinary procedures which subject disciplinary and dismissal decisions to hearing and appeal. These can be enforced as express terms of the contract of employment and operate as legal constraints on managerial decisions to dismiss.[8]

Secondly, the authority of employers under the implied term is not absolute. Where an order is unlawful or not within the employer's contractual authority,[9] or palpably unsafe,[10] or not sufficiently direct[11] the employee's refusal to obey will not necessarily be repudiatory. Furthermore, employers too are subject to an implied term that they 'will not, without reasonable and proper cause, conduct themselves in a manner calculated or likely to destroy or seriously damage the relationship of confidence and trust between employer and employee'.[12]

This implied term does not require the employer in issuing instructions to treat an employee reasonably in all respects.[13] Rather it requires employers not to be extremely unreasonable in the way they exercise their contractual authority. To take one example, at common law, courts are unwilling to ask whether an employer's decision for requiring an employee to move to another place of work is for a genuine operational reason,[14] but they will imply an obligation that an employer must give reasonable notice of such a transfer.[15]

Thirdly, protective legislation, generally operates as a limit upon managerial prerogative. In particular, as we shall see in Chapter 8, the unfair dismissal provisions of the Employment Rights Act 1996 allow a complaint by an employee to an industrial tribunal to determine whether the employer's decision to dismiss an employee for refusing to obey an order was reasonable in all the circumstances - a test which appraises the reasonableness of the employer's decision to dismiss even if the employer has contractual authority for that dismissal. Moreover, s 100 of the

7 See Ch 5.
8 See Ch 4.
9 *Pepper v Webb* [1969] 2 All ER 216, [1969] 1 WLR 514, CA.
10 See *Gregory v Ford* [1951] 1 All ER 121.
11 See *Laws v London Chronicle (Indicator Newspapers) Ltd* [1959] 2 All ER 285, [1959] 1 WLR 698, CA (order distinguished from advice).
12 *Woods v W M Car Services (Peterborough) Ltd* [1981] ICR 666, [1981] IRLR 347, EAT approved by the Court of Appeal in *Lewis v Motorworld Garages Ltd* [1986] ICR 157, [1985] IRLR 465.
13 *Post Office v Roberts* [1980] IRLR 347, EAT.
14 *Courtaulds Northern Spinning Ltd v Sibson* [1988] ICR 451, [1988] IRLR 305, CA.
15 *United Bank Ltd v Akhtar* [1989] IRLR 507, EAT; see discussion of the interaction of this term with express terms in Ch 4.

Employment Rights Act 1996 may give protection to an employee against dismissal in a situation where the employee refuses to obey an instruction which is reasonably believed to be seriously or imminently dangerous and that fact has been brought to the employer's attention.

Subject to these limitations, the common law duty of obedience remains fundamental to the employment relationship. Assuming an order is within the contractual authority of the employer - the employee has the obligation to obey or run the ultimate risk of losing his or her job. A basic disagreement with the policy or the chosen method of implementation, even based on conscientious objection,[16] is not necessarily a justification for an employee's refusal to obey an instruction.

## (b) The duty of cooperation and adaptability

In recent years, the courts have also enlarged the duty of obedience into a wider duty of co-operation and adaptability. This has taken two forms. A duty not to be deliberately non-cooperative has been developed particularly in the context of industrial action. In *Secretary of State for Employment v ASLEF (No 2)*[17] a group of train drivers attempting a 'work to rule' were held by the Court of Appeal to be in breach of an implied term in their contract. Buckley LJ described it as the duty to perform the contract in such a way as not to frustrate its commercial objectives. Roskill LJ's view was that the implied term was 'that each employee will not, in obeying his lawful instructions, seek to obey them in a wholly unreasonable way which has the effect of disrupting the system, the efficient running of which he is employed to ensure'. Lord Denning MR was willing to limit it to a more specific prohibition upon wilful disruption by the employee.

Second, the duty to obey orders has been enhanced by a duty of adaptability on the part of employees. In *Cresswell v Board of Inland Revenue*[18] a group of tax officers who brought an action against the Inland Revenue for refusing to pay them unless they worked a new computerised system for administering PAYE were informed that the employer had not broken the contract since there was an implied contractual duty on their part 'to adapt themselves to new methods and techniques' introduced in the course of employment. The employer had in turn an obligation to train the employee, if the change required it. The judges have been clearly predisposed towards flexibility and a view of employment as consisting

16 See eg *Owen v Coventry Health Authority* (1986) Lexis Transcript, 19 December; see too *UCATT v Brain* [1981] IRLR 224, CA on the issue of confidentiality.

17 [1972] 2 QB 455, [1972] ICR 19, CA; see too *British Telecommunications plc v Ticehurst* [1992] ICR 383, [1992] IRLR 219, CA (discussed on p 343 below).

18 [1984] ICR 508, [1984] IRLR 190.

of a commitment by employees and employers to the common purpose of the efficient running of the enterprise.

Lord Justice Watkins expressed the policy behind this judicial development when he stated: in *Wood*'s case:[19]

> 'Employers must not, in my opinion, be put in a position where through the wrongful refusal of their employees to adopt change they are prevented from introducing improved business methods in furtherance of seeking success for the enterprise.'

## (c) Implied terms in fact and flexibility

A similar urge to ensure flexibility in employment contracts can be observed in the development of implied terms in fact. In theory, terms implied in fact were supposed to be justified by reference to a finding that the parties would have agreed to such a term if they had been asked,[20] or where it could be shown to be necessary to give to the transaction such business efficacy as the parties must have intended.[1] In such cases the contractual intentions of the parties were regarded as strict limits upon the possibilities of judges to find an implied term. Yet the requirement of intent appears to have been relaxed by more recent decisions as the courts appear to be increasingly prepared to use the method of implication of terms in fact to fill in unexpressed terms in employment contracts. As Browne-Wilkinson LJ (as he then was) put it in *Howman & Son v Blyth*:[2]

> 'The industrial tribunals are not limited solely to implying terms as fact by the test of obvious intention of the parties - so called "Moorcock type" terms. They are also expected to imply terms in fact where the relationship requires that there be some agreed term which has not in fact been agreed but both parties would have agreed if asked. In such a case the court implies a reasonable term.'

This statement was made in the course of implying a term in relation to a contract with no express provision for sick pay, but the technique has also been used to imply flexibility in employment contracts 'reasonable'.

For example, in the case of *Jones v Associated Tunnelling Co Ltd*[3] the question arose of whether or not the employer was entitled under the contract to change the place of work of Mr Jones who was taken on initially to work at a particular pit. The contract was originally silent as to the extent

19 *Woods v W M Car Services (Peterborough) Ltd* [1982] ICR 693, [1981] IRLR 413, CA.
20 *Shirlaw v Southern Foundries (1926) Ltd* [1939] 2 KB 206, [1939] 2 All ER 113.
1 *The Moorcock* (1889) 14 PD 64.
2 [1983] ICR 416, [1983] IRLR 139, EAT.
3 [1981] IRLR 477, EAT.

of mobility. The employer notified the employee later in writing that he could be required to work 'at any place in the UK the employer may decide'. The EAT would not accept the later communication as a variation of terms of the contract, but decided nevertheless that since the contract was unclear on the question of mobility it was necessary to imply some terms in order to give the contract business efficacy. The test, it suggested, was 'a term which the parties, *if reasonable* would probably have agreed to if they had directed their minds to the problem'. The term it found was that Mr Jones could be moved anywhere within reasonable daily commuting distance from his home.[4]

Similarly, in *Courtaulds Northern Spinning Ltd v Sibson*,[5] a lorry driver who resigned his trade union membership was told by the employer either to rejoin the union or transfer to another depot which was one mile away. He refused to do either and resigned claiming that the employer's insistence on the move was a breach of contract. The industrial tribunal, and the EAT, found that he was constructively dismissed but the Court of Appeal overturned that decision. The Court reasoned that since the contract was silent on the issue of mobility, some term had to be implied to deal with the issue and the implied term had to be, as Slade LJ put it, 'one which the parties would probably have agreed if they were being reasonable, not one which the parties, if asked, would have agreed to before entering the contract'.[6] Here too the court decided that the employer had the power to direct the employee to move anywhere within commuting distance. This power, the court said, was unfettered by law in the sense that the employer's reason for, or reasonableness in, giving the order could not be questioned. The only limit on the managerial decision was the requirement that he be employed within reasonable commuting distance.

Despite the rhetoric of unfettered managerial powers in *Sibson*,[7] the implied terms of mobility and flexibility are often accompanied by certain implied obligations placed upon the employer. For example in *Prestwick Circuits Ltd v McAndrew*[8] an employer ordered a process operator in Ayr to move to another factory in Irvine 15 miles away. He was told on Friday 1 May to go to the Irvine factory on the following Tuesday, later extended to a week. The employer was held to have constructively dismissed him because of the failure to give reasonable notice. The mobility term implied into the contract was conditional upon reasonable distance and reasonable

4 See too *Managers (Holborn) Ltd v Hohne* [1977] IRLR 230, EAT; cf *Solihull Metropolitan Borough v NUT* [1985] IRLR 211.

5 [1988] ICR 451, [1988] IRLR 305, CA.

6 Ibid at 309.

7 See *O'Brien v Associated Fire Alarms Ltd* [1969] 1 All ER 93, [1968] 1 WLR 1916; see discussion 1988 ILJ 255.

8 [1990] IRLR 191, Ct of Sess. See too *United Bank Ltd v Akhtar* [1989] IRLR 507, EAT.

notice. Further, in *Cosslett Contractors Ltd v Quinn*[9] the EAT was prepared to imply a term into the contract of a mobile crane operator to be entitled to 'all expenses, losses and liabilities' incurred in the performance of his duties as the correct basis for calculating 'away pay'.

Nevertheless, the net effect of such implied terms is to create contractual support for a widened area of managerial discretion which allows the employer to reorganise certain of the employees terms and conditions of work without breaking the contract. This managerial discretion, as we shall see, is subject only to the limits established by the employer's implied obligation of mutual trust and confidence.

## (d) The duty of fidelity

Another implied fundamental obligation of employees at common law is the duty owed to their employers of'fidelity' and good faith. This duty, an adaptation of the duty of faithful service in Master-Servant law, requires the employee not to work in competition with the employer,[10] even, in certain situations, outside working hours;[11] not to disclose or make use of confidential information such as trade secrets acquired in the course of employment, while the employment continues and after the employee has left;[12] a duty of a manager to disclose the misconduct of other employees;[13] a duty to account to his employer for property entrusted to him;[14] and finally a duty to disclose to the employer and surrender the property right to an invention made during working hours which relates to the employment.[15]

Again, each of these duties has its limits.[16] For example, while an employee may be restrained from disclosing confidential information in the nature of 'trade secrets', he may take away with him his individual skill and knowledge when he leaves employment.[17] As Lord Parker stated in *Herbert Morris Ltd v Saxelby*:[18]

> 'Wherever such covenants have been upheld it has been on the ground, not that the servant or apprentice would, by reason of his employment or

9 [1990] IRLIB 413.
10 *Thomas Marshall (Exports) Ltd v Guinle* [1979] Ch 227, [1978] ICR 905.
11 *Hivac Ltd v Park Royal Scientific Instruments Ltd* [1946] Ch 169, [1946] 1 All ER 350, CA. Cf *Marshall v Industrial Systems and Control Ltd* [1992] IRLR 294, EAT.
12 See eg *Faccenda Chicken Ltd v Fowler* [1987] Ch 117, [1986] IRLR 69, CA.
13 *Sybron Corpn v Rochem Ltd* [1983] ICR 801, [1983] IRLR 253.
14 *Boston Deep Sea Fishing and Ice Co v Ansell* (1888) 39 Ch D 339.
15 See eg *British Syphon Co Ltd v Homewood* [1956] 2 All ER 897, [1956] 1 WLR 1190.
16 *Nova Plastics Ltd v Frogatt* [1982] IRLR 146.
17 *Printers and Finishers Ltd v Holloway* [1964] 3 All ER 731, [1965] 1 WLR 1.
18 [1916] 1 AC 688 at 709, HL; *Faccenda Chicken Ltd v Fowler* [1987] Ch 117, [1986] IRLR 69.

training, obtain the skill and knowledge necessary to equip him as a possible competitor in the trade, but that he might obtain such personal knowledge of an influence over the customers of his employer, or such an acquaintance with his employer's trade secrets as would enable him, if competition were allowed, to take advantage of his employer's trade connection or utilise information confidentially obtained.'

In *Fowler v Faccenda Chicken Ltd*[19] confidential information was described by Goulding J as falling into one of three classes:

(i) information which, because of its trivial character or its easy accessibility from public sources of information, cannot be regarded by reasonable persons or by the law as confidential at all;
(ii) information which the servant must treat as confidential but which once learned necessarily remains in the servant's head and becomes part of his skill and knowledge;
(iii) specific trade secrets so confidential that, even though they may necessarily have been learned by heart, and even though the servant may have left the service, they cannot lawfully be used for anyone's benefit but the master's.

In that case, the Court of Appeal held that after the employee leaves employment the implied term of fidelity could only extend to information in the third class, ie trade secrets.[20] In *Lansing Linde Ltd v Kerr* Lord Justice Staughton suggested a view of trade secret as 'information which if disclosed to a competitor, would be liable to cause real (or significant) harm to the owner of the secret'. In *Lancashire Fires Ltd v SA Lyons & Co Ltd* the Court of Appeal, per Sir Thomas Bingham MR, was prepared to apply the definition to a highly technical production process 'where information about the process was not public, and was not available from any other source and there was no evidence that competitors were experimenting with anything similar'.[1] In the event, as we shall see, employers prefer to enlarge the implied duty of fidelity by using express non-competition and non-solicitation clauses in employment contracts.

Moreover, the duty not to work in competition with the employer requires the employee to refrain from responding to the approaches of customers or soliciting customers or competitors during working hours.[2] In an employee's spare time, however, if there is no express restriction

19 [1985] 1 All ER 724, [1984] ICR 589; affd [1987] Ch 117, [1986] 1 All ER 617, CA.
20 [1991] IRLR 80 at 84 CA.
1 [1997] IRLR 113 at 120; moreover the court reaffirmed that the test of a 'trade secret' is objective and not one which is dependent upon the employer's subjective view. Cf *Thomas Marshall (Exports) Ltd v Guinle* [1978] IRLR 174, HC.
2 See eg *Wessex Dairies Ltd v Smith* [1935] 2 KB 80, CA.

and the moonlighting activity causes no serious harm or prejudice to the employer, employees remain free to take on such work.[3]

In the case of the duty to disclose information about the misconduct of other employees, there is an obvious increase in strictness for those in general management and executive positions[4] but employees are not required to disclose their own defective conduct or breaches of duty.[5]

At common law, designs and inventions made by the employee during working hours belong to the employer; an employee's invention could remain his own property only if it did not arise from the nature of his employment or involve the use of the employer's trade secrets.[6] The inequity of this common law rule prompted the Patents Act 1977,[7] which provides that an invention made by the employee shall be taken to belong to the employer only if the invention was made in the course of the employee's normal duties or those assigned to him and it could 'reasonably be expected to result from that work'.[8]

Alternatively, if the invention was not made in the normal course of the employee's duties, it must be made in the course of a duty specifically assigned to the employee such that an invention would be expected to result. For example, in *Reiss Engineering Co Ltd v Harris*[9] an employee inventor of a valve was able to retain the rights to his invention because, although he was made manager of a valve department, it was not made in the course of his normal duties. Moreover, the nature of his duties did not involve a special obligation to further the interests of his employer's undertaking.

In all other cases the employee inventor can apply for compensation to the Patent Office or the courts for a 'fair share' of the results of the exploitation of the patent by the employer. The Act further provides that any agreement excluding the employee's statutory rights is unenforceable unless a trade union of which the employee is a member negotiates a result in collective agreements which is different from the guidelines established in the Act.[10]

3 *Nova Plastics Ltd v Frogatt* [1982] IRLR 146.
4 *Sybron Corpn v Rochem Ltd* [1983] ICR 801, [1983] IRLR 253.
5 *Bell v Lever Bros Ltd* [1932] AC 161.
6 *British Syphon Co Ltd v Homewood* [1956] 2 All ER 897, [1956] 1 WLR 1190; *Re Selz Ltd's Application* (1953) 71 RPC 158.
7 See now Wotherspoon 'Employee Inventions Revisited' (1993) ILJ 11a (discussing three 1992 cases brought by employees). See also Phillips, J (ed) *Employees' Inventions: A Comparative Study* (1981). A similar statutory protection has not been included in the Copyright, Designs and Patents Act 1988.
8 *Byrne v Statist Co* [1914] 1 KB 622; *Stevenson Jordan and Harrison Ltd v MacDonald and Evans* [1952] 1 TLR 101.
9 [1985] IRLR 232.
10 Section 40(3).

While there have been few cases reaching trial under the Patents Act thus far, it should eventually prove a fertile field for litigation. At all events it offers a good example of the way legislation can be used to place reasonableness limits on the contractual rights of employers. The unfair dismissals legislation also applies a test of reasonableness to dismissals for working in competition, but as we shall see this is a less stringent test.[11]

### (e) The duty of skill and care

Finally, the common law imposes upon employees an implied obligation to perform their duties with skill and care. Thus in *Lister v Romford Ice and Cold Storage Co Ltd*,[12] an employee who negligently drove his lorry and injured a fellow employee was held to be responsible to the employer to indemnify him for the loss caused by his vicarious liability for the employee's conduct. The right of indemnity in practice is limited by a 'gentlemen's agreement' amongst insurers not to exercise subrogated rights of indemnity against employees.

## THE EMPLOYER'S IMPLIED OBLIGATIONS

As mentioned, the implied obligations of the employee at common law are accompanied by reciprocal implied obligations owed by the employer to the employee. The first and most important of these is the employer's obligation to pay wages for the performance of work according to the terms of the contract.

### (a) The obligation to pay contractually agreed remuneration

An employer's duty to pay agreed remuneration is a fundamental obligation under the contract of employment.[13] A failure to pay agreed remuneration is a breach of contract giving rise to action for damages or

11 See eg *Skyrail Oceanic Ltd v Coleman* [1980] ICR 596, [1980] IRLR 226, EAT.

12 [1957] AC 555, [1957] 1 All ER 125; but *Jones v Manchester Corpn* [1952] 2 QB 852, [1952] 2 All ER 125 (need for adequate supervision); see *Harvey v R G O'Dell Ltd* [1958] 2 QB 78, [1958] 1 All ER 657 (limited exception to rule of idemnity) *McNally v Welltrade International Ltd* [1978] IRLR 497.

13 The employer must give details of the rate of pay and the method of calculating pay in the written statement of particulars (see Ch 4) and give the employee an itemised pay statement upon payment of wages and salary.

debt or unlawful deduction[14] and can amount to repudiation, justifying constructive dismissal. For example, in *Miller v Hamworthy Engineering Ltd*,[15] a foreman put on short-time work for a period of time was able to claim for the net loss of earnings suffered during the short-time working period. Similarly in *Rigby v Ferodo Ltd*,[16] an employee subjected to a unilateral wage cut was able to sue the employer for the difference between the amount paid to him and contractual earnings owed to him. Moreover in *R F Hill Ltd v Mooney*[17] a salesman employed on a contract stipulating a salary plus 1% commission on sales was forced to accept a change in the system of commission whereby it would be paid only for sales over a target figure. The EAT upheld the industrial tribunal's decision that there was a constructive dismissal because the employer had failed to perform his obligation to pay remuneration by altering the formula whereby wages were calculated.

The principles that apply to the employer's duty to pay agreed remuneration also extend to other elements of pay and fringe benefits as long as they are contractual obligations; for example, commission or bonuses,[18] overtime pay,[19] etc. The failure of an employer to meet any such obligations could amount to a repudiation entitling employees to terminate their contracts.

Yet the employer's basic obligation is to pay only contractually agreed remuneration. Thus, where an employer has contractual authority to suspend an employee without pay for disciplinary reasons,[20] to lay off on guarantee payment,[1] or to institute short-time working,[2] the employee will have no recourse. Similarly, where employers can show that an employee has taken part in industrial action and is therefore not entitled to pay, they may refuse to pay remuneration without being in breach of contract.[3]

The precise terms of the employer's obligation are determined by the nature of the wage-work bargain between the parties and this will vary with the type of employment. Salaried workers will generally be entitled to a monthly payment often regardless of the variations in the quantum of work actually produced by the hours actually worked. Their contractual status reflects the view that the employee's loyalty and commitment makes

14 See Employment Rights Act 1996, Part II (see Ch 2 below).
15 [1986] IRLR 461, CA.
16 [1988] ICR 29, [1987] IRLR 516, HL.
17 [1981] IRLR 258, EAT. See also *Gillies v Richard Daniels & Co Ltd* [1979] IRLR 457, EAT; *Adams v Charles Zub Associates Ltd* [1978] IRLR 551, EAT.
18 *Logabax Ltd v Titherley* [1977] ICR 369, [1977] IRLR 97, EAT.
19 *Stokes v Hampstead Wine Co Ltd* [1979] IRLR 298, EAT.
20 *Bird v British Celanese Ltd* [1945] KB 336, [1945] 1 All ER 488, CA.
1 *Powell Duffryn Wagon Co Ltd v House* [1974] ICR 123.
2 *Browning v Crumlin Valley Collieries Ltd* [1926] 1 KB 522.
3 *Miles v Wakefield Metropolitan District Council* [1987] ICR 368, [1987] IRLR 193, HL; see further Ch 17, pp 342-347.

unnecessary the controls of a salary tied directly to levels of input or hours of work. Instead of 'clocking in' there is often flexitime. Instead of payment by results, there is a salary structure including increments for periods of service and merit, and in recent years performance appraisal systems are spreading.

For salaried employees income is generally maintained as employers have tended historically to regard such employees as 'fixed costs'.

Manual workers on the other hand have traditionally been regarded as variable costs. They are either paid by the hour or the week or paid by results with a fall-back rate. For example, in *Miller v Hamworthy Engineering Ltd*[4] the Court of Appeal was unprepared to accept that a newly promoted foreman on staff status could still be held to be bound by the short time agreement in the collective agreement which applied when the employee was a weekly paid engineer. In recent years the upgrading of manual workers to staff status, harmonising terms and conditions of both groups of employees, has become a personnel management objective. It is thought to engender greater loyalty and commitment. It is helpful as a defence to equal pay claims. Moreover, it has been used as a device to convince employees to move from collective bargaining to individual bargaining.

## (b) Lay offs

Whatever the type of payment system, where the employee is ready and willing to perform, and the contract of employment has not been terminated, contractual wages must be paid unless the employer can point to an express or implied term entitling him to lay off without pay or put the employee on short time.[5] Where an employer is unable to offer work to the employee 'for reasons outside his control' such as when government-ordered power cuts compelled employers to adopt a three-day week, the courts might imply a term suspending his obligation to pay wages.[6] Moreover, where collective agreements provide lay off or short-time working provisions, these may be incorporated into employment contracts to give employers a right to lay off on guaranteed payment rates[7] or to introduce short-time working involving proportionate reductions in earnings. But where an employer attempts to introduce such steps unilaterally for reasons of trade, the employee may have an action for

4 [1986] ICR 846, [1986] IRLR 461, CA.
5 *Devonald v Rosser & Sons* [1906] 2 KB 728.
6 *Browning v Crumlin Valley Collieries Ltd* [1926] 1 KB 522.
7 In addition, there is a specific statutory right to a guarantee payment in the event of lay off or short time. See Employment Rights Act 1996, ss 28-35.

breach of contract to recover earnings or even wrongful or constructive dismissal under the theory that the breach amounted to a repudiation.[8]

## (c) Sick pay

Sick pay is treated somewhat differently in the absence of an express contractual provision. At one point there appeared to be authority for the proposition that employment contracts contained an implied presumption that pay would accrue during sickness absence,[9] though the employer could negate the presumption by an express term.[10] In *Mears v Safecar Security Ltd*,[11] however, the Court of Appeal rejected a common law presumption in favour of continued pay during the period of sickness. The Court of Tribunal had to look at such factors as the knowledge of the parties at the time the contract was made, whether the employment was daily, indefinite or for a fixed term of years and on occasion what the parties actually did during the contractual period. And in *Howman & Son v Blyth*[12] the EAT decided that there was an implied obligation to pay sick pay for a reasonable period of time. In this case, the period chosen was the period specified in the relevant collective agreement for the industry - the National Joint Working Rule Agreement.

The development of statutory sick pay schemes (SSP) makes the clarification of contractual sick pay entitlements more likely in many cases. An employer can incorporate SSP within a contractual payment, but cannot contract out of this statutory obligation.[13]

## (d) Pay and industrial action

In cases where the employer decides to withhold pay in response to various forms of industrial action the common law rules apply with equal force to salaried and manual workers. If the employee stops work completely or refuses to work in accordance with instructions issued within the employer's contractual authority, the employer can dismiss summarily or withhold payment. For example, in *Cresswell v Board of Inland Revenue*[14] the employee's action for payment was rejected by the court because they

8 *Devonald v Rosser & Sons* [1906] 2 KB 728.
9 *Marrison v Bell* [1939] 2 KB 187, [1939] 1 All ER 745; *Orman v Saville Sportswear Ltd* [1960] 3 All ER 105, [1960] 1 WLR 1055.
10 *Petrie v MacFisheries Ltd* [1940] 1 KB 258, [1939] 4 All ER 281.
11 [1983] QB 54, [1982] ICR 626, CA.
12 [1983] ICR 416, EAT.
13 Social Security Contributions and Benefits Act 1992, ss 151-163.
14 [1984] ICR 508, [1984] IRLR 190.

were not working the new computerised equipment in accordance with their employer's contractual instructions and therefore the employer was entitled to withhold pay according to the principle of 'No work - no pay'. As the court put it:

> 'This is such an obvious principle, founded on the simplest consideration of what the plaintiff would have to prove in any action for recovery of pay in respect of any period where he was deliberately absent from work of his own accord.'[15]

There is in fact an extensive body of case law on this issue which is discussed at length in Chapter 17.

## (e) The employer's obligation to provide work to do

The employer's obligation to ensure that employees receive contractually agreed remuneration sometimes creates an ancillary obligation to provide work in order to ascertain the remuneration, as in cases of commission, piecework, etc. To what extent, however, is an employer obliged to provide an employee with work even where he otherwise meets his duty to pay the contractually agreed remuneration?

At common law, the general rule was that the employer's duty was to pay wages, not to provide the employee with work to do as well.[16] However, in certain exceptional cases where the nature of the employee's work required actual work as well as wages to meet the employer's obligations and employee's interests it has been held that there is a positive duty to provide work. Thus, the need of entertainers for publicity,[17] the need of skilled workers to work so as to maintain their skills,[18] the need to preserve contacts and reputation in a trade or profession[19] and the need of apprentices for work[20] have all given rise to a positive obligation to provide work.

In *Breach v Epsylon Industries Ltd*,[1] the EAT made the point that it was necessary for industrial tribunals to look into the circumstances of the case to decide whether, owing to the nature of the employment, a term should be implied to the effect that there was an obligation on the employer to provide work suitable for the employee in the position he held. For

15 See also *Miles v Wakefield Metropolitan District Council* [1987] ICR 368, [1987] IRLR 193, HL, discussed further in Ch 16, pp 304-309.
16 *Collier v Sunday Referee Publishing Co Ltd* [1940] 2 KB 647, [1940] 4 All ER 234.
17 *Herbert Clayton and Jack Waller Ltd v Oliver* [1930] AC 209, HL.
18 *Langston v AUEW (No 2)* [1974] ICR 510, [1974] IRLR 182, NIRC.
19 *Bosworth v Angus Jowett & Co Ltd* [1977] IRLR 374, IT.
20 *Dunk v George Waller & Son Ltd* [1970] 2 QB 163, [1970] 2 All ER 630, CA.
1 [1976] ICR 316, [1976] IRLR 180.

example, in *Bosworth v Angus Jowett & Co Ltd*,[2] an obligation to provide work was implied in a sales director's contract under the criterion in *Breach's* case to entitle the employee to work during the remainder of his fixed term contract. Such cases appear to be authority for the proposition that particular types of employment, by their nature, give rise to an obligation to provide work.

On the other hand, under-employment of an employee on certain duties contained within his job description may not necessarily amount to a repudiation,[3] particularly where there is no contractual entitlement to exercise particular duties at a particular time.

## (f) The employer's obligation to exercise care

Under the contract of employment there is a general implied duty of employers to exercise care. Under certain circumstances a failure to perform this obligation is repudiatory. As the EAT put it in *British Aircraft Corpn Ltd v Austin*,[4] as part and parcel of the employers' duty to take reasonable care for the safety of their employees, they are also under an obligation to act reasonably in dealing with matters of safety or complaints about lack of safety which are drawn to their attention by employees. For example, in the *British Aircraft Corpn* case, an employer's failure to investigate an employee's complaint about the inadequacy of protective eyewear made available for use was conduct entitling the employee to resign without notice. Further in *Pagano v HGS*,[5] the employer's failure to maintain vehicles in a roadworthy state in spite of numerous complaints by the employee about the state of the vehicles amounted to a contractual repudiation. In *Graham Oxley Tool Steels Ltd v Firth*,[6] the fact that employers left an employee working for several months in intolerably cold conditions was a breach of their implied contractual obligation to provide a proper working environment. However, in *Reid v Rush & Tompkins Group plc* the Court of Appeal was unwilling to imply a term into the contract of employment to provide insurance or even advise an employee to obtain insurance in the case of work abroad.[7]

2 [1977] IRLR 374, IT.
3 See eg *Peter Carnie & Son Ltd v Paton* [1979] IRLR 260, EAT; *Hemmings v International Computers Ltd* [1976] IRLR 37, IT.
4 [1978] IRLR 332, EAT; cf *Wilsons and Clyde Coal Co Ltd v English* [1938] AC 57, [1937] 3 All ER 628, HL.
5 [1976] IRLR 9, EAT.
6 [1980] IRLR 135, EAT.
7 See *Reid v Rush & Tompkins Group plc* [1989] 3 All ER 228, [1990] ICR 61, CA.

Moreover, it was also stated in the *Graham Oxley Tool Steels*[8] that there was no principle that a breach of a statutory duty under the Factories Act or a breach of the common law duty to take reasonable care for the safety of his workers by providing them with a safe system of work and proper plant and materials *by itself* results in a fundamental breach of contract by one employer.

Finally, in the case of *Spring v Guardian Assurance plc*[9] the House of Lords held that in certain circumstances there was an implied duty of care upon employers not to be negligent in the preparation and presentation of references for employees.

## (g) The duty not to undermine the trust and confidence of the employee

In recent years, as courts and tribunals have increasingly encountered factual examples of unreasonable and abusive conduct by employers they have decided that employers have a fundamental implied obligation not to destroy or seriously damage the mutual trust and confidence between employer and employee. This new implied obligation derived from the widened obligations of employees to co-operate, has been developed by the judiciary into a duty of mutual respect.[10]

In *Robinson v Crompton Parkinson Ltd*,[11] Kilner Brown LJ took up the suggestion that an obligation of trust and confidence might be mutual and applied it to the cases of constructive dismissals:

> 'In a contract of employment, and in conditions of employment, there has to be mutual trust and confidence between master and servant. Although most of the reported cases deal with the master seeking remedy against a servant or former servant for acting in breach of confidence or breach of trust that action can only be upon the basis that trust and confidence is mutual. Consequently, when a man says of his employer, "I claim that you have broken your contract because you have clearly shown that you have no confidence in me and you have behaved in a way which is contrary to the mutual trust which ought to exist between master and servant", he is entitled in these circumstances, it seems to us, to say that there is conduct which amounts to a repudiation of contract.'[12]

8 [1980] IRLR 135, EAT. See now *Johnstone v Bloomsbury Health Authority* [1991] ICR 269, [1991] IRLR 118, CA. See also Employment Rights Act 1996, s 100 which provides that dismissal of an employee who leaves in response to an employers failure to respond to a serious health and safety complaint could amount to an automatically unfair dismissal.

9 [1994] IRLR 460, HL.

10 *Wilson v Racher* [1974] ICR 428, [1974] IRLR 114, CA.

11 [1978] ICR 401, [1978] IRLR 61, EAT.

12 Ibid at 65.

Lord Denning in *Woods v W M Car Services (Peterborough) Ltd*[13] endorsed this view of a parallel between the law of wrongful dismissal and constructive dismissal:

> 'Now under modern legislation we have the converse case. It is the duty of the employer to be good and considerate to his servants. Sometimes it is formulated as an implied term not to do anything likely to destroy the relationship of confidence between them, see *Courtaulds Northern Textiles Ltd v Andrew* [1979] IRLR 84. But I prefer to look at it in this way: the employer must be good and considerate to his servants. Just as a servant must be good and faithful, so an employer must be good and considerate. Just as in the old days an employee could be guilty of misconduct justifying his dismissal, so in modern times an employer can be guilty of misconduct justifying the employee in leaving at once without notice. In each case it depends on whether the misconduct amounted to a repudiatory breach as defined in *Western Excavating (ECC) Ltd v Sharp* [1978] QB 761, [1978] IRLR 27.'

This implied obligation has been an umbrella category applied quite widely to find abusive or arbitrary treatment repudiatory conduct by the employers. In certain cases the employer's repudiatory conduct has involved a failure to perform specific positive obligations. Thus in *Post Office v Strange*[14] a failure by the employer to provide the employee with the right of appeal to an appropriate level within the disciplinary procedure was viewed as a clear failure to perform the contract and hence a repudiation entitling the employee to resign.[15]

Similarly, a failure by an employer to provide adequate support to employees during busy periods,[16] to provide an appraisal to probationers during a trial period,[17] to respond to an employee's complaints about the lack of adequate safety equipment,[18] to undermine a supervisor's authority by criticising him in front of other employees,[19] and to protect an employee against harassment, including sexual harassment,[20] from other employees[1] have all been characterised as breaches of the particular implied terms of mutual trust and confidence.

13 [1982] ICR 693, [1982] IRLR 413, CA.

14 [1981] IRLR 515, EAT.

15 See also *Wetherall (Bond St W1) Ltd v Lynn* [1978] 1 WLR 200, [1978] ICR 205 (a breach of grievance procedure). See further *W A Goold (Pearmak) v McConnell* [1995] IRLR 516, EAT, discussed in Ch 4.

16 *Seligman and Latz Ltd v McHugh* [1979] IRLR 130, EAT.

17 *White v London Transport Executive* [1982] QB 489, [1981] IRLR 261, EAT.

18 *British Aircraft Corpn v Austin* [1978] IRLR 332, EAT.

19 *Associated Tyre Specialists Ltd v Waterhouse* [1977] ICR 218, [1976] IRLR 386, EAT.

20 See eg *Bracebridge Engineering Ltd v Darby* [1990] IRLR 3, EAT, discussed in Ch 13.

1 See eg *Wigan Borough Council v Davies* [1979] ICR 411, [1979] IRLR 127, EAT. See too *Bracebridge Engineering*.

Furthermore, in *Scally v Southern Health and Social Services* Board[2] the House of Lords was prepared to imply into the contracts of employment of doctors an obligation of the employer to take reasonable steps to inform them of a new right which requires action by them to obtain the benefits, though Lord Bridge indicated that this implied term was conditional upon the circumstance that the terms of the contract of employment have not been negotiated with the individual employee but result from negotiation with a representative body or are otherwise incorporated by reference. Lord Bridge was attempting to retain a 'necessity' test for such implied terms rather than a 'reasonableness' test but he did accept that the test of necessity had been shifted to that of a necessary incident of a definable category of contractual relationship rather than the traditional test of necessity to give business efficacy to the contract of employment as a whole.

In some other cases certain critical remarks by the employer to the employee have been held to be sufficiently abusive in the circumstances to amount to a repudiation. As Lord Denning remarked in *Wood*'s case a certain amount of trenchant criticism can reasonably be regarded as part of the day-to-day exchange between employee and employer.[3] Yet there can come a point when the remarks in context can reach the point where they make continued employment intolerable for the employee and entitle him or her to resign and be constructively dismissed.

To take one rather extreme example, in *Isle of Wight Tourist Board v Coombes*,[4] an employee of 15 years' standing resigned when the director to whom she was personal secretary stated, within her hearing to another employee, 'she is an intolerable bitch on a Monday morning'. The EAT per Bristow J agreed that this was conduct entitling the employee to resign particularly since there was no attempt to make an apology because it shattered the relationship which in this particular case was one of 'complete confidence'.

Moreover in *Courtaulds Northern Textiles Ltd v Andrew*[5] where a manager exclaimed to an employee 'you can't do the bloody job anyway' and he used these words maliciously - with no belief in their truth - in order to get rid of him, then it might be sufficient to justify a resignation as constructive dismissal because those words seriously damaged the relationship of confidence and trust between employer and employee.

In *Fyfe and McGrouther Ltd v Byrne*,[6] the EAT stated that where an employer makes a false accusation to the police without having any

2 [1991] ICR 771, [1991] IRLR 522, HL.
3 [1982] ICR 693, [1982] IRLR 413, CA; see too *Chesham Shipping Ltd v Rowe* [1977] IRLR 391, EAT; *Palmanor Ltd v Cedron* [1978] ICR 1008, [1978] IRLR 303, EAT.
4 [1976] IRLR 413, EAT.
5 [1979] IRLR 84, EAT.
6 [1977] IRLR 29, EAT; *Robinson v Crompton Parkinson Ltd* [1978] ICR 401, [1978] IRLR 61, EAT.

evidence to back up his suspicion, that could entitle an employee to resign and claim to be constructively dismissed, because in such a case 'by adopting this attitude in a situation for which [the employee] was not responsible [the employer] had destroyed any basis of confidence that could ever exist between them and him in the future'.

Another category of constructive dismissal case is where the employer imposes a penalty for disciplinary offences which is grossly out of proportion to that offence. Thus in *BBC v Beckett* the exercise of a contractual power to downgrade for disciplinary reasons was viewed as so disproportionate to the misconduct itself that it amounted to a repudiation.[7]

A further category of abusive conduct consists of cases where an employee has been subjected to a sustained pattern of harassment by his or her employer. For example in *Garner v Grange Furnishing Ltd*[8] an employee resigned after being treated badly for a sustained period by the employer in circumstances of some mutual friction. The EAT upheld the industrial tribunal's finding of constructive dismissal commenting that a series of small incidents over a period of time can eventually amount to a repudiation. In such circumstances 'the employer is making it impossible for the employee to go on working for him'.[9]

In *Wadham Stringer Commercials (London) Ltd and Wadham Stringer Vehicles Ltd v Brown*[10] an employee was gradually demoted from fleet sales director to a retail salesman and moved to a very small office. He protested in writing about his treatment. He was given instructions relating to his continued work as salesman and warned that unless he accepted them it would be presumed that he wished to resign. He replied that he was not resigning. He was then moved again to a smaller office with no ventilation, initially no telephone or light and situated next to the gentleman's lavatory. When he finally resigned in response to the employer's treatment, the EAT upheld the industrial tribunal's finding that he had been constructively dismissed.

In more recent years, the duty of mutual trust and confidence has been expanded to include further limits to the exercise of contractual authority by the employer. For example, in relation to pension schemes, employers have been held to have an *implied obligation of good faith* using their

7 [1983] IRLR 43, EAT; see also *Cawley v South Wales Electricity Board* [1985] IRLR 89, EAT.

8 [1977] IRLR 206, EAT.

9 Ibid.

10 [1983] IRLR 46, EAT. See too *Lewis v Motorworld Garages* [1985] IRLR 465, CA; see discussion by H Carty in 'Contract Theory and Employment Reality' [1986] 49 MLR 240.

discretion. In *Imperial Group Pension Trust Ltd v Imperial Tobacco Ltd*[11] the employers had refused to consent to the trustee's request to increase the benefits to employees from a surplus. Browne-Wilkinson VC held that this was a breach of their obligation of good faith to their employees. The employer was not entitled to exercise their discretion in administering the pension fund solely to further the financial interests of the company but had to take the interests of the employees into account sufficiently not to undermine the trust and confidence of employees in their employ.

In *United Bank Ltd v Akhtar*[12] an express mobility clause was subject to an implied term of reasonable notice and an obligation by the bank not to exercise its discretion so as to make the employee's performance a practical impossibility. Knox J made the point that there was a clear distinction between implying a term which negates an express term and one which controls the exercise of a discretion which is expressly enforced by the contract.[13]

The introduction of such wide standard implied obligations on the part of employer and employee makes the employment relationship into a hybrid relationship with strong elements of status; a relationship where individual employees are working under a code of rights and obligations pre-established by the judiciary and on occasion at odds with employees' contractual expectations. That said, it is at least as important to establish how the rules themselves strike a balance between employers' decisions and workers' rights under the contract. On the one hand, as we have seen, the implied obligations of co-operation and flexibility placed on the employee suggest that the judges quite consciously consider that employers should continue to be given a wide enabling power to determine the most appropriate method of running a business.

On the other hand, possibly as a quid pro quo, the new duties of mutual trust and confidence do create constraints on the way management goes about the implementation of decisions, as if the judges had decided to exercise a civilising influence on employers in employment matters.

As Napier sums it up:

> '. . . the courts have to a much greater extent than in the past been given opportunities of passing judgment on the orders given by an employer to his employees. Under the influence of these rights - the prevailing view

11 [1991] 1 WLR 589, [1991] IRLR 66, Ch D; see too *Stannard v Fisons Pension Trust Ltd* [1992] IRLR 27, CA, in which it was held that pension trustees had a general legal duty to give properly informed consideration to the exercise of their powers; see also *Mihlenstedt v Barclays Bank International* [1989] IRLR 522, CA.

12 [1989] IRLR 507; see discussion in Ch 4.

13 See also *Johnstone v Bloomsbury Health Authority* [1991] ICR 269, [1991] IRLR 118, CA. Both the implied term and its effect upon express terms are discussed further in Ch 4.

> which has emerged favours a much more restrictive interpretation of the right to command than was previously found acceptable. The right to command is seen as more limited in scope and is itself subject to the employer's contractual duty to maintain the employees' trust and confidence.'[14]

Yet is this not to say that these two lines of authority are of equal weight and effect? For on the one hand the new implied terms tend to widen employee flexibility, mobility, loyalty and co-operation and thereby expand the scope of employer discretion within the parameters of the contract. On the other hand, in contrast, the new common law limits on the employer's exercise of this form of prerogative are constraints on the way the employer takes and implements decisions. It is true that they are sufficiently powerful at times to regulate the way the employer exercises discretion even under express contractual terms. Nevertheless, they leave considerable contractual authority to employers to determine the substance of decisions since they intervene only in cases where the exercise of discretion has been extremely unreasonable.

That being so, the next question to investigate is precisely how the implied terms interact with the express terms of the legal contract.

14 Napier, B 'The Contract of Employment' in Lewis (ed) *Labour Law in Britain* (1986) p 348. See too Brodie 'Beyond Exchange: The New Contract of Employment' (1998) ILJ 79.

CHAPTER 4

# The terms of employment contracts: express terms

## INTRODUCTION

In theory, the express terms of the contract are jointly agreed by the parties. In practice, however, the contracting process leaves considerable scope for the employer to enhance the powers given by the implied terms. Where collective bargaining results in collective agreements which contain terms for incorporation within contracts of employment, the employer's discretion is limited by a jointly agreed term as to pay or other conditions of employment. In unusual cases, when employees have sufficiently rare skills individual bargaining produces genuine mutually agreed terms between employer and employee. However, legislation often operates in a field where the employer drafts many terms of the contract and presents them to the employee on a 'take it or leave it' basis. This drafting power of the employer is, as we shall see, subject to certain constraints at common law and under statute law. Yet, statute law does not always give adequate recognition to the actual reach of the employer's drafting power in forming the contract.

The contract of employment is only rarely reduced to a formal written document setting out the terms and conditions of employment. For most employees the reality of employment consists of a hiring interview with a job offer, sometimes in writing, giving the essential terms of the job. When this has been accepted and the employee has begun to work, the employer is required to issue, not later than two months after the first day of work, a written statement setting out certain basic initial employment particulars such as the name of the employee and employer, the date employment began, the date the employee's continuous service began, including any service with a former employer if it counts, pay rates, the method of calculating pay, how often remuneration is paid, hours of work, including normal hours of work, entitlement to holidays and holiday pay, sick leave or sick pay, pensions, length of notice, job title or brief job description, expected length of employment if not permanent, the place of work and any relevant collective agreements.[1] Most of the above particulars must be included in a single document.[2]

The employer may however, refer the employee to other documents in relation to the provisions of collective agreements, sick pay provisions and pension arrangements but only if those documents are made reasonably accessible to the employee.[3] Most of the written particulars are not compulsory. An employer has the option of either providing them or stating that there are no relevant particulars.[4] There are three main exceptions to this rule. The minimum period of notice of termination is prescribed by ERA, ss 86-89. The written statement must include a note specifying existing disciplinary rules if any and in addition specify a 'disciplinary procedure' ie a person to whom the employee can appeal if dissatisfied with a disciplinary decision and the manner of such an appeal and a 'grievance procedure,' ie a person to whom an employee can apply to redress any grievance relating to his or her employment and the manner of such an application. Moreover, if there are further steps of appeal they must be explained. The employer can notify the employee either in the written statement or by reference to another document which is reasonably accessible.[5]

The statutory power to issue written information to the employee was meant to help employees by providing them with information about their contractual terms and conditions. Now, as modified by the EC directive, it should result in more information being given to employees. Nevertheless, it also has the effect of facilitating the employer's power to shape the contents of the contract of employment. The written statements, it is true, are not technically contracts themselves. They only constitute 'very strong prima facie evidence' of the terms of the contract and can be refuted by evidence submitted by the employee,[6] even some time after having received a written statement.[7]

Further, statements made in the course of the early stages of forming the contract, whether oral or in writing, can be regarded as express terms of the contract outweighing a subsequent written statement. For example,

1 ERA, s 1.
2 ERA, s 2(4).
3 ERA, s 2(3).
4 ERA, s 2(1). An employee who is dissatisfied with written particulars cannot compel the employer to insert a particular but can only apply to the industrial tribunal for finding whether or not the particulars in a written statement accurately reflect the real position. See eg *Eagland v British Telecommunications plc* [1992] IRLR 323, CA. See too *Morley v Heritage plc* [1993] IRLR 400, CA.
5 ERA, s 3.
6 *System Floors (UK) Ltd v Daniel* [1982] ICR 54, [1981] IRLR 475, EAT; cf *Eagland v British Telecommunications plc* [1990] ICR 248, [1990] IRLR 328, EAT.
7 *Jones v Associated Tunnelling Co Ltd* [1981] IRLR 477, EAT.

in *Hawker Siddeley Power Engineering Ltd v Rump*[8] an employee who had received an oral promise when he was hired that his work would be confined to southern England was held not bound by written particulars later issued by the employer which required countrywide mobility in accordance with a collective agreement. Similarly in *Robertson v British Gas Corpn*[9] a letter from the Gas Board indicating that 'incentive bonus scheme conditions will apply' was held to supervene a subsequent statement of written particulars issued by the employer which applied the provisions of a collective agreement - the NJC agreement - and relating bonuses to the scheme agreed by it. These and other cases seem to suggest that representations made in the formation stage of the contract will be honoured as representations which tended to induce the bargain.

Nevertheless, where the employers are sufficiently careful to distinguish between an initial exploratory stage and a formal offer and acceptance stage, the courts have been willing to honour their exercise of their drafting power. For example, in *Deeley v British Rail Engineering*[10] the Court of Appeal was prepared to disregard the fact that the original advertisement, the employee's letter of application and the employer's acknowledgment all specified 'Sales Engineer (Export)' in determining the scope of the employee's contractual duties where the employer could show that he had issued a formal offer of employment and terms and conditions of employment all headed 'Sales Engineer' which contained an express clause to the effect that "the duties will be as required by the Managing Director of British Rail Engineering Ltd or as the Railway Board may from time to time determine", and the employee's acceptance of the offer was headed 'Sales Engineer'. The case apparently was regarded as one of a written contract rather than written statement under ERA, s 1.

## CHANGING THE TERMS OF EXISTING CONTRACTS

Finally where there is a change in any of the terms of employment, the employer is required to inform the employee again either in writing or by reference to another document made reasonably accessible to the employee.[11]

This statutory obligation is meant only to provide information to employees about actual changes in the existing contractual relationship, yet in practice it can be brought in as part of that process. It is useful to distinguish between four separate legal categories:

8 [1979] IRLR 425, EAT.
9 [1983] IRLR 302, CA.
10 [1980] IRLR 147, CA.
11 ERA, s 4.

(1) The employer may introduce a unilateral change in employment conditions such as pay, hours at work or pay but nevertheless be entitled to do so by virtue of an express or implied term of the contract. This may or may not involve a change in the written statement.

(2) The employer may propose a change in the existing contractual terms in which case acceptance by the employee is necessary in order for there to be a mutually agreed variation of the contract. This must be followed up by a written statement of the change.

(3) The employer may choose (*using the written statement*) to introduce a change outside the contract to which the employee is unwilling to agree. The employee may defend his or her rights under the existing contract by an action for breach of contract, an action for unlawful deduction under Part II of ERA 1996 or by treating it as a repudiation and a constructive dismissal for the purposes of a claim for unfair dismissal or redundancy. In such a case employees must be careful not to conduct themselves in such a way as to impliedly assent to the breach or appear to waive the repudiation.

(4) Finally, the employer may decide to terminate the existing employment contract by giving the appropriate notice of termination and offer the employee a new contract on new terms (with a new written statement of particulars).

The act of the employee in not objecting to a unilateral variation of the original written statement will not itself be taken as committing him to these varied terms. As Browne-Wilkinson J (as he then was) put it in *Jones v Associated Tunnelling Co Ltd*:

> 'it would be unrealistic to expect employees to read and react to erroneous changes in their written particulars so that their effective consent could be inferred from their silence.'[12]

At all events, while the process of issuing information to the employee does not itself amount to a contracting power, in many cases it provides the employer with the opportunity to prepare the main elements of the contractual bargain and present them to the employee on a 'take it or leave it' basis at the start of employment. In so far as there are trade union representatives negotiating collective agreements with the employer, remuneration, hours, holiday entitlement, etc may be jointly determined, and indeed, in practice, trade union representation results in common terms for all employees covered by the agreement. But there are areas of managerial decision-making which are not always dealt with by trade union negotiation. Moreover, in the absence of a trade union, the employer has considerable scope to formulate the rules of the relationship as express

12 [1981] IRLR 477 EAT.

terms of the employment contract. To illustrate the drafting power of the employer and its regulation at common law, we can take three prominent examples:

(a) express mobility and flexibility clauses;
(b) restraints on working in competition; and
(c) disciplinary terms in the employment contract.

## EXPRESS MOBILITY AND FLEXIBILITY CLAUSES

Where an employee agrees to take a job at a place of work and for specified hours it is possible for employers, if left unhindered by collective bargaining or legislation, to draft the express terms of the contract so as to widen their powers of unilateral decision-making under the contract in terms of hours of work, type of work to be performed and the place at which the work can be performed.

For example in *Dowsett Engineering Construction Ltd v Fowler*[13] an employee's contract contained a term incorporated from the staff handbook that read: 'If you are employed on site you may be required to work overtime on being given reasonable notice'. Although the employee had been working weekend overtime on a voluntary basis for some time, the EAT held that the clause 'required' the employee 'to work overtime if overtime was asked to be done', and hence required him to accept a new weekend rota scheme as part of his existing contractual duties. The wider contractual authority conferred upon the employer by the clause meant that the employee's resignation in the face of the employer's insistence upon a change was not a 'constructive dismissal' by the employer.

In contrast, if an employee is covered by collective bargaining, then overtime is usually subject to joint regulation either by placing a premium on overtime pay or by restricting the employer's discretion to require employees to work overtime. For example, a clause may read, 'The employee shall work only such overtime as is mutually agreed,' in which case the employee has a veto right over overtime. Alternatively, if the clause says, 'The employee agrees to work a reasonable amount of overtime as and when production requires it', the employee has some legal basis for objecting to the amount of overtime required as it moves towards an 'unreasonable' level.

The clause in *Dowsett* gave complete discretion as to the amount of overtime that could be required; the only fetter upon managerial discretion in the clause was the requirement of reasonable notice. In practice, good personnel management would ensure in most cases that there would be

13 [1977] EAT 425/76.

limits to the employer's demands. Moreover, considerations of health and safety might intervene at the extremes of hours worked. The employer's decision must also take into account contractual obligations of mutual respect and duty not to impair the employee's health.[14] Within these limits, however, such an express overtime clause, combined with the employee's duty to obey orders, creates a formidable contractual basis for unilateral managerial authority.

Employers also use express contract terms to ensure obligations of flexibility in the type of work to be performed and mobility in the place at which work can be performed. Flexibility can be achieved by choosing a wide job title, eg 'copy typist/general duties clerk'.[15] Alternatively, it can be secured by the device of a flexibility clause.

For example in *Deeley's* case[16] the flexibility clause specifying that the employee's 'duties will be as required by the Managing Director of British Rail Engineering Limited or as the Railway's Board may from time to time determine' was held to allow the employer the discretion to transfer Mr Deeley from export sales to domestic sales despite the first three years of employment being exclusively concerned with export sales. And in *Nelson v BBC*[17] a BBC Caribbean Service producer who worked under a flexibility clause requiring him 'to serve when, how and where the BBC demanded' discovered when the Caribbean Service was discontinued that the BBC had contractual authority to treat him as a general producer rather than a producer in the Caribbean Service. In that case an industrial tribunal finding that the actual work that the employee had been doing provided evidence of an implied term limiting the scope of the flexibility clause was swept aside by the Court of Appeal. Roskill LJ stated:

> 'With great respect to the Tribunal, that seems to me to be an impossible conclusion as a matter of law, for this reason: it is a basic principle of contract law that if a contract makes express provision (as clause 8 did) in almost unrestricted language, it is impossible in the same breath to imply into that contract a restriction of the kind that the Industrial Tribunal sought to do.'

Similarly, in the case of mobility clauses, employees may be required 'to transfer to another location',[18] or even to work anywhere in the United Kingdom,[19] it would appear that the courts are reluctant to constrain the

14 See *Johnstone v Bloomsbury Health Authority* [1991] ICR 269, [1991] IRLR 118, CA.
15 *Glitz v Watford Electric Co Ltd* [1979] IRLR 89, EAT; see also *Peter Carnie & Son Ltd v Paton* [1979] IRLR 260, EAT.
16 [1980] IRLR 147, CA.
17 [1977] ICR 649, CA.
18 *Rank Xerox Ltd v Churchill* [1988] IRLR 280, EAT.
19 *Sutcliffe v Hawker Siddeley Aviation Ltd* [1973] ICR 560, [1973] IRLR 304, NIRC.

employers' discretion by examining their reasonableness in exercising contractual authority under such express terms.

In *Rank Xerox Ltd v Churchill*,[20] for example, secretaries were required to move from Central London to Marlow. Their contracts provided that 'The Company may require you to transfer to another location'. The industrial tribunal found that the mobility clause was subject to an implied term that transfers had to be within reasonable distance from the employee's home. The EAT however held that the express contractual term was so clear that there was no room for an implication which would vary the unambiguous words of the contract.

On occasion, however, the courts have shown an awareness of the drafting power of employers and have been prepared to place limits on the scope of express terms. For example, in *Cowen v Haden Ltd*[1] the Court of Appeal was faced with an express contractual term providing that 'The employee's job title will be regional surveyor - southern region. He will be required to undertake, at the direction of the company, any and all duties which reasonably fall within the scope of his capabilities.'

In deciding the scope of the employee's work under the contract, for the purpose of determining whether the employee was redundant, the Court of Appeal held that the effect of the flexibility clause 'was not to give the employers the right to transfer him from his job as regional surveyor to any job as a quantity surveyor in their organisation, but only to require him to perform any duties reasonably within the scope of his job as regional surveyor'. This was an example of the technique of strict construction.

More recently, however, in *United Bank Ltd v Akhtar*[2] an implied term was applied inventively to limit more directly the employer's discretion under an express term, in the context of a constructive dismissal claim. In that case the employer had inserted a mobility clause in the contract of a junior bank clerk working in Leeds which provided that 'the bank may from time to time require an employee to be transferred temporarily or permanently to any place of business which the bank may have in the UK for which a relocation allowance or other allowances may be payable at the discretion of the bank'. On 2 June, Mr Akhtar was told that he was required to work at Birmingham with effect from 8 June. Although his wife was ill, and he had difficulties selling his house, the bank refused to postpone the move at his request. The EAT was prepared to accept that the industrial tribunal could imply into the contract a requirement that

20 [1988] IRLR 280, EAT; see too *Express Lift Co Ltd v Bowles* [1977] ICR 474, [1977] IRLR 99, EAT. In *Sibson*'s case the mobility clause was implied but the effect was the same as an express clause.

1 [1983] ICR 1.

2 [1989] IRLR 507, EAT. See too *McLory v Post Office* [1992] ICR 758 in which the contractual right to suspend the employee was viewed as subject to an implied term of 'reasonableness' in its exercise.

reasonable notice should be given in the exercise of the employer's power under that clause and that the bank's discretion in respect of mobility allowances would not be exercised so as to make the employee's performance a practical impossibility. It found, therefore, that the industrial tribunal was entitled to hold that the employer's insistence upon immediate transfer was a fundamental breach of the general implied contractual duty of maintaining confidence and trust between employer and employee. The EAT described the term of mutual trust and confidence as 'an overriding obligation... independent of and in addition to the literal interpretation of the employer's actions permitted under the terms of the contract.' It added however, that there was a clear difference between implying a term which negatives a provision which is expressly stated in the contract and implying a term which controls the exercise of discretion which is expressly contained in a contract.[3]

Moreover in *Johnstone v Bloomsbury Health Authority*,[4] a doctor whose contract required him to work 40 hours per week and remain on call for another 48 hours per week claimed that 88 hours per week was an unreasonably long period to work each week, and by requiring him to work such long hours the employer was in breach of its contractual duty to take reasonable care for the employee's health and safety because this would foreseeably injure his health.

The Court of Appeal would not imply a reasonable limit of 72 hours to the maximum hours of work specified in the contract. However, a majority were prepared, in permitting the case to go to full trial, to hold that the discretion of the employer conferred by the express terms of the contract could be circumscribed by the implied terms of the employment contract. Only Leggatt in dissent maintained that reliance on a clear express term could not be used to find the employer in breach of an implied term. Browne-Wilkinson V-C, started from the position that the express and implied terms must be capable of co-existence without conflict and held that while the employee's absolute duty to work 40 hours could not be subject to a restrictive implied term, the employer's exercise of his discretion in allocating additional hours was subject to the implied limitations of health and safety. Stuart Smith LJ went further and held that even an express contractual power could be subject to the implied duty of care both in contract and tort not to injure the employee's health and safety.

Moreover, the court accepted the argument that in so far as the employee could be viewed as accepting the risk of personal injury by agreeing to the excessive hours, then the clause of the agreement could fall within s 2(1) of the Unfair Contracts Terms Act 1977.[5]

3 [1989] IRLR 507 at 512.
4 [1991] ICR 269, [1991] IRLR 118, CA.
5 Cf *Chapman v Aberdeen Construction Group plc* [1991] IRLR 505, Ct of Sess (re s 10 of UCTA).

The net effect of these and other cases is to suggest that there are limits imposed by his implied terms upon to the exercise of managerial discretion having express contractual authority. In *Akhtar* the effect of the implied term was to place merely a *procedural* limit upon the employers express authority. This procedural dimension of the implied term was confirmed by the House of Lords in *Scally v Southern Health and Social Services Board* when it found that it was an implied obligation of the employer to inform the employee of his rights to a new pension term because the employee could not reasonably be expected to be aware of the term unless it is drawn to his attention.[6] Yet, *Johnstone* offered an example of the implied term being used to override the *substance* of the employer's decision-making under the express term. This substantive dimension could also be found in the decision by Brown Wilkinson V-C, in *Imperial Tobacco*[7] to the effect that the employer could be required by the implied term of a good faith to award some increase to the employees of the old scheme despite the apparently complete discretion conferred by the express term.

These limits are imposed only at the outer reaches of the exercise of managerial authority where the factual circumstances are extreme because the implied obligations of trust and confidence or good faith do not impose a general condition of reasonableness but only apply to extremely unreasonable exercises of discretion.[8] Hence, in any but the more extreme cases, the employer's exercise of discretion in respect of hours of work, place of work, etc will be non-repudiatory. Consequently, if the employee resigns in the face of such an instruction, there would be no claim of a wrongful dismissal or constructive dismissal. If, on the other hand, the employee refuses to carry out the instruction and is dismissed, the employee can claim unfair dismissal or redundancy and have an industrial tribunal determine the reasonableness of the employer's decision to dismiss (Ch 8) or the issue of whether the dismissal was for redundancy (Ch 9).

6 [1991] ICR 771 at 781, [1991] IRLR 522 HL; see H Collins 'Implied Duty to give Information During Performance of Contracts' [1992] 55 MLR 556; cf *W A Goold (Pearmak) v McConnell* [1995] IRLR 516 in which the EAT upheld an industrial tribunal which held that the employer had an implied obligation to 'reasonably and promptly afford a reasonable opportunity to their employees to obtain redress' of grievances. See discussion by D Brodie [1996] ILJ 121 at 124.

7 [1991] IRLR 66, Ch D.

8 See, eg *White v Reflecting Roadstuds Ltd* [1991] ICR 733, [1991] IRLR 331, EAT: in which Wood P emphasised that the test applied only to "capricious" decisions of the employer and that the test was only that 'discretionary power should not be exercised in such a way as to make it impossible for the employee to carry out his part of the contract.'

## RESTRAINTS ON WORKING IN COMPETITION AND TRADE SECRETS

Employers can also make use of their power to draft contract terms to extend their authority, through the device of covenants to restrain employees from making use of confidential information or working in competition. In theory, employees' duty of fidelity at common law requires them not to divulge confidential information in the nature of the trade secrets of the employer even after they have left employment.[9] This duty extends to include secret formulae for the manufacture of products as well as the names of customers and the contents of their orders,[10] and the detailed knowledge of the workings of a business.[11] However, employees are entitled to take away with them information which remains in their heads and has become part of their skill and knowledge as long as it is not a trade secret.[12] In practice, therefore, there are considerable difficulties in defining trade secrets with sufficient precision to obtain an injunction.[13]

In general, employers are reluctant to rely solely on a covenant of non-confidentiality, in part because of the difficulties of defining trade secrets to prove a breach of an implied term,[14] in part because of the difficulties of enforcement.

They tend to make use of an express covenant not to compete or to work for a competitor as a means of ensuring that confidential information in the form of trade secrets is kept confidential after employment has terminated.[15] Employers also make use of post-termination non-solicitation clauses to complement non-competition clauses because of the limited reach of the implied term.[16]

9 *Printers and Finishers Ltd v Holloway* [1964] 3 All ER 731, [1965] 1 WLR 1; *Roger Bullivant Ltd v Ellis* [1987] ICR 464, [1987] IRLR 491; *Cranleigh Precision Engineering Ltd v Bryant* [1964] 3 All ER 289, [1965] 1 WLR 1293; *Herbert Morris Ltd v Saxelby* [1916] 1 AC 688, HL; *Faccenda Chicken Ltd v Fowler* [1987] Ch 117, [1986] 1 All ER 617, CA.

10 See eg *Lansing Linde Ltd v Kerr* [1991] ICR 428, [1991] IRLR 80, CA.

11 *Littlewoods Organisation Ltd v Harris* [1978] 1 All ER 1026, [1977] 1 WLR 1472, CA.

12 Ibid.

13 *Lawrence David Ltd v Ashton* [1989] ICR 123, [1989] IRLR 22, CA.

14 Ibid.

15 *Littlewoods Organisation Ltd v Harris* [1978] 1 All ER 1026, [1977] 1 WLR 1472 at 1479; *Printers and Finishers Ltd v Holloway* [1965] 1 WLR 1 at 6: see too *PSM International plc and McKechnie plc v Whitehouse and Willenhall Automation Ltd* [1992] IRLR 279, CA (where an ex-employee was restrained from fulfilling a contract already made with a third party).

16 *John Michael Design plc v Cooke* [1987] 2 All ER 332, [1987] ICR 445, CA. See too *Scully UK Ltd v Lee* [1998] IRLR 259, CA; *Dawnay, Day & Co Ltd v De Braconnier D'Alphen* [1997] IRLR 285, CA.

Unlike mobility and flexibility clauses, however, such covenants are subjected to a 'reasonableness' test at common law imposed by the doctrine of restraint of trade. This doctrine attempts to balance employees' freedom to work for whom they like with employers' interest in protecting their business against ex-employees' use of trade secrets and confidential commercial information by applying the rule that such covenants must be (i) reasonable as between the parties, and (ii) in the public interest.[17] One reason for this is that employers can, in most cases,[18] only enforce such clauses by seeking an interlocutory injunction on equitable principles. In *Herbert Morris v Saxelby* Lord Parker said:

> 'Wherever covenants against competition by a servant or apprentice have been upheld it has been on the ground, not that the servant or apprentice would, by reason of his employment or training, obtain the skill and knowledge necessary to equip him as a possible competitor in the trade, but that he might obtain such personal knowledge of and influence over the customers of his employer or such an acquaintance with his employers' trade secrets as would enable him, if competition were allowed, to take advantage of his employers' trade connection or utilise information confidentially obtained.'[19]

On the other hand,

> 'an employer has no legitimate interest in preventing an employee, after leaving his service, from entering the service of a competitor merely on the ground that the new employer is a competitor.'[20]

The courts are prepared to enforce such covenants only if the employer can show:

(i) that there is a clear proprietary interest requiring protection, ie there are genuine 'trade secrets' or confidential information involved;[1]
(ii) that restraint is reasonably necessary to protect such trade secrets, ie that there is a real possibility that the information will be improperly used or if used would have a damaging effect;[2] and
(iii) that the restraints are reasonable in scope, ie no greater than is necessary to protect the proprietary interest taking into account the

17 *Herbert Morris Ltd v Saxelby* [1916] 1 AC 688 at 707, HL.
18 The employer of course can dismiss an employee for setting up in competition: see eg *Marshall v Industrial Systems and Control Ltd* [1992] IRLR 294, EAT.
19 Ibid at 709.
20 *Kores Manufacturing Co Ltd v Kolok Manufacturing Co Ltd* [1959] Ch 108 at 125.
1 *Faccenda Chicken Ltd v Fowler* [1987] Ch 117, [1986] IRLR 69, CA; *Johnson & Bloy Holdings Ltd v Wolstenholme Rink plc* [1987] IRLR 499, CA; *Roger Bullivant Ltd v Ellis* [1987] ICR 464, [1987] IRLR 491; *Cantor Fitzgerald (UK) Ltd v Wallace* [1992] IRLR 215; *Dawnay, Day & Co Ltd v De Braconnier D'Alphen* [1997] IRLR 285.
2 *Provident Financial Group plc v Hayward* [1989] ICR 160, [1989] IRLR 84.

nature of the activities which are being restrained,[3] the position of the employee,[4] the period of time for which the employee is restricted and the geographic scope of the restriction.

For example, in *Hinton & Higgs (UK) Ltd v Murphy and Valentine*,[5] a clause inserted in the contracts of two health and safety consultants precluding them from working for 18 months for any previous or present client of the group of companies was too wide to be enforced because it referred to previous as well as present customers, it placed no geographic limits on the restriction and it restricted the employee from working for the clients of any other company in the same group.

Moreover, in *Greer v Sketchley Ltd*[6] a restriction covering the whole of the UK was too wide because the company had branches only in the Midlands and the South of England. Similarly in *Spencer v Marchington*[7] a 25-mile restriction was too wide where a 20-mile restriction was adequate.

In general, the higher the position of the employee the wider the restriction allowed, because there may be more information which is of a trade secret nature. Thus, in *Lansing Linde Ltd v Kerr*,[8] a senior marketing executive's attendance at monthly board meetings, and access to plans for developing new products were factors to be taken into account in supporting a covenant against competition in the UK. However, the length of the restriction must take into account the time it will take for the confidential information to grow stale. Thus in *Provident Financial Group plc v Hayward*, a financial director in an estate agency business could not be stopped from ending his 'garden leave' ten weeks early to take up a similar post with another estate agency. The job was an administrative one and very confidential information would be relevant to the other employer. The geographic scope will also have to be reasonable given the nature of the company's activities.[9]

Related to this is the willingness of the courts to take into account the respective bargaining power of the parties to the contract. For example, in *Bridge v Deacons*[10] an equity partner was held bound by a five-year

3 *Mason v Provident Clothing and Supply Co Ltd* [1913] AC 724 at 742, HL.
4 *M and S Drapers v Reynolds* [1956] 3 All ER 814 at 817E; *Sybron Corpn v Rochem Ltd* [1984] Ch 112, [1983] 2 All ER 707.
5 [1989] IRLR 519.
6 [1979] IRLR 445.
7 [1988] IRLR 392 (Ch D).
8 [1991] ICR 428, [1991] IRLR 80, CA (injunction refused for other reasons); see too *Office Angels Ltd v Rainer-Thomas and O'Connor* [1991] IRLR 214, CA; *Littlewoods Organisation Ltd v Harris* [1978] 1 All ER 1026, [1977] 1 WLR 1472; *Spafax Ltd v Harrison* [1980] IRLR 442, CA.
9 [1989] IRLR 84.
10 [1984] AC 705; cf *Allied Dunbar (Frank Weisinger) Ltd v Weisinger* [1988] IRLR 60; *Systems Reliability Holdings plc v Smith* [1990] IRLR 377.

restraint. Bargaining weakness in turn will make the courts look more closely at the width of the prohibition and the extent of the prohibition.[11]

Generally, where a restrictive clause is too widely drawn it will be declared unenforceable as against public policy and the employer will be left solely with the ex-employee's implied duty of confidentiality.[12] In some cases, however, an unreasonable clause can be altered to a reasonable clause either by a limiting interpretation, ie by restricting the geographic scope[13] or by the use of a blue pencil, ie a deletion which leaves 'the clause standing fully grammatical, having full effect in its other parts and not in any way so radically altering it as to make it a different covenant from that entered into'.[14] For example, in *Business Seating (Renovations) Ltd v Broad*,[15] a non-solicitation clause applying to 'customers' of 'the company or any associated company' could be 'blue pencilled' by deleting the reference to 'any associated company'.[16]

Employers sometimes insert a clause to the effect that 'in the event that any restriction found to be void would be valid if some part thereof was deleted . . . such restrictions shall apply with such modifications as may be necessary to make them valid or effective'. However, the courts may nevertheless be unwilling to rewrite the contract.[17]

Finally, an issue can arise when an employer attempts to enforce a restrictive covenant after a wrongful dismissal.[18]

In principle, when the employee leaves accepting the repudiation and putting an end to the contract, the outstanding obligations of the employee are in law discharged along with the contract.[19] Moreover, even if an employer attempts to avoid this result by inserting a clause which provides that the express restraint shall apply for a fixed period after termination, 'whatever the reason for the termination' it is by no means certain that the clause will be honoured.[20]

11 *NIS Fertilisers Ltd v Neville* [1986] 2 NIJB 70.
12 See eg *Provident Financial Group plc v Hayward* [1989] ICR 160, [1989] IRLR 84; *Office Angels Ltd v Rainer-Thomas and O'Connor* [1991] IRLR 214, CA.
13 *Littlewoods Organisation Ltd v Harris* [1978] 1 All ER 1026, [1977] 1 WLR 1472, CA.
14 *Systems Reliability Holdings plc v Smith* [1990] IRLR 377.
15 [1989] ICR 729; see *Attwood v Lamont* [1920] 3 KB 571 where blue pencil was not possible.
16 *Business Seating (Renovations) Ltd v Broad* [1989] ICR 729 but see *Attwood v Lamont* [1920] 3 KB 571 (blue pencil not possible).
17 See eg *Hinton & Higgs (UK) Ltd v Murphy and Valentine* [1989] IRLR 519.
18 It would seem that breach of contract isn't enough. There must be a repudiation. *Spencer v Marchington* [1988] IRLR 392 (Ch D); *Rex Stewart Jeffries Parker Ginsberg Ltd v Parker* [1988] IRLR 483.
19 See *Rock Refrigeration Ltd v Jones* [1996] IRLR 675, CA. *General Billposting Co Ltd v Atkinson* [1909] AC 118, HL.
20 *Briggs v Oates* [1990] ICR 473, [1990] IRLR 472; see discussion in M Jefferson [1997] ILJ 62.

The net effect of the principles which apply to express restraints is that even parties with bargaining power are forced to draft contract terms with a close eye to reasonableness in order to ensure that they will be enforced. To what extent can the same be said of case law relevant to an employee in respect of employee flexibility and mobility?

## ENFORCEMENT

In the case of working in competition and no-solicitation clauses, the employer cannot use self-help disciplinary measures such as dismissal to any effect. Instead they must seek assistance from the courts in the form of an injunction.

The enforcement of non-competition and non-solicitation clauses often takes place on an interlocutory basis.[1] Although it will be difficult to obtain an Anton Piller order in such cases[2] the usual rules of interlocutory injunctions will apply. The plaintiff must first show that there is a serious question to be tried.[3] This requires evidence that there is a repudiatory breach by the employee which was accepted. Furthermore, the clause or clauses must be shown not to be obviously void given the nature of the trade secrets, or confidential information and the area of restraint.

The second step is to consider whether damages is an appropriate remedy. This will usually be satisfied by the showing of irreparable harm or at least harm for which the defendant does not have the resources to pay.[4] Connected with this is the balance of convenience: this test is sometimes described as the balance of irreparable harm, ie which party would be more seriously damaged by irreparable harm as a result of the grant of the injunction. Thus, in the *Lawrence David Ltd v Ashton*[5] case, the High Court decided that while the damage caused to the company would not be very extensive, the financial loss Ashton would suffer for being out of work during the period which he had been wrongly enjoined if the company lost the case at trial, was not irreparable because the company would be able to compensate him.

In *Lawrence David Ltd v Ashton*[6] the point was made that in cases of such interlocutory relief it should be possible to move to a speedy trial,

1 *Lawrence David Ltd v Ashton* [1989] ICR 123, [1989] IRLR 22, CA.
2 *Lock International plc v Beswick* [1989] 3 All ER 373, [1989] IRLR 481; but see *PSM International plc v Whitehouse* [1992] IRLR 279, CA (where an Anton Piller order was obtained to search for and remove documents).
3 *American Cyanamid Co v Ethicon Ltd.*
4 See eg *PSM International plc v Whitehouse* (above).
5 [1989] ICR 123, [1989] IRLR 22, CA.
6 Ibid.

thus reducing the harm to the employee that would occur from loss of employment during the period of the interlocutory injunction.

In theory employees' contracts of employment cannot be specifically enforced. Historically, however, employers have been able to obtain negative injunctions against employees and enforce express covenants - not to work in competition as well as the implied obligation of fidelity. The courts have long maintained that an injunction will not be allowed against an employee if the consequences of that injunction would be to put the employee in a position that he would have to go on working for his former employers or starve.[7]

However, in a case where the employer has agreed to an extended notice period and the employer gives the employee 'garden leave' for that period, the court may decide to enforce an injunction restraining the employee from working for another employer until the notice period is complete. In *Evening Standard Co Ltd v Henderson*[8] an employee was offered a job with a rival London evening paper. The employers argued that since they were prepared to provide Mr Henderson with all contractual benefits during the notice period and allow him to work if he wished, they were entitled to an injunction compelling him to refrain from working for anyone else until the notice period was complete.

One influential factor in the case was the court's concern not to allow employees to take advantage of the specific performance inhibition. As Lawton LJ put it:

> 'As the law stands at present they can snap their fingers at their old employers because they can say you cannot obtain an injunction against me ... and damages are impossible to quantify.'

On the other hand, the employers were prepared to allow Mr Henderson to work at his job if he wished during the notice period, a point which was important given that his job was such that the employer owed him a duty to provide work as well as contractual remuneration.

However, judicial reservations have been expressed about the practice of long periods of 'garden leave', even where contractual benefits were provided.

In *Provident Financial Group plc v Hayward*[9] the Court of Appeal refused the employers an injunction where a financial controller and finance director, having agreed 'not to undertake any other business or profession or become an employee or agent of any other person or persons, or assist or have any financial interest in any other business or profession ...' submitted his resignation to take employment with ASDA, a retail firm, after only three months of an agreed six months notice period.

7 See eg *Warner Bros Pictures Inc v Nelson* [1937] 1 KB 209, [1936] 3 All ER 160.
8 [1987] ICR 588, [1987] IRLR 64, CA.
9 [1989] ICR 160, [1989] IRLR 84, CA.

The employers were refused an injunction to enforce the clause even though they had established an arguable case for breach of contract because the proposed new employment was not likely seriously to damage the existing employee's business.

## DISCIPLINARY TERMS IN THE EMPLOYMENT CONTRACT

The earliest field in which employers made use of their drafting power to shape express terms in employment contracts to their advantage was in the field of works rules, employee handbooks and disciplinary rules and disciplinary procedure.

Employers' disciplinary powers, as we have seen, are well developed in the terms implied in employment contracts. Even if nothing is put into the express terms of employment contracts, the employer's disciplinary control is carefully preserved in the employee's duty to obey as an implied fundamental term of the contract. Moreover, acts of dishonesty and carelessness etc, as well as disobedience can, if sufficiently serious, be regarded as repudiatory breaches of implied terms by employees, entitling the employer to dismiss summarily for gross misconduct: technically accepting the employee's repudiation and terminating the contract without notice.

In the disciplinary context, the power to draft express terms can nevertheless enhance managerial authority in at least three important respects. First, the employer may reserve certain rights of investigation of employee's conduct or capability such as a 'right to search the person or property of the employee', or the entitlement to insist upon a medical examination. In such cases, without contractual authority, the employer would not have the right to insist upon the particular investigative step.

Second, the employer may draft a code of disciplinary offences in the works rules, employee handbook or disciplinary procedure specifying which offences are to be viewed as serious misconduct warranting summary dismissal. Although there are certain forms of conduct which are repudiatory even without specification in the contract - such as fighting, theft, dangerous activity at the work place, etc[10] nevertheless, specification in a disciplinary code both reinforces the limits in the minds of employees and allows the employer to add to the more obvious common law categories, for example, hygiene rules in a food manufacturing or pharmaceutical firm, no-smoking rules in a chemicals firm, no-betting rules

10 See eg *C A Parsons & Co Ltd v McLoughlin* [1978] IRLR 65, EAT (fighting); *Bailey v BP Oil (Kent Refinery) Ltd* [1980] ICR 642, [1980] IRLR 287, CA (act of violence); *Denco Ltd v Joinson* [1992] 1 All ER 463, [1991] IRLR 63 (unlawful access to computer information).

in a betting shop,[11] till-reading rules for cashiers,[12] clocking-out procedures in a factory[13] and offences committed outside the scope of employment.[14] These rules, if incorporated into the contract of employment, enlarge the category of dismissible offences within the contractual authority of the employer, although, as we shall see, such dismissals may still be subject to certain limits both at common law and under the law of unfair dismissal.

Third, an employer can use express terms to provide disciplinary measures short of dismissal as part of the contractual relationship.[15] For example, suspension without pay as a disciplinary measure requires express authority because it suspends the employer's obligation to pay wages as long as the employee is ready and able to perform work.[16] Moreover, authority for a demotion or downgrading as an alternative to dismissal would generally have to be an express term to avoid being repudiatory.[17] In such cases, express terms are often used to provide alternative disciplinary penalties not in isolation, but rather as part of a disciplinary procedure consisting of a system of warnings, hearings and appeals, which as we shall see creates added constraints upon managerial authority.[18]

In the past thirty years managers have changed their approach to discipline, particularly in the larger firms, moving from a model of disciplinary control exercised by a supervisor directly and personally with 'full rights to hire and fire, intervene in production, direct workers, . . . etc', to a 'company rules' approach to discipline. This approach is an attempt to secure compliance, co-operation and greater self-discipline on the part of employees by emphasising the non-arbitrary nature of employer decisions and their acceptance of the principles of fairness. The process of dismissal in this model becomes subject to 'the rule of (company) law', ie the impersonal force of 'company rules' and 'company policy' are established as the basis for control.[19] The right to dismiss remains, but it is reshaped to incorporate a formal 'corrective' approach whereby, apart from cases of gross misconduct, workers can be dismissed only if they

11 *Ladbroke Racing Ltd v Arnott* [1983] IRLR 154, Ct of Sess.

12 *Jones v London Co-operative Society Ltd* [1975] IRLR 110, IT.

13 *Elliott Bros (London) Ltd v Colverd* [1979] IRLR 92, EAT.

14 *Singh v London Country Bus Services Ltd* [1976] IRLR 176, EAT.

15 Any deduction from pay for poor workmanship must be authorised by 'mutual agreement' under Part II of the Employment Rights Act 1996, see discussion in next section.

16 See eg *Bird v British Celanese Ltd* [1945] KB 336, [1945] 1 All ER 488, CA.

17 See eg *BBC v Beckett* [1983] IRLR 43, EAT; cf *Wadham Stringer Commercials (London) Ltd v Brown* [1983] IRLR 46, EAT.

18 See discussion in Chs 6 and 9.

19 Dickens, L, Jones, M, Weekes, B and Hart M *Dismissed: A Study of Unfair Dismissal and the Industrial Tribunal System* (1985) Oxford, p 143.

continue to 'misbehave' after receiving written warnings specifying improper behaviour.[20]

Alan Fox suggests that the reason for this change is that management decided that in their own interest they had to moderate their use of coercion and authoritarianism and search for other ways of promoting compliance among the rank and file because of the ability of even workers in low discretion jobs to raise the cost to management of openly coercive strategies of discipline (control) - responses such as high staff turnover, absence, sickness and wastage which are individual forms of protest and can, in sufficient numbers, approximate a collective expression of protest. He later pointed out that: 'Even in the high unemployment of the 1980s there was a need to retain such a changed approach to discipline because of the dependence upon employee co-operation and goodwill for effective performance.' In other words, these consent strategies which were originally introduced to deal with cyclical changes in employee bargaining power have also proved to be useful in the current conditions where labour has a higher trust, has become more skilled, handles more expensive equipment and receives information of greater commercial value.[1]

The disciplinary procedures which are a product of this change in managerial practice create positive contractual rights for employees enforceable as terms of the contract at common law using the remedies of damages, declaration and even injunction.[2] However, that is a by-product of a process in which management uses its drafting power to underpin its system of maintaining discipline.

## DEDUCTIONS AND PART II OF THE EMPLOYMENT RIGHTS ACT 1996

Deductions from pay by employers were regulated historically by the Truck Acts which required employers to pay manual employees 'the whole of the wages due in coin' avoiding alternative methods of payment in kind.[3] These statutes also provided a system of protection against arbitrary deductions requiring all deductions from pay for manual workers to be notified in advance and 'fair and reasonable in the circumstances.'[4]

In Part II of the Employment Rights Act (formerly the Wages Act 1986), this protection has been 'deregulated' to some extent. At first glance, the

20 Ibid.

1 Fox, A *Beyond Contract: Work, Power and Trust Relations* (1974); *Man Mismanagement* (2nd edn, 1985).

2 See Ch 6.

3 See Truck Acts 1831-1940.

4 The Truck Acts did not preclude contractual provision for disciplinary suspension without pay. See *Bird v British Celanese Ltd* [1945] 1 All ER 488.

Act appears to provide a wide 'right' not to suffer unauthorised deductions by employers. Thus, under s 13(1) of the Act employers are not allowed to make any 'deduction' from any 'wages' of any worker[5] employed by them. However this rule is subject to two main conditions (s 13(1)(a) and (b)) and a series of exceptions (s 14). The two conditions are (a) that the deduction is not required or authorised to be made by virtue of any statutory provision or any relevant provision of the worker's contract; and (b) that the worker has not previously signified in writing his agreement or consent to the making of it. The second condition may be useful in the case of truly agreed deductions but it also gives wide rein to employers to use their superior bargaining power to impose deductions. In partial recognition of this point, the Act provides that in the case of one group of particularly vulnerable workers, retail workers, deductions for cash shortages or stock deficiencies can only be made if they do not exceed one-tenth of the gross wages payable on any pay day save the last in that employment.[6] This only serves to underline the vulnerability of employees to 'agreed' deductions in other sectors. The one safeguard provided by s 13 lies in the timing of the contractual provision for the deduction. Section 13(6) provides that the worker's agreement or consent to the making of a deduction cannot apply to any conduct of the worker or any other event occurring before the agreement or consent was signified.[7] Section 13(5) applies a similar rule to variations in the worker's contract.

In cases where the employee considers that an unlawful deduction has been made, he or she can bring a complaint to an industrial tribunal to recover compensation. The definition of deduction for the purposes of the Act is 'the deficiency': '... where the total amount of any wages that are paid on any occasion by an employer to any worker employed by him is less than the total amount of wages that are properly payable by him to the worker on that occasion' after legitimate deductions and apart from 'an error of computation'. This definition extends to all non-payment of wages as well as specific deductions since the statute specifically provides that deficiencies other than computational errors 'shall be treated as deductions'.[8]

However the deficiency must be one in 'wages' that are properly payable. Wages are defined as 'a sum payable to the worker by his

5 Defined in s 8 as an individual who has entered into or works (worked) under a contract of service, apprenticeship or any other contract whereby he undertakes to do or to perform personally any work or service.

6 ERA, s 17(4).

7 Cf *Discount Tobacco and Confectionery Ltd v Williamson* [1993] ICR 371, [1993] IRLR 327, EAT.

8 *Delaney v Staples (t/a De Montfort Recruitment)* [1992] 1 AC 687, [1992] IRLR 191, HL; see too *Home Office v Ayres* [1992] IRLR 59; *Greg May (Carpet Fitters and Contractors) Ltd v Dring* [1990] ICR 188, [1990] IRLR 19, EAT.

employer in connection with his employment.' And on occasion this wide definition has been rigorously applied. For example in *Kent Management Services Ltd v Butterfield,*[9] when Mr Butterfield was dismissed and the company refused to pay him commission owed under a company 'discretionary and ex gratia' bonus and commission scheme, the EAT held that this was an unlawful deduction because the commission was 'a sum payable to the worker by his employer in connection with his employment as the employee would normally have expected to receive commission for the work done.'

In contrast, in *Delaney v Staples*[10] the House of Lords held that 'wages' did not include payment in lieu of notice which amounts to damages for wrongful dismissal. The House of Lords drew a distinction between a case of summary dismissal with money paid in lieu and "garden leave" where the employee is given notice that his employment will terminate in four weeks but he need not work out that notice and he is paid wages for that period. The former is money in lieu paid for the period after the contract has been terminated and is to be treated as damages for breach of contract and not wages; the latter is wages for work done and payable in connection with the employment.

Finally, even if deductions are caught by s 13(1), they are still subject to the series of exceptions in s 14 eg overpayments of wages (s 14(1)); 'checkoffs' (s 14(4)) and industrial action (s 14(6)). At one point, it seemed that these exceptions could apply only if the employer could show that he or she was lawfully entitled to make an excepted deduction. For example, in *Home Office v Ayres*[11] the EAT thought that an overpayment claimed by the employer could only be excepted under s 14(1) if the overpayment was lawfully demanded. In *Sunderland Polytechnic v Evans*[12], however, a case concerning a deduction from pay owing to the industrial action of the employee, the EAT decided that the reasoning in *Ayres* could no longer stand. The legislative history made it plain that the exception in s 14(6) and by implication the other exceptions were to be applied without any qualification of lawfulness being read into the section. If an employee has a claim as to the legality of the deduction it must be taken to a county court. If an employee is dismissed for bringing a claim under s 13, such a dismissal will be automatically unfair and the qualifying period will not apply.[13]

9 [1992] IRLR 394, EAT.

10 [1992] 1 AC 687, [1992] IRLR 191, HL. See discussion in Ch 6. See Honeyball 'Wages, Payments in Lieu of Notice and Deductions', [1991] ILJ 143.

11 [1992] ICR 175, [1992] IRLR 59, EAT.

12 [1993] ICR 392, [1993] IRLR 196, EAT; see too *SIP (Industrial Products) Ltd v Swinn* [1994] IRLR 323.

13 ERA 1996 ss 104, 108 see Ch 8.

Despite its weaknesses, Part II of the ERA 1996 can be used on occasion as a weapon to contest an employer's attempt unilaterally to reorganise the terms and conditions of employees contracts.[14]

14 See eg *Whent v T Cartledge Ltd* [1997] IRLR 153 (attempt to change post TUPE pay negotiations); see too *Bruce v Wiggins Teape (Stationary) Ltd* [1994] IRLR 536 (shift bonus withdrawn) see further Miller [1995] ILJ 162.

CHAPTER 5

# Collective agreements and contracts of employment

## COLLECTIVE AGREEMENTS AND THE LAW

In practice, collective bargaining operates as the main social constraint upon managerial discretion in labour relations. That workers can organise into trade unions and by bargaining with employers provide a measure of countervailing power to the powers of management has long been understood as fundamental to industrial relations. Equally clear has been the understanding that the power to bargain collectively is underpinned by the right to strike of employees. As Kahn Freund put it 'If the workers could not, in the last resort, collectively refuse to work they could not bargain collectively'.[1] And as Lord Wright stated in *Crofter*'s case 'the right to strike is an essential element of collective bargaining'.[2] Collective bargaining, underpinned by the threat of collective action, is essentially a system of conflict resolution which results in collective agreements imposing joint regulation upon unilateral managerial decision making.[3]

What is perhaps less well understood in labour law circles, however, are the precise ways in which collective bargaining through collective agreements places social constraints upon managerial discretion. One type of constraint upon managerial decision making is fairly familiar. It consists of the labour standards or norms established by collective agreements relating to pay and hours which are translated into the terms and conditions of employment for employees represented by trade unions and other employees affected by collective agreements. The second type of constraint is less well developed in the labour law literature. It consists of the rules established by collective agreement or custom and practice which regulate the relationship between management and trade union or unions creating

1 O Kahn Freund *Labour and the Law* (3rd edn, 1983).
2 *Crofter Hand Harris Woven Tweed Co Ltd v Veitch* [1942] AC 435 at 463, HL.
3 Allan Flanders *Industrial Relations: What is Wrong with the System?* (1965) p 12.

rights and obligations more directly between the parties. Let us consider each in turn.

## (i) The establishment of labour standards

Industrial relations commentators have referred to the establishment of labour standards through substantive provisions in collective bargaining - pay, hours, holiday entitlement etc as bargaining over 'market relations'.[4] Labour lawyers have at times described this aspect of collective agreements as their 'normative aspect' providing a 'source of rules for terms and conditions of employment, for the distribution of work and for the stability of jobs'.[5] Collective agreements establish not only standards for trade union members in their employment relationship, but also provide a standard which can be extended to other employees either through contract, in the case of other non-unionised employees covered by the collective agreement, or by statute law which used the substantive terms of collective agreements as standards to be applied to other groups of workers.[6] In either guise, collective agreements establish standards which operate to limit managerial discretion in setting wage, hours and other substantive terms of employment. At the same time, these standards also offer the advantage to management of harmonising labour costs throughout an industry.

## (ii) The establishment of the rules of the collective relationship

The second function of collective bargaining consists of the bargaining over 'managerial relations', ie the rules which govern the continuing relationship between unions and employers.[7] These rules are often recorded in procedure agreements or the procedural clauses of collective agreements: negotiating procedures, disputes procedures, bargaining rights and management rights clauses, shop stewards' facilities, redundancy, disciplinary and grievance procedures. Labour lawyers have sometimes referred to these as the 'contractual function' of collective agreements because this dimension of bargaining creates rights and obligations more directly between employees and trade unions.[8] These rules establish rights

4 *Flanders*, p 13.
5 *Kahn Freund*, p 154.
6 See eg Fair Wages Resolutions; Sch 11 to the Employment Protection Act 1975 (now repealed).
7 *Flanders*, p 13.
8 *Kahn Freund*, p 154.

and responsibilities for trade unions; they also place limits upon managerial discretion.

The 'contractual' function of collective agreements in regulating managerial relations has only been partially developed in the labour law literature. There has been a tendency to equate the contractual function mainly with the 'peace obligation' or 'no strike clause' in collective agreements, that is, the obligation of the trade union not to take industrial action until procedure is exhausted, and to view as the principal expectations of the two sides to the collective agreement as an exchange of a no strike promise for improved terms and conditions of employment. It is undoubtedly true that the peace obligation is extremely important from the employer's point of view. As Wedderburn has pointed out:

> 'what is invariably at issue when enforcing a collective agreement is whether the employer can enforce against the union by legal as well as economic means, the agreed procedure, commonly the peace obligation not to strike until a dispute procedure is exhausted.'[9]

Yet there are other quite significant 'contractual' obligations owed by employers to trade unions which are contractual in nature. For example collective agreements, particularly negotiation and disputes procedures, are often agreements by the employer to recognise the trade union as the representative of a given group of employees for the purpose of collective bargaining, as long as the agreement remains in force.[10]

Moreover, disputes procedures can confer rights upon trade unions to be consulted either before a decision is taken or once management's attention has been drawn to a dispute. An example of the former comes from the 1922 EEF CSEU Agreements.

> 'When management contemplates alterations in recognised working conditions ... The management shall give the work people directly concerned, or their representatives in the shop, introduction of their intentions and afford an opportunity for discussion. The alternatives shall not be implemented until settlement has been reached or until the procedure has been exhausted.'

An example of the latter concerns the Engineering 1976 Agreement

> 'It is agreed that in the event of any difference arising which cannot immediately be disposed of, then whatever practice or agreement existed prior to the difference shall continue to operate pending a settlement or until the agreed procedure has been exhausted.'[11]

9 *The Worker and the Law* (3rd edn, 1986) p 319.
10 See Ch 16.
11 See further Anderman 'The Status Quo Issue and Industrial Disputes Procedures: Some Implications for Labour Law' [1975] ILJ 131.

Finally, collective agreements can provide a joint policy for redundancies or the introduction of new technology providing consultation rights for trade union representatives as well as rights governing seniority, job guarantees and measures to avoid redundancies.[12]

These recognition, consultation and status quo clauses are given in exchange for no strike obligations by the union. They are also given in return for management rights clauses which recognise the rights of management to take initiatives and to direct the workforce. Sometimes such clauses are very general. For example the 1922 Engineering Agreement merely states: 'Management has the right to manage the enterprise.' Sometimes these clauses are more specific and apply to flexibility arrangements and working practices.

In countries like the USA and Sweden, the contractual function of collective agreements in regulating managerial relations has been given far greater recognition in industrial relations literature and case law. In the USA, for example, 'the collective bargaining agreement unlike most other contracts, is an instrument of government, as it were, the industrial constitution of the enterprise, setting for the broad general principles upon which the relationship of employer and employee is conducted'.[13]

In Sweden, Fahlbeck has written too of a 'constitutional concept' for collective agreements; they are viewed in constitutional terms, containing 'rules to govern the relationship between trade unions and employers ...' involving 'some kind of co-responsibility for the running of the business, as a minimum the right to be consulted before management decide'.[14]

In these countries, moreover, the parties to collective agreements can use legal means directly to enforce the "managerial" rules in collective agreements, including the peace obligation. In the US, the promise to go to arbitration on issues of interpretation of disputed contents of collective agreements can be specifically enforced[15] and trade unions can obtain an injunction to stop the employer from breaking a collective agreement.[16] In turn the employer has the option of enforcing the collective agreement directly against the unions either by an action for damages[17] or an injunction.[18] In Sweden the managerial rules in collective agreements are enforceable in part as peace obligations undertaken by unions and members as well as employers. Moreover, the law on the Joint Regulation of Working

12 See eg *Lee v GEC Plessey Telecommunications* [1993] IRLR 383, HL.

13 A Cox 'The Legal Nature of Collective Bargaining Agreements' (1958-9) 57 Mich L Rev 1.

14 R Fahlbeck 'Legal Nature of Collective Agreements' at p 27.

15 *United Steelworkers v Warrior and Gulf Navigation Co* 363 US 574 (1960).

16 See eg Cantor 'Buffalo Forge and Injunctions against Employer Breaches of Collective Bargaining Agreements' [1980] Wisconsin L Rev 247.

17 Labour Management Relations Act, s 301.

18 *Boys Market Inc v Retail Clerks Union Local* 770 398 US 235 (1970).

Life places limits upon managers in the form of statutory trade union rights of negotiation or consultation which include a legal right for the union to demand postponement of a managerial decision until negotiations have been held, and a right of veto over subcontracting.[19]

## THE LEGAL STATUS OF 'CONTRACTUAL' COLLECTIVE TERMS

In Britain, unlike many other countries[20] there has been little impetus to make the 'contractual' obligations contained in collective agreements, whether no strike clauses or 'managerial relations' provisions, legally enforceable. From 1871 to 1971 the legal status of collective agreements between one employer and trade unions was surprisingly unclear.[1] There were few cases, which suggested that employers were disinclined to use legal means to enforce the peace obligation in collective agreements. Moreover, there was no tendency for trade unions to regard the collective agreements as legally binding in any other respect. Indeed, the TUC was extremely wary about legal enforceability of collective agreements.

In 1968, the Donovan Commission reported a consensus of opinion against an assumption of intention for legal enforceability. And in 1969 when the Ford Motor Company[2] attempted to test the issue directly, the Court decided, after looking inter alia at the Donovan report and the TUC's evidence to the Commission, that it was

> 'clear that the climate of opinion was unanimous to the effect that no legally enforceable contract resulted from the collective agreements. Without clear and express provisions making them answerable to legal action they remain in the realm of undertakings binding in honour.'

The consensus suggested in the *Ford* case that collective agreements could be presumed not to be legally binding was first challenged in the Industrial Relations Act 1971. This Act, concerned with reducing industrial action generally and unofficial industrial action in particular, chose to give legal weight to the peace obligation contained in collective agreements by creating a statutory presumption that collective agreements were legally binding unless the parties stipulated otherwise.

Section 34 of the Industrial Relations Act 1971 provided that a collective agreement which 'does not contain a provision which (however expressed) states that the agreement or part of it is intended not to be legally

19 Fahlbeck 'The Swedish Act on the Joint Regulation of Working Life' in *Law and the Weaker Party* Vol I (Professional Books, 1981).
20 Eg see Schmidt and Neal. See Kahn Freund, op cit, pp 154-158.
1 See eg Hepple 'Intention to Create Legal Relations' (1970) Camb LJ 122.
2 *Ford Motor Co Ltd v AEU* [1969] 2 QB 303, [1969] 2 All ER 481. There were other cases before this but none which dealt with the issue so directly.

enforceable, shall be conclusively presumed to be intended by the parties to it to be a legally enforceable contract'. The Act also made certain that a trade union's liability for the no-strike clause extended to unofficial action. Under s 36 trade unions were required to take all reasonably practicable steps to prevent their members from contravening such agreements.

Yet, in 1971, the legislators misjudged the mood of employers. As research on the Act has shown, there was an almost universal tendency for employers to join with trade unions to negate the statutory presumption by inserting into the agreement the phrase 'This agreement is not intended to be legally enforceable'.

When the Labour party was returned to power in 1974, s 34 of the 1971 Act was replaced by s 18 of the Trade Union and Labour Relations Act 1974 which restored the presumption against legal enforceability. In its present form, as s 179 of TULR (C)A, it reads as follows:

'(1) any collective agreement shall be conclusively presumed not to have been intended by the parties to be a legally enforceable contract unless the agreement -
  (a) is in writing, and
  (b) contains a provision which (however expressed) states that the parties intend that the agreement shall be a legally enforceable contract.

(2) Any collective agreement which does satisfy these conditions in subsection (1)(a) and (b) above shall be conclusively presumed to have been intended by the parties to be a legally enforceable contract.'

These statutory provisions concentrate on the intentions of the parties. If the collective agreement is to be legally enforceable, it must contain a provision which states that the parties so intend. If the collective agreement does not contain such a provision, it is not legally enforceable between the trade union and employer. A similar statement of intention is required for the parties to have the no strike promise in the collective agreement incorporated into the individual contract of employment (TULR(C)A s 180). Interestingly enough the presumption in s 179 has not been disturbed in the six rounds of labour legislation from 1980 to 1993. Yet the idea is not completely removed from the agenda.

At the same time, however, labour legislation since 1980 has progressively increased trade union responsibility for industrial action generally and has provided the employer with legal sanctions directly against unofficial strikes to the point where the introduction of legal enforceability of collective agreements would not add much to employers' armories against trade unions in cases where the no-strike clause is broken.[3]

3 See Ch 17.

In the event, while employers have not been unduly inconvenienced by the non availability of a means to enforce no strike clauses directly against trade unions, trade unions have suffered from the absence of the possibility of legal action whether in the form of injunctive relief, declaration or damages against employers who breach or repudiate their 'managerial' obligations to trade unions in collective agreements.

In particular, employers have been under no legal obligation to maintain their recognition arrangements under an existing collective agreement. For example Times Newspapers International could respond to a strike by closing down its Fleet Street sites, dismissing its workforce and starting up operations at Wapping without giving the NUJ, the NGA and SOGAT any legal recourse under existing collective agreements. Moreover, the National Coal Board was found to be legally free to terminate its collective agreement providing exclusive recognition to the NUM when in 1985/86 it began negotiations with the breakaway unions in Nottinghamshire and South Derbyshire.[4] Nor are there any major obstacles to a company's decision to derecognise a trade union and move to individual bargaining. Indeed, by withdrawing recognition, employers can ensure that statutory rights to consultation and disclosure of information, which are based on a trade union's recognition by an employer in collective agreements can be withdrawn without the union having any legal recourse directly against the employer.[5] Moreover, the procedural rights to prior consultation obtained by unions in collective agreements cannot be enforced directly by trade unions against employers. A union cannot as in other countries[6], get an injunction against the employer for breach of the status quo clause. As to rights of prior consultation, trade unions have to rely on statutory rights provided in the two specific cases of redundancies[7] and transfer of undertakings.[8]

In cases of takeover or transfer, furthermore, there is no guarantee that a successor employer will honour the agreements with the trade unions which were recognised by the transferor employer. The Transfer of Undertakings Regulations 1981, stipulate that in the case of a 'transfer' under the Regulation, recognition of the existing union and the collective agreement must pass to the transferee with the undertaking and the employee's contract together with any acts done under it and orders made in respect of it (reg 6). It is still the case, however, that the transferee

4 *National Coal Board v National Union of Mineworkers* [1986] ICR 736, [1986] IRLR 439.

5 See Ch 16. See too proposals for change in *Fairness at Work* Appendix, below.

6 See eg the position in the USA. Cantor 'Buffalo Forge and Injunctions Against Employer Breaches of Collective Bargaining Agreements' [1980] Wisconsin L Rev 247; for the position in Sweden see Fahlbeck 'The Swedish Act on the Joint Regulation of Working Life' in *Law and the Weaker Party* Vol I Professional Books (1981).

7 See Ch 16.

8 See Ch 11.

employer may withdraw recognition and renounce the collective agreement not long after the transfer. It is true that cases of transferee employers doing this are rare but the fact remains that if an employer were to take such a step, even without notice of termination of the collective agreement, there would be no legal redress for the union.

## COLLECTIVE AGREEMENTS AND CONTRACTS OF EMPLOYMENT

Although the contractual functions of collective agreements are not *directly* enforceable between trade union and employer, some terms and conditions established for employees in collective agreements can achieve legal weight by being incorporated into individual contracts of employment by the judiciary applying common law principles.[9]

In carrying out that task, British judges, unlike those in many other countries, have shown little interest in an 'agency' model, ie that the union acts as an agent of the employee in concluding a collective agreement with the employer.[10] Instead, the courts have preferred to proceed on the basis that the normative terms of collective agreements could by express or implied agreement of employer and employee be incorporated in the individual contract of employment. In such a case, however, only a limited range of collectively agreed terms can, in fact, meet the tests of incorporation. For the contract between the individual employee and his employer becomes the primary contract and the extent of incorporation of collective terms is left to be determined by reference to principles of employment contract law, a process which inevitably distorts the meaning and effect of collectively agreed rules.[11] The courts claim to be applying two main criteria to the issue of incorporation. In the first place, there must be sufficient evidence of contractual intention for incorporation of any term of the collective agreement to be possible. In theory this is meant to include an investigation of implied as well as express intent. Secondly, even if there is sufficient evidence of contractual intention for a collective agreement

9 See eg Wedderburn 'Inderogability, Collective agreements and Community Law' [1992] ILJ 245.

10 The fact of membership alone under British law is not enough to create an agency; evidence of something more - ie the creation of a specific agency is needed before the courts will accept an agency analysis in any case. (See eg *Burton Group Ltd v Smith* [1977] IRLR 351; *Edwards v Skyways Ltd* [1964] 1 All ER 494, [1964] 1 WLR 349 (ex gratia redundancy payment negotiated by trade union viewed as 'standing offer' by employer to individual employees.)) Moreover, the legal effect of collective agreements upon individual contracts is generally not limited to trade union members, though in rare cases non-membership limits the application of collective agreements: eg *Ellis v Brighton Co-operative Society* [1976] IRLR 419, EAT.

11 See eg *Hooper v British Railways Board* [1988] IRLR 517, CA.

to be incorporated, there is a further question to be answered: is the particular term of the collective agreement appropriate for incorporation in an individual employment contract? In theory this is meant to be an inquiry as to whether the term is truly normative in character. In both instances, practice does not always match up with theory.

## Contractual intention to incorporate

While there are cases of an express term incorporating a collective agreement which employers have inserted into contracts of employment,[12] the most common evidence of intention to incorporate is the reference by employers to collective agreements in written statements of particulars. For example in *Robertson v British Gas Corpn*[13] the statement read

> 'The provision of the agreement of the National Joint Council . . . relating to remuneration and increments will apply to you . . .'

This, together with similar language in the employee's letters of appointment, was sufficient to incorporate the terms of an incentive bonus agreement negotiated between the employer and the unions into the contract of employment and to give the individual employee a right to sue for the bonus payments.

While it is rare for an agency relationship between trade union and employee to be accepted[14] something approaching an agency relationship occurs when the form of the incorporation gives advance authority to the union to negotiate not only the original agreement but also subsequent agreements. Thus, if the phrase used to incorporate a collective agreement makes reference to 'agreements from time to time in force', this virtually delegates authority to the union to negotiate new agreements which are automatically incorporated into the terms of individual contracts as they are concluded between employer and trade unions. The employee's contractual terms an be varied without any further consent on his part.[15]

As Ackner LJ described such an arrangement in *Robertson*'s[16] case

> 'From time to time the collective scheme modified the bonus which was payable and when that occurred . . . that variation became a part of the employer's obligations to pay and the employer's obligation to accept on satisfaction . . . the collective scheme provided the tariff which . . . had been imported into the agreement, first when the agreement was originally made and then altered as time went by; by the consensual agreement between the

12 *NCB v Galley* [1958] 1 All ER 91, [1958] 1 WLR 16, CA.
13 [1983] ICR 351, [1983] IRLR 302, CA.
14 *Edwards v Skyways Ltd* [1964] 1 All ER 494, [1964] 1 WLR 349.
15 As to the possible limits to automatic incorporation see eg *Singh v British Steel Corpn* [1974] IRLR 131.
16 [1983] IRLR 302, CA.

> trade union and the employer, it being implied in the contract [of employment] that that variation should bind the parties to this contract of employment.'

As we have seen, however, the statutory statement is not itself the contract. It only provides very strong prima facie evidence of what the terms of the contract are between the parties.[17] But the way in which it refers to the documents to be incorporated will fall to be analysed according to contractual principles, particularly where contractual remedies are sought.

For example in *Alexander v Standard Telephone and Cables Ltd (No 2)*[18] the written statement contained the following clause:

> 'The basic terms and conditions of your employment by this Company are in accordance with and subject to the provisions of relevant Agreements made between and on behalf of the Engineering Employers Federation and the Trade Unions (National Agreements) or by Agreements made by the Joint Industrial Council for the Cable Making Industry (National Agreements); the Collective Agreements made between the Company at plant level and the Trade Unions (Plant Agreements); Company Orders; the Handbook "Working with STC"; . . .'[19]

It then added that 'alterations in the terms and conditions of employment, particulars of which are given in any of the documents referred to above, will be duly notified after (within) one month of the date of any such alteration.'

The numbered paragraphs in the statement had the following headings:

> '1 Date of Commencement of Employment
> 2 Continuity of Employment
> 3 Job Title
> 4 Wages
> 5 Normal Working Hours
> 6 Holidays
> 7 Sickness and Accident Pay
> 8 Social Security Pensions Act 1975
> 9 Grievances and Procedures
> 10 Disciplinary Rules and Procedures
> 11 Notice.'

Mr Justice Hobhouse accepted that, given the reference to basic conditions in its introductory clause, the written statement was sufficient

17 *System Floors (UK) Ltd v Daniel* [1982] ICR 54. (At most they place a heavy burden on the employer to show that the actual terms of the contract are different from those which he has set out in the statutory statement, per Browne Wilkinson at 58).
18 [1991] IRLR 286.
19 The written statement also incorporated the provisions of certain statutes.

to incorporate the provisions from the collective agreements which related to paras 1-11 of the written statement.

Moreover, a term in the redundancy agreement relating to wage rates for employees compulsorily transferred to new shifts was incorporable because wages were incorporated by para 4 of the written statement. However, another clause of the same redundancy agreement which provided that 'In the event of compulsory redundancy, selection will be made on the basis of service within the group covered by the term agreement' could not be incorporated because the written statement did 'not deal with redundancy matters' and hence there was no express intention to incorporate.

In contrast, in *Anderson v Pringle of Scotland*[20]where the written statement provided that 'The terms and conditions of your employment are in accordance with and subject to the provisions of the agreement' [between Pringle and the GMB union]. The Court of Session held in an action for interim relief that this clause incorporated the agreement as a whole and 'there would be no problem in treating the terms of the redundancy selection criteria as terms of the individual contract of employment.'

The courts have been extremely wary about implying specific collective terms. In *Alexander (No 2)*, Hobhouse J was not prepared to *infer* an intention to incorporate the seniority clause in the collective agreement into the contract of employment in a situation where there was no evidence of prior acceptance by management of this clause as a 'normative term'. Although recognising that redundancy issues could be regarded as basic terms in some contexts, he was unwilling to view them as equivalent to the more regularly observed 'basic terms' such as wages and hours. He was concerned that the seniority clause had not been applied before in redundancy situations and hence was not custom and practice.[1] It is arguable, however, that this is too narrow a view of implied intent, relying entirely on the past conduct of the parties.

Moreover, in *Ali v Christian Salversen Food Services Ltd*[2] the Court of Appeal refused to allow the EAT to imply a term to fill a gap left by the negotiators. The court stressed that where a collective agreement negotiated on behalf of a substantial labour force leaves a topic uncovered the natural inference is not that there is an omission which requires judicial correction. The court was understandably cautious about opening the door to such claims,[3] but left open the possibility of implication where 'the contractual

20 [1998] IRLR 64 at 66.
1 [1991] IRLR 286, HL.
2 [1997] IRLR 17, 1997 ICR 25, CA.
3 Wynne-Evans 1997 ILJ 166 at 168.

documents create by their wording an internal context in favour of... the implication of the proposed term.'[4]

This requirement of an explicit showing of contractual intention also extends to collective agreements negotiated by employer associations. Merely because an employer is a member of an employer's association which has negotiated a collective agreement, there is no assurance that the agreement is capable of incorporation into that employer's contracts of employment with his employees. In *Hamilton v Futura Floors Ltd*[5] an executor claimed a death benefit under the deceased's contract of employment because the employers association of which the firm was a member had provided such a benefit in the National Labour Agreement of the Joint Industrial Council for the Furniture Trades. The employers claimed they were unaware of the agreement and the death benefit provision. The court held that membership alone was not enough to establish that the collective term was incorporated into the individual contract of employment.

## IS THE TERM OF THE COLLECTIVE AGREEMENT APPROPRIATE FOR INCORPORATION?

Even where courts can find prima facie consent to incorporate a collective agreement, they will still ask whether the particular term is apt for incorporation. In deciding the question of aptness a distinction is drawn between terms of a collective agreement which are of their nature apt to become enforceable by individuals such as terms fixing rates of pay, hours of work, etc and terms which are meant to govern managerial relations such as conciliation schemes and which are therefore inapt for incorporation.[6] In theory the courts claim to be asking the question: 'is this collective term of a type intended to have a "normative effect" on individual contracts?'. In practice, the courts' concern about employer intention tends to influence their decisions about appropriateness.

For example, in *British Leyland UK Ltd v McQuilken*[7] the employer had an agreement with the union that following the closure of a department, employees would be interviewed to determine whether they wished to opt for retraining or redundancy. After a change in management policy, McQuilken was offered a choice between transfer to another location or retraining, without an interview being given. The EAT overturned the

4 [1997] IRLR 17 at 20.
5 [1990] IRLR 478, CA. See too *Burroughs Machines Ltd v Timmoney* [1977] IRLR 404.
6 See Scott J in *NUM v NCB* [1986] IRLR 439 at 454.
7 [1978] IRLR 245, EAT.

tribunal's finding of constructive dismissal, stating that the terms of the agreement had not altered the employee's contract of employment. The agreement was a long-term plan dealing with policy rather than the rights of individual employees. The decision turned on the argument that the right to an interview with a choice between redundancy and transfer arising from the planned reorganisation had not sufficiently crystallised into an individual right *because the company had not yet begun to implement the policy*. In *McQuilken*'s case, the issue of policy versus agreement aside, the procedural rights provided by the plan were themselves sufficiently individualised in form to be attributable to employees. In effect, the decisive issue was the lack of assurance that the employer had actually reached the stage of agreeing to be bound by the collective term.

Similarly in *Alexander (No 2)*[8] the seniority clause in the collective agreement was sufficiently individualised to be incorporable into a contract of employment and formulated sufficiently explicitly to justify incorporation; it regulated the order of compulsory redundancies in a production department on the 'basis of service within the group.'

However, Hobhouse J chose to look essentially to employer intent to decide the question of aptness. He said that the wording of the clause was insufficiently cogent to give rise to an inference of incorporation, the context suggested a lack of intent and it could find no prior practice of strict observance by management and trade union. Having no reassurance that management had taken on that norm as a legally binding constraint upon its discretion, he was unwilling to find it "apt" for incorporation.

Yet, in these cases the normative form of the collective term was not really in question. Indeed, in *Alexander (No 1)*[9] Aldous J was prepared to find that there was an arguable case that the provisions applying LIFO to redundancy selection were part of the employee's contract of employment because they had the effect of benefiting employees who had seniority and put at risk those who did not and hence were not only intended to govern the relationship between the union and the employer. Moreover, in *Anderson v Pringle of Scotland*[10] the Court of Session was prepared to regard the 'last in first out' seniority clause in the collective agreement as having contractual force between employee and employer for the purpose of an interim injunction restraining the employer from applying its own selection criteria for redundancy. Furthermore in *Marley v Forward Trust Group Ltd*[11] an express provision in the manual relating to redundancy including a mobility clause reserving the right for relocated employees to

8 [1991] IRLR 286, HC.

9 [1990] ICR 291, [1990] IRLR 55. As we have seen, however, an injunction was refused on the issue of the limits of the written statements.

10 [1998] IRLR 64.

11 [1986] IRLR 369, CA.

opt for redundancy within six months of relocation was viewed as contractually enforceable. Finally the mere fact that the provisions are 'procedural' cannot itself preclude incorporation. The provisions of certain formal disciplinary and grievance procedures which have been jointly agreed have long been accepted as incorporable into contracts of employment because they create recognisable rights for individual employees.[12]

Thus on closer inspection the courts have not always applied the test of aptness to distinguish between normative and contractual terms. Rather they have used it to filter out those cases where they are uncertain that the employer has agreed to accept the collective term as a normative term.

This is not to say that the courts will always slavishly follow the employer's views. For example in *Marley v Forward Trust Group Ltd*[13] the employer argued that an enhanced redundancy payment clause for employees who had tried out an offer of alternative employment and rejected it was not incorporated from the collective agreement into the employee's contract of employment because the collective agreement was meant to be binding 'in honour only'. In that case the clause itself was individualised in its content and the employer made claim that that specific clause in the collective agreement was not apt for incorporation.

Where however employers raise an issue about a particular clause while conceding that the collective agreement in other respects has been incorporated in the employment contract, they may find a more receptive judicial ear.

## THE COLLECTIVE TERM AS A TERM OF THE INDIVIDUAL CONTRACT

Once a collective term has been successfully incorporated into the employee's contract of employment it can take on a life of its own, 'vesting' in the individual contract and binding the employer vis-à-vis the individual employee for all collective terms intended to benefit that employee.[14] Thus,

12 See eg *Irani v Southampton and South West Hampshire Health Authority* [1985] ICR 590, [1985] IRLR 203.

13 [1986] IRLR 369, CA. See too *Lee v GEC Plessey Telecommunications* [1993] IRLR 383, HC, where the employer was held to be bound by his omission of an express incorporation clause in a new written statement.

14 In which case the language in the collective agreement will be looked at in contractual terms. See eg *Hooper v British Railways Board* [1988] IRLR 517, CA. If the employer has reserved an express discretion in the collective agreement to amend the existing bonus scheme 'only after consultation' this may amount to prior consent to unilateral variation of the individual contract of employment. See eg *Airlie v City of Edinburgh District Council* [1996] IRLR 516, EAT.

if the employer should rescind or attempt to vary the collective agreement, for example by imposing a wage cut[15] or introducing short time work on an unwilling trade union[16] or leaving the employers association which negotiated the collective agreement[17] these actions will not automatically vary the individual contract of employment.[18] To vary the terms of the employment contract, the employer must either obtain the consent of an employee individually to a mutual variation or terminate the contract by notice to the employee.[19] As Kerr LJ stated in *Robertson*'s case:

> 'The terms of an individual contract are in part to be found in the agreed collective agreements as they exist from time to time and if these cease to exist as collective agreements, then the terms as expressly varied between the individual and the employer will remain as they were by reference to the last agreed collective agreement incorporated into the individual contracts.'

For example in *Miller v Hamworthy Engineering Ltd*[20] an employer who imposed short time working on an employee without the agreement of the employee's trade union was liable for net loss of pay. The Court of Appeal reasoned that where there was an admitted contract of employment with a salary payable in accordance with a collective agreement, if the provision of payment of salary in that contract was to be displaced, the employer had to show some agreed variation of the contractual term binding upon the employee. Similarly in *Robertson and Jackson v British Gas Corpn*[1] where an employer gave notice to the union terminating a bonus scheme originally agreed with the union and stopped bonus payments altogether, the employee was able to succeed with the argument that the original bonus scheme remained incorporated in his contract of employment and survived the ending of the scheme at the collective level. The court first found that the collective agreement had been expressly incorporated in the employees' contract of employment by a letter stating that 'incentive bonus scheme conditions will apply to meter reading and collective work' and that this meant that the contract did not contemplate the absence of a bonus. It then decided that the termination by the employer of the *collective* scheme did not affect the individual terms of the employee's contract. The changes at collective level gave the employers no right to abrogate the bonus scheme unilaterally at the individual level.

15 *Rigby v Ferodo Ltd* [1988] ICR 29, [1987] IRLR 516, HL.
16 *Miller v Hamworthy Engineering Ltd* [1986] ICR 846, [1986] IRLR 461, CA.
17 *Burroughs Machines Ltd v Timmoney* [1977] IRLR 404, CA.
18 Unless of course the employer has inserted a clause stating that 'terms and conditions of your employment contract are subject to collective agreements from time to time in force.'
19 *Rigby v Ferodo Ltd* [1988] ICR 29, [1987] IRLR 516, HL.
20 [1986] ICR 846, [1986] IRLR 461, CA.
1 [1983] ICR 351, [1983] IRLR 302, CA.

The employees could claim their pay under the old scheme until the individual agreement was either mutually varied or terminated.[2]

Further in *Lee v GEC Plessey Telecommunications*[3] three employees made redundant were able to argue that their redundancy payment should be calculated on the basis of their first, 1985, collective agreement incorporated in their employment contracts (£26,643) rather than a subsequent agreement (£8,193). Connell J accepted that the earlier redundancy payment entitlement was like remuneration generally not capable of unilateral alteration by the employer but could only be removed by agreement or specific right found within the agreement.

Finally, in *Whent v T Cartledge Ltd*[4] the EAT held that a transferee employer who, after a transfer of the undertaking, terminates the existing collective agreement not only continues to be bound by it because it was incorporated in the employees' contracts of employment, but also can be bound by wage increases awarded by a collective agreement made subsequent to the transfer.[5] The employer was bound until there was an appropriate change in the individual contract.

Even where the union terminates the collective agreement the employer continues to be liable under the contract of employment until mutual variation or termination of the employment contract. In *Gibbons v Associated British Ports*,[6] the employee, a registered dock worker who received a weekly minimum basic wage by virtue of a local collective agreement incorporated into his contract of employment, did not lose that contractual right simply because the union terminated the collective agreement. The High Court held that once the term was incorporated in the contract of employment it could only be varied with the *employee's* agreement.

The individualisation of collective terms can also, however, work to the disadvantage of employees. For, in such cases, the employer is only bound by the incorporated, collective pay rates as long as the individual contract of employment remains in effect. An employer who wishes to reorganise terms and conditions without breach of contract may serve notice of termination of the employment contract upon the individual employee and offer a new contract on revised terms.[7] If employees refuse the new contract, their only recourse will be a claim for unfair dismissal

2 See too *Rigby v Ferodo Ltd.* [1988] ICR 29, [1987] IRLR 516, HL. But see *Airlie v City of Edinburgh District Council* [1996] IRLR 516, EAT.

3 [1993] IRLR 383, HL.

4 [1997] IRLR 153, EAT.

5 The incorporation clause referred to the terms of the National Joint Council 'as amended from time to time.'

6 [1985] IRLR 376, QB.

7 See eg *Whent v T Cartledge* [1997] IRLR 153, EAT.

or possibly redundancy as contractual rights have been extinguished by the notice of termination, as long as it is of proper length.[8]

The rights of employees to collective terms under their contracts of employment can also be taken away if the employer is able successfully to show that they are severable from the main body of contractual rights under the collective agreement. For example in *Land v West Yorkshire Metropolitan County Council*,[9] the contracts of employment of some West Yorkshire fireman were held to be divisible into two parts, one relating to whole time service on full pay and the other a supplemental part relating to retained duties in the employee's spare time. The second part was severable from the first and could be terminated separately on reasonable notice. However, in *Gibbons v Associated British Ports*[10] the court found that a six day guarantee could not be severed from the overall remuneration arrangements as it was part of a package deal agreement designed to close up earnings between two groups of workers covered by the agreement and hence an integral part of the terms of remuneration of the dock workers.

On balance, however, the current legal framework in the UK, unlike the law in the USA and in many continental EC member states,[11] provides little assurance that the 'normative' terms of collective agreements will provide a legal underpinning for individual contracts of employment. UK law allows the employer to alter the individual employment contract by negotiation with the employee or by termination and the offer of a new contract upon new terms and thereby 'derogate' from the collectively agreed norm.

8 See Ch 9.

9 [1981] ICR 334, [1981] IRLR 87; *Bond v CAV Ltd* [1983] IRLR 360.

10 [1985] IRLR 376; see also *Burroughs Machines Ltd v Timmoney* [1977] IRLR 404, CA.

11 See *Wedderburn* [1992] ILJ 245.

CHAPTER 6

# Wrongful dismissal: remedies and consequences for statutory claims

The main legal constraint upon managerial decisions contained in employees' contracts of employment is the prospect of an action for breach of contract or wrongful dismissal. What remedies are available to enforce such actions? (Part A).

A second related issue is how does a wrongful dismissal or breach of contract by the employer affect the determination of an employee's rights under statute law? (Part B).

## A REMEDIES FOR WRONGFUL DISMISSAL

Prior to 1971, the normal remedy for employees who were wrongfully dismissed was damages. Specific performance was not available because contracts of employment were viewed as personal contracts and the courts were unwilling to 'compel persons who are not desirous of maintaining continuous personal relations with one another to continue these personal relations'.[1]

This attitude to specific performance went hand in hand with the view that an employer's action in dismissing the employee *automatically* terminated the contract. In *Sanders v Ernest A Neale Ltd*[2] Sir John Donaldson, President of the NIRC at the time, stated:

> 'The obvious, and indeed, the only explanation is that the repudiation of a contract of employment is an exception to the general rule. It terminates the contract without the necessity for acceptance by the injured party.'

1 *De Francesco v Barnum* (1890) 45 Ch D 430 at 438.

2 [1974] ICR 565 at 571, NIRC. This wasn't a unanimous view. See eg *Decro-Wall International SA v Practitioners in Marketing Ltd* [1971] 2 All ER 216, [1971] 1 WLR 361, CA.

A corollary of the 'automatic theory' was the notion that upon repudiation the right to remuneration under the contract was extinguished. The employee dismissed without adequate notice was left only with the remedy of damages for breach of contract. This issue as we shall see is particularly relevant to certain claims under statute law.[3]

As a remedy for wrongful dismissal, damages were generally limited to compensation for the loss of remuneration during the notice period which the employee had been wrongfully denied.[4] The courts proceeded under the assumption that the employer could end the contract lawfully at any time merely by giving appropriate notice of termination. In the case of fixed term contracts for higher paid employees, or employees with big salaries and long notice periods, the amounts could be considerable.[5] In most cases, however, the amount was and is measured by loss of income for the notice period due under the contract, which since 1963 has been subject to the standard minima established by s 86 of the ERA 1996 and its predecessors of one to twelve weeks.

Damages for loss of reputation or to compensate for the distress caused by the manner of dismissal were rarely if ever obtained.[6] One exception that survives today is the case where an employee is deprived of a claim under statute law owing to a wrongful dismissal precluding eligibility because of the time limit.[7] Furthermore, the courts have placed defendants under a duty to mitigate their loss of remuneration, by looking for new employment even during the period corresponding to the notice entitlement.[8] In the event, at common law, the restraints placed upon employers deciding to dismiss without proper notice or otherwise repudiate the employment contract were exceedingly weak, a factor which contributed to the decision to introduce a statutory protection against unfair dismissal in 1971.[9]

3 See Part B of this chapter.

4 *Addis v Gramophone Co Ltd* [1909] AC 488, HL; *Lavarack v Woods of Colchester Ltd* [1967] 1 QB 278, [1966] 3 All ER 683.

5 See eg *O'Laoire v Jackel International Ltd (No 2)* [1991] ICR 718, [1991] IRLR 170, CA; see too *Hopkins v Norcross plc* [1993] 1 All ER 565, [1992] IRLR 304 (pension payments are not deductible from damages).

6 *Addis v Gramophone Co Ltd* [1909] AC 488, HL; *Cox v Philips Industries Ltd* [1976] 3 All ER 161, [1976] ICR 138, overruled in *Bliss v South East Thames Regional Health Authority* [1987] ICR 700, [1985] IRLR 308, CA; see too *Marbe v George Edwardes (Daly's Theatre) Ltd* [1928] 1 KB 269, CA; *Dunk v George Waller & Son Ltd* [1970] 2 QB 163, [1970] 2 All ER 630, CA.

7 *Robert Cort & Son Ltd v Charman* [1981] ICR 816, [1981] IRLR 437, EAT, approved in *Stapp v Shaftesbury Society* [1982] IRLR 326, CA. But see *Morran v Glasgow Council of Tenants Associations* [1998] IRLR 67, CS.

8 See eg *Yetton v Eastwoods Froy Ltd* [1966] 3 All ER 353, [1967] 1 WLR 104.

9 See Ch 9.

In recent years, however, the courts have indicated that they are prepared, in certain circumstances, to view the employer's repudiatory act as not automatically terminating the contract, but rather presenting employees with an option either to accept the employer's repudiatory conduct as terminating the contract, or to choose to keep certain terms, or the whole, of the contract on foot so as to enforce their contractual or statutory rights.[10]

In the case of certain dismissals, as a matter of fact, employees have no option other than to accept the employer's repudiation as terminating the contract and accept a remedy of damages. Nevertheless, in principle, the adoption of an 'elective theory' had the advantage of bringing the law of repudiation of employment contracts into line with the general law of contract, even if its application in practice would be circumscribed.[11]

With the adoption of the 'elective theory', even in a limited number of factual situations, moreover, the courts could view the remedies for employers' breaches of contract in a different light. They could begin to introduce a legal basis for a larger measure of damages. For example, the courts could add to the amount the employer would have been bound to pay had the employee's contract been lawfully terminated, the loss of pay during the period the proper operation of the contractual disciplinary aggrievance procedure would have required.[12] They could also contemplate the possibility of an interlocutory injunction specifically enforcing a term or even the whole of the employment contract, pending a trial on the action for damages.

The first hint of a new remedy of specific performance was *Hill v C A Parsons & Co Ltd*[13] in which the Court of Appeal held that in a case where the employer, reluctantly enforcing a closed shop arrangement, gave inadequate notice of termination to a senior employee of long service, an injunction could be granted to the employee restraining the employer from terminating the employment contract. Lord Denning was careful to state that this was an exceptional case, in which the court found that both employer and employee had continued confidence in one another.

Nevertheless, it established an exception to the general rule that courts would not grant specific performance of contracts of service. Sachs LJ made the point that it was necessary for the plaintiffs to establish at trial

10 *Gunton v Richmond-upon-Thames London Borough Council* [1981] Ch 448, [1980] ICR 755.

11 Ibid; see also *Thomas Marshall (Exports) Ltd v Guinle* [1979] Ch 227, [1978] ICR 905.

12 See eg *Gunton v London Borough of Richmond Upon Thames* [1980] IRLR 321, CA; *Boyo v London Borough of Lambeth* [1995] IRLR 50, CA. This did not allow for damages for loss of opportunity to succeed in the appeal procedure. See *Janciuk v Winerite Ltd* [1998] IRLR 63.

13 [1972] Ch 305, [1971] 3 All ER 1345, CA.

that the employer's repudiation of the contract did not terminate the contract in the absence of it being accepted; and that the contract would continue to subsist until the end of the period of proper notice to which the employee was entitled.[14]

Shortly afterwards, in *Chappell v Times Newspapers Ltd*,[15] this window for employee injunctions appeared to be closed again. Lane LJ stated:

> 'Very rarely indeed will the court enforce, either by specific performance or by injunction, a contract for services; either at the behest of the employers or of the employee. The reason is obvious: if one party has no faith in the honesty or integrity or the loyalty of the other to force him to serve or to employ that other is a plain recipe for disaster.'

In the 1980s, however, a number of injunctions were granted to employees whose contracts of employment had been repudiated by employers. In the early stages, employers' breaches of employees' rights in disciplinary or grievance procedures incorporated in their contracts offended the judges' sense of contractual obligation.

In *Jones v Lee and Guilding*[16] a Roman Catholic head teacher was granted an injunction against the Local Education Authority to defer a dismissal decision until his employer had honoured his contractual right to a hearing. The Court of Appeal's decision was quite straightforward. The employers' failure to follow their own procedure - an express term - was a breach of contract and the appropriate remedy was a form of interim specific performance. There was no mention of the long-standing strictures of *Hill v Parsons* that employment contracts should not be specifically enforced unless mutual confidence existed between the parties to the employment contract. Nor was there much discussion of the elective theory of wrongful dismissal.

In *Gunton v Richmond-upon-Thames London Borough Council*[17] a college registrar was dismissed on a contract terminable by one month's notice, by a local authority for disciplinary reasons without complying with the authority's own regulations incorporated in the employee's contract of employment, providing a procedure for disciplinary dismissals. The Court of Appeal took the view that the employee could enforce his contract of employment for the proper period of notice and the period which would have been due had a proper disciplinary procedure been followed because only then would the employer's termination have been lawful. The majority of the Court held that the employer's repudiation did not terminate the contract of employment because it was not 'accepted' by the employee as

14 Ibid.
15 [1975] 2 All ER 233, [1975] IRLR 90, CA.
16 [1980] ICR 310, [1980] IRLR 67, CA.
17 [1981] Ch 448, [1980] ICR 755, CA.

terminating the employment contract. This was effectively a rejection of the automatic theory of repudiation. Buckley LJ stated that

> 'the adoption of the disciplinary regulations and their consequent incorporation in the plaintiff's contract of service did disable the council from dismissing the plaintiff on disciplinary grounds until the procedure prescribed by these regulations had been carried out.'[18]

In effect, the majority chose to bring employment contracts into line with the general law of contract in respect of wrongful repudiation, setting the stage for a further elaboration of the doctrine of specific performance of employment contracts as well as the remedy of damages for the failure to follow a contractual disciplinary procdure.

In *R v BBC, ex p Lavelle*[19] an employee, charged with misconduct, and dismissed subject to her appeal under an internal disciplinary procedure, sought to stay the hearing of her appeal pending the results of a criminal proceeding relating to the alleged misconduct. The BBC argued that the wrongful dismissal action could only be enforced by the remedy of damages. Woolf J stated, however, that when the employer 'engrafted onto the ordinary principles of master and servant an elaborate framework of appeals', it restricted its power 'as an employer to terminate the employee's employment'. The employer's decision to give the employee a right to be heard and to agree to a restriction on its rights to dismiss, although procedural, nevertheless altered her rights substantially from the pure common law position, and made her contract more akin to that of an office holder. Consequently a breach by the employer could be remedied not only by damages but where appropriate 'by way of injunction and certainly by way of declaration'.

Then, in *Irani v Southampton and South West Hampshire Health Authority*[20] the High Court, Chancery Division, granted an injunction under the Court's normal equity jurisdiction where an employer gave an employee six weeks' notice but failed to follow the dispute procedure laid down by the joint trade union management negotiating committee for the health service, which was incorporated into the employee's contract of employment. To hold otherwise, Warner J stated would, in effect, be to hold that the defendant employer would be 'entitled to snap its fingers at the rights of the employee under the blue book'. In this case, the decision was qualified by the condition of *Hill v Parsons* that the employer continued to have confidence in the employee.

18 Ibid at 765. Cf *Boyo v London Borough of Lambeth* [1995] IRLR 50, CA (in which *Gunton* was applied with some misgivings.

19 [1983] 1 All ER 241, [1983] ICR 99.

20 [1985] ICR 590, [1985] IRLR 203. For vain attempts to use Order 53 to obtain judicial review in such situations see *R v East Berkshire Health Authority, ex p Walsh* [1985] QB 152, [1984] IRLR 278, CA; Collins, H [1984] 13 ILJ 174.

Later, in *Robb v Hammersmith and Fulham London Borough Council*[1] Marland J, citing Warner J in *Irani*, granted an injunction where the plaintiff was dismissed in breach of the disciplinary procedure incorporated within his contract of employment. The order restrained the employers from giving effect to the purported dismissal of the plaintiff and treated him as suspended on full pay until they properly complied with the disciplinary procedure contained in the contract. In *Jones v Gwent County Council*[2] after receiving a defective notification for a hearing and a notice of dismissal, the employee was able to obtain an interim injunction preventing the dismissal and a permanent injunction restraining the dismissal.

In the late 1980s a second category of cases emerged, in which the courts were prepared to restrain attempts by the employer unilaterally to vary *substantive* terms of the contract, pending a court resolution of the contractual issue. In *Hughes v London Borough of Southwark*[3] a local authority was restrained from transferring specialised social workers in Maudsley Hospital to general social work in Southwark because there was a serious issue to be tried as to whether the work was within the employees' contractual obligations. And in *Powell v Brent London Borough Council*[4] the Court of Appeal approved an injunction to restrain the local authority from advertising and filling the post of Principal Benefits Officer after having already appointed the plaintiff to the post and later rescinding the appointment.[5] Finally, in *Anderson v Pringle of Scotland Ltd*[6] the Court of Session granted an interim injunction enforcing an employee's rights under a 'last in–first out' redundancy selection provision incorporated from a collective agreement which the employer had ignored in its managerial selections for redundancy. The injunction required the employer not to select employees for redundancy on any other basis than the 'last in–first out' principle in the contract.

## Injunction procedure

In such cases, in order to obtain an interim injunction, certain procedural conditions have to be satisfied. The plaintiff employee must show that

1 [1991] ICR 514, [1991] IRLR 72, HC.
2 [1992] IRLR 521. Cf *Newns v British Airways* [1992] IRLR 575, CA (Steyn LJ '... If a particular proposal by an employer is a breach of his obligation of good faith, it may be that an employee can apply for an injunction to restrain the proposal as being an apprehended breach of the ... obligation of good faith.')
3 [1988] IRLR 55.
4 [1988] ICR 176, [1987] IRLR 466, CA.
5 See too *Jones v Gwent County Council* [1992] IRLR 521.
6 [1998] IRLR 64.

damages would be an inadequate remedy,[7] ie that the loss would not be readily compensatable. This requirement is often met in cases where the employee can claim the loss of an opportunity to put his side of the issue in a hearing or appeal.[8] There must be evidence of a prima facie case or at least a 'serious issue to be tried'.[9] Finally, the balance of convenience must be shown to be in favour of the plaintiff. Again, the change in contractual terms or failure to provide an express procedural entitlement can usually meet this procedural obstacle.[10]

The final hurdle, however, is the most difficult. Even if there is a breach of contract by the employer, before an injunction can be granted there must usually be a finding that the trust and confidence between the employer and employee continue to exist. For example, in *Powell*'s case, the court emphasised that such an injunction would not be granted,

> 'unless there exists sufficient confidence on the part of the employer in the servant's reliability and other necessary attributes for it to be reasonable to make the order. Sufficiency of confidence must be judged by reference to the circumstances of the case, including the nature of the work, the people with whom the work must be done and the likely effect upon the employer and the employer's organisation if the employer is required by an injunction to suffer the plaintiff to continue in the work.'[11]

In *Alexander v Standard Telephones and Cables plc*,[12] a group of employees were able to show that there was a serious issue to be tried: that the employer had repudiated a term of the plaintiff's contract, which stipulated that no redundancies would occur without the principle of 'last in - first out' being applied. An injunction was denied because

> 'it could not be said that the employer had complete confidence in the plaintiffs since they had less confidence that they can do the work than the other members of the work-force that had been retained.'

On the other hand, in *Anderson v Pringle of Scotland*,[13] Lord Prosser dealt with the confidence point in the following way:

7 See eg *McGoldrick v London Borough of Brent* [1987] IRLR 67, CA; *Dietman v Brent London Borough Council* [1988] ICR 842, [1988] IRLR 299, CA.

8 Cf *Jakeman v South West Thames Regional Health Authority* [1990] IRLR 62, where damages were adequate and no injunction granted.

9 *American Cyanimid Co v Ethicon Ltd* [1975] AC 396, HL; *Alexander v Standard Telephones and Cables plc* [1990] ICR 291, [1990] IRLR 55.

10 *Irani v Southampton and South West Hampshire Health Authority* [1985] ICR 590, [1985] IRLR 203; *Robb v Hammersmith and Fulham London Borough Council* [1991] ICR 514, [1991] IRLR 72.

11 [1987] IRLR 466, CA.

12 [1990] ICR 291, [1990] IRLR 55, HC.

13 [1998] IRLR 64 at 67.

> 'If there were any question of mistrust, the position would no doubt be very different; but at least on the material before me, I am not persuaded that there is any true analogy between the respondents' preference for other employees and the need for confidence which is inherent in the employer/employee relationship...'

In other situations, this condition creates a considerable hurdle for plaintiffs to surmount, even if courts will not automatically accept an employer's allegation that there has been a breakdown in trust and confidence.[14] There have been cases where no mention has been made of this requirement but these have been rare.[15] In recent cases however, another criterion has begun to emerge: where the court decides that a Court order is 'workable'.[16] Thus, in *Robb v Hammersmith and Fulham London Borough Council*[17] the High Court granted an injunction restraining an employer from summarily dismissing an employee until the requisite steps in the disciplinary procedure had been completed, but this was a case where the employee had already been suspended on full pay and the effect of the injunction was simply to continue the suspension until the disciplinary procedure was completed. Marland J stated:

> 'In my judgment, although the court will only rarely grant the plaintiff injunctive relief against his employer, the all important criterion is whether the order sought is workable.'

Similarly, in *Powell*[18] the fact that the employee had been working satisfactorily in the post made it difficult to argue that the injunction was not workable.

Finally in *Jones v Gwent County Council*[19] Chadwick J in the High Court (QBD) was prepared to grant an injunction restraining a dismissal under Ord 14, r 1 following an invalid letter of dismissal without reference to the issue of trust and confidence.

Whatever the basis used, employee injunctions will continue to be a fairly rare remedy. Moreover, even where injunctive relief is granted its effect is often limited. In the widest category of case, breach of procedure, the remedy is essentially an interim measure. As Roskill LJ indicated in

14 See eg *Hughes v London Borough of Southwark* [1988] IRLR 55; *Robb v Hammersmith and Fulham London Borough Council* [1991] ICR 514, [1991] IRLR 72.

15 See eg *Jones v Lee and Guilding* [1980] ICR 310; *R v BBC, ex p Lavelle* [1983] 1 All ER 241, [1982] IRLR 404.

16 See eg *Robb* (above); *Wadcock v London Borough of Brent* [1990] IRLR 223.

17 [1991] IRLR 72 at 75. See too *Jones v Gwent County Council* [1992] IRLR 521.

18 [1987] IRLR 466, CA.

19 [1992] IRLR 521. Under Ord 14A, r 1 a court may at any stage of any proceedings determine any question of law or the construction of any document: (i) where such a question is suitable for determination without a full trial; and (ii) where the determination will finally determine the entire cause of action.

*Jones v Lee and Guilding*[20] injunctive relief does not preclude the employer from dismissing the employee, provided that the employer follows a correct procedure. There is little basis for review of the substance of the employer's decision if the procedure is followed. One cannot argue that the employer has prejudged the case.[1] The net effect of these decisions is only to ensure that employers perform their contractual obligations.

Nevertheless, the availability of injunctive relief, even on a highly limited basis, cannot be dismissed out of hand. For in such cases the courts have dramatically changed the calculus for managers. They know that their decisions can be overturned by the courts, albeit temporarily, as opposed to being subject to a remedy merely requiring a higher price to be paid for an already implemented decision in the form of financial compensation to the employee.

## B WRONGFUL DISMISSAL AND STATUTORY CLAIMS

The development of the elective theory of wrongful dismissal has also affected certain statutory rights. In the first place, it has had to be reconciled with the definition of dismissal for the purposes of unfair dismissals and redundancy. Second, it has affected the time of termination for the purposes of other statutory time limits. Third, it has affected the entitlement of employees to bring an action under Part II of the Employment Rights Act 1996 (formerly the Wages Act 1986). Let us look at each of these points in turn.

### Wrongful dismissal and the definition of dismissal

For the purposes of the unfair dismissals and redundancy payments law, two statutory modes of dismissal overlap with the common law concept of wrongful dismissal. The first is the case where the employer terminates the employee's contract without proper notice (ERA, s 95(1)(a)). The second is where employees terminate the contracts with or without notice but in circumstances entitling them to do so by reason of the employer's conduct (ERA, s 95(1)(c)).

Both sections can be applied consistently with the ground rules of the elective theory of repudiation. If the employee repudiates the contract by say an act of gross misconduct, it is terminated by the employer's

20 [1980] ICR 310, [1980] IRLR 67, CA.

1 See eg *White v Kuzych* [1951] AC 585, [1951] 2 All ER 435, PC; *Ali v Southwark London Borough Council* [1988] ICR 567, [1988] IRLR 100; cf *Longley v NUJ* [1987] IRLR 109, CA.

acceptance of the repudiation and consequently the employer has terminated the contract in the meaning of s 95(1)(a). This would defeat any claim by the employer that employees have dismissed themselves by their repudiation of the contract.[2] If, on the other hand, the employer has repudiated the contract it is not the employer's act which terminates the contract but the employee's act in accepting the repudiation and treating it as a termination of the contract. This type of employee termination of the contract is 'constructive dismissal' under s 95(1)(c).[3]

## Wrongful dismissal and the effective date of termination

On the other hand, in the determination of the precise date of dismissal for various statutory purposes, courts have insisted upon the retention of the automatic theory of repudiation. The reason for this is partly the limited reach of the statutory provision which regulates the 'effective date of termination', ie the final date of the period of continuous service for many statutory rights.[4]

ERA, s 97(2) provides that where an employee is entitled to a statutory minimum period of notice from the employer,[5] the date at which *the notice would have expired if duly given* will for certain purposes[6] be treated as the effective date of dismissal, rather than the date the employee actually left his employment. This statutory deeming provision for the date of effective termination under s 97(2) applies whether the dismissal was without adequate notice, without any notice at all or with pay in lieu of notice.[7]

It therefore offers an example of the statutory technique of removing the employer's discretion to affect the scope of the employee's rights by 'structuring' the transaction. Under this section the only case where the employer can legitimately end the period of the employee's service by a dismissal without notice is where, in fact, the conduct of the employee justified a termination without notice, an issue which must itself be decided by a tribunal should the employee complain.[8]

2 *Rasool v Hepworth Pipe Co Ltd* [1980] ICR 494, [1980] IRLR 88, EAT.
3 *Western Excavating (ECC) Ltd v Sharp* [1978] QB 761, [1978] ICR 221, CA.
4 In the case of redundancy payments, the equivalent of the effective date is called the 'relevant date' (see s 145) but similar principles apply.
5 ERA, s 86.
6 Eg qualifying period of continuous service, ERA, s 108(1); calculation of the basic award, ERA, s 119(1); maximum amount of a week's pay, ERA, s 227(3).
7 See eg *Secretary of State for Employment v Staffordshire County Council* [1989] IRLR 117, CA (contractual waivers of notice do not alter the date for statutory purposes).
8 See eg *Lanton Leisure Ltd v White and Gibson* [1987] IRLR 119, EAT.

While s 97(2) applies to determine the date of termination of many specified statutory rights,[9] it does not apply to all.[10] And in most cases where s 97(2) does not apply, the courts have adopted an automatic theory of repudiation.[11] In *Robert Cort & Son Ltd v Charman*[12] the EAT held that, where an employer dismissed an employee summarily and without giving the period of notice required by the contract, for the purposes of applying s 97(1) to determine the time period to present a complaint of unfair dismissal 'the effective date of termination is the date of summary dismissal whether or not the employer makes a payment in lieu of notice'.

It reasoned that s 97(1) seems to have been drafted on the footing that the unilateral view is correct, ie dismissal even without the contractually required notice terminates the contract. Furthermore it considered it important that there should be no doubt or uncertainty as to the date which is the 'effective date of termination' for an issue such as the calculation of the time period for presenting a complaint of unfair dismissal not covered by s 97(2).

Consequently, if an employer *clearly* notifies an employee that his employment will terminate immediately[13] or on a specific date,[14] the date that the notification is actually received[15] or the date that is stated will normally be regarded as the date when dismissal takes effect, even if the employer's action in prematurely terminating the contract was wrongful. The timing of the dismissal is unaffected by the wrongfulness of the dismissal or by the fact that the employee can recover damages for breach of contract.[16] Nor, assuming that the employer's letter is unambiguous does the fact that the employer offers to pay wages in lieu of notice affect the

9 See n 6 above.

10 It does not apply, for example, to the date of dismissal for the calculation of the time period for submitting a complaint of unfair dismissal or a redundancy payment to an industrial tribunal.

11 In cases of contructive dismissal the test is partly statutory and 'deemed' (see s 97(4)) and partly based on an elective theory for cases falling outside the deemed notice period. See eg *BMK Ltd v Logue* [1993] ICR 601, [1993] IRLR 477, EAT.

12 [1981] ICR 816, [1981] IRLR 437, EAT.

13 *Dedman v British Building and Engineering Appliances Ltd* [1974] 1 All ER 520, [1974] ICR 53; *Adams v GKN Sankey Ltd* [1980] IRLR 416, EAT.

14 *Dixon v Stenor Ltd* [1973] ICR 157, [1973] IRLR 28.

15 Where the dismissal is communicated in a letter, the effective date of communication is the date when the employee has actually read the letter or the date when he has a reasonable opportunity of reading it: *Brown v Southall and Knight* [1980] ICR 617, [1980] IRLR 130, EAT.

16 *Stapp v Shaftesbury Society* [1982] IRLR 326, CA (damages for wrongful dismissal at common law could include the loss of the right to complain of unfair dismissal which the employee would have had had he not been summarily dismissed); see too *Octavius Atkinson & Sons Ltd v Morris* [1989] ICR 431, [1989] IRLR 158, CA. For the test that applies to grievance and disciplinary procedures see *J Sainsbury Ltd v Savage* [1980] IRLR 109, CA.

timing of the dismissal since, in such a case, the pay in lieu of notice is viewed as a matter of law as damages for breach of contract.[17]

On the other hand, if the employer's dismissal notification is ambiguous and suggests that the arrangement may be regarded as a form of paid leave, the date of dismissal will be the end of the period of contractual notice. For example, in *Adams v GKN Sankey Ltd*[18] a letter of dismissal sent by the employer dated 2 November 1979 said: 'You are given 12 weeks' notice of dismissal from this company with effect from 5 November 1979. You will not be expected to work out your notice but will receive money in lieu of notice.' This letter was interpreted to mean that the employee's employment did not end until 12 weeks after the 5 November. The period of notice was a paid leave and the reference to money in lieu was construed as payment in lieu of working out notice.

If the paid leave exception does help to ameliorate the unfairness of the automatic termination rule it does not extinguish it entirely. Moreover, both the rule and the distinction are now also relevant for the purposes of determining the jurisdiction of industrial tribunals under the Part II of the ERA 1996. In *Delaney v Staples*[19] the House of Lords held that the question of whether a payment in lieu of wages was within the statutory definition of wages depended upon the distinction between (a) an employee who is summarily dismissed and given wages in lieu (in which case the ERA, s 13 does not apply), and (b) an employee given notice that his or her employment will terminate in four weeks and paid in advance but he or she need not work that period for garden leave (in which case the ERA, s 13 will apply). The importance of this distinction for the purposes of ERA, s 13 has lessened now that the government has extended the jurisdiction of industrial tribunals to claims for damages for a breach of contract of employment.[20]

Nevertheless, we have here examples of two statutory provisions, ie ERA, s 97(1) and ERA, s 13 which, as formulated, leave to the discretion of the employer the choice of arranging a letter or interview so as to determine the date of dismissal for the purpose of the employee's statutory rights.

17 *Adams v GKN Sankey Ltd* [1980] IRLR 416, EAT. See discussion below.

18 [1980] IRLR 416, EAT; see also *Chapman v Letheby and Christopher Ltd* [1981] IRLR 440, EAT (per Brown-Wilkinson, and ambiguity in the dismissal notice should be construed against the employer); see too *Leech v Preston Borough Council* [1985] IRLR 337.

19 *Delaney v Staples (t/a De Montfort Recruitment)* [1992] 1 AC 687, [1992] IRLR 191, HL. See Honeyball, 'Wages, Payments in Lieu of Notice and Deductions' [1991] ILJ 143.

20 See Industrial Tribunal Extension of Jurisdiction Order 1994, SI 1994 No 1623; in Scotland SI 1994 No 1624.

PART II

# Individual employment legislation

# Introduction

Individual employment legislation takes the form of statutory rules imposed directly upon a wide range of management decisions, inter alia, to hire and fire, to promote and discipline, to grant leave or time off, to reorganise terms and conditions of employment and establish the physical conditions of work. Such laws also impinge upon collective bargaining. As Hepple once described it:

> '. . . matters which were entirely in the sphere of managerial prerogatives or collective bargaining are now directly regulated by positive rights and duties.'[1]

While we know with some precision which spheres are regulated, we know less about how this layer of legislation regulates managerial prerogatives and collective bargaining. The policy debate portrays employment protection legislation almost entirely in terms of establishing worker 'rights' or labour 'standards' as if they applied generally to establish minimum levels of protection or a 'floor of rights' throughout the workforce. In practice, however, the statutory rules have certain features which can result in different standards of protection and constraints upon managerial prerogative than those suggested by a more cursory reading of the statute. In a sense, a measure of 'deregulation' or managerial flexibility is built into the very structure of the statutory standards. On the other hand, the rights of workers can be reinforced by particular statutory formulations of the standards, the inclusion of collective rights in the formulation of individual rights and purposive interpretations of such legislation whether based upon the application of European Community standards to UK legislation or upon a judicial recognition of a method of interpretation which strives to effect the purposes of national legislation.

1 Hepple 'Individual Employment Law' in Bain *Industrial Relations in Britain* (1983) p 394.

The following features of individual employment protection legislation are particularly worth noting:

(1) their qualifying conditions;
(2) their relationship with the contract of employment;
(3) the points of discretion embedded in the statutory standards;
(4) the statutory remedies;
(5) individual employment protection legislation and collective bargaining;
(6) the relationship between UK and EC law.

## THE QUALIFYING CONDITIONS FOR INDIVIDUAL EMPLOYMENT LEGISLATION

Many statutory rights are restricted in their scope to 'employees' ie those who work under a contract of employment, for a minimum period of continuous service.

By creating these preconditions for eligibility, statute law allows employers to retain considerable discretion to structure work relationships so as to avoid legislation, as well as creating inequities in the incidence of protection for a workforce which is becoming increasingly short-term working arrangements and self-employment. The issue is considered in Chapter 6.

## THE CONTRACT OF EMPLOYMENT AND LEGISLATIVE STANDARDS

An important feature of individual employment protection legislation is the extent to which and the way in which it relies upon contractual elements to shape legislative standards. Given that, as we have seen, the contract of employment often provides a ready platform for managerial discretion, reliance upon contract by statute law can result in an undermining of the statutory standards of protection.

Both unfair dismissals law and redundancy payment law, for example, define dismissal as 'termination of the contract of employment'. Moreover, the concepts of 'type of work' and 'place of work' in the statutory definition of redundancy can be interpreted to a greater or a lesser extent as dependent upon contract. In such cases, it is important to study to what extent judicial decisions take into account the fact that the legislation was meant to be an employment protection and that employers are placed in a position to use contract to reduce the scope of the statutory protection.

Although employment protection legislation contains an express restriction against the parties contracting out of the provisions of the relevant Act (Employment Rights Act, s 203(1)) employers can achieve such a result indirectly by use of their greater bargaining and 'drafting' powers. These issues are highlighted in the study of unfair dismissal and redundancy in Chapters 7 and 8.

## DISCRETIONARY STATUTORY STANDARDS AND MANAGERIAL PREROGATIVES

Even where statutes are drafted to impose 'contract free' statutory norms upon the employment relationship, there is still a need to examine the discretionary elements in the statutory standard and how that discretion has been defined and interpreted.

One important test is how the judiciary approaches the issue of examining the reasoning and 'justification' for management decisions. To what extent is the statutory standard interpreted to provide protections for employees' interests at the expense of employers' interests? To what extent is the legislation interpreted to give autonomy to business decisions at the expense of worker protections? Does judicial concern for the managerial inefficiencies of intervention run counter to the legislative intention to improve managerial efficiency by insisting on certain minimum standards of management?

### The scope of the statutory remedies

In addition the nature of the statutory remedies has a decisive influence upon the effectiveness of statutory standards.

If the remedies are set too low the legislation can be ignored with impunity by management or avoided by action which gives the appearance of compliance but not the reality. The analysis of remedies requires several steps to capture all the nuances. First of all, to what extent does legislation adopt a remedy of specific performance or a court order requiring the employer to take certain actions? To what extent does it consist of a purely financial penalty? To the extent that the legislation relies solely on financial penalties it places the employer in the position to pay for the costs of non-compliance as an alternative to the business costs of compliance. In other words, the limitations of its remedies are in turn a limit to the capacity of the legislation to influence managerial decisions.[2] To what extent is this taken into account in setting the scale of financial compensation?

2 See eg *Marshall v Southampton and South West Hampshire Area Health Authority (No 2)* [1993] IRLR 445, ECJ.

## Individual employment protection legislation and collective bargaining

The structural relationship between individual employment legislation and collective bargaining has not always been accurately described. At one stage individual employment legislation was portrayed as 'deferring to' collective bargaining as if there was little overlap or intermingling between the two spheres.[3] The individual employment protections were viewed as providing minimum substantive standards of protection to employees whether trade union members or not in the form of statutory rights to be adjudicated by industrial tribunals. Collective bargaining operating alongside the legislation was to produce improved results for employees with good organisation and bargaining power. There was provision for the extension of collective bargaining results to other more weakly organised sectors by a process of arbitration under Sch 11 to the Employment Protection Act 1975 and public sector contracting obligations under the Fair Wages Resolution. However, there was little recognition that individual employment legislation was actually intended to impinge upon collective bargaining.

Initially it must have been supposed that the statutory protections could be isolated from collective bargaining by a statutory system of exclusions. Thus the legislation on unfair dismissals (ERA, s 110), redundancy payments (ERA, s 157) and guarantee payments (ERA, s 35) all provide that the Secretary of State for Employment could confer exemptions upon the parties to collective agreements and thereby exclude individual employees from making a complaint to the industrial tribunal under the relevant statutory provisions where the collective arrangements satisfied the requirements of the particular statute, in that they provide comparable or more favourable protection than the statutory enactment. However, with the exception of the guarantee payment legislation, these statutory exclusions have rarely, if ever, been resorted to.

The failure of the policy of statutory exclusions, however, was only part of the reason for the subsequent influence of the legislation upon collective bargaining arrangements. For the legislation had always had the ambition of improving and reforming collective bargaining and managerial practice as well as establishing rights for employees. A good example of this is the redundancy payments legislation which provided a minimum lump sum of compensation for employees dismissed for redundancy. At first glance this legislation appeared to be concerned with compensating long-serving employees who had been dismissed through no fault of their own. Yet the lump sum payment also was designed to reduce collective

3 See eg Deakin and Wilkinson *Labour Law, Social Security and Economic Inequality* (1989) IER p 35.

worker resistance to managerial redundancy decisions. Similarly the unfair dismissals provisions were designed to stimulate managerial reforms of disciplinary procedures and thereby lessen collective industrial conflict over disciplinary issues as well as to improve the extent of legal protection of employees.

Moreover, certain legislation, such as the Equal Pay and Sex Discrimination Acts has been quite specifically designed to override collective bargaining as well as managerial practice where they violated the statutory provisions. For example, section 6 of the SDA 1986, as amended by s 32 of TURER 1993, gives individuals a right to a declaration that a discriminatory term of a collective agreement or employer rule is void.[4]

In the area of equal pay too, collective arrangements are not completely isolated from the individual's rights. Section 3(4) of the Equal Pay Act stipulates that where provisions in collective agreements or pay structures apply 'specifically to men only or to women only' the CAC is given powers to amend collective agreements so as to eliminate the sex discrimination in the pay structures.[5] Moreover, Article 119 has been held to apply directly to collective agreements.[6] In these and other respects, the so-called individual employment rights have a marked inter-relationship with collective bargaining and this factor too is relevant to any assessment of the impact of statute law upon managerial decisions. Some employment legislation was always intended to have some impact upon managerial efficiency and reform collective bargaining as part of the process of establishing minimum standards.

At a more technical legal level, moreover, there is a noticeable overlap between individual employment legislation and collective bargaining. For example the unfair dismissals law provides that employers should dismiss employees only after ensuring that the procedure they adopt is fair - and where the disciplinary procedure provides for a right of trade union representation or a right of trade union participation in an appeal panel, these 'collective' features are given weight in the test of reasonableness built into the statute (see Chapter 8).

In the case of redundancy law the in-built collective features are also evident. Under ERA, s 98(4), in a test of unfair redundancy, the question of whether the employer behaved with procedural propriety in consulting the trade union representative is a factor. Further, the redundancy payment provisions calculate pay on the basis of contractual payment and this is

4 See eg Lester and Rose 'Equal Value Claims and Sex Bias in Collective Bargaining' (1991) ILJ 163.

5 Ibid.

6 See eg *Nimz v Freie und Hansestadt Hamburg*: C-184/89 [1991] ECR I-297, [1991] IRLR 222, ECJ.

influenced by the rates established in the contract of employment by collective bargaining. It is clearly the case that the trade union rights and employee rights in the UK are not as closely integrated as in Sweden[7] and Italy,[8] but there is nonetheless a significant overlap.

## EUROPEAN LAW AND UK LAW

Finally, as we have seen, European Community law and UK labour law have become closely intertwined in the past few years in certain fields of labour law. It may be accurate to describe domestic UK legislation and Community law as two facets of an integrated system in certain spheres of law. These points are explored in greater depth in Chapters 10 ('Transfers of undertakings'), 13 ('Sex discrimination') and 14 ('Equal pay').

7 Anderman 'Labour Law in Sweden: A Comment' in Neal (ed) *Law and the Weaker Party* Vol I (1981) p 193.

8 Wedderburn 'The Italian Workers' Statute: Some British Reflections' (1990) ILJ 154.

CHAPTER 7

# The coverage of individual employment protection legislation

## INTRODUCTION

In recent decades, there has been a dramatic shift in the labour market away from the model of full-time, long-term employment to an emphasis upon more flexible forms of employment and new contractual relationships, such as part-time, short-term and self-employment contracts. Since 1965 self-employment has increased from 1.6 million to almost 3.5 million and part-time employment has increased from 1.5 million to approximately 5 million. In addition, other forms of temporary, agency, casual work and home workers have dramatically increased. Together these new forms of so-called 'atypical' or 'marginal' employment now account for more than one-third of the entire workforce.[1]

These changes have occurred against the backdrop of a major shift in employment from manufacturing to services (in the period from 1965 to 1985, manufacturing jobs declined by 3 million; from 1970 to 1983 service jobs rose by 2 million) and from manual jobs, predominantly semi-skilled and unskilled, to non-manual jobs. During this period, moreover, there was a marked increase in the proportion of women in the workforce, rising from 36% in 1961 to 75% in 1985. Moreover, it is likely that these trends will continue. Forecasts of employment trends to 1995 suggested an annual increase of 2% for part-time employment.

What is striking about these now 'flexible' forms of employment is that they are predominantly occupied by female workers. Hakim estimates that women constitute almost two-thirds of the 'flexible workforce',[2] ie part-time, short-time, casual and home workers. These new forms of

1 See Hakim 'Trends in the flexible workforce' Employment Gazette, Nov 1987, pp 549-560, see also Leighton 'New Employment Relations "Marginal Workers"' in Lewis (ed) *Labour Law in Britain* (1986). See Dickens 'Whose Flexibility'.

2 Hakim C, 'Trends in the Flexible Workforce' Employment Gazette, Nov 1987, pp 549-560.

employment are associated with generally lower levels of fringe benefits and pension entitlements and fewer rights under employment legislation and social security than are enjoyed by workers in traditional jobs.[3] Moreover, there is a markedly lower level of unionisation and coverage by collective bargaining in the 'flexible workforce'. In all these respects the flexible workforce includes a significant proportion of second-class workers, generally weaker and considerably more vulnerable than full-time employees.

## Why has this segmentation occurred?

The main reason for this segmentation is that employers have taken decisions to reduce fixed commitments to labour costs and to shift more of their labour costs into 'variable flexible' obligations.[4] The recession of the early 1980s brought home to firms how competitive pressures had intensified and that there was a need to look more closely at their cost structures and their capacity to respond to changes in product demand. Employers were affected by the redundancies and lay-offs of the early 1980s and made use of their new bargaining power to reassert their 'right to manage' in the sense of determining the size of the workforce. The introduction of new technology also created opportunities to reorganise work in both manual and clerical occupations.

Along with this was the tendency for employers to subscribe to the image of the 'flexible firm': a firm which combined a 'core' of stable and committed workers and a 'periphery' of casual, short-term and self-employed workers.[5] This image held forth the prospect that employers could enjoy flexibility in determining the numbers of employees to meet the vicissitudes of competition in the product market. It also incorporated a vision of greater flexibility within the core group of workers. These relatively well paid, relatively secure and highly-trained employees, the model suggested, would accept greater flexibility in the work they did, the hours they worked and the skills that they could be called upon to use. Whether or not this image corresponded to the reality,[6] it shaped management and perhaps even government attitudes during the 1980s.

A second factor in the development of new forms of work has been the attitudes of workers themselves. There is abundant evidence that married women with young children prefer part-time rather than full-time work.[7]

3 See Fredman *Women and the law* (Clarenden Press, Oxford, 1997).
4 Atkinson 'Flexibility, Uncertainty and Manpower Management' IMS Report No 89, 1985; Meager 'Temporary work in Britain' Employment Gazette, Jan 1986.
5 See Atkinson, op cit.
6 The reality may have been for example a growth of 'peripheral' workers on a large scale in certain sectors without any corresponding 'core' of any significance.
7 Martin and Roberts *Women and Employment: A Lifetime Perspective* (1984, HMSO).

There is also evidence of certain groups of workers subscribing to the advantages of self-employment as opposed to employment.[8] Yet alongside these voluntary part-timers and self-employed, there are many workers on whom a part-time, self-employed, temporary or casual status has been imposed. It has been estimated for example that almost one-third of part-time and self-employed work is involuntary.[9] Moreover, several commentators have indicated that the preference of women for part-time work is less 'voluntary' than it appears.[10]

Finally, the demographic changes of the late 1980s and early 1990s foreshadow a huge decline in new entrants to the labour market, creating problems with traditional recruitment patterns. Working mothers and retired people are being viewed with increased interest as recruits and greater flexibility is offered in terms of employment contract eg job sharing, networking from home and part-time work for professionals.[11]

## THE QUALIFICATIONS IN THE EMPLOYMENT LEGISLATION

The emergence of these new forms of employment throws into bold relief the pre-conditions of employment protection legislation.

In the first place, only a minority of employment protections (eg the Sex Discrimination Act, the Race Relations Act, the Health and Safety at Work etc Act and Part II of the Employment Rights Act 1996 (the Wages Acts 1986)), apply comprehensively to employed and self-employed workers, part-time and full-time and temporary or permanent employment, regardless of length of service, ie: 'Any contract to personally execute any work or labour' (SDA, s 82(1); RRA, s 98(1)).

The majority, consisting of the overwhelming majority of statutory rights in the Employment Rights Act 1996, are far more restricted, applying only to those workers who are 'employees', ie individuals who work under (or who have worked under) a contract of employment (ERA, 230(11)).

Second, most of these statutory rights are further qualified by the requirement that employees must work a particular period of unbroken or 'continuous' service. Let us consider each requirement in turn.

8 Leighton P 'Marginal Workers' in Lewis (ed) *Labour Law in Britain* (1986) p 505.
9 Rajan 'Restructuring the workforce to meet the demographic challenge' NEDO 1990.
10 See eg Dickens pp 33-36.
11 Leighton *New Employment Relationships* (1991); Rajan '1992 A Zero Sum Game' Industrial Society (1990).

## Employment or self-employment?

In so far as legislation has been drafted to apply only to individuals who work under a contract of employment, self-employed workers are clearly excluded from the statutory protection. While self-employed status is sometimes openly preferred by individuals because of the tax advantages of Schedule D status, there are many individuals who have self-employment status imposed upon them or accept it without understanding its full implications.

Another category of work affected by this distinction is casual or intermittent work. Very often this type of work consists of a series of jobs for the same 'employer', or contractor, punctuated by periods of no work. Again some workers actually prefer this form of work. For example some 'temps' prefer the higher rates and freedom to decide when and where to work. However, to many casual workers the employer has simply imposed upon them the burden of coping with the uncertainty of non-regular employment.

A further category is that of home workers. They have the advantage, if they have children, of working at home. However, they have the disadvantage of low pay and non-existent fringe benefits. Moreover, they have little choice about the form of their working arrangements.

For these groups of workers the definition of statutory protections as applying solely to 'employees' raises the threshold of qualification for eligibility. Do they work under a contract of employment or a contract for services?

### *(a) The criteria for identifying a contract of employment*

Historically, the test to determine whether a contract was one of employment or services was whether or not the employer controlled or had the right to control the job that the employee did and the way that it was done. This traditional control test was soon outdated by changes in the nature of employment. The early industrial relationships presupposed a high degree of operating knowledge and skill on the part of the employer. With the development of the wider education and training of the workforce, such assumptions could no longer apply.[12]

A second test of whether the work was an 'integral part of the business' was introduced partly to meet this point, but this test was too imprecise about the facts necessary to establish whether a worker's work was integral to a business as opposed to merely an accessory to it to be widely accepted.[13]

12 Kahn Freund (1951) 14 MLR 505.

13 See eg *Stevenson Jordan and Harrison Ltd v MacDonald and Evans* [1952] 1 TLR 101 at 111, CA.

Latterly, the courts have moved to a multiple factor test, one which retains the test of control but combines it with a test of mutual obligation. In *Ready Mixed Concrete (South East) Ltd v Minister of Pensions and National Insurance*,[14] McKenna J suggested that the issue of whether there is a contract of service should be decided in these terms:

> 'A contract of service exists if these three conditions are fulfilled. (i) The servant agrees that, in consideration of a wage or other remuneration, he will provide his own work and skill in the performance of some service for his master. (ii) He agrees, expressly or implied, that in the performance of that service he will be subject to the other's control in a sufficient degree to make that other master. (iii) The other provisions of the contract are consistent with its being a contract of service.'

In *Market Investigations Ltd v Minister of Social Security*,[15] Cooke J suggested that in certain cases it would be equally valid to define what is a contract for services rather than a contract of employment by asking whether or not there was an entrepreneurial element in the relationship. He summarised the test in the following terms:

> 'Is the person who has engaged himself to perform these services performing them as a person in business on his own account? If the answer to that question is "yes", then the contract is a contract for services. If the answer is "no", then the contract is a contract of service. No exhaustive list has been compiled and perhaps no exhaustive list can be compiled of the considerations which are relevant in determining the question nor can strict rules be laid down as to the relative weight which the various considerations should carry in particular cases. The most that can be said is that control will no doubt always have to be considered, although it can no longer be regarded as the sole determining factor; and that factors which may be of importance are such matters as whether the man performing the services provides his own equipment, whether he hires his own helpers, what degree of financial risk he takes, what degree of responsibility for investment and management he has, and whether and how far he has an opportunity of profiting from sound management in the performance of his task. The application of the general test may be easier in a case where the person who engages himself to perform the services does so in the course of an already established business of his own; but this factor is not decisive . . .'

In *Lee Ting Sang v Chung Chi-Keung*[16] this latter approach was specifically endorsed by the Privy Council.

In other recent employment protection cases, however, the Court of Appeal has been concerned to ensure that the entrepreneurial test has not been applied in isolation and that there has also been an assessment of the issue of 'mutuality of obligation'. Thus in *Nethermere (St Neots) Ltd v*

14 [1968] 2 QB 497, [1968] 1 All ER 433.
15 [1969] 2 QB 173, [1968] 3 All ER 732.
16 [1990] ICR 409, [1990] IRLR 236, PC.

*Taverna and Gardiner*,[17] a majority of the Court of Appeal was willing to find that there was an irreducible minimum of obligation on each side, the employer to provide work and remuneration and the employee to do the work provided under the employer's control. In *O'Kelly v Trusthouse Forte plc*[18] the court noted that the industrial tribunal, whilst directing itself in terms of determining 'whether the person was carrying on business on his own account', was also careful to give due weight to the issue of whether or not there was 'mutuality of obligation'.

There appears to be little predictability in the test or tests which tribunals will use. The courts have rejected any one test as 'the fundamental test'. Hence tribunal chairpersons will tend to instruct the tribunals that consideration should be given to all the factors including the degree of control, the risk of loss and chance of profit, the provision of equipment, the methods of tax and national insurance payment, and the parties' intentions. As the court put it in *O'Kelly*, the industrial tribunal should 'consider all aspects of the relationship, no single feature being in itself decisive and each of which may vary in weight and direction.'[19]The test however is basically contractual, often applied without weight being given to its statutory context.

Consequently, as in *O'Kelly*, the requirement of mutuality of obligation can operate as an obstacle to less conventional forms of work qualifying as employment for the purposes of the statutory protections.

### *(b) The intention of the parties*

Despite the discrepancy in bargaining power between employer and employee, the way in which they draw up their agreement and express it may be a very important factor in determining what the true relation is between them. This can be seen in *Massey v Crown Life Insurance Co*,[20] a case where a branch office manager who had agreed to self-employed status for tax purposes was found not to be an employee for the purposes of an unfair dismissal claim. Lord Denning made the point that the manager, 'having made his bed as being self-employed he must lie on it'. He cannot 'come along afterwards and say it is something else in order to claim that he has been unfairly dismissed'. However, while the parties' intentions are an important factor, they are not conclusive.[1] In *Young and Woods Ltd v West*,[2] for example, the judiciary showed a greater willingness

17 [1984] ICR 612, [1984] IRLR 240, CA.
18 [1983] ICR 728, [1983] IRLR 369, CA.
19 [1983] ICR 728, [1983] IRLR 369, CA.
20 [1978] ICR 590 at 596.
1 See eg *Warner Holidays Ltd v Secretary of State for Social Services* [1983] ICR 440 at 454.
2 [1980] IRLR 201, CA.

to take into account the policy implications of the identification process. In that case too an employee chose to be paid as self-employed when he was 'hired' and offered a choice between employment or self-employment. No deductions were made from his pay for tax, he was responsible for his own National Insurance contributions and he did not receive any holiday pay or sickness benefit from the company. Moreover, the agreement was made with the knowledge of the Inland Revenue who treated him for tax purposes as self-employed. Nevertheless when the employee's services were terminated by the company and he complained of unfair dismissal, a tribunal held that he was an employee as defined by the statute and entitled to bring a claim of unfair dismissal.

Upon appeal to the Court of Appeal, employer's counsel argued that Mr West could not resile from the position he had established for himself. The Court of Appeal, however, upheld the industrial tribunal's decision. Lord Justice Ackner stated:

> 'It is by now well settled law that the label which the parties chose to use to describe their relationship cannot alter or decide their true relationship but in deciding what that relationship is, the expression by them of their true intention is relevant but not conclusive.'[3]

The Court was impressed by the point that a failure to allow the employee to resile from his earlier position would amount to allowing the employer and employee to contract out of the Act and this would make employees vulnerable to being pressed into self-employment 'by employers anxious to escape from their statutory liabilities'. Moreover the Court was prepared to accept the industrial tribunal's decision because it did not think that the employee could avoid the tax implications of his belated claim of employee status.

There has been evidence of a similar 'policy' approach in other cases. Thus, in *Ferguson v John Dawson & Partners (Contractors) Ltd*,[4] a worker claiming damages for injuries at work was told that his labour-only subcontracting or 'lump' arrangement with the employer would not stand in the way of a finding that the remainder of the contractual terms governing the realities of the relationship show the relationship of employer and employee. Megaw LJ underlined the point that:

> '... the parties cannot transfer a statute-imposed duty of care for safety of workmen from an employer to the workman himself merely because the parties agree, in effect that the workman shall be deemed to be self-employed, where the true essence of the contract is, otherwise, a contract of service.'[5]

3 [1980] IRLR 201 at 208.
4 [1976] 3 All ER 817, [1976] IRLR 346, CA.
5 Ibid.

Nevertheless, the contractual view of the statutory test set out in *Massey*'s case is not completely lacking support. As Lawton LJ argued in his dissenting judgment in *Ferguson*:

> 'Anyway public policy is an awkward horse for a judge to ride, particularly when it wants to go in more than one direction. Maybe the law should try to save workmen from their folly; but it should not encourage them to change a status which they have freely chosen when it suits them to do so. In my judgment it would be contrary to public policy to allow a man to say he was self-employed for the purpose of avoiding the incidence of taxation but a servant for the purpose of claiming compensation.'[6]

The public policy espoused by Lawton was the public policy of sanctity of contract, one which in his view appears to override the public policy declared in statute law. This view has found its way into a string of cases concerned with the effects of a finding that the parties deliberately and intentionally set about to defraud the Inland Revenue not so much in artificial arrangements of self-employment but in more clear-cut deceits such as false expenses. Such a contract is illegal though the effect of the illegality varies. In some cases involving false expenses, where the employee knows of the tax evasion it operates to deprive an employee entirely of employee status, since the employee is viewed as not working under a valid contract of service.[7] In other cases, eg a short-term lodging allowance, it operates only during the period of the fraud and has the effect of breaking continuity of service.[8]

However, as Mogridge has persuasively argued, the courts could take into account to a far greater extent the legislative context when they analyse the effects of the illegality.[9]

### *(c) Is the test one of law or fact?*

Adding to the unpredictability of the issue of employment versus self-employment has been its shift from a question of law to one of fact. At one point it was regarded as entirely a question of law, which would allow an appellate court to look at the facts as found, both written agreement and oral evidence, and decide for itself that the court of first instance took the wrong view of the true nature of the agreement.[10]

6 Ibid.
7 See eg *Tomlinson v Dick Evans U Drive* [1978] ICR 639, [1978] IRLR 77, EAT.
8 See eg *Hyland v J H Barker (North West) Ltd* [1985] ICR 861, [1985] IRLR 403. See now *Hewcastle Catering Ltd v Ahmed and Elkamah* [1992] ICR 626, [1991] IRLR 473, CA.
9 Mogridge, C 'Illegal employment contracts - loss of statutory protection' (1981) 10 ILJ 23; see also discussion in Smith and Wood *Industrial Law* (5th edn, 1996) pp 80-84.
10 Stephenson LJ in *Young and Woods Ltd v West* [1980] IRLR 201,CA.

Today, however, at least in the cases of unfair dismissal and other forms of statutory employment protections, the test is regarded as a question of fact for industrial tribunals to determine, subject to an appeal on the grounds that the tribunal misdirected itself or came to a perverse decision on the evidence.[11] This widening of the sphere of fact makes it less easy to correct the decision of the industrial tribunals should they decide to make a finding of fact without regard to the context of the statute for which the indemnification of the relationship is being made. For example, in *O'Kelly*'s case the industrial tribunal appeared to treat the issue of employment status in isolation from the fact that the workers in question were looking for protection of their rights of trade union membership and activity.

On the other hand, the widening of the issue of fact is not always inconsistent with a more considered view being given to the economic realities of the parties' positions and the purpose for which the test is applied. Indeed in *Nethermere*, a case which was decided at roughly the same time as *O'Kelly*, the industrial tribunals were prepared to decide that home workers were employees for the purpose of the unfair dismissal law despite the intermittent nature of the work that they did. The two workers having previously worked in the company's factory began working at home on the basis that they could indicate how much work they wanted each week as long as there was an amount sufficient to make it worthwhile for the driver to call on them to pick up their work. This was sufficient evidence for the tribunal to find an irreducible minimum obligation on each side - the employer to provide work and the employee to do the work provided under the employer's control. Unlike *O'Kelly*, the Court of Appeal in *Nethermere* was prepared to support the EAT's concern not to unduly limit the protective legislation in the case of workers who were in irregular or casual employment. As Stephenson LJ put it at 246:

> 'I cannot see why well grounded expectation of continuing home work should not be hardened or refined into enforceable contracts by regular giving and taking of work over periods of a year or more and why outworkers should thereby become employees under contracts of service like those closed workers in the factory.'[12]

Nevertheless, the overall effect of the rules governing the identification of a contract of employment is to leave us with a line between employment and self-employment which is not consistently drawn in relation to the purposes of the legislation and introduces an element of unpredictability into what should be a more settled field.

11 See now *Lee Ting Sang v Chung Chi-Keung* [1990] ICR 409, [1990] IRLR 236, PC.
12 [1984] IRLR at 369.

## CONTINUITY OF SERVICE

A second condition of many employment protections consists of the requirement of a minimum period of continuous service with an employer or an associated employer, typically, a qualifying period of at least two years. In other cases, for example the minimum period of notice of termination, the redundancy payment or the calculation of a basic award for unfair dismissal, the period of continuous service determines the extent of the statutory benefit or remedy.

These statutory rules allow for a number of breaks in service which do not necessarily cause a break in continuity for the purposes of calculating the period of continuous service. Thus, for example, where an employee has been absent owing to sickness or injury,[13] a temporary cessation of work, such as lay-off,[14] owing to pregnancy or confinement,[15] or by arrangement or custom,[16] the weeks away are counted towards, and there is deemed to be no break in, the period of continuous employment. Moreover, certain absences such as weeks in strike do not break continuity although they do not count towards the total period of service.[17]

Nevertheless, the requirements of continuous service tend to bear down heavily upon short-term and casual workers. Even where such individuals are able to meet the test of working under a contract of employment, the interruptions to their employment can operate to cause a break in their continuous service.

On occasion, it has been accepted that expected temporary breaks in the context of a long-term relationship do not break continuity. In *Ford v Warwickshire County Council*[18] the House of Lords was prepared to find that in the case of a longer service part-time lecturer in a further education college, the regular summer breaks did not constitute a break in service because of the length of service, the mutual expectation of work and the shortness of the break.

A series of temporary cessations of work in the context of a longer-term relationship can, however, be viewed as a succession of separate short-term or task contracts at different intervals. For example, in *O'Kelly*'s case the court rejected the argument that the contracts in question were anything other than separate contracts of short duration. In *Hellyer Bros Ltd v McLeod*,[19] trawlermen were held to work on a series of successive 'task contracts', one for each trip. In *Lewis v Surrey County Council*,[20] teachers

13 ERA, s 213(3)(a). *Pearson v Kent County Council* [1993] IRLR 165, CA.
14 ERA, s 213(3)(b).
15 ERA, s 213(3)(d).
16 ERA, s 213(3)(c).
17 ERA, s 216.
18 [1983] 2 AC 71, [1983] ICR 273.
19 [1987] 1 WLR 728, [1987] ICR 526, CA.
20 [1988] AC 323, [1987] 3 All ER 641, HL.

were held to be employed on different contracts at different sites. In such cases it was not possible to establish continuous service of any significant length despite the existence of a long-term relationship between worker and employer.

## PART-TIME EMPLOYEES

At one time, many employment protection provisions were qualified by the requirement that part-time employees must be working under a contract which normally involves 16 hours a week or more,[1] or where an employee was continuously employed for 5 years or more under a contract normally involving 8 hours employment per week.[2] The net effect of these pre-conditions to employment protection legislation was to withdraw from part-time employees the protection of statutory job rights in a situation where they were already discriminated against in terms of pay rates, overtime rates, sick pay entitlement and pensions.

Now these minimum hour requirements have been removed to comply with the decision of the House of Lords in *R v Secretary of State for Employment, ex p EOC*[3] that they were contrary to article 119 and the Equal Treatment Directive because they were indirectly discriminatory to female employees.[4]

## CONCLUSIONS

The changing trends in the labour market combined with the retention of 'employee' status and significant periods of continuous service, as pre-conditions to statutory employment protection ensure that, if insufficient is done, an ever increasing proportion of the workforce will be left without the cover of many legislative protections. This will reinforce existing trends towards a dual sector labour market consisting of a primary sector of employees protected by collective bargaining as well as legislation and a secondary sector consisting of individuals who receive the protection of neither.

The Conservative Government appeared to view this prospect more as an opportunity than as a cause for concern, since the trends themselves would have furthered their policy of 'deregulation'.

Moreover, within Community law, there is strong support for an alternative legislative strategy of attempting to ensure that protective

1 See eg *Green v Roberts* [1992] IRLR 499, EAT.
2 EPCA, s 146(5).
3 [1994] IRLR 176, HL.
4 See Employment Protection (P/t Employees) Regulations 1995, SI 1995 No 31.

legislation applies more generally despite the variation in the forms of employment.[5]

The EC approach includes certain efforts to regulate the employer's decision to resort to atypical forms of employment reflecting the regulatory experience in member states such as France, Germany and Italy.[6] For example in its proposals for directives on atypical workers, the Commission suggests an obligation for employers to give reasons for temporary work in temporary employment contracts and to inform worker representatives before resorting to part-time work.[7]

However, the main thrust of the current Action Programme, reflecting the concerns of the 1986 Action Programme, is to attempt to secure rights for atypical workers such as part-timers and short-term workers which are comparable to or proportionate with those of full-time workers. Thus the Commission has proposed three directives for protections for atypical workers. One directive, based on Article 100A, attempts to ensure treatment for part-time and temporary employees which is comparable to that of full-time, long-term employees in terms of rights to paid holidays, dismissal allowances and seniority allowances and occupational pensions. A second directive, based on Article 100, includes comparable provisions for access to training and benefits for such workers.[8] A third directive, based on Article 118A, which proposes equality of treatment for temporary workers and permanent workers in establishments or undertakings in respect of health and safety, has now been adopted.[9] The logic of the Action Programme is that atypical work relationships must be regulated not only to avoid unfairness but also to avoid 'social dumping' and 'distortions of competition' at the Community level.

At one stage, any extension of social legislation by the Community, apart from the limited realm of health and safety, was subject to the veto of the UK Conservative Government. However, that veto on legislation did not preclude the possibility that EC law might produce a change in UK law by a process of judicial interpretation. Thus in *Rinner-Kühn v FWW Spezial-Gebaüdereinigung GmbH & Co KG*[10] the ECJ held that a West German law permitting employers to exclude employees working

5 For example, the proposed Directive on Part-time Working (OJ C18, 22/1/1983) was designed to extend to *part-time workers* the rules which apply to full-time employees - to avoid discrimination and secure the observance of the principle of *proportionate* rights. Similarly, the Directive of Temporary Work and Fixed Term Employment Contracts (OJ C133, 21/5/1986) was designed to protect *temporary workers* by giving them rights comparable to those of permanent workers.

6 See a summary of relevant developments in Wedderburn 'The Social Charter in Britain' [1991] MLR 1 at 10-12.

7 Nielsen and Szysczak *The Social Dimension of the European Community* (1991).

8 OJ 1990 C224/4 and OJ 1990 C224/6.

9 See too Fitzpatrick (1995) ILJ 296.

10 171/88: [1989] IRLR 493, ECJ.

less than 10 hours per week (or 45 hours per month) from sick pay schemes was indirectly discriminating against women when such a measure affected a far greater number of women than men. Member states have a defence where they can demonstrate that such legislation was justified by objective factors unrelated to sex discrimination, in which case the criteria of *Bilka-Kaufhaus* will be applied.[11] In the event, the qualifying conditions in employment protection legislation for part-time employees may be further contested in litigation.[12]

Until inequalities in the legislative framework are rectified on a wider basis, the trends in the labour market ensure that a core of full-time and higher-paid workers will receive the benefits of legislation and collective bargaining while a large group of individuals, usually women, in less traditional forms of work will be given significantly less favourable treatment.

11 *Bilka-Kaufhaus GmbH v Weber von Hartz*: 170/84 [1987] ICR 110, [1986] IRLR 317, ECJ, see discussion in Ch 12.

12 See eg statement by Dillon J in *R v Secretary of State for Employment, ex p EOC* [1993] IRLR 10, CA, that a *Francovich* type action may be possible for part-time employees dismissed after two years of service and not qualified to bring claims of redundancy or unfair dismissal.

CHAPTER 8

# Maternity rights

At the heart of the gender inequalities on the UK labour market lies the social pattern whereby women have been allocated the major share of responsibility for the rearing of children. Historically, women would leave work on the birth of the first child and not resume work until the last child reached school age or school leaving age. When mothers re-entered the labour market after this break in continuity, it was often to a lower paid or lower status job than before the break, either because the new job was part time or required little training.

Starting in the late 1960s women began to opt to continue work up to and shortly after pregnancy because they began to define their lives as including uninterrupted participation in working life as well as family life.[1]

Starting with the Employment Protection Act 1975, legislation was enacted which attempted to give statutory protection for women with such an aim. This Act was amended in the 1980s and subjected to major reform in TURER 1993, which implemented the EC Directive on the Protection of Pregnant Women at Work.[1a]

Today there are three major statutory protections[2] in relation to maternity:

(i) protection against dismissal on grounds of pregnancy and childbirth (s 99);
(ii) maternity leave (s 71) and the right to return after maternity leave (s 79);
(iii) statutory maternity pay.

1 See, eg, Fredman *Women and the Law* (Clarendon Press, Oxford, 1997) Ch 5.
1a EEC 92/85.
2 In addition, there are two other provisions: a right to suspension on medical grounds (s 66); and a right to time off for ante-natal care (s 55).

## A PROTECTION AGAINST DISMISSAL ON GROUNDS OF PREGNANCY AND CHILDBIRTH

Under s 99 of the Employment Rights Act, all employees have a right from the start of employment not to be dismissed on grounds of pregnancy and childbirth. Section 99 provides that a dismissal is automatically unfair if the reason or principal reason for the dismissal is that she is pregnant or any reason connected with her pregnancy; she is dismissed during her maternity leave because of the childbirth or a reason connected to it; she is dismissed after her maternity leave because of taking that leave or because she extended her leave by certificated absence for four weeks or less; she is dismissed in circumstances when she is entitled to medical suspension for maternity; she is dismissed for redundancy during her maternity period and not offered an existing suitable vacancy; she is dismissed in connection with exercising her right of return to work. Thus, this statutory right overlaps with a claim for direct discrimination under the Sex Discrimination Act.[3]

## B MATERNITY LEAVE AND THE RIGHT TO RETURN TO WORK

### (1) Maternity leave

Under the Employment Rights Act, an employee has the right to 14 weeks' maternity leave irrespective of length of service.[4] The pregnant woman must notify the employer of her intended starting date and can choose the date as long as it is after the 11th week before the expected week of childbirth. Moreover, if she is absent from work for a day during the six weeks before the expected week of childbirth, she is deemed to have started the leave and, if she has not notified the employer by the date of childbirth, the leave is deemed to have started by that date and she must notify the employer as soon as reasonably practicable after the birth.[5]

To qualify for the right, the employee must notify the employer 21 days before the leave commences of the fact of her pregnancy, her expected week of childbirth and, if requested, supply a certificate from a doctor or

3 See Ch 13. Note that the Labour Government proposes to remove the maximum limits for compensation for unfair dismissal which should make the decision to choose between the two statutory rights less difficult.

4 Section 73 stipulates that the period can be extended if statute prohibits the employee from working after that period because of the birth.

5 See below.

midwife.[6] Any return before the end of the leave must be notified to the employer seven days in advance.[7]

## (2) The right to return to work

The Employment Rights Act also creates a right for a qualified employee to return to her 'job' with her original employer or his successor at any time during the period starting after her period of maternity leave and before the end of a period of 29 weeks beginning with the week in which the date of her confinement falls.[8] Under ERA, s 79(2) she is ostensibly entitled to 'return to the job' in which she was originally employed on terms not less favourable than would have been applicable to her had she not been absent. Moreover, under s 96 if she is entitled to return to work and has exercised her right to return to work in accordance with the Act then a failure by her employer to allow her to return to work will be treated as a dismissal with effect from the day she was due to return for the reason which she was not permitted to return.

Yet the detailed qualifications of this particular employment might make it less promising than it first appears.

### *(1) The pre-conditions*

In the first place the entitlement to return to work is subject to certain exclusions and pre-conditions.

The first pre-condition is that the individual must have continued to be employed by the employer (whether or not she is at work) until immediately before the beginning of the 11th week before the expected week of childbirth.[9] It is not necessary for the employee actually to be at work until the beginning of the 11th week as long as she continues to be contractually employed until that date. As Lord McDonald put it in *Satchwell Sunrie Ltd v Secretary of State for Employment*[10] she may be absent for reasons of

> 'sickness, whether connected with pregnancy or not, holidays, compassionate or special leave with or without pay and others. The existence

6 Section 75.
7 Section 76.
8 Section 79.
9 ERA, s 79(1)(b).
10 *Satchwell Sunnie Ltd v Secretary of State for Employment* [1979] IRLR 455, EAT; see too *Secretary of State for Employment v Doulton Sanitaryware Ltd* [1981] ICR 477, [1981] IRLR 365, EAT

of a contract of employment does not depend upon what the employee actually does. It depends upon what the parties agree that each should do'.

Yet whilst absence prior to the 11th week *as such* does not extinguish the right, there is a risk that where a woman notifies her employer that she will be absent prior to the 11th week before the expected week of confinement she may be regarded as having resigned and hence having extinguished here right.[11] An employee's general statement that she does not intend to return when she leaves because of the unexpected confinement will probably not be sufficiently specific to amount to a resignation.[12] But as the EAT has indicated, 'where a woman has resigned ... not in error, not ignorant of her rights but in full understanding ... it may be that resignations taking effect before the 11th week *before* the expected week of confinement are binding and irrevocable'.[13]

On the other hand where an employee is dismissed prior to the 11th week before the expected week of childbirth[14] because owing to her pregnancy she has become incapable of adequately doing her work, and is not re-engaged in suitable alternative work, then (in addition to having a right under ERA, s 99, she will also have a right to return to work subject to three conditions.[15]

The first pre-condition is that, at the beginning of the 11th week before the expected week of childbirth, the employee must be *continuously* employed for a period of not less than 2 years.[16] Continuous employment will include previous periods of maternity leave.[17]

The second pre-condition is that she must, along with her notice of pregnancy under s 71, inform her employer in writing at least 21 days before her maternity leave begins or if that is not practicable as soon as is reasonably practicable, that she intends to return to work with her employer.[18]

In *Nu-Swift International Ltd v Mallinson*[19] the EAT indicated that the phrase 'reasonably practicable' would be applied in accordance with the

11 See eg *J Williams & Co Ltd v Secretary of State for Employment* [1978] IRLR 235, IT.

12 See eg *Hughes v Gwynedd Area Health Authority* [1978] ICR 161, [1977] IRLR 436, EAT; see too *Secretary of State for Employment v Doulton Sanitaryware Ltd* [1981] ICR 477, EAT.

13 Ibid. Resignations *after* the 11th week do not have such an effect, see *Mitchell v Royal British Legion Club* [1981] ICR 18, [1980] IRLR 425, EAT.

14 Note that the date of the dismissal is defined by ERA, s 97 but s 97(2) does not apply.

15 ERA, s 79.

16 ERA, s 79(1)(b). See now *Fairness at Work* proposal

17 ERA, s 212.

18 ERA, s 80 and s 75(1).

19 [1979] ICR 157, [1978] IRLR 537, EAT.

interpretation given by the Court of Appeal to the same phrase in respect of late applications for unfair dismissal. Thus where an employee knows of her rights but fails to give notice because of uncertainty about her ultimate decision, she will be disentitled,[20] whereas ignorance would make it not reasonably practicable.[1]

The third condition is that if she receives a request in writing[2] from her employer, at any time after 21 days before the end of her maternity leave, the employee must give written confirmation of her intended return to work within 14 days of receiving the request or if that is not reasonably practicable, as soon as reasonably practicable.[3]

Finally, to avoid disentitlement the employee must exercise her right to return to work by giving written notice 21 days before the day she proposes to return to work indicating that she proposes to return on that day (the notified day of return).[4] Both the employer and the employee then have the right to postpone her return to work by up to four weeks.[5]

### *(2) The extent of the right to return to work*

Assuming that she has met these pre-conditions the employee has a right to return to work with her original employer or his successor in the 'job' in which she was previously employed and on terms and conditions 'not less favourable than' those which she would have enjoyed had she remained in employment during the period of absence.[6]

Strictly speaking, however, the right to return to work cannot be said to be a right to re-instatement in the original job. In the first place, the ERA defines the 'job' as 'the nature of the work which she is employed to do in accordance with her contract and the capacity and place in which she is so employed'.[7] Therefore, depending upon the contents of the employee's contract of employment and in particular any 'flexibility' clauses, her right to return could be satisfied by an offer of a number of alternative jobs of a similar contractual nature.[8]

Where the employer offers a job which is contractually different in kind, the offer of re-engagement will not meet that test. For example in *McFadden v Greater Glasgow Passenger Transport Executive*[9] an offer

20 Ibid.
1 This remark was obiter.
2 The request must also be accompanied by a written statement of the effect of ERA, s 80(2).
3 ERA, s 80(2).
4 ERA, s 82.
5 ERA, ss 82(2) and (3).
6 ERA, s 79.
7 ERA, s 235(1).
8 *Edgell v Lloyd's Register of Shipping* [1977] IRLR 463, IT.
9 [1977] IRLR 327, IT.

of a non-established post before taking maternity leave was held not to be an offer of the same job in accordance with s 96. The difference in status and the greater vulnerability to redundancy were enough to make the jobs different even if the pay, hours of work and holiday entitlement were the same. ERA, s 96 also provides, however, that where it is not reasonably practicable for the employer, or his successor to reinstate an employee in her old job for a reason other than redundancy, and she is offered suitable alternative employment by the employer or an associated employer which she either accepts or unreasonably refuses, then she shall not be regarded as dismissed. In both cases, the alternative employment offered must not only be suitable in relation to the employee and appropriate for her to do in the circumstances but also the terms must not be substantially less favourable than if she had returned to work in accordance with ERA, s 79.

Finally, whilst s 79(2)(a) states that the employee is entitled to return to work on terms and conditions 'not less favourable' than those which would have been applicable to her if she had not been absent, it also explicitly provides that as regards seniority, pension rights and other similar rights, the period or periods of employment prior to the employee's absence will be regarded as continuous with her employment following that absence.[10] In contrast, in respect of continuity of employment for statutory purposes, her period of maternity leave is counted in computing her period of continuous employment.[11]

## (3) The statutory rights and the contract of employment

The employee's statutory rights to maternity leave and to return to work may be combined with any rights of the employee under her contract of employment to form a composite right, allowing the employee to take advantage of whichever right is more favourable in any particular respect.[12] Certainly, if the contractual right is more favourable in any respect, it will apply to that extent. For example if the employee fails to meet the notification requirements of the statutory right, she may nevertheless exercise any contractual right to maternity leave or a right to return to work she may have.[13] Yet, there are limits to the construction of a composite right in the sense that once an accommodation has been reached

10 ERA, s 79(2)(b).
11 ERA, s 212(2) and s 79(2)(a).
12 Section 78.
13 See eg *Lucas v Norton of London Ltd* [1984] IRLR 86, EAT.

contractually, it may not be possible to use the statute to introduce a further variation to that contractual accommodation.[14]

Finally, there is an important difference in the status of the contract under the statutory right to maternity leave (s 71) and the statutory right to maternity absence prior to the exercise of the right to return to work (s 79). In the case of the former, s 71 states that apart from pay, the employee must be entitled to the benefit of the terms and conditions of employment which would have been applicable to her *if she had not been absent*. In contrast, under s 79, there is no specific provision and the courts have held that the issue of whether the contract continues during the maternity period of absence must be determined by reference to the contract. If there is an express or implied agreement that the contract continues, the employee may have a claim for unfair dismissal if the employer refuses to take the employee back, even if the employee has failed to qualify under the statutory right.[15] However, there is no presumption that the contract continues to exist during this period,[16] and, if no express or implied agreement can be proved, a failure by the employee to comply with the statutory notification requirements could result in no protection for the employee should the employer refuse to take the employee back.[17]

## C STATUTORY MATERNITY PAY

Along with the 14 weeks' minimum statutory maternity leave, legislation now provides for 18 weeks' statutory maternity pay. To qualify, the employee must be in employment for 26 weeks by the qualifying week, ie the 15th week before the expected week of childbirth. If qualified, the employee is entitled to six weeks' maternity pay at the higher level[18] and the remainder of the 18 week period at the lower level.[19]

The relatively low level of statutory maternity pay reflects, as Fredman rightly puts it, 'the low priority given to maternity and parenthood within the market order.'[20] In the *Gillespie* case,[1] the ECJ held that the special position of women during this period made it not comparable to men or women at work and therefore it was not unlawful for national legislatures

14 See eg *Bovey v Board of Governors of the Hospital for Sick Children* [1978] IRLR 241, EAT.
15 See eg *Hilton Hotels International v Kaissi* [1994] IRLR 79, EAT.
16 See eg *Crouch v Kidsons Impey* [1996] IRLR 79, EAT.
17 See eg *Lavery v Plessey Telecoms Ltd* [1983] IRLR 202, CA.
18 Ie nine-tenths of her week's pay.
19 Ie fixed by regulation from time to time; currently £54.55 per week.
20 *Fredman* p 199.
1 [1996] IRLR 214, ECJ.

to set SMP at less than full pay as long as it was not set at levels which would undermine the purpose of maternity leave.

The field of maternity leave and parenthood calls for fundamental reform; however the prospects are more marginal. The Parental Leave Directive will provde three months' leave for either parent available up to the child's eighth year. Moreover, the Labour Government's *Fairness at Work* proposes a reform of the notice requirements and an extension of maternity leave to 18 weeks to match maternity pay.

CHAPTER 9

# Unfair dismissals

## INTRODUCTION

Statutory protection against unfair dismissals legislation was first enacted in 1971, and has remained a prominent part of the array of legislative employment protections despite wide fluctuations in the overall legal framework for labour relations.

One reason for the retention of this employment protection has been the acceptance by both Labour and Conservative governments of the need for domestic British legislation to meet UK obligations under the ILO Convention 119 (1963) which provides that an employer should not dismiss an employee without valid reason and sufficient cause and without the dismissed employee having a right to have recourse to an independent tribunal to determine the issue and decide an appropriate remedy.

The key section of the UK statute, ERA, s 98, provides that an employee who considers that he has been dismissed unfairly can, if suitably qualified, complain about the dismissal to an industrial tribunal which will determine whether the employer acted 'reasonably' in the circumstances in taking the decision to dismiss. If the tribunal decides that the dismissal was unfair it may order reinstatement or re-engagement or award compensation.[1]

The enactment of this law was a conscious attempt to create a statutory protection which improved upon the position at common law in the 1960s.[2] At common law,[3] as we have seen, as long as employers gave proper contractual notice of termination, they could dismiss the employee for whatever reason they chose. There was no requirement placed upon the employer to give reasons for dismissal at the time of dismissal, much less to justify the dismissal. There was no obligation to give warnings, provide

1 ERA, ss 111-132.
2 See discussion in Ch 5.
3 See eg Freedland *The Contract of Employment* (1976) OUP.

a hearing or an appeal and no test of the reasonableness of dismissal as a response to the employee's misconduct. If the employer dismissed the employee wrongfully because of inadequate notice or a mistaken summary dismissal, the employee could bring a claim for wrongful dismissal, but the remedy was limited solely to damages for the loss of pay for the period of notice required under the contract.[4]

The introduction of the statute, however, had a second aim, and that was to improve managerial practice in disciplinary matters by convincing managers to develop and improve their approach to disciplinary and dismissal disputes in line with the more enlightened practice of management in the larger firms.

The legislators had discerned that managers had begun to change their approach to discipline, particularly in the larger firms, and thought that a statute would provide managers with a clear incentive to introduce and improve such procedures, partly as a means of convincing employees not to bring complaints to the statutory procedure and partly so as to be prepared to make a good case to a tribunal should a complaint be brought.[5]

In furtherance of this aim, they compiled a Code of Practice on disciplinary procedures to accompany the statute[6] and provided the incentive of exemption to employers and trade unions who established voluntary procedures which provided remedies on the whole as beneficial as those provided by the statute.[7]

The legislators had the further hope that a fairer and more systematic treatment of disciplinary issues by management, combined with the possibility of an appeal to a statutory tribunal to resolve dismissal disputes, might have an impact upon the incidence of industrial action over dismissals. The theory was that, by providing an acceptable alternative channel whereby contested decisions could be challenged without the need for industrial action, such action would become unnecessary.[8]

The statute has produced an enormous increase in the number of formal disciplinary procedures. Estimates range from 84% to 99% of the larger firms in industry now to have such procedures.[9]

These procedures also operate with a close eye upon the stream of judicial decisions. As Daniels and Milward[10] have written:

4 See Ch 6.

5 See eg Royal Commission on Trade Union and Employers' Associations 1968, para 533.

6 Now replaced by ACAS Code of Practice No 1 'Disciplinary practice and procedures in employment'.

7 ERA, s 110. See Anderman *Law of Unfair Dismissal* (2nd edn) 198, Appendix III.

8 RCTUEA, para 528.

9 L Dickens, M Jones, B Weekes and M Hart *Dismissed: A Study of Unfair Dismissal and the Industrial Tribunal System* (1985) Oxford p 224.

10 W W Daniels and Neil Milward *Workforce Industrial Relations in Britain* DE/PSI/SSRC Survey, London, p 126.

> 'the form and operation of voluntarily agreed norms and procedure have been effectively modified and guided by an awareness of the legal provisions and their operation.'

Moreover, Dickens et al, describe the way in which the unfair dismissals provisions have stimulated:

> 'the development, formulation and modification of procedure for handling discipline/dismissal issues, incorporating notions of due process and natural justice and encouraging the quasi-judicial managerial review of decisions.'[11]

In such a setting, the statutory test of fairness has operated not only to decide individual cases but also as an influence upon organisational rules and decisions.

However, while the legal rules regulating unfair dismissal have this wider impact, it is necessary to understand them as legal norms determined by a process of tribunal and court interpretation of statutory standards.[12] To examine how the main elements of the statutory test have been interpreted it is useful to look at the case law under four heads:

(1) Which individuals are qualified to bring a complaint of unfair dismissal?
(2) How has 'dismissal' been defined?
(3) What is the statutory test of unfairness?
(4) What are the remedies for unfair dismissal?

## (1) Which individuals are qualified to bring a complaint of unfair dismissal?

The unfair dismissals legislation falls short of providing a universal right to complain of unfair dismissal. To be qualified to bring such a claim an individual must be an employee with at least two years' continuous service at the effective date of termination.[13] Moreover, employees must not have reached the normal retiring age for their position (providing that it is the same for men and women) or, if there is no such normal retiring age for employees in their position, then they must not have reached the statutory

11 Dickens et al, n 8 at p 252.
12 See generally Collins *Justice in Dismissal* (OUP, 1992).
13 ERA, s 108. See *Roach v CSB (Moulds) Ltd* [1991] ICR 349, [1991] IRLR 200, EAT. This may be reduced to one year by the new Labour government or by the ECJ in its decision on the reference to it by the House of Lords in *R v Secretary of State for Employment, ex p Seymour Smith and Perez* [1997] IRLR 315, HL.

retiring age of sixty-five (s 64(1)(b)).[14] They must not normally be working outside Great Britain,[15] and, if working on a fixed term contract of at least one year's duration, have not agreed in writing to exclude any claim to a right of unfair dismissal.[16]

In addition, workers who do not meet the statute's technical definition of 'employee', that is, an individual who works under or who has worked under a contract of employment, are excluded from its protection.[17]

## (2) How has 'dismissal' been defined?

Before an industrial tribunal will examine the fairness or unfairness of a dismissal, it must be satisfied by the employee that he has been dismissed in accordance with ERA, s 95. According to s 95 an employee shall be treated for the purposes of the Act as dismissed by his employer only if any one of three events occur:

(i) the employer terminates the employee's contract, whether with or without notice (s 95(1)(a));
(ii) the employer fails to renew a fixed term contract under which the employee is employed (s 95(1)(b)); or
(iii) the employee terminates his contract in circumstances entitling him to terminate it without notice by reason of the employer's conduct (whether the employer does so with or without notice)(s 95(1)(c)).

To fit within s 95(1)(a) employees may show that their employer terminated the contract with or without notice, but they must show that the contract was in fact terminated by the employer. Thus, if the employer succeeds in showing that the contract was terminated by the resignation of the

14 ERA, s 109 was amended by Sex Discrimination Act 1986 in response to *Marshall v Southampton and South West Hampshire Area Health Authority (Teaching)*: 152/84 [1986] QB 401, [1986] IRLR 140, ECJ. Note that the statutory retiring age is not interchangeable with the pensionable age under occupational or state pension schemes. For a discussion of the relationship between the statutory and normal retiring ages see the following: *Waite v Government Communications Headquarters* [1983] ICR 653, [1983] IRLR 341, HL; *Brooks v British Telecommunications plc* [1991] ICR 286, [1991] IRLR 4, EAT; *Hughes v Department of Health and Social Security* [1985] AC 776, [1985] IRLR 263, HL. But see now *Barber v Thames Television plc* [1991] ICR 253, [1991] IRLR 236, EAT.

15 ERA, s 196(2).

16 ERA, s 197(1). Other excluded categories are set out in ERA, ss 199 and 200 (share fisherman and police), ERA, s 110 (statutorily approved collective Industrial Tribunals Act 1996 dismissals procedure), s 18 (agreement precluding a complaint).

17 ERA, s 230(1). See discussion in Ch 7.

employee,[18] the operation of the doctrine of frustration[19] or by mutual agreement,[20] or if the contract was not terminated at all but was simply consensually varied, the employee will not be treated as dismissed for the purpose of this provision.

Where the employee repudiates the contract and the employer asks the employee to leave, it is not open to the employer to argue that the employee had dismissed himself owing to the repudiation. Technically under s 95(1)(a) the employer has terminated the contract, ie has accepted the employee's repudiation.

Similarly, where the employee resigns this would not normally be a termination by the employer under s 95(1)(a).[1] It might, however, be a constructive dismissal under s 95(1)(c), if the employee resigns in circumstances entitling him to do so without notice by reason of the employer's conduct.[2]

Section 95(1)(c) extends the statutory definition of dismissal to resignations by the employee in response to repudiatory conduct by the employer. The section was introduced to prevent employers from forcing employees to resign as a method of avoiding claims for unfair dismissal or redundancy. As interpreted, however, it applies only to employees who can show that the employer's conduct that forced them to leave amounted to a contractual repudiation.

As Lawton LJ said in *Western Excavating*[3] the words 'entitled' to terminate the contract of employment 'without notice' in the statute are 'the language of contract; language which has a significant meaning in law in that it confers a right on an employee to be released from his contract and extinguishes the right of the employer to hold the employee to it'. And as Lord Denning put it:

> 'If the employer is guilty of conduct which is a significant breach going to the root of the contract of employment or which shows that the employer no longer intends to be bound by one or more of the essential terms of the contract then the employee is entitled to treat himself as discharged from

18 See eg *Martin v Glynwed Distribution Ltd* [1983] ICR 511, [1983] IRLR 198, CA; *Sothern v Franks Charlesly & Co* [1981] IRLR 278, CA.

19 See eg *F C Shepherd & Co Ltd v Jerrom* [1986] IRLR 358, CA. *Tarnesby v Kensington and Chelsea and Westminster Area Health Authority* [1981] ICR 615, [1981] IRLR 369, HL; *Norris v Southampton City Council* [1982] ICR 177, [1982] IRLR 141, EAT; *Williams v Watsons Luxury Coaches Ltd* [1990] ICR 536, [1990] IRLR 164, EAT.

20 See eg *Igbo v Johnson Matthey Chemicals Ltd* [1986] ICR 82, [1985] IRLR 189, EAT; *Midland Electric Manufacturing Co Ltd v Kanji* [1980] IRLR 185, EAT: *Hellyer Bros Ltd v Atkinson and Dickinson* [1992] IRLR 540, EAT.

1 See eg *Martin v Glynwed Distribution Ltd* [1983] ICR 511, [1983] IRLR 198, CA; *Kwik-Fit (GB) Ltd v Lineham* [1992] ICR 183, [1992] IRLR 156, EAT; *Staffordshire County Council v Donovan* [1981] IRLR 108, EAT.

2 See *Alcan Extrusions Ltd v Yates* [1996] IRLR 327, EAT.

3 *Western Excavating (EEC) Ltd v Sharp* [1978] IRLR 27 at 30, CA.

> any further performance of the contract. The employee is entitled in these circumstances to leave at the instant without giving any notice at all or, alternatively, he may give notice and say that he is leaving at the end of the notice. But the conduct must in either case be sufficiently serious to entitle him to leave at once.'[4]

The Court of Appeal has indicated quite forcibly that industrial tribunals are to decide whether or not the employer's conduct amounted to a repudiation as a question of fact rather than one of law.[5]

However, the fact to be found, ie repudiation, is more of an admixture of law and fact than would have been a reasonableness test. As Arnold J (as he then was) remarked in *Courtaulds Northern Textiles Ltd v Andrew*:[6]

> 'Now it is of course true, applying the Court of Appeal's test, that in order to decide that the conduct is sufficiently repudiatory to justify a conclusion of constructive dismissal one has to consider whether the conduct complained of constitutes either a fundamental breach of the contract or a breach of a fundamental term of the contract: two somewhat elusive conceptions which figure in our modern contract law.'

Consequently, industrial tribunals run a risk of reversal if they misdirect themselves in law upon the relevant principles of repudiation in two important respects: first, the difference between breach and repudiation; and, secondly, the difference between 'acceptance' of the repudiation and affirmation of the contract by the employee.[7]

Repudiatory conduct by an employer can consist first of all of a failure by the employer to meet a positive contractual obligation (express or implied) such as the duty to pay agreed remuneration[8] or to provide a safe system of work[9] or the duty to provide a proper grievance procedure, etc,[10] or that the employee would not be transferred to another location except on reasonable notice.[11] It can also consist of an insistence by the employer upon a fundamental change in the nature of the employee's contractual performance such as the kind of work he could be required to perform, or his hours or place of work.[12] This includes conduct by the employer which

4 Ibid at 29.

5 *Woods v W M Car Services (Peterborough) Ltd* [1982] ICR 693, [1982] IRLR 413, CA.

6 [1979] IRLR 84, EAT.

7 See eg *W E Cox Toner (International) Ltd v Crook* [1981] ICR 823, [1981] IRLR 443, EAT. See discussion of the 'elective' theory of contract termination in Ch 6.

8 *R F Hill Ltd v Mooney* [1981] IRLR 258, EAT.

9 *British Aircraft Corpn Ltd v Austin* [1978] IRLR 332, EAT. See too *Walker v Northumberland County Council* [1995] IRLR 35, HC.

10 See eg *W A Goold v Pearmak Ltd v McConnell* [1995] IRLR 516, EAT.

11 *Prestwick Circuits Ltd v McAndrew* [1990] IRLR 191, Ct of Sess.

12 *McNeill v Charles Crimm (Electrical Contractors) Ltd* [1984] IRLR 179, EAT; *Warnes v Trustees of Cheriton Oddfellows Social Club* [1993] IRLR 58, EAT.

amounts to a breach of a particular implied obligation such as the duty not to destroy the mutual confidence and trust of the employment relationship.[13] In principle any of these actions by the employer will entitle the employee to resign and claim constructive dismissal.

The duty not to destroy the mutual confidence and trust of the relationship has been extended to a particularly wide range of employer mistreatment of employees including false accusation of dishonesty and theft,[14] harsh language,[15] and harassment,[16] including sexual harassment.[17]

Moreover, the EAT has on one occasion held that it was possible for tribunals to imply a term that employers will not treat their employees arbitrarily, capriciously or inequitably in matters of remuneration where an increase was refused.[18]

Furthermore, the way employers exercise their express contractual authority has become a potential source of constructive dismissal.

In *BBC v Beckett*,[19] for example, the EAT found that even where an employer had an express term in the contract entitling him to downgrade the employee in cases of misconduct, the industrial tribunal was entitled to find that the punishment was grossly out of proportion to the offence and therefore a repudiation of the contract by the employer. It did not matter that the employer did not intend to repudiate, for as had been said by Lord Wilberforce in *Federal Commerce and Navigation Co Ltd v Molena Alpha Inc*:[20]

> 'If a party's conduct is such as to amount to a threatened repudiatory breach, his subjective desire to maintain the contract cannot prevent the other party from drawing the consequences of his actions.'

Moreover, in *Cawley v South Wales Electricity Board*,[1] an arbitrator in an internal disciplinary procedure found a dismissal too severe a penalty and ordered re-engagement on a lower grade at another location. Management's subsequent offer of a job at a salary three grades lower with £1,400 a year less than his previous salary was found to be a constructive dismissal.

Thus, while the EAT has regularly insisted that the contractual approach to s 95(1)(c) must prevail, the development of the implied term of mutual

13 *Woods v W M Car Services (Peterborough) Ltd* [1982] ICR 693, [1982] IRLR 413, CA.
14 *Robinson v Crompton Parkinson Ltd* [1978] ICR 401, [1978] IRLR 61, EAT.
15 *Palmanor Ltd v Cedron* [1978] ICR 1008, [1978] IRLR 303, EAT.
16 See *Garner v Grange Furnishing Ltd* [1977] IRLR 206, EAT.
17 *Bracebridge Engineering Ltd v Darby* [1990] IRLR 3, EAT.
18 See eg *F C Gardner Ltd v Beresford* [1978] IRLR 63, EAT.
19 [1983] IRLR 43, EAT.
20 [1979] AC 757 at 780, HL.
1 [1985] IRLR 89, EAT.

trust and confidence has tended to outflank the contractual test imposed by *Western Excavating*.[2]

These cases provide a corpus of precedent for the proposition that extremely unreasonable managerial conduct towards employees may amount to constructive dismissal. However, under the statutory procedure, this confirms only that there has been a dismissal; there is still the further step to be taken of testing the reasonableness of the employer's decision.

## (3) What is the statutory test of unfairness?

Once an employee succeeds in proving that he or she has been dismissed under the statute, the industrial tribunal must determine whether or not that dismissal was fair. The Employment Rights Act, s 98 asks the tribunal to test the fairness of a dismissal in two stages. First, the employer must show his reason for dismissal s 98(1) and that it fits into one of the reasons listed in s 98(2), that is: the capability or qualifications of the employee for performing work of the kind he was employed by the employer to do; the conduct of the employee; that the employee was redundant; that the employee could not continue to work in the position he held without contravention (either on his part or on that of his employer) of a statutory duty or restriction; or some other substantial reason of a kind such as to justify the dismissal of an employee holding the position which that employee held (s 98(1)(b)). Normally this stage requires employers only to provide sufficient evidence to prove what in fact their motive was and not to justify it. Nevertheless, a dismissal can be found to be unfair at the first stage if employers fail to show that their reason for dismissal was one which was presumptively valid under the statute.[3] Employees may be able to show that the employer's reason for dismissal was one which is automatically unfair under the statute if they can show that the reason related to trade union membership or activity or non-membership (s 152);[4] selection for redundancy in breach of an agreed procedure (s 105); pregnancy (s 99); assertion of a statutory right (s 104); health and safety (s 100); trustees of occupational pension schemes (s 102); employee representatives (s 103); and a 'rehabilitated person' under the rehabilitation of Persons Act.[5] There are also separate statutory protections for dismissals

2 See eg *United Bank Ltd v Akhtar* [1989] IRLR 507, EAT; cf *W A Goold (Pearmak) v McConnell* [1995] IRLR 516, EAT.

3 See eg *UCATT v Brain* [1981] IRLR 224, CA; *Polentarutti v Autokraft Ltd* [1991] ICR 757, [1991] IRLR 457, EAT; see further Anderman *Law of Unfair Dismissal* (2nd edn) Ch 4.

4 See Ch 15.

5 Rehabilitation of Offenders Act 1974, s 4(3).

based on sex or race discrimination[6] or disability discrimination[7] and dismissal caused by a transfer of an undertaking.[8]

If the employer succeeds in showing that his reason for dismissal was a potentially valid reason for dismissal in accordance with s 57(1), the next stage, s 57(3), requires industrial tribunals to determine whether the dismissal was fair or unfair, 'having regard to the reason shown by the employer'. The tribunal's decision must take into account 'whether in the circumstances (including the size and administrative resources of their undertaking) the employer acted reasonably or unreasonably in treating their reason as a sufficient reason for dismissing the employee'. This question must be determined in accordance with equity and the substantial merits of the case.

In determining as a question of fact whether or not the employer's decision to dismiss was reasonable or unreasonable in the meaning of the subsection, industrial tribunals enjoy considerable discretion. They are viewed as 'industrial juries' applying the accepted standards of industry operating at the relevant time and place.[9] Thus, even where the Employment Appeal Tribunal or a court of higher instance may disagree with an industrial tribunal's decision on the facts, they have no right to substitute their views for those of the tribunal. As Lord Donaldson put it in *Union of Construction Allied Trades and Technicians v Brain*:[10]

> 'whether someone acted reasonably is always a pure question of fact, so long as the tribunal deciding the issue correctly directs itself on matters which should and should not be taken into account. But where Parliament has directed a tribunal to have regard to equity, which means common fairness, the tribunal duty is very plain. It has to look at the question in the round and without regard to lawyer's technicalities. It has to look at it in an employment and industrial relations context. It should therefore be very rare for any decision of an industrial tribunal under this section to give rise to any question of law, and where Parliament has given to the tribunals so wide a discretion appellate courts should be very slow to find that the tribunal has erred in law.'

In a number of cases, moreover, the Court of Appeal has warned that care must be taken to avoid dressing up points of fact as points of law[11] and searching around with a fine toothcomb for some point of law.[12]

6 See discussion in Ch 13.

7 Disability Discrimination Act 1995, s 4.

8 Reg 8 of TUPE 1991 as amended; see discussion in Ch 10.

9 See eg *Grundy (Teddington) Ltd v Willis* [1976] ICR 323, [1976] IRLR 118, EAT.

10 [1981] ICR 542, [1981] IRLR 224, CA; *British Telecommunications plc v Sheridan* [1990] IRLR 27, EAT. See now *Piggott Bros & Co Ltd v Jackson* [1992] ICR 85, [1991] IRLR 309, CA.

11 See eg remarks of Lord Denning in *Hollister v National Farmers' Union* [1979] ICR 542 at 553.

12 See eg *Retarded Children's Aid Society Ltd v Day* [1978] ICR 437, [1978] IRLR 128 at 130, CA; *Kent County Council v Gilham* [1985] IRLR 18 at 22.

Yet the discretion of industrial tribunals under s 98(4), while extremely wide, is not unlimited. An appeal may still be allowed from an industrial tribunal decision on either of two grounds: misdirection or perversity.

The traditional definition of perversity as a basis of appeal where an industrial tribunal is engaged in making a finding of fact is that a tribunal can only be successfully overturned if the evidence for its decision is obviously so inadequate that 'no reasonable tribunal properly directing itself could, upon the facts before it, have come to the conclusion which it did'.[13]

As far as misdirection is concerned, it has also been made quite plain by the House of Lords, the Court of Appeal and the EAT, that industrial tribunals do not have complete carte blanche in interpreting s 98(4). For even the pure language of s 98(4) places certain limits upon the exercise of tribunal discretion. Thus, as has been clearly indicated by the House of Lords in *W Devis & Sons Ltd v Atkins*[14] the actual language of the section directs the tribunal to focus its attention upon the conduct of the employers, not on whether the employee in fact suffered any injustice.

This places three main legal constraints upon the way it must go about determining the reasonableness of the employer's decision to dismiss. First, in judging the reasonableness of an employer's action an industrial tribunal must normally take into account only those circumstances actually known to the employer at the time of dismissal or circumstances of which he could and should have known at the moment of dismissal.[15] As Viscount Dilhorne put it in *W Devis & Sons Ltd v Atkins*:[16]

> '"It" [s 98(4)] must refer to the reason shown by the employer and to the reason for which the employee was dismissed. Without doing very great violence to the language I cannot construe this paragraph as enabling the tribunal to have regard to matters of which the employer was unaware at the time of dismissal and which therefore cannot form part of his reason or reasons for dismissing an employee.'

Thus, clearly any event that occurs subsequent to the decision to dismiss, even though it may bear upon the correctness or incorrectness of the dismissal, will not normally be admissible in evidence either to support

13 The standard has sometimes been described as 'where there was no evidence upon which a reasonable tribunal could have reached its conclusion of fact' or where the evidence was 'wholly contradictory to that conclusion' or plainly wrong. See now *East Berkshire Health Authority v Matadeen* [1992] ICR 723, [1992] IRLR 336, EAT; *Piggott Bros & Co Ltd v Jackson* [1992] ICR 85, [1991] IRLR 309, CA. See also *Retarded Children's Aid Society Ltd v Day* [1978] ICR 437, [1978] IRLR 128, CA.

14 [1977] AC 931, [1977] ICR 662, HL.

15 *Earl v Slater and Wheeler (Airlyne) Ltd* [1973] 1 All ER 145, [1972] IRLR 115, NIRC; *St Anne's Board Mill Co Ltd v Brien* [1973] ICR 444, [1973] IRLR 309, NIRC; *Chrystie v Rolls-Royce (1971) Ltd* [1976] IRLR 336, EAT.

16 [1977] AC 931, [1977] ICR 662, HL.

or to deny the reasonableness of the employer's decision to dismiss. For example, in misconduct cases where an employee is dismissed for an alleged criminal offence, although the fact that the police had arrested and charged the employee before the dismissal may be both relevant and important,[17] any development that occurs *after* the dismissal, whether a conviction, an acquittal or even a refusal of the police to take action, would not be a relevant circumstance in the determination of the reasonableness of the employer's decision to dismiss.[18] Moreover, in cases of redundancy, if an employer dismisses employees and at a later date the business recovers and new men are taken on, these events subsequent to the dismissal are only 'indirectly relevant if relevant at all'.[19]

Further, any information that becomes available to the employer after the dismissal is normally not admissible on the question of the reasonableness of his decision to dismiss, even if the information consists of evidence of misconduct by the employee or injustice to an employee[20] which occurred prior to the dismissal. For example, where, as in *Devis*'s case, an employee is dismissed for a failure to comply with directions and is subsequently discovered to have been dishonest, the evidence of dishonesty may not normally be allowed on the question of the reasonableness of the employer's decision to dismiss. The test for the tribunal was the reasonableness of the employer's behaviour at and leading up to the time of dismissal.[1]

This constraint, however, does not operate to preclude evidence of which the employer ought to have known from being held against the employer even if he did not actually know of it. This point was first acknowledged by the NIRC in *St Anne's Board Mill Co Ltd v Brien*[2] when Sir Hugh Griffiths pointed out that the reasonableness of an employer's decision to dismiss was to be decided not only in the light of the circumstances known to the employer at the moment of dismissal, but also in the light of circumstances 'of which he ought reasonably to have known

17 *Carr v Alexander Russell Ltd* [1979] ICR 469n, [1976] IRLR 220, Ct of Sess.

18 See *West Midlands Co-operative Society Ltd v Tipton* [1986] IRLR 112, HL; *Bates Farms and Dairy v Scott* [1976] IRLR 214, EAT. At the same time, it would be relevant to the question of the employee's entitlement to compensation.

19 *O'Connell and Wood v Hiltop Steel Structures Ltd* (1976) EAT 27/76.

20 *W Devis & Sons Ltd v Atkins* [1977] AC 931, [1977] ICR 662, HL.

1 [1977] AC 931, [1977] IRLR 314, HL. *Devis*'s case was decided under TULRA. Several law lords expressed reservations about their willingness to extend it to that Act as amended by EPA because of the entitlement of the employee to a basic award. At common law, the opposite rule applies for cases of wrongful dismissal. See eg *Boston Deep Sea Fishing and Ice Co v Ansell* (1888) 39 Ch D 339, 59 LT 345, CA; *Cyril Leonard & Co v Simo Securities Trust Ltd* [1971] 3 All ER 1313, [1972] 1 WLR 80, CA.

2 [1973] ICR 444, [1973] IRLR 309, NIRC.

at the moment of dismissal'. It was later supported by the House of Lords in *W Devis & Sons Ltd v Atkins*,[3] in which Viscount Dilhorne stated:

> 'it cannot, in my opinion, be said that the employer acted reasonably in treating (the reason shown as sufficient) if he only did so in consequence of ignoring matters he ought reasonably to have known and which would have shown that the reason was insufficient.'

In *W Weddel & Co Ltd v Tepper*[4] however, the Court of Appeal per Stephenson LJ added the cautionary note that:

> 'Reading that passage as a whole I understand that last sentence to mean "what reasonably (the employers) ought to have known if it was a proper case to carry out a further investigation and if they had carried out that investigation".'

Furthermore, since the decision of the EAT in *National Heart and Chest Hospitals Board of Governors v Nambiar*[5] there may be an exception in a case where an employer provides an internal appeals procedure.

In *National Heart and Chest Hospitals Board of Governors v Nambiar*, the EAT held that in a case where the employer provided an internal appeal procedure with the employee suspended on full pay pending the results of an appeal, the employer could rely on the new information discovered in the course of the appeal particularly where it confirmed the decision to dismiss for the original reason. The decision that the time of dismissal was the date the dismissal was finally confirmed rather than the date it was originally decided appeared to turn on the issue that technically the contract of employment as a whole had continued during the course of the appeal.[6]

In contrast, in *Monie v Coral Racing Ltd*,[7] a case involving an internal appeal procedure, the Court of Appeal held that information that emerged after the decision to dismiss but before the decision was confirmed in the appeal was inadmissible to support a *different* reason for dismissal following the rule in *Devis*. Moreover, the particular appeal procedure in *Monie* made no provision for keeping the employee on until the final confirmation of the dismissal.

Apart from this, the constraint in *W Devis & Sons Ltd v Atkins* applies pervasively to tribunals applying s 98(4). It does not apply, however, to exclude evidence on the later question of the amount of compensation to which an employee is entitled.[8]

3 [1977] AC 931, [1977] ICR 662, HL.
4 [1980] ICR 286, [1980] IRLR 96, CA.
5 [1981] ICR 441, [1981] IRLR 196, EAT; see also *Turner v Newham London Borough* (1984) EAT 786/83; *Greenall Whitley plc v Carr* [1985] ICR 451, [1985] IRLR 289, EAT.
6 See too *West Midland Co-operative Society v Tipton* [1986] IRLR 112, HL.
7 [1981] ICR 109, [1980] IRLR 464, CA.
8 See discussion under 'Remedies for Unfair Dismissal' supra.

The second constraint upon tribunal discretion in applying s 98(4) is that it must not impose upon an employer its view of what is a more reasonable decision. It must restrict itself to looking at what the employer has decided and ask itself whether the employer has acted reasonably in the circumstances in taking his decision to dismiss. The duty of the industrial tribunal is to hear the evidence, putting itself in the position, as it were, of the employer. Having heard the evidence it must not fall into the error of asking itself the question, 'If we had been the employer would we have done it this way?' Instead, the industrial tribunal has to judge by the objective standard of whether the employer has acted as a reasonable employer in those circumstances would act in taking a decision to dismiss the employee. These propositions have been emphatically supported by the Court of Appeal. Thus as Lord Justice Donaldson put it in *Union of Construction Allied Trades and Technicians v Brain*:[9]

> '. . . this approach of tribunals, putting themselves in the position of the employer, informing themselves of what the employer knew at the moment, imagining themselves in that position and then asking the question, "Would a reasonable employer in those circumstances dismiss?" seems to be a very sensible approach - subject to one qualification alone, that they must not fall into the error of asking themselves the question, "Would we dismiss?", because you sometimes have a situation in which one reasonable employer would and one would not. In those circumstances, the employer is entitled to say to the tribunal, "Well, you should be satisfied that a reasonable employer would regard these circumstances as a sufficient reason for dismissing because the statute does not require the employer to satisfy the tribunal of the rather more difficult considerations that *all* reasonable employers would dismiss in those circumstances."'

As the EAT summed up this approach:

> 'The function of the tribunal as an industrial jury, is to determine whether in the particular circumstances of each case the decision to dismiss the employee fell within the band of reasonable responses which a reasonable employer might have adopted. If the dismissal falls within the band it is fair; if it falls outside it is unfair.'[10]

On the other hand, industrial tribunals are entitled to consider the alternative courses of action open to the employer given the employer's assessment of the employee's conduct. As Lord Donaldson MR suggested in *Piggott Bros & Co Ltd v Jackson*:

> 'In deciding whether the employer has acted reasonably or unreasonably in treating the employee's conduct, an industrial tribunal will have to

9 [1981] ICR 542, [1981] IRLR 224, CA.
10 *Iceland Frozen Foods Ltd v Jones* [1982] IRLR 439 at 442. See too *British Leyland v Swift* [1981] IRLR 91, CA.

> consider what alternative courses of action were open to the employer - should he, for example, not have dismissed at all or should he have taken further steps to persuade the employee to desist from such conduct and only have dismissed if that proved ineffective'.[11]

Nevertheless a range of reasonable employer responses test operates as a limit upon tribunal discretion in the main substantive elements of the test of reasonableness, viz:

(1) the test of the employer's factual basis for his conclusions;
(2) the sufficiency of the employer's reason for dismissal on the merits.[12]

### *(1) The factual basis of the employer's conclusions*

In the first place, an industrial tribunal must ascertain whether an employer acted reasonably in forming his view of the facts, for example in concluding that an employee in a misconduct case had committed an act of misconduct, or that an employee in a capability case was actually incompetent or too ill to warrant continued employment.

This does not require the employer to prove to the satisfaction of the tribunal that the employee was actually guilty of the alleged misconduct or was in fact incapable. Instead, it has been interpreted to require of the employer only that he acted reasonably in the sense of having reasonable grounds for his belief that an employee had actually committed an act of misconduct or was incapable as alleged. As the EAT put it in *British Home Stores Ltd v Burchell*,[13] in determining whether a dismissal is unfair, what an industrial tribunal has to decide is, broadly expressed, whether the employer who discharged the employee on the ground of the misconduct in question entertained a reasonable suspicion amounting to a belief in the guilt of the employee of that misconduct at that time.[14]

> 'That is really stating shortly and somewhat compendiously . . . more than one element. First of all, there must be established by the employer the fact of that belief; that the employer did believe it. Secondly, that the employer had in mind reasonable grounds upon which to sustain that belief.[15] And thirdly, we think, that the employer, at the stage which he formed that belief on those grounds, at any rate at the final stage at which he formed that belief on those grounds, had carried out as much investigation into the matter as was reasonable in all the circumstances of the case.'[16]

11 [1991] IRLR 309 at 310-311, CA.
12 See this point in connection with dismissals for some other substantial reasons and reorganisations: Ch 11.
13 [1980] ICR 303n, [1978] IRLR 379, EAT.
14 Cf *Distillers Co (Bottling Services) Ltd v Gardner* [1982] IRLR 47, EAT.
15 See *British Home Stores Ltd v Burchell* [1980] ICR 303n, [1978] IRLR 379, EAT; *Monie v Coral Racing Ltd* [1981] ICR 109, [1980] IRLR 464, CA.
16 [1980] ICR 303, [1978] IRLR 379, EAT.

Since *Burchell*'s case, s 98(4) has been amended to remove from the employer the formal burden of proving the reasonableness of the dismissal.[17] Industrial tribunals continue to be guided that they must not make their own determination of the fact whether or not employees had committed an act or acts for which they have been dismissed; they must limit themselves to determining whether the belief of the employer at the time the employer took the decision to dismiss was justified in the light of the evidence available and the extent of the investigation undertaken.[18] They do not themselves have to be convinced of the employee's guilt.[19]

The *Burchell* test consists partly of a test of the employer's subjective belief. However, it also includes a residual objective test, ie that the employer had reasonable grounds for that belief and had conducted a reasonable investigation. This test of the balance between the employer's investigation and his belief by itself is a significant feature of the statutory test of unfair dismissal.

For example, in *ILEA v Gravett*[20] a swimming instructor summarily dismissed on grounds of indecent exposure to and indecent assault upon a 13-year-old girl was found by an industrial tribunal to be unfairly dismissed because the employer, though clearly genuinely believing that the employee had committed the act, had failed to show either a reasonable ground for that belief or that a reasonable investigation had been made. There had been a series of interviews with witnesses but nothing conclusive had emerged. Moreover, the investigation had been unsystematic and disjointed. By the objective test of whether a reasonable employer could have reached the conclusion upon the available relevant evidence,[1] the employer had failed.

On the other hand, as long as the employer's efforts to investigate are reasonable in the sense of falling within the range of reasonable employer investigations the industrial tribunal cannot insist upon a more elaborate investigation which it would have preferred.[2] Moreover, as long as reasonable grounds for belief have been produced, then industrial tribunals are not in the position to question the employer's assessment of the evidence.

17 *Boys and Girls Welfare Society v McDonald* [1996] IRLR 129, EAT.

18 *W Weddel & Co Ltd v Tepper* [1980] ICR 286, [1980] IRLR 96, CA; *Monie v Coral Racing Ltd* [1981] ICR 109, [1980] IRLR 464, CA.

19 *British Gas plc v McCarrick* [1991] IRLR 305, CA.

20 [1988] IRLR 497, EAT; see also *Henderson v Granville Tours Ltd* [1982] IRLR 494, EAT; *Louies v Coventry Hood and Seating Co Ltd* [1990] ICR 54, [1990] IRLR 324, EAT.

1 See eg *Murray Mackinnon v Forno* [1983] IRLR 7, EAT; *Clarke v Trimoco Motor Group Ltd* [1993] ICR 237, [1993] IRLR 148, EAT.

2 See eg *Ulsterbus Ltd v Henderson* [1989] IRLR 251, NICA.

For example, in *Morgan v Electrolux Ltd*[3] a tribunal was found to have erred in law when it found an employee dismissed for overbooking her work assembling microwave ovens was unfairly dismissed because it thought that the employer's assessment of the evidence of another employee was unreasonable. The tribunal's error according to the Court of Appeal was that it substituted its own evaluation of the witness for that of the employee.

This logic has led on occasion to allowing employers, being entitled upon reasonable investigation and having reasonable grounds for suspicion, to dismiss several employees fairly where all were reasonably suspected but the evidence was such that no one person could be proved to be guilty of the misconduct in question.[4]

A similar constraint is placed upon tribunals determining the factual basis of dismissals for other reasons. For example in the case of the employer's assessment of the employee's work performance, all an employer must prove is that he 'honestly and reasonably held the belief that the employee was not competent' and that 'there were reasonable' grounds for that belief.[5] The reasonable ground test does not allow the industrial tribunal to determine whether the employee was in fact incompetent. In so far as tribunals are thus circumscribed in deciding the 'facts' of the case, the description of tribunals as 'industrial juries' may be somewhat misleading. Their test of reasonableness has been shifted by interpretation to a test of whether on the basis of a largely subjective assessment of the facts, the employer acted reasonably in taking the dismissal decision.

### *(2) The merits of the case*

Assuming that an employer has acted 'reasonably' in forming his conclusions of fact, to what extent may an industrial tribunal question the exercise of management discretion in taking the decision to dismiss? Section 98(4) states that the tribunal must determine whether the employer acted reasonably or unreasonably in treating his reason as sufficient for dismissal. This implies that a tribunal should be satisfied that in all the circumstances a management response as drastic as dismissal was a reasonable response.

3 [1991] ICR 369, [1991] IRLR 89, CA; see also *Linfood Cash and Carry Ltd v Thomson* [1989] ICR 518, [1989] IRLR 235, EAT.

4 *Parr v Whitbread & Co plc* [1990] ICR 427, [1990] IRLR 39, EAT; *Monie v Coral Racing Ltd* [1981] ICR 109, [1980] IRLR 464, CA; see also *Frames Snooker Centre v Boyce* [1992] IRLR 472, EAT.

5 *Alidair Ltd v Taylor* [1978] ICR 445, [1978] IRLR 82, CA; see further Anderman *The Law of Unfair Dismissal* (2nd edn) Ch 6 (ill health) pp 186-188.

Industrial tribunals may consider the alternative courses of action open to the employer.[6] However, they have also been reminded that in deciding the issue of reasonableness they must not ask themselves what they would have done had they been the management, rather they must look at what the employer has decided and ask whether the employer's decision in the circumstances was reasonable;[7] remembering that in these cases 'there is a band of reasonableness within which one employer might reasonably take one view; another quite reasonably take a different view. And as long as it was quite reasonable to dismiss him then the dismissal must be upheld as fair even though some other employers may not have dismissed him'.[8]

In so far as these points are established by the authorities as principles of law, an industrial tribunal which fails to apply them will be regarded as having erred in law and be susceptible to an appeal on that ground.[9]

In cases of dismissals for misconduct industrial tribunals applying the sufficiency test or the test of whether the employer acted as a 'reasonable employer' will ask two questions. First, looking solely at the conduct of the employee, was it reasonable to dismiss an employee for that conduct? The employee may have been dismissed for gross misconduct, for a single breach of discipline, or for misconduct constituting a series of acts and following a series of warnings, but in principle the first element of the test is the same. Would a reasonable employer have decided that the employee's conduct, taken on its own, was sufficiently serious to warrant the penalty of dismissal?

A good example is the application of the test where an employee is dismissed for gross misconduct. Normally an employee may be dismissed for a first offence if the act is an act of gross misconduct. Not only may employers dispense with a warning in such cases; they may also dismiss without notice. For the concept of gross misconduct in industry is rooted in the common law notion of repudiation and includes such conduct as theft, fighting, etc.

However, the statutory test (whether a reasonable employer would in the circumstances have dismissed the employee for that misconduct) does not simply ask if this act of misconduct was gross misconduct in the sense of being a repudiation. It goes beyond the contractual test and applies an overriding rule of reasonableness.

The industrial tribunals can find that the disciplinary rule itself is unreasonable, or that the employer's application of the disciplinary rule

6 *Piggott Bros & Co Ltd v Jackson* [1992] ICR 85, [1991] IRLR 309, CA.

7 *Union of Construction Allied Trades and Technicians v Brain* [1981] ICR 542, [1981] IRLR 224, CA.

8 *British Leyland (UK) Ltd v Swift* [1981] IRLR 91, CA.

9 See eg *Piggott Bros & Co Ltd v Jackson* [1992] ICR 85, [1991] IRLR 309, CA; *Iceland Frozen Foods Ltd v Jones* [1982] IRLR 439 at 442, EAT.

is unreasonable. For example, in *Ladbroke Racing Ltd v Arnott*,[10] three employees were dismissed for breach of a company rule which stated that employees were not permitted to place bets, or allow other staff to do so, and that breach of the rule would result in immediate dismissal. Yet the bets had been placed with the knowledge of the office manager; only minor infringements of the rule had involved no personal advantage to the employees. In these circumstances the Court of Session upheld the EAT's decision which stated that, notwithstanding the mandatory terms of the disciplinary rule, the employers had not acted reasonably within the meaning of the statute in dismissing the employees for breach of the rule.

As the Court of Session put it:

> 'While the appropriate rule in each case specifically stated that a breach of the rule would result in dismissal that cannot in itself necessarily meet the requirements of [s 98(4)] which calls for the employer satisfying the Tribunal that in the circumstances (having regard to equity and the substantial merits of the case) he acted reasonably in treating it as sufficient reason for dismissal. This seems to me to predicate that there may be different degrees of gravity in the admitted or proved offence, and, as each case has to be considered on its own facts, consideration has to be given inter alia to the degree of culpability involved.'[11]

In effect this was a test of the reasonableness of the application of the rule.

A variant on this theme is offered in *Jones v London Co-operative Society Ltd*[12] in which an employee was dismissed for incorrectly ringing up a purchase even though this was found to be an honest mistake. The employer had relied upon a disciplinary rule which was a term of the employee's contract of employment, and which stated that an incorrect till reading was a serious offence meriting summary dismissal 'unless the employee could be proved to be justified in such reading'. The tribunal found the dismissal unfair despite the evidence of the rule as a term of employment. The employee's act had been a truly honest mistake, and the rule was unreasonable in failing to make an exception for an honest mistake and not drawing a distinction between that and an intentional act 'or a persistent failure to maintain cash control standards'.[13]

The test of reasonableness will also apply to the employer's classification of particular offences within the accepted categories of gross misconduct. A tribunal can examine whether the employee's conduct was sufficiently serious in the circumstances to warrant inclusion within the

10 [1983] IRLR 154, Ct of Sess; *Trusthouse Forte (Catering) Ltd v Adonis* [1984] IRLR 382, EAT.

11 See also *Taylor v Parsons Peebles NEI Bruce Peebles Ltd* [1981] IRLR 119, EAT.

12 [1975] IRLR 110, IT.

13 As to the reasonableness of the rule, see *Schmidt v Austicks Bookshops Ltd* [1978] ICR 85, [1977] IRLR 360, EAT; *Silentnight v Pitfield and Pitfield* (1983) EAT 106/82.

category of gross misconduct, though this examination is subject to the range of reasonable employer responses limit.[14]

For example, in *Clarkson v Brown Muff & Co Ltd*[15] an employee was dismissed for dishonesty because she failed to report her absence from work. The employers had indicated in the employee's conditions of employment that instant dismissal would be the normal penalty for cases of gross misconduct and had specified certain offences as amounting to gross misconduct, viz dishonesty, arson, violence.

Moreover, even where the conduct of the employee taken by itself may have been sufficient to justify dismissal, a tribunal may nevertheless find a dismissal unfair because the employer gave inadequate consideration to one or more important extenuating factors.

The conduct or performance of the employee cannot be looked at in isolation. In taking a decision to dismiss, an employer may not take an unduly narrow view of the circumstances that should affect his decision. As the Court of Appeal suggested in *Vokes Ltd v Bear*[16] the net must be cast fairly wide:

> 'The circumstances embrace all relevant matters that should weigh with a good employer when deciding at a given moment in time whether he should dismiss an employee.'

Any important circumstance that mitigates the fault of the employee or otherwise calls into question the wisdom of dismissal should be taken into account in any reasonable decision to dismiss. For example, an employee's past record of good service, an explanation or excuse, provocation or inadvertence, a lowering of standards induced by the employment setting or the extent to which management by its own action or inaction was itself partly to blame for the employee's alleged deficiencies, are all important mitigating circumstances. A further factor may be the employer's consistency in the application of disciplinary rules.[17]

At the same time, however, the phrase 'in the circumstances' can be a two-edged sword. As s 98(4) makes explicit, the circumstances that must be taken into account include the size and administrative resources of the firm.[18] Particularly in cases of dismissals for reasons other than misconduct, such as ill health, redundancy, or some other substantial reason, an

14 See eg *United Distillers v Conlin* [1992] IRLR 503, EAT; *East Berkshire Health Authority v Matadeen* [1992] IRLR 336, EAT.

15 [1974] IRLR 66, IT. See also *Trusthouse Forte (Catering) Ltd v Adonis* [1984] IRLR 382, EAT.

16 [1974] ICR 1, [1973] IRLR 363, NIRC.

17 See eg *Procter v British Gypsum Ltd* [1992] IRLR 7, EAT; *United Distillers v Conlin* [1992] IRLR 503, EAT.

18 This had already been indicated in cases prior to the 1980 amendment. See eg *Royal Naval School v Hughes* [1979] IRLR 383, EAT.

employer may argue that these factors may be important to take into account. In the Court of Appeal's view the general rule in the test under s 98(4) is that the dismissal must be fair in the circumstances – fair to the employee and fair to the business.[19] By introducing a range of reasonable responses test, the courts have created a balance between these two interests which is tilted too far in the direction of the employer.

The judicial interpretation of the statutory test of reasonableness in s 98(4) on the issue of fact and merits offers a good case study in the power of the judiciary to shift the regulatory line by interpretation. Cases such as *British Home Stores Ltd v Burchell* and *Monie v Coral Racing Ltd* establish quite clearly that the courts were concerned to interpret the statute not to require the employer to meet the objective test of establishing on the balance of probabilities that the employee had in fact committed the act(s) or omission(s) complained of, but to establish a relatively subjective test, with only a minimum residual standard of objectivity. This, in effect, is to select from the range of possible interpretations that which is the most favourable from the employer's point of view. It suggests that the courts have been willing to sacrifice the 'protective' function of the statute because of their preoccupation that the statute should not place too great a limitation upon managerial authority.

The 'range of reasonableness test' suggested by the Court of Appeal in *British Leyland (UK) Ltd v Swift* is further evidence that the courts are determined to limit the extent to which tribunals may use unfair dismissals legislation to interfere with management discretion. In effect the judiciary has read into the Act a self-denying ordinance which attempts to ensure that rather than imposing upon employers an objective notion of fairness in the interpretation of the statutory standard, it is to be limited to reflecting the lowest common denominator of acceptable managerial practice.[20] The balance struck between the competing policies of protecting employees from arbitrary managerial decisions and avoiding an undue interference with managerial prerogative clearly favours the latter policy.

### *(3) The procedural test of fairness*

A third legal constraint in the application of s 98(4) by industrial tribunals to cases of alleged unfair dismissals is a test of procedural reasonableness.

In *Polkey v A E Dayton Services Ltd*[1] the House of Lords made it plain that the procedure adopted by the employer in the course of dismissing an employee falls to be considered in deciding whether a dismissal is unfair

19 See eg *Retarded Children's Aid Society Ltd v Day* [1978] ICR 437, [1976] IRLR 128, CA.
20 See remarks by Elias 'Fairness in Unfair Dismissal Trends and Tensions' (1981) ILJ 201.
1 [1988] ICR 142, [1987] IRLR 503, HL.

since, per Lord Mackay, the action of the employer in treating the reason as sufficient for dismissal of the employee will include at least part of the manner of the dismissal.[2] As Lord Bridge put it:

> 'An employer having prima facie grounds to dismiss will in the great majority of cases not act reasonably in treating the reason as a sufficient reason for dismissal unless and until he has taken the steps, conveniently classified in most of the authorities as procedural, which are necessary in the circumstances of the case to justify that course of action.'[3]

Thus in the case of incapacity the employer will normally not act reasonably unless he gives the employee fair warning and an opportunity to mend his ways and show that he can do the job. In the case of misconduct the employer will normally not act reasonably unless he investigates the complaint of misconduct fully and fairly and hears whatever the employee wishes to say in his defence or in explanation or mitigation.

The key to the procedural test is whether the procedure adopted is one which a reasonable employer would adopt in the circumstances not what is a just procedure from the point of view of the employee.

This is influenced by the guidelines laid down by the ACAS Code of Practice on Disciplinary Practice and Procedures. The Code states that employers should have formal disciplinary procedures which provide that before dismissal an employee is given adequate warnings in the case of misconduct short of gross misconduct, as well as a fair hearing and a right of appeal. The recommendations of the Code do not have the force of law, though they must be taken into account by tribunals when relevant. Consequently, while industrial tribunals have the discretion to decide that an important procedural omission by itself makes a dismissal unfair,[4] a procedural omission does not necessarily make a dismissal unfair under the statutory test of reasonableness.[5]

The criteria for deciding when an employer can omit an important procedural step and nevertheless be found to have fairly dismissed have been clearly defined by the *Polkey* decision. As Lord Bridge stated, the test is whether,

> '. . . the Tribunal is able to conclude that the employer himself at the time of the dismissal, acted reasonably in taking the view that, in the exceptional circumstances of the particular case, the procedural steps normally appropriate would have been futile, could not have altered the decision to dismiss and therefore could be dispensed with.'[6]

2 At 507, para 19.
3 At 508, para 28.
4 *W Devis & Sons Ltd v Atkins* [1977] ICR 662, [1977] IRLR 314, HL; *Williams v Compair Maxam Ltd* [1982] ICR 156, [1982] IRLR 83, EAT.
5 See *Bailey v BP Oil (Kent Refinery) Ltd* [1980] ICR 642, [1980] IRLR 287, CA; *Harris v Courage (Eastern) Ltd* [1982] ICR 530, [1982] IRLR 509, CA.
6 [1988] ICR 142, at 163B.

This gave the imprimatur to a long-standing category of cases, in which industrial tribunals were allowed to find a dismissal fair despite the employer's failure of procedure, because the particular procedural step, viewed from the point in time of dismissal, was clearly unnecessary or pointless. For example, where the employer already has strong evidence of misconduct[7] or the employee has already indicated his views in another context, the omission of a formal hearing has not been conclusively unfair conduct.[8] In such cases the procedural failure has been considered to be either superfluous or unimportant by comparison with the substantive merits of the case and the employer could not be said to have acted unreasonably in the circumstances, judged by what was known at the time of dismissal, by dismissing in spite of the procedural omission.

However, *Polkey* sounded the death knell for another line of cases which had been influenced by the doctrine in *British Labour Pump v Byrne*.[9] This doctrine provided that even where the case was not obvious at the time of dismissal it would be proper for tribunals to ask whether it would have made any difference to the outcome of the case if the procedural mistake had been corrected. Under this test, dismissals were held to be fair even where the employer had failed to meet his agreed procedural obligation to include an employee's trade union official at a hearing,[10] or to give an employee an opportunity to be heard in the case of serious misconduct,[11] or to give a warning,[12] because in these cases the industrial tribunals found that the procedural defect was not likely to have affected the outcome of the decision.

In *Polkey* the House of Lords made it plain that such an approach was inconsistent with the language of s 98(4) which requires the test to be whether, at the time of the dismissal, the employer acted reasonably in dismissing an employee after having omitted an important procedural step. To attempt to decide whether the correction of a procedural omission would have made a difference was, the Law Lords indicated, to apply a test conditioned upon the consequence of the failure; it was essentially a test of whether the employee suffered an injustice which was not the same as whether the employer acted reasonably.[13] On the other hand as Lord McKay put it, 'if the employer would reasonably have concluded in the light of the circumstances known to him at the time of dismissal that

7 [1987] IRLR 503 at 508.

8 Eg *James v Waltham Holy Cross UDC* [1973] ICR 398, [1973] IRLR 202, NIRC; *Retarded Children's Aid Society Ltd v Day* [1978] ICR 437, [1978] IRLR 128, CA.

9 [1979] ICR 347, [1979] IRLR 94, EAT.

10 *Bailey v BP Oil (Kent Refinery) Ltd* [1980] ICR 642, [1980] IRLR 287, CA.

11 *W & J Wass Ltd v Binns* [1982] ICR 486, [1982] IRLR 283, CA.

12 *Retarded Children's Aid Society Ltd v Day* [1978] ICR 437, [1978] IRLR 128, CA.

13 [1988] ICR 142 at p 161F.

consultation or warning would be utterly useless he may well act reasonably even if he did not observe the provisions of the code.'[14]

The effect of the *Polkey* decision is to place a far higher premium upon procedural propriety. The only excuse for a procedural omission is that the step would have been futile in any event judging from the time of the dismissal. An omitted warning will rarely pass this test because an employer can rarely be certain how an employee would respond to a warning. In *Tower Hamlets Health Authority v Anthony*[15] the Court of Appeal allowed an appeal against the EAT for overturning a tribunal decision that an employer was unfair in dismissing an employee while her appeal against a former warning was still pending and the employer's own procedure required a formal warning before dismissal.

Furthermore, the omission of a hearing, or the inadequate preparation for a hearing, will often raise the point that the employer could rarely be certain that he hadn't missed obtaining significant further evidence. In *Spink v Express Foods Group Ltd*[16] the EAT found a tribunal in error for holding a dismissal fair where the employer had failed to give a sufficiently clear indication of the charges before the hearing to the employee to allow him to know the case against him.

Finally, in *Stoker v Lancashire County Council*[17] the Court of Appeal held that an industrial tribunal had erred in law in finding that an employer had acted reasonably when dismissing in spite of a failure to provide the employee with the full external stages of the appeal procedure in its own disciplinary code. In this case the reasonableness test was viewed as insufficiently flexible to allow the employer to ignore the full requirements of the appeal stage of its own disciplinary procedure.

At the same time, the test of whether an employer had omitted an essential procedural step or committed an important procedural error can occasionally be influenced by the relativism of the application of the range of reasonable employer responses standard. For example, in *Slater v Leicestershire Health Authority*[18] the industrial tribunal were held to have erred in holding a dismissal unfair where the manager, who had carried out the preliminary investigation, also conducted the disciplinary hearing. It could not be held that this precluded the possibility of a fair inquiry.

14 [1988] ICR 142 at 153G.

15 [1989] ICR 656, [1989] IRLR 394, CA; see too *Louies v Coventry Hood and Seating Co Ltd* [1990] ICR 54, [1990] IRLR 324, EAT.

16 [1990] IRLR 320, EAT; see too *McLaren v National Coal Board* [1988] ICR 370, [1988] IRLR 215, CA (procedure unreasonably ignored in the context of the miners' strike).

17 [1992] IRLR 75, CA.

18 [1989] IRLR l6, CA, but see *Byrne v BOC Ltd* [1992] IRLR 505, EAT, where the close involvement of the same manager at both stages was the basis for the EAT to overturn a tribunal decision.

Moreover, as the Court of Appeal put it, while it was a general principle that a person holding an inquiry must be seen to be impartial, the rules of natural justice do not provide an independent ground upon which a decision to dismiss may be attacked. Furthermore in *Sartor v P&O European Ferries (Felixstowe) Ltd*[19] similar reasoning was applied to the involvement of managers in the appeal stage who had been active in a previous stage.

The effect of this reasoning is to treat procedure almost entirely in terms of its functional importance in influencing the mind of the employer. For where, at the time of the dismissal, the employer could reasonably conclude that the procedural step was unnecessary because it could not have changed the decision, then a dismissal could be held to be fair despite the procedural omission.[20] The test subordinates the requirement of equity in s 98(4) to the reasonable employer test. Even if the judges view 'equity' in the test of s 98(4) as meaning equity to the employee and equity to the business, where the substantive test is based on a range of reasonable responses framework, the procedural safeguards should be scrupulously applied. Nevertheless, in most cases, this test does not prevent a clear message being sent to employers that, whatever the reasoning behind it, procedural propriety is viewed as essential in the conduct of a reasonable employer in the course of dismissing an employee.

On the other hand, in cases where a dismissal is unfair largely for reasons of procedural failure, the conduct of the employee both before and after the dismissal can be taken into account in the test of compensation. One issue this raises is whether this second message sent to employers may not dilute the effects of the first.

### *(4) Remedies for unfair dismissal*

Once an industrial tribunal finds that an employee has been unfairly dismissed, it must choose between three remedies: reinstatement, re-engagement or compensation. The statute gives formal priority to reinstatement (ie a return to the same job as if not dismissed) (s 112) and re-engagement (ie a return to a comparable job with the same employer) (s 114). Industrial tribunals are required first to determine whether the employee wishes to obtain re-employment in either form and then whether it is practicable to order such a remedy (s 116(1)(a) and (b)).[1] When looking at the practicality of reinstatement, tribunals ought to consider the industrial relations consequences of making such an order,[2] the likelihood of friction

19 [1992] IRLR 271, CA, but see *Byrne v BOC Ltd* [1992] IRLR 505, EAT.

20 See eg *Ulsterbus Ltd v Henderson* [1989] IRLR 251, NI CA; *Mathewson v R B Wilson Dental Laboratory Ltd* [1988] IRLR 512, EAT.

1 *Port of London Authority v Payne* [1993] ICR 30, [1992] IRLR 447, EAT.

2 *McGrath v Rank Leisure Ltd* [1985] ICR 527, [1985] IRLR 323.

with supervisors or fellow employees,[3] as well as the size and scale of the organisation,[4] the capabilities of the individual and the availability of the job itself, though the absence of a vacancy cannot be decisive.[5] Moreover, where the tribunal finds that an employee has caused or contributed to some extent to the dismissal it must determine whether it could be 'just' to make such an order (s 116(1)(c)). A high contributory element by the employee, say 75%, could preclude an order for re-employment.[6]

However, even where re-employment is ordered under ss 114 or 116, the penalty for non-compliance with the order is purely financial. An employer who, without good cause, refuses to comply, will only be required to pay compensation to the employee in the form of an 'additional' award, amounting, in most cases, to 13 to 26 weeks' pay, on top of the compensatory and basic awards (s 117(3)).[7] In cases where the reinstatement order is combined with a loss of earnings payment award, that award can be enforced in a county court even if it exceeds the additional award.[8] In cases of dismissals on grounds of racial or sex discrimination, the scale of the additional award is raised from 26 to 52 weeks' pay. But before an industrial tribunal can make an additional award, it is open to an employer to show that it was not practicable for him to comply with the order.[9] In cases of dismissal for trade union membership and activity or non-membership there is in addition, a 'special' award of compensation and the possibility of a remedy of 'interim relief.' (Ch 14).

If an industrial tribunal finds that a dismissal is unfair and makes no order of reinstatement or re-engagement, it must make an award of compensation under two headings: a 'basic award' and 'a compensatory award' (s 118). The basic award is designed to provide compensation for the loss of accrued rights owing to past service and in particular to compensate for the decrease in the value of a redundancy payment should the employee ever be made redundant in the future (s 119). It is therefore calculated normally[10] before deductions as the equivalent of a redundancy payment (see Ch 9). The basic award can be reduced even to a nil award by four types of deductions: a proportionate reduction representing the

3 *Pirelli General Cable Works Ltd v Murray* [1979] IRLR 190, EAT.
4 *Coleman v Magnet Joinery* [1975] ICR 46, CA.
5 *Nothman v Barnet London Borough (No 2)* [1980] IRLR 65, CA.
6 See eg *Nairne v Highland and Islands Fire Brigade* [1989] IRLR 366, Ct of Sess.
7 *Mabirizi v National Hospital for Nervous Diseases* [1990] IRLR 133, EAT.
8 *Conoco (UK) Ltd v Neal* [1989] ICR 114, [1989] IRLR 51, EAT. See too *Mabirizi* (above); *O'Laoire v Jackel International Ltd (No 2)* [1991] ICR 718, [1991] IRLR 170, CA.
9 See *Timex Corpn v Thomson* [1981] IRLR 522, EAT; *Freemans plc v Flynn* [1984] ICR 874, [1984] IRLR 486; *Cold Drawn Tubes Ltd v Middleton* [1992] IRLR 160, EAT.
10 Section 120 provides a minimum award of £2,770 and s 121 provides a minimum award of two weeks' pay in special circumstances.

tribunal's judgment of the extent to which the employee contributed to his own dismissal; a reduction by the amount of any redundancy payment either awarded by a tribunal or made by the employer; a failure by the employee to mitigate his loss by accepting a reasonable offer of reinstatement; or a reduction for any conduct which was not taken into account in calculating the basic award because it was discovered after the dismissal but would make it just and equitable to reduce the basic award.[11]

The compensatory award in principle is designed to compensate an employee for all other financial loss to the employee caused by the employer's decision to dismiss the employee. In such cases tribunals are entitled to add a sum to account for a loss of earnings for the period for which consultations should have been given,[12] or which another procedural step would have required, but it cannot second guess the reasonableness of an employer's decision to close down a business.[13] Section 123(2) states that such loss should include any benefit which the dismissed employee might reasonably be expected to have had but for the dismissal and any expense incurred as a result of the dismissal. In practice this award includes mainly loss of earnings and other benefits before the hearing and for a period into the future owing to unemployment or obtaining a lower-paid job. It also includes loss of pension entitlement and expenses where relevant. Yet the compensation which an employee receives under this head can be reduced when 'just and equitable' in all the circumstances.[14] The *Polkey* decision makes it clear that the chance that the employee may well have been dismissed in any case despite the procedural fairness can be reflected in a reduction under s 123(1) as well as s 123(2)(b).[15] Furthermore, there is a maximum limit to the compensatory award, currently £11,300.[16] Moreover, for all employees there are a number of deductions from the sum which is determined to be the 'actual financial loss'. First employees have a duty to mitigate their loss by making reasonable efforts to find new

11 Section 122 See eg *Chelsea Football Club and Athletic Co Ltd v Heath* [1981] ICR 323, [1981] IRLR 73, EAT.

12 See eg *Mining Supplies (Longwall) Ltd v Baker* [1988] ICR 676, [1988] IRLR 417, EAT. A further element of compensation for inability to make a claim for two years is offered in *SH Muffett Ltd v Head* [1987] ICR 1, [1986] IRLR 488, EAT, usually amounting to £100.

13 See *James W Cook & Co (Wivenhoe) Ltd (in liquidation) v Tipper* [1990] ICR 716, [1990] IRLR 386, CA.

14 *Tele-Trading Ltd v Jenkins* [1990] IRLR 430, CA. See Collins (1991) ILJ 201.

15 See eg *Campbell v Dunoon and Cowal Housing Association* [1993] IRLR 497, CS; *Rao v Civil Aviation Authority* [1994] IRLR 240, CA; *O Dea v ISC Chemicals Ltd* [1995] IRLR 599, CA.

16 ERA, s 124. The Labour government has suggested in its white paper 'Fairness at Work' that this maximum could be removed.

employment.[17] Second, where an employee to some extent causes or contributes to the dismissal, the compensatory award may be proportionately reduced including in extreme cases a reduction to nil.[18] Finally, where an employer paid an employee an ex gratia award or a redundancy payment over and above the employee's entitlement to a basic award, these sums can be deducted from the compensatory award.[19] This is designed to encourage employers to be generous in making ex gratia payments.

The tribunals and the judges have tended to apply the remedies for unfair dismissal conservatively. Although the statutory provisions were amended specifically to make reinstatement the primary remedy, the tribunals have been reluctant to order this remedy in practice.[20] Reinstatement and re-engagement have been ordered in less than 5% of successful cases, and the proportion of re-employments secured at the conciliation stage has been about 8%.[1] In those cases where tribunal orders have been made, about one-half have been effective in the sense that the employees continued in employment for six months or more.[2]

While the rarity of re-employment is largely due to the reluctance of tribunals to make appropriate orders, it is also true that employees do not always take advantage of the option when it is offered to them.[3] One factor that undoubtedly influences the majority of non-unionised complainants of unfair dismissal is that they may be isolated and vulnerable where there is no organisation at workplace level that could help them face up to the day to day pressures of being back at work after a reinstatemnt or re-engagement order. At all events, the statistics puncture the myth that the statute offers a form of job security by providing an effective remedy of reinstatement. At most it provides a form of compensation for loss of employment, though at levels which are barely adequate. The median award of compensation tends to be little more than the equivalent of a few months' average wages. Moreover, some employers may be wary about

17 Section 123(4). See eg *Fyfe v Scientific Furnishings Ltd* [1989] ICR 648, [1989] IRLR 331, EAT. This does not require mitigation after repudiation and before dismissal *Prestwick Circuits v McAndrew* [1990] IRLR 191, Ct of Sess; *Savoia v Chiltern Herb Farms Ltd* [1981] IRLR 65, EAT.

18 Section 123(6). *Hollier v Plysu Ltd* [1983] IRLR 260, CA; *Polentarutti v Autokraft Ltd* [1991] ICR 757, [1991] IRLR 457, EAT.

19 Section 123(7). *McCarthy v British Insulated Callenders Cables plc* [1985] IRLR 94, EAT; *Rushton v Harcros Timber Building Supplies Ltd* [1993] ICR 230, [1993] IRLR 254, EAT.

20 *Dickens et al*, pp 111-113.

1 *Dickens et al*, p 158.

2 Williams and Lewis *The Aftermath of Reinstatement* (1981) Res Paper 23, Department of Employment, p 24.

3 *Dickens et al*, pp 114-119.

hiring an employee who has taken an unfair dismissal complaint to an industrial tribunal.

## EFFECTS OF THE LEGISLATION

One measure of the effectiveness of the unfair dismissal law is the 'success rate' of complainants. From 1976 to 1981 there was a decline in the rate of successful complaints of unfair dismissal as a proportion of all such complaints from 37.6% to 23.3%. This decline has been explained by the fact that employers screened out the more obvious unfair decisions and then made greater use of legal counsel at tribunal hearings.[4] Also, redundancy dismissal complaints, with their greater propensity for failure, have increased as a proportion of all unfair dismissal complaints.[5] However, one should not entirely exclude the impact of the judicial interpretation of the test of fairness on the success rate of complainants. With the reintroduction of a more stringent procedural test after *Polkey*, it is to be expected that the success rate will increase.

The impact of the legislation upon collective labour relations has been complex. The legislative aim to reform management procedures has clearly been realised at least in the larger firms.[6] The effects of this increase in formal procedures upon management have been partly to restrict the discretion of supervisors and lower-line management to dismiss and partly to give greater importance to the personnel function in companies.[7] This in turn has operated as a control over arbitrary decisions by first-line management and has resulted in the introduction of greater due process and natural justice in industry.[8]

Evans, Goodman and Hargreaves, moreover, have found that trade union reactions to the legislation were that where workplace organisation was weak 'the law has achieved what was beyond the unions' resources …'. Procedures had brought improvements and more predictability to management behaviour, greater notice of impending dismissals, greater opportunity for representation, and in some cases had removed the need to resort to industrial action.[9]

4 Williams, K 'Unfair Dismissal: Myths and Statistics' [1983] ILJ 160.
5 *Davies and Freedland*, (1984) p 507.
6 Daniel and Stilgoe *The Impact of Employment Protection Laws* (1978) PSI, p 49 found that 84% of the firms they studied had adopted formal procedures for discipline and dismissals. A Warwick University survey found that between 94-99% of firms with a hundred or more employees had adopted written disciplinary and dismissals procedures (Dickens et al, p 236).
7 *Daniel and Stilgoe*, p 41; *Dickens et al*, p 264.
8 *Dickens et al*, p 252.
9 'Unfair Dismissal Law and Changes in the Role of Trade Unions and Employer Associations' [1985] ILJ 91, 95.

Yet voluntary procedures do not solely operate as an employee protection. They also provide a basis for processing dismissals more effectively by management. They tend to centralise control in higher management and help to legitimise management decisions to the workforce.[10]

It has been argued, however, that the direct impact of the statutory procedure upon the trade union sector and collective action has been relatively insignificant: that whatever the intention of the unfair dismissals legislation to 'individualise' potential collective disputes, the law has not been put into effect in practice for organised workers.[11]

Evans, Goodman and Hargreaves[12] found that in workshops where there is strong workplace union organisation, eg printing and engineering, 'traditional bargaining' over disciplinary matters continued, emphasising custom and practice, reciprocal understandings with managers and including threats of industrial action.

It is true that those employees making the most of the tribunal procedures have tended to be non-unionised employees, with the highly unionised sectors being under-represented in the complaints of unfair dismissals to industrial tribunals. Most claims come from small firms and in industrial sectors with a below average union density. At one point only 16% of applicants were trade unionists.[13] It is also true that there is little hard evidence that the legislation has reduced the incidence of industrial conflict over disciplinary dismissals. Strikes over non-redundancy dismissals which on average constituted about 10% of stoppages in the 1964-1966 period still accounted for about 9% of stoppages in 1982.[14] This in turn may be related to the low rate of success of complainants and the paucity of reinstatement orders. As the statute has been interpreted, it fails to offer employees, collectively dissatisfied with a managerial decision, a credible alternative.[15]

Nevertheless, it would be a mistake to conclude from this evidence that the overall impact of dismissals legislation upon collective labour relations has been minimal. For the procedural reforms concerning discipline and dismissal introduced by management in response to the legislation have occurred in the unionised as well as in the non-unionised sectors. These reforms, while providing formal trade union representation in disputes

10 *Dickens et al*, p 266.

11 See eg Clark and Wedderburn 'Modern Labour Law' in *Labour Law and Industrial Relations* (1983) p 189.

12 'Unfair Dismissals Law and Changes in the Role of Trade Unions and Employer Associations' [1985] ILJ 91, 97.

13 Hepple, B 'Individual Labour Law' in Bain (ed) *Industrial Relations in Britain* (1983) p 395; Davies and Freedland *Labour Law Cases and Materials* (2nd edn, 1984) p 510.

14 *Dickens*, pp 224-227.

15 Anderman *The Law of Unfair Dismissal* (2nd edn) pp 326-327.

procedures, have made a significant contribution to managerial control over discipline and dismissal in the organised sectors.[16]

Evans, Goodman and Hargreaves indicate the wide-ranging effects of formal disciplinary procedures upon discipline handling; that shop stewards in some cases were getting involved in formal legalistic investigations with management to the detriment of their bargaining role; management's insistence upon conformity with the disciplinary procedure; the isolation of disciplinary matters in the adjudication of the disciplinary procedure and a move away from the disputes procedure with its potential for negotiation with higher management; finally, the fact that full time officials coming in late have been met by a claim in which the shop steward arguments had been well rehearsed and managements had themselves weeded out the cases of procedural impropriety. Moreover, they argue that these factors help to explain the low rate of resort of trade unionists to industrial tribunals.

It may be difficult to evaluate which of the two effects of the disciplinary procedural reforms have been more pronounced: the greater control given to management over discipline or the greater protection to workers from the removal of the arbitrary control of their immediate supervisor. What is indisputable, however, is that this so-called individual employment protection has had a profound impact on 'collective' procedures and managerial practice.

The procedural reforms in industry have now taken on a life of their own being sustained as managerial reforms. They cannot, however, be viewed entirely as self-sustaining. Before *Polkey*, there was a risk that the legal standard had become so low that it no longer underpinned the voluntary procedures. Employers, particularly in the smaller and medium-sized firms, had less of an incentive to introduce a formal procedure.

One of the ironies of the judicial resistance to strong measures of social protection is that such legal rights in fact have a dual effect: they provide a stimulus to managerial efficiency along with the burdens they create. In any case, this area of labour law offers good examples of how the judiciary through interpretation effectively substitute their views of appropriate balance for those of the legislators.

16 *Dickens*, pp 250-252.

CHAPTER 10

# Redundancy decisions and the law

## INTRODUCTION

Redundancy decisions, whether full plant closures or more limited workforce reductions, are essentially the consequences of prior managerial investment decisions. They can be caused by a fall in demand in the product market. They can also be prompted by a change in corporate strategy in which an overall reorganisation of existing production patterns results in a decision to close down a particular manufacturing unit. They can also result from a takeover when a change in ownership puts a new managerial team in place to reorganise and rationalise. They are, in other words, decisions which are the result of a view taken by managers about how to manage invested capital.

The criteria used by managers to make such investment decisions are not free of a certain degree of subjectivity. While, of course, in extreme cases, eg insolvency, redundancies are compelled by the facts, it is far more often the case that such decisions are determined by the preferences of decision-makers at boardroom level.

In the first place, expected rates of return for investment prospects can vary considerably from firm to firm. Moreover, even if a particular profit centre falls below an expected rate of return, there is always the possibility of cross-subsidies within a group. The question of how much and how long a cross-subsidy will be forthcoming depends upon subjective views at boardroom level. Further, within groups of companies it is common to levy a share of group headquarters costs upon subsidiary profit centres - an item that affects rates of return. Indeed management buy-outs are sometimes attractive investments for city finance, even where subsidiaries have been unprofitable, partly because the 'bought-out' firm will be free of its group carrying charge. And the scale of the charge levied upon subsidiaries varies from group to group.

Finally, along with these quantitative questions there are qualitative questions of corporate strategy. There are times when groups, particularly multinationals, can decide to close down firms or establishments which may themselves be profitable, simply because they no longer fit within a particular corporate strategy. Sometimes these units can be sold as going concerns. However, companies can decide to prevent the plant and trained workforce from being acquired by competitors and offer to sell the plant only on the condition that it will not be used for its original purpose.

These types of investment decisions have important social consequences. The loss of jobs often leads to periods of unemployment. Workers must often retrain or relocate to find new employment. Older workers have difficulties obtaining employment. The lives of individuals, families and sometimes communities are disrupted. Yet these social costs are rarely taken into account in investment decisions because they do not affect the individual firm in balance sheet terms. In the private sector, the main calculation is the comparison of the total costs of the redundancy payments package, as a once and for all payment, with the reduction in the annual flow of labour costs, over a period of years, which would have been incurred if the same employees had been retained. There is little room for social costs to be factored into this equation. It is only in the public sector redundancies such as those formerly in British Steel or British Coal that a large share of the social costs of closure may be taken into account in decisions because of the ultimate responsibility of the Exchequer for public expenditure such as unemployment pay and Social Security etc. For the firm in the private sector however, the human costs of redundancy are, as the economists put it 'externalities', tending to take second place to considerations of financial return.

Because of their social costs, however, redundancy decisions have become increasingly subject to legal regulation. The resultant legislation has not sought single mindedly to create workers' rights to income or employment protection, but instead has struck a careful balance between employment protection and the interests of employers in implementing the investment decisions they have taken. To understand the nature of the balance which has been struck it is useful to examine the legislation in respect of two fundamental issues. First, to what extent does the legislation question the basis of managerial decisions on redundancies? Second, to what extent are employers taking redundancy decisions forced to contribute to the social costs which are incurred as a consequence of managerial decisions?

## QUESTIONING MANAGERIAL DECISIONS

Even if the legislation avoids questioning the underlying investment decision, there is scope for questioning the way management has taken steps to implement those decisions. Have managers got their calculations right? Have all possible steps been taken to avoid or minimise redundancies? For example, it is often the case that managers have agreed in advance in redundancy procedure agreements with trade unions in cases of proposed redundancies to restrict recruitment, retrain and redeploy workers in disappearing jobs, reduce overtime, explore early retirement, reduce or terminate contracting out work and the use of temporary staff. Has the selection of employees been fair and appropriate? A starting point for legislation as well as collective bargaining could be to ensure that all such steps have been taken.

All these steps presuppose acceptance of the underlying thrust of investment decisions. The issue is whether management has planned the implementation of its decision sufficiently carefully so as to create the maximum employment security consistent with the manpower flexibility 'which was required'.[1]

The current legislation relating to redundancy decisions can be analysed under three main heads:

(1) the statutory redundancy payment and related employment protections;
(2) the collective consultation provisions of TULR(C)A 1992 (see Ch 16); and
(3) the unfair redundancy provisions of the unfair dismissals law.

The first category of legislation consists of the statutory redundancy payment together with related legislation. In form, this category deals exclusively with the consequences or effects of managerial redundancy decisions. Thus the Employment Rights Act (ERA) makes provisions for: a lump sum redundancy payment (ss 135-165); a right to a minimum period of notice of dismissal or pay in lieu (s 86); a right to reasonable time off from work with pay during the notice period to look for another job or make arrangements for training for future employment (s 52); a right to a guaranteed weekly payment in case of lay-off or short time (s 28); protection for employees in cases where the employer has become insolvent (s 182). Moreover, in cases of transfers of undertakings, protection is provided for employees by the Transfers of Undertakings (Protection of Employment) Regulations 1981.[2]

In form, the second and third heads appear to provide a legal platform to question the substance of managerial decisions. Thus TULR(C)A 1992 requires employers to inform appropriate employee representatives, about, inter alia the reasons for the redundancy and to consult with them in advance of redundancies. The unfair dismissals provisions relating to redundancies appear to provide a basis for complaint by employees against

1 ACAS Annual Report 1986, p 24.
2 See Ch 11.

the reasonableness of the employer's selection for redundancy as well as the employer's timing of the redundancy decision and the procedure adopted by the employer in implementing the employer's decision.

Yet legislative appearances can be deceptive. In practice legal measures providing a basis to challenge managerial decisions have had more of an effect on levels of compensation than redundancy decisions. And the statutory redundancy payment has not solely had the effect of helping to provide compensation to employees; it has also helped reduce the capacity of trade unions and workforces collectively to resist and modify managerial redundancy decisions.

## A THE STATUTORY REDUNDANCY PAYMENT[3]

The redundancy payments legislation was enacted in 1965, prompted by a concern that employees who suffered unemployment as a result of redundancy should be protected from the effects of management decisions by a form of compensation for the loss. Yet the legislation was also impelled by a concern to improve managerial efficiency, by helping managers to convince employees to accept redundancy as a necessary concomitant of industrial change. Trade union policies of resisting redundancies at the time stood in the way of managerial attempts to introduce greater efficiencies in the use of manpower. At a time of high employment, legislators thought that they were providing a basis for a more efficient utilisation of labour and its movement to expanding sectors. For that reason, a lump sum payment rather than an enhanced unemployment benefit was chosen as the payment to be made to employees management decided to make redundant. The lump sum is payable whether or not such employees are able to obtain employment with another employer immediately after losing their existing job through redundancy.[4]

The redundancy payment is calculated on the basis of the employee's age, length of continuous service (up to a maximum of 20 years) and weekly pay (currently up to a maximum of £210) and payable to qualified employees with a minimum of two years' service over the age of 18 who were 'redundant' owing to dismissal[5] or lay-off or on short time.[6] Thus employees who are made redundant between the ages of eighteen and twenty-one are entitled to half a week's pay for each year of service;

3 For two specialist works on the subject see Grunfeld *The Law of Redundancy* (3rd edn, 1990); Bourn *Redundancy Law and Practice* (1983).

4 Fryer *Redundancy and Public Policy*; Martin and Fryer *Redundancy and Paternalist Capitalism* (1973) pp 216-260; Fryer 'The Myths of the Redundancy Payment Act' [1973] ILJ.

5 ERA, ss 135-136.

6 ERA, ss 135 and 147.

employees between ages 21 and 41 a week's pay for each year of service; and between ages 41 and 64 one-and-a-half week's pay for each year of service. Upon reaching the age of 65 employees are excluded from a right to redundancy payment and they lose one-twelfth of their entitlement for every month they have worked after their sixty-fourth birthday.[7]

The lump sum redundancy payment has both a legal and an industrial relations dimension. At the legal level, in order for an employee to claim a redundancy payment, that individual must show that he or she has been dismissed (or laid off or put on short time) by the employer by reason of redundancy as defined by the statute.

## Dismissal

'Dismissal', the most common mode of redundancy, is defined in ERA, s 136 the same way as the claim for unfair dismissal, that is to say where the employer terminates the employee's contract with or without proper notice, or fails to renew a fixed-term contract on the same terms or constructively dismisses the employee by repudiating the contract of employment.[8]

In the redundancy context, the important legal issues raised by the dismissal requirement occur in situations where the employee leaves in response to an announcement of redundancy by the employer. Technically, to qualify for dismissal the employee must wait until being served with a formal notice of termination of contract. Where employees decide to leave in response to an announcement of redundancy and do not wait until being served formal notice of termination of contract, they may lose their claim to a redundancy payment, because the employer's announcement will be viewed as a warning of future redundancy rather than as a repudiation of the contract.[9]

If employees wish to leave before their notice period expires they must wait until their 'obligatory' period of notice commences, ie the period to which they are entitled under the statute by virtue of the period of continuous service. For a counter notice given before the statutory notice period commences will be invalid and the employee's departure at that stage will be viewed as a resignation, not a dismissal. This is a potential trap for the unwary employee. If the employer agrees, the two can arrange a consensual variation of the notice period to avoid the effects of s 85.

7 See ERA, s 162.
8 See Ch 9. Other modes of redundancy include layoffs or short time (ERA, ss 147-8).
9 *Haseltine Lake & Co v Dowler* [1981] ICR 222, [1981] IRLR 25, EAT. It would seem that unlike other cases of constructive dismissal the formalities of redundancy preclude the argument of anticipatory repudiation.

## Redundancy

A dismissal is taken to be by reason of 'redundancy' under ERA, s 139(1) only if it is attributable wholly or mainly to:

(a) the fact that the employer has ceased, or intends to cease to carry on the business for the purposes of which the employee was employed by him, or has ceased, or intends to cease, to carry on that business in the place where the employee was so employed; or
(b) the fact that the requirements of that business for employees to carry out work of a particular kind in the place where they were so employed, have ceased or diminished or are expected to cease or diminish.

In other words, redundancy as defined in the Act can consist of one or more of three basic managerial decisions: (i) the closure of an entire business or part of a business; (ii) a decision that an employee, or group of employees, is surplus to requirements of his business at a particular place of work; and (iii) a decision to move a business or part of a business to a new location.

## Offers of suitable alternative employment

In most large-scale redundancies including closures there is generally little difficulty in meeting the technical test of redundancy in s 139(1). The one residual issue, however, may be whether a redundancy payment is not payable under ERA, s 139(2) because 'suitable alternative employment' has been offered to employees by their employer or an associate employer or by a new transferee employer and they have unreasonably refused to accept such an offer.

In practice an employer with more than one establishment may wish to transfer certain employees to a second site rather than make them redundant. The negotiation between manager and individual employee occurs in the shadow of the law of 'suitable alternative employment'. For an unreasonable refusal of suitable alternative employment has the legal consequence that an employee is disqualified from a claim for a statutory redundancy payment. Acceptance of the offer means that there is no dismissal and no break in continuous service.

To constitute an offer of 'suitable alternative employment' a job must be offered to take effect immediately or within four weeks of the date of termination. It must be either the same job or substantially similar in respect of working hours, place of work, status and pay etc, but it can be offered with less attractive terms and conditions. In particular the job may be a completely different job,[10] it may be a job with only a short-term future[11] and it may involve increased travelling[12] and still be viewed as suitable by a tribunal. In other words this is a statutory category not limited by the 'kind of work' or 'place of work' defined in the employee's contract of employment. On the other hand if the move is too far from the individual's home, or the job too different or the pay too unfavourable by comparison, it may be found to be unsuitable.[13] Suitability is a question of fact for the tribunal to decide with the burden of proof on the employer[14] to show substantial equivalence with the employment which has ceased.[15]

## The statutory trial period

A second feature of the offer of alternative employment is that employees are entitled to a trial period as of right[16] for four calendar weeks[17] during which they may try out the new job without prejudice to their chances of refusing it and still be entitled to a redundancy payment. This statutory trial period can occur without prejudice to the entitlement of an employee for the purposes of constructive dismissal to consider an imposed change in terms by an employer before agreeing to a variation or deciding to treat it as a repudiation.[18] The trial period can be extended by mutual agreement in writing for a specified period for the purpose of retraining.[19] Yet at the end of the trial period the employee must still make a decision whether or not to accept the offer knowing that a refusal could constitute an unreasonable refusal and hence disqualify him or her from a redundancy payment. On the other hand, if neither party terminates the contract by the end of the trial period, the termination of the contract prior to the offer of alternative employment is treated as if it never happened and the employee loses his or her claim for a redundancy payment.[20]

10 See eg *O'Loughlin v Fitzpatrick & Son (Contractors) Ltd* [1976] IRLR 39 (place of work), *Harris v E Turner & Sons (Joinery) Ltd* [1973] ICR 31 (loss of status), *E & J Davis Transport v Chattaway* [1972] ICR 267 (loss of bonus payment). See also Grunfeld *Law of Redundancy* (3rd edn).

11 *Dutton v Hawker Siddeley Aviation Ltd* [1978] ICR 1057, [1978] IRLR 390.

12 *Morganite Crucible Ltd v Street* [1972] 2 All ER 411, [1972] ICR 110.

13 See fns 9-11.

14 *Jones v Aston Cabinet Co Ltd* [1973] ICR 292.

15 *Cambridge & District Co-operative Society v Ruse* [1993] IRLR 156.

16 *Elliot v Richard Stump Ltd* [1987] ICR 579, [1987] IRLR 215.

17 See eg *Benton v Sanderson Kayser* [1989] ICR 136, [1989] IRLR 19.

18 Section 138. See eg *Turvey v C W Cheyney & Son Ltd* [1979] ICR 341, [1979] IRLR 105; *Coopkind (UK) Ltd v Buckland* [1981] EAT 403/89.

19 Section 138(3). *McKindley v William Hill (Scotland) Ltd* [1985] IRLR 492.

20 Section 138(1), (5). See eg *Meek v J Allen Rubber Co Ltd* [1980] IRLR 21.

## Reasonable refusals of offers of alternative employment

Even where offered alternative employment employees may be able to argue that their refusals are reasonable given their domestic circumstances: for example where the new job involves considerably longer travel times or a change of residence.

The same factors are often looked at under the two heads - suitability of employment and reasonableness of refusal - but whereas the first head involves a comparison of the two jobs and is an objective issue, the test of unreasonable refusal entails a close look at the personal circumstance of the individual and 'is a subjective matter to be considered from the employee's point of view'.[1] Consequently the reasonableness of the location of the alternative work can be affected by family arrangements,[2] the kind of work can be affected by employee preferences[3] and the change in working conditions when cuts are introduced and work is reorganised can be suitable alternative employment under ERA, s 139 and nevertheless be reasonably refused if the employees feel that the change is unacceptable to them because they can no longer do the job properly under the new conditions.[4] Moreover, where a number of employees are made redundant and offered similar work, some may be able to reasonably refuse and others not.

This is one of those rare elements of the statute where the rationality of the employee's family interest is given considerable weight in the legal test.

## Diminished requirements of the business for employees

The striking feature of the statutory definition of redundancy is that it consists solely of whether, *in the employer's opinion*, fewer employees are required to perform the kind of work that the employees do at their place of work. The only restraint provided by s 139[5] is to specify the minimum cost of the redundancy payment, a cost which is offset against profit for tax purposes. Moreover, there are certain technicalities in the statutory test of redundancy which may adversely affect an employee's

1 See eg *Cambridge and District Co-operative Society Ltd v Ruse* [1993] IRLR 156 at 158, EAT. See also *Hindes v Supersine* [1979] IRLR 343 ; *Executors of J F Everest v Cox* [1980] ICR 415.

2 *Brennan v Mott Hay & Anderson* [1975] IRLR 305.

3 *National Carriers Contract Services v Urey* 14.9.90 EAT 233/89.

4 *Spencer and Griffin v Gloucestershire County Council* [1985] IRLR 393, EAT.

5 In principle, the obligation placed with employers to consult with employee representatives might result in a second opinion being put forward prior to the final decision. See discussion in Ch 16.

claim for a payment (or a determination of whether a case is one of redundancy for the purpose of unfair dismissal).

The first point of interpretation of the statutory definition under ERA, s 139(1) of diminished requirements for employees to do work of a particular kind at their place of work is that the management decision must result in a decrease in the *number of employees* performing a particular kind of work; the change in the overall requirements of managers for the quantum of work of a particular kind by itself is not significant. For example in *Carry All Motors Ltd v Pennington*,[6] an 'efficiency restructuring' of a motor-car transport department resulted in a decision that the work of the transport manager and that of a transport clerk could be done by one person. The industrial tribunal accepted the argument that the consequent dismissal of the extra employee after the reorganisation was not redundancy because there was no reduction in the overall amount of work. The EAT overturned the tribunal's decision remarking that undue emphasis had been placed upon 'work of a particular kind' without giving proper effect to the preceding words 'the requirements of that business for *employees* to carry out that work'.

On the other hand, where a job has ended but there has been no reduction in the overall number of employees in a firm, there can nevertheless be a redundancy because the firm's requirements for employees doing *that particular job* have diminished. Everything depends on how the job or the work of a particular kind is defined. For example, in *Murphy v Epsom College*[7] a plumber replaced with a heating technician when he indicated he was unable to maintain the modernised heating system of the college was held to be redundant. The work had changed, it was held, from general plumbing to heating maintenance and therefore there had been a reduction in plumbers.

## Work of a particular kind and place of work

The second point of interpretation under s 139(1) concerns the judicial interpretation given to the phrase 'place of work' and 'work of a particular kind'.

In the earlier cases, the courts chose to give a contractual definition to the statutory term 'work of a particular kind' rather than taking it to refer to the job that the employee was actually performing. As a consequence, where employees worked under a contract with a flexibility clause providing that they could be transferred to other types of work, the work

6 [1980] ICR 806, [1980] IRLR 455, EAT. See too *McCrea v Cullen & Davison Ltd* [1988] IRLR 30, NICA.

7 [1985] ICR 80, [1984] IRLR 271, CA.

that they were actually doing or even their job description was given little legal weight. What counted in defining the phrase 'work of a particular kind' was the width of the contractual flexibility clause, that is, the work the employee could be contractually required to perform. For example, in *Nelson v BBC*[8] a BBC Caribbean Service producer worked under a contract of employment with a flexibility clause requiring him to serve when, how and where the BBC demanded. His position was viewed as general producer rather than that of producer in the Caribbean Service. When the Caribbean Service job ended and he refused another production job with the BBC, his dismissal could not be regarded as dismissal for redundancy, since his job, as defined by the contract, had not disappeared.

Similarly, where the contract provided an express geographic mobility clause, the place of work was not confined to the place where the employee is currently working.

For example in *Rank Xerox Ltd v Churchill*[9] secretaries working at the company's London headquarters were asked to move to Marlow in accordance with a clause in their contract which read: 'The company may require you to transfer to another location.' Though the company offered financial assistance with the move the employees refused to move. They left their employment claiming redundancy payments. The EAT reversed the industrial tribunal's ruling that the clause was ambiguous and should be construed to provide authority to transfers only within reasonable daily travel distance. The EAT held that the clause was clear and therefore the place of employment under the contract was 'anywhere under the contract of employment he could be required to work.'[10]

Historically, the courts have been prepared to place some limits on very wide express flexibility clauses in the redundancy context. For example, in *Cowen v Haden Ltd*[11] the employee was a regional surveyor with a flexibility clause in his contract that said: 'the employee's job title will be regional surveyor - Southern Region. He will be required to undertake, at the direction of the company, any and all duties which reasonably fall within the scope of his capabilities.' The Court of Appeal decided that when his job as regional surveyor ended, his dismissal was for redundancy despite the flexibility clause. This was because the effect of that clause was not to entitle the employer to transfer the employee to any job as quantity surveyor within the organisation but only to require him to

8 [1977] ICR 649, [1977] IRLR 148, CA.

9 [1988] IRLR 280, EAT.

10 [1988] IRLR 280; see also *Sutcliffe v Hawker Siddeley Aviation Ltd* [1973] ICR 560, [1973] IRLR 304, CA.

11 [1983] ICR 1, [1982] IRLR 314, CA. But see too *Deeley v British Rail Engineering Ltd* [1980] IRLR 147. See further *Curling v Securicor Ltd* [1992] IRLR 549 where employer did not consistently rely upon the mobility clause. See discussion in Ch 2.

perform any duties reasonably within the scope of his capabilities as a regional surveyor.

More recently, the courts have been prepared to view the question of place of work and type of work under the statutory redundancy provisions as factual tests with the contractual provisions providing guidance rather than a decisive role. Thus, in *Bass Leisure Ltd v Thomas*,[12] Mrs Thomas was a driver based in Coventry but the contract of employment included a clause reserving to the employer the right to transfer the employee to a suitable alternative place of work. When the company closed the Coventry depot, she was asked to operate from Erdington, 20 miles away. After a trial period, she found she could not cope and left the employment claiming redundancy. The EAT upheld the industrial tribunal's finding of redundancy, preferring a 'factual' test to a 'contractual test' for s 139(1), stating that the place where the employee was employed for the purposes of s 139(1) 'is to be established by a factual inquiry, taking into account the employee's fixed or changing place or places of work and any contractual terms which go to evidence or define the place of employment and its extent, but not those (if any) which make provision for the employee to be transferred to another' (p 112). The Court of Appeal in *High Table Ltd v Horst*,[13] per Peter Gibson LJ, indicated that it was in broad agreement with this interpretation of the statutory language, stressing that the question of where the employee was employed was to be answered primarily by a consideration of the factual circumstances which obtained prior to the dismissal. The Court added that: 'It would be unfortunate if the law were to encourage the inclusion of mobility clauses in contracts of employment to defeat genuine redundancy claims.' Furthermore, in *Johnston v Peabody Trust*[14] a roofer who worked under a contract with a wide flexibility clause, reading 'Where possible, trade persons will be expected to carry out multiskill operations,' was dismissed for redundancy as a roofer. He claimed that the dismissal could not have been for redundancy because of the flexibility clause and that under the 'contractual test' test all contractual functions should have ended before redundancy could be declared. The EAT upheld the industrial tribunal's finding of redundancy, stating that the 'the basic task which the employee has contracted to perform' should be the test. The essential nature of the job was that of a roofer and the mobility clause was only a subsidiary obligation. These cases suggest that the courts in adopting a factual test in place of a contractual test have finally moved to a method of statutory interpretation which does justice to both the statutory language and the statutory purpose.

12 [1994] IRLR 104.
13 [1997] IRLR 513, CA.
14 [1996] IRLR 387.

In the absence of an express term on mobility or flexibility, courts may be willing to imply flexibility and mobility terms on the basis of reasonableness. In *Courtaulds Northern Spinning Ltd v Sibson*[15] the Court of Appeal was prepared to read into Sibson's contract an implied right for the company to transfer its employees within reasonable travelling distance. In *North Riding Garages Ltd v Butterwick*,[16] a workshop manager supervising maintenance work had his job drastically reorganised. He was asked to take on the extensive administrative as well as maintenance work after another firm took over his employer. When he proved unable to match up to the new type of job, he was dismissed. The court held that he could not qualify for a redundancy payment. His job had not disappeared. His employer still had a continued need for workshop managers, albeit of a different type. For the purpose of the Act, the court said an employee who remained in the same kind of work was expected to adapt himself to new methods and techniques, and could not complain if his employer insists on higher standards of efficiency than those previously required. If, however, the employee can show, as in *Murphy*'s case, that the nature of the job has changed, eg from plumber to heating technician, then there is a redundancy.

The courts have also tended to give a strict reading to the nature of 'work' in the statutory definition. Thus, when an employer reorganises work so as to retain the need for the specific tasks performed by employees but drastically changes their hours of work or terms of remuneration, despite the blow to the employees' contractual expectations the courts have not always been prepared to recognise that this constitutes a change in 'work of a particular kind'. They have viewed the statutory phrase quite narrowly in terms of the tasks performed in the job rather than seeing the work as a contractual bundle of job-related rights.[17] In *Johnson v Nottinghamshire Combined Police Authority*,[18] for example, the working hours of two women were reorganised from a five-day week to a shift system and a six-day week. The change was held not to be a change in the 'kind of work', it was only a change in hours, which was not mentioned specifically in the statute. For the purposes of the statute, it was held that a change in hours of work did not cause a change in the particular kind of work unless it was so fundamental as to change the nature of the work. Furthermore, in *Chapman v Goonvean and Rostowrack China Clay Co Ltd*,[19] an employer's withdrawal of free transport was held not to be a

15 [1988] ICR 451, [1988] IRLR 305.

16 [1967] 2 QB 56, [1967] 1 All ER 644, DC.

17 See Davies and Freedland's useful discussion of this point in *Labour Law: Text and Materials* (2nd edn) p 540.

18 [1974] 1 All ER 1082, [1974] ICR 170, CA; see also *Lesney Products & Co Ltd v Nolan* [1977] ICR 235, [1977] IRLR 77, CA.

19 [1973] 2 All ER 1063, [1973] ICR 310, CA.

reduction in the requirement for an employee to carry out 'work of particular kind', even though it was an important part of his package of rights under his contract of employment and the decision was a consequence of a prior redundancy. Today, such cases could be the basis of a claim[20] for unfair dismissal, but there is no assurance that a dismissal in the context of a work reorganisation will necessarily be unfair.

Employers are thus entitled to reorganise their business so as to improve its efficiency and in so doing to propose to their staff a change in terms and conditions, and to dismiss them if they do not agree, without necessarily triggering the right to a statutory redundancy payment. Moreover, where employees resign because of the denial of their contractual expectations they may be regarded as constructively dismissed, but still denied redundancy pay. In the event, employees dismissed for economic reasons and through no fault of their own can end up with no compensation.

The strictness of the interpretation of the definition of redundancy is ironic given the withdrawal of the contribution from the Redundancy Fund to employers and the wider industrial relations purpose of the legislation. It also has the effect of making it more difficult for employers to prove that redundancy is their reason for dismissal in unfair dismissal cases.

## Bumping or transferred redundancy

The contractual element in the definition of a particular kind of work under ERA, s 139(1) can also be relevant where as a result of a transferred redundancy, an employee is 'bumped' out of a job, ie where in accordance with a redundancy selection procedure, possibly based on a collective agreement, the employer has applied the criterion of seniority, ie length of continuous service, or some other more complex set of criteria including skill levels, to transfer the employee whose job has ceased into the job of the employee who is dismissed.[1] From an industrial perspective, the practice of bumping if based on seniority can be viewed as 'industrial justice.' Moreover, in so far as the dismissal is in accordance with the redundancy procedure, it will be viewed as qualifying for a voluntary redundancy payment under the collective agreement or employer's unilateral redundancy procedure. However, is it redundancy within the meaning of s 139(1)? Technically, there has been no reduction in the work that the dismissed employee has been performing; he or she has been dismissed because of the reduction in the number of employees needed for the first job. However, s 139(1)(b)(i) stipulates only that there should

20 See Ch 12.

1 The issue is treated separately under the test of unfair redundancy.

be a reduction in the requirements of the employer for work of a particular kind; it does not add that the decline must be in the work for which the dismissed employee is employed. Section 139(1)(b)(ii), in contrast, does require that the reduction in the employer's requirements for employees must be at the place of work where the employee was employed by the employer. Section 139(1) thus appears to envisage transferred redundancy as 'redundancy.' Moreover, it could even apply to a transferred redundancy from one site to another in the employer's business. The definition of redundancy in s 139(1)(b)(i) is an alternative to s 139(b)(ii). Moreover, s 139(2) specifies that for the purpose of s 139(1) the business of the employer should be treated as extending to the business of associated employers in the interpretation of s 139(1). In *Church v West Lancashire NHS Trust*,[2] a helpdesk operator in a computer services department was replaced by a redundant senior coordinator after refusing to compete for his own job. The EAT held that this was not a redundancy but a dismissal for reorganisation because the definition of the kind of work of the employee should be held to be limited to that work performed by the dismissed employee. Leave to appeal has been granted.

## Impact of redundancy legislation on collective bargaining

Away from the margins of statutory interpretation in the case law, the impact of the redundancy payments legislation upon collective bargaining and managerial practice in the context of larger workforce reductions has been profound. In the first place there has been a strong tendency in private industry to improve upon the statutory level of lump sum compensation for redundancy, for example by providing higher rates of payment, often multiples of the statutory rate, by removing the minimum and maximum periods of service and other qualifications, and by providing other enhancements in certain cases such as closure bonuses, hardship and unemployment allowances.

According to the Labour Research Department surveys, more than half of all agreements improved on one or more features of the statutory entitlements of employees. The form these enhanced payments took varied from agreement to agreement. A common approach was to give some multiple of statutory redundancy pay (see Table 1 opposite).

It can be seen from Table 1 that whereas in 1981 53% of the schemes considered paid more than statutory redundancy pay, in 1984 90% improved on the legal minimum. And whereas in 1981 one-third paid twice the statutory redundancy pay or better, in 1984 the figure was well over half.

2 [1998] IRLR 4; but see *Safeway Stores Ltd v Burrell* [1997] IRLR 200, EAT.

*Table I*

Number of redundancy agreements providing more than minimum statutory redundancy pay (source:Labour Research Department 1981, 1984).

| | *Enhancement* | | | |
|---|---|---|---|---|
| | *No of agreements* | | *% of agreements* | |
| | 1981 | 1984 | 1981 | 1984 |
| At least 4 times statutory redundancy pay | 15 | 17 | 9 | 15 |
| At least 3 times statutory redundancy pay | 6 | 15 | 3 | 14 |
| At least twice statutory redundancy pay | 33 | 31 | 19 | 28 |
| At least 1 times statutory redundancy pay | 23 | 19 | 13 | 17 |
| Better than statutory minimum | 15 | 15 | 9 | 14 |
| No enhancement | 83 | 11 | 47 | 10 |
| Total number of agreements assessed | 175 | 110 | 100 | 100 |

Supplements based on age or service were also common; often no notice was taken of the statutory minimum age or service or maximum weekly earnings. In some cases part-time workers were made eligible for redundancy payments. In some exceptional cases individual company agreements offered closure bonuses, hardship and unemployment allowances.

Also, the statutory payment and its enhancements have had the effect of helping to win wider acceptance among employees of the practice of redundancy. The Industrial Relations Code of Practice accompanying the 1971 Industrial Relations Act prescribed specific procedures for consultation and selection. And 'procedures for redundancy' have usually been agreed to in collective agreements with an enhanced redundancy payment. These procedures usually provide for some form of collective notice and consultation and resort to other methods of workforce reduction such as redeployment, natural wastage and early retirement. However, they also contain agreed criteria for selection such as 'last in–first out', implying that redundancies would be acceptable in certain situations. The lump sum severance payment made redundancy less unattractive to employees, especially long-service employees, and contributed to the growth of the practice of voluntary redundancy.

This practice consisted of giving workers in certain grades the opportunity to volunteer to be made redundant and receive a payment. If sufficient numbers stepped forward in the case of partial plant closure, this practice made it possible to avoid compulsory redundancy and a possible industrial dispute. It was perhaps insufficiently appreciated at the time, however, that eventually collective resistance to compulsory redundancies in plant closures might also be undermined by the practice of the lump sum redundancy payment as workers became divided in their views about the importance of resisting redundancies where compensation was available.[3]

As Daniel described it, the trade union representatives after a while were 'caught in a pincer movement between managerial strategy and individualist opportunism on the part of its members' and 'had no alternative but to adopt two stances' in relation to redundancy. The first was to insist upon 'No compulsory redundancy'. The second was to bargain over the inducements to volunteer and, in particular, to try to bid up the size of the employer's supplement to the statutory minimum payments. This made it more difficult to fight plant closures when they began to occur with increasing frequency in the late 1970s and early 1980s.[4]

During this period, too, managers began to publicise more widely the fact that those who engaged in industrial action in an effort to resist compulsory redundancies could if dismissed during such action, lose their redundancy pay entitlement. A dismissal for industrial action prior to receiving formal notice of dismissal for redundancy can result in a complete loss of redundancy pay. Even a dismissal for industrial action during the obligatory notice period can result in a complete or partial loss of payment subject to the discretion of industrial tribunals.[5] In these ways the so-called 'individual' employment law of redundancy payments has developed into a significant factor in managing collective redundancies, giving employers greater control over redundancy than in previous periods.

## B UNFAIR REDUNDANCY

An employee's claim that a dismissal for redundancy is unfair is the second tier of the 'individual' statutory rights which regulate managerial redundancy decisions.

Even where an employer has successfully shown that an employee has been dismissed for redundancy and received a redundancy payment in accordance with the statute, the employee may also be entitled to complain that the redundancy was an unfair dismissal, and this under either of two

3 Gennard 'Great Britain' in Yemin (ed) *Workforce Reductions in Undertakings* (1982).
4 Daniel W W 'The United Kingdom' in Cross (ed) *Managing Workforce Reduction* (1985).
5 See Ch 17.

heads. In the first place, the redundancy may be an automatically unfair selection under s 105. Second, the redundancy may have been 'unreasonable' under s 98.

## Automatically unfair selection

Under s 105[6] a dismissal for redundancy can be automatically unfair if the employee can show that the redundancy applied to other employees in similar positions, and that the real reason for the selection of redundancy was trade union membership and activity or non-membership[7] or some other inadmissible reason under ss 99-104, eg pregnancy, health and safety, shop worker, trustees of a pension scheme, employee representatives or assertion of a statutory right.

Formerly, an employee selected in unjustified contravention of a customary arrangement or agreed procedure relating to redundancy could also claim an automatically unfair dismissal but this ground was repealed in 1995.[8] Now this ground can be asserted under the reasonableness test of s 98(4).

## The reasonableness of the employer's redundancy dismissal under s 98(4)

If a dismissal for redundancy fails to satisfy the conditions for an automatically unfair dismissal under s 151, an employee may still claim under s 98(4) that it was unreasonable in all the circumstances.

In exercising their discretion under s 98(4), industrial tribunals have been urged to act as 'industrial juries', taking everything into account subject only to an appeal on a matter of law.[9] Yet they have also been told that they must not judge the employer's decision on the basis of what they would have done had they been the employer. Rather they must apply the standard of the reasonable employer, that is to say, they must judge by 'the objective standard of the way in which a reasonable employer in those circumstances in that line of business would have behaved'.[10] In other words they must judge the reasonableness of the employer's decisions on the basis of whether their actions fell within the range of reasonable

6 Selection for redundancy can also be contrary to the Sex Discrimination Act, see Ch 12.
7 See s 153 TULRCA; see further Ch 15.
8 Deregulation and Contracting Out Act 1994, s 36 took effect January 1995.
9 *Bessenden Properties Ltd v Corness* [1977] ICR 821n, [1974] IRLR 338, CA.
10 *BL Cars Ltd v Lewis* [1983] IRLR 58, EAT.

responses of employers generally and not judge the employer's decisions on the basis of what it would have done had it been the employer.

In *BL Cars Ltd v Lewis*,[11] for example, an industrial tribunal was found to have erred in law when it decided that an employee's selection for redundancy was unfair because the employer had given insufficient weight to the employee's length of service. The criteria applied by the employer had consisted of a combination of service, occupation, and skill on apparatus all on equal bases. By insisting on greater points for the criteria of service, the tribunal had in effect asked itself whether it would have made that selection rather than the proper question which was, was the selection one which a reasonable employer would have made?

This test of reasonableness under s 98(4) applied in unfair redundancy cases in four separate lines of inquiry.

(1) Did the employer follow a reasonable procedure in making the redundancy decision?
(2) Was there a reasonable investigation of the possibilities of alternative employment?
(3) Was the selection reasonable?
(4) Was the timing and financial basis reasonable?

### *(a) Reasonable procedure and unfair redundancy: warnings and consultation*

In addition to asking whether management acted reasonably in selecting an employee for redundancy, an industrial tribunal may also ascertain whether the procedure used by the employer was that of a reasonable employer in the circumstances, that is to say, that the employer acted reasonably in warning and consulting with employees. The obligation to warn is separate from the obligation to consult.[12]

The EAT has stressed the importance of consultation to explore the possibilities of avoiding the redundancy decision in the case of the individual employee. As the EAT put it in *Grundy (Teddington) Ltd v Plummer*:[13]

> 'In the particular sphere of redundancy, good industrial practice in the ordinary case requires consultation with the redundant employee so that the employer may find out whether the needs of the business can be met in some other way than by dismissal and, if not, what other step the employer can take to ameliorate the blow to the employee.'

11 Ibid.
12 See eg *Rowell v Hubbard Group Services Ltd* [1995] IRLR 195, EAT.
13 [1983] ICR 367, [1983] IRLR 98, EAT. See too *Rolls Royce Motor Cars Ltd v Price* [1993] IRLR 203, EAT.

Further, in *Williams v Compair Maxam Ltd*[14] the EAT indicated that where the employer recognises an independent union there are certain principles of good industrial practice which reasonable employers will follow, eg:

> '1. The employer will seek to give as much warning as possible of impending redundancies so as to enable the union and employees who may be affected to take early steps to inform themselves of the relevant facts, consider possible alternative solutions and, if necessary, find alternative employment in the undertaking or elsewhere.
>
> 2. The employer will consult the union as to the best means by which the desired management result can be achieved fairly and with as little hardship to the employees as possible. In particular, the employer will seek to agree with the union the criteria to be applied in selecting the employees to be made redundant. When a selection has been made, the employer will consider with the union whether the selection has been made in accordance with those criteria...'

In *Rowell v Hubbard Group Services Ltd*[15] the EAT made the point that fair consultation 'involves giving the body consulted a fair and proper opportunity to understand fully the matters about which it is being consulted, and to express its views on those subjects, with the consultor thereafter considering those views properly and genuinely.'[16]

In *Mugford v Midland Bank*,[17] the EAT added that, consultation with the trade union over selection criteria will not of itself release the employer from considering with the employee individually his or her selection for redundancy.

> 'Experience shows that trade unions rarely if ever wish to be involved in the actual selection of individuals for redundancy (other than on the basis of the LIFO principle) since to do so would involve choosing between their members, though they will provide representatives to employees identified for redundancy in their individual consultations with management. Individual consultation should take place before a final decision is reached and allow the employee an opportunity to put his or her case to the relevant managers so that the latter may make a fully informed decision.'[18]

Furthermore, consultation with the individual also presupposes adequate information to allow the individual to understand fully the matters upon which he or she is being consulted. In *John Brown Engineering Ltd v Brown*,[19] the EAT upheld an industrial tribunal which had found that

14 [1982] ICR 156, [1982] IRLR 83, EAT.
15 [1995] IRLR 195 at 197; see too *King v Eaton Ltd* [1996] IRLR 199, CS.
16 This adopted the statement by Glidewell LJ in *British Coal Corpn v Price* [1994] IRLR 72 at 75.
17 [1997] IRLR 208, EAT.
18 Ibid at 210.
19 [1997] IRLR 90.

employees had been unfairly selected for redundancy on the basis of a points system when they had not been informed of their own marks.

Although the guidelines of the EAT are clearly not rules of law in the sense that a failure by an employer to meet each procedural standard will invariably lead to a finding of unfair dismissal, they may nevertheless be applied by industrial tribunals under s 98(4) as long as they take into account all the relevant circumstances of the case.[20]

In *Polkey v A E Dayton Services Ltd*[1] the House of Lords held that the procedural test was an important component of the test of s 98(4) in redundancy cases. Lord Bridge first made the general point that 'an employer . . . will in the great majority of cases not act reasonably in treating the reason as a sufficient reason for dismissal unless and until he has taken the steps, conveniently classified in most of the authorities as "procedural" which are necessary in the circumstances of the case to justify that course of action'. He then added that in the case of redundancy, the employer will normally not act reasonably unless he warns and consults any employees affected or their representative, adopts a fair basis on which to select for redundancy and takes such steps as may be reasonable to avoid or minimise redundancy by redeployment within his own organisation.

Moreover, as Lord Mackay emphasised in *Polkey*'s case:

> 'the statutory test shows that at least some aspects of the manner of the dismissal fall to be considered in considering whether a dismissal is unfair since the action of the employer in treating the reason as sufficient for dismissal of the employee will include at least part of the manner of the dismissal.'

Indeed, in an extreme case, it might be legally perverse for an industrial tribunal to find a dismissal fair where the employer has failed to follow the canons of good industrial practice. Thus in *Williams v Compair Maxam Ltd*[2] the EAT reversed an industrial tribunal which had found a dismissal not unfair despite the employer's failure to consult the union on the criteria for selection of employees for redundancy and to look for alternative employment for the employees made redundant. And in *Freud v Bentalls Ltd*[3] the EAT decided that an industrial tribunal's decision was legally perverse where it found a dismissal for redundancy fair and the employers had intentionally omitted to consult the employee and failed to give any good reason justifying this omission. The company had simply indicated that it was company policy not to consult employees at managerial level over redundancy.

20 *Grundy (Teddington) Ltd v Plummer* [1983] ICR 367, [1983] IRLR 98, EAT.
1 [1988] ICR 142, [1987] IRLR 503, HL.
2 [1982] ICR 156, [1982] IRLR 83, EAT.
3 [1983] ICR 77, [1982] IRLR 443, EAT.

For many years, in determining whether a procedural omission makes a dismissal for redundancy unreasonable, industrial tribunals were 'guided' that they should seek a further question: were the circumstances such that the procedural step if taken would have made a difference?[4]

In *Polkey*'s case, however, the House of Lords made it clear that the *British Labour Pump* principle and all decisions supporting it were 'inconsistent with the statute and should be overruled'. Lord Mackay indicated that the test involved an impermissible reliance upon matters not known to the employers before the dismissal and a confusion between unreasonable conduct in reaching the conclusion to dismiss which is a necessary ingredient of an unfair dismissal, and injustice to the employee which is not a necessary ingredient of an unfair dismissal although its absence will be important in relation to the compensatory award.

The House of Lords suggested a far stricter test of fair dismissal when an important procedural step was omitted by the employer. As Lord Mackay stated:

> '. . . if the employer could reasonably have concluded in the light of the circumstances known to him at the time of dismissal that consultation or warning would be *utterly useless* he might well act reasonably even if he did not observe the provisions of the code. Failure to observe the requirement of the code relating to consultation or warning will not necessarily render a dismissal unfair. Whether in any particular case it did so is a matter for the industrial tribunal to consider in the light of the circumstances known to the employer at the time he dismissed the employee.'[5]

And as Lord Bridge said:

> 'it is quite a different matter if the tribunal is able to conclude that the employer himself, at the time of dismissal, acted reasonably in taking the view that, in the exceptional circumstances of the particular case, the procedural steps normally appropriate would have been *futile*, could not have altered the decision to dismiss and therefore could be dispensed with. In such a case the test of reasonableness under section [98(4)] may be satisfied.'[6]

In the event, the manner of the dismissal is to be judged in accordance with the test of reasonableness generally under ERA, s 98(4). Lord Bridge's test of futility is an objective test, ie whether the employer acted reasonably in 'taking the view at the time of the decision' that the decision would not have been altered had the correct procedure been followed. In *Duffy v Yeoman's & Partners Ltd*[7] however, the Court of Appeal, per Lord Balcome, emphasised that Lord Mackay's test was the one upon which all the law Lords agreed and that this test did not require the employer, *as*

4 See eg *British United Shoe Machinery Co Ltd v Clarke* [1977] IRLR 297, EAT.
5 [1987] IRLR at 504.
6 [1987] IRLR at 508.
7 [1994] IRLR 642, CA at 645; see Wynn [1995] ILJ 272.

*a matter of law*, take a deliberate decision at the time of dismissal that consultation would be useless. Instead, it was enough to determine whether the employer acting reasonably could have failed to consult in the given circumstances, ie on the basis of the facts known to him at the time the decision was taken. This test, if followed would downgrade the importance within the reasonableness test, of the fact that the employer had actually considered the consultation step. Yet it is still open to employees to argue before industrial tribunals as opposed to on appeal as in *Duffy*, that a failure by the employer to consider the consultation option in the circumstances of *that* case was unreasonable.

For as the EAT pointed out in *Heron v Citylink-Nottingham*[8] there may be circumstances known to the employee, and not the employer which could influence the outcome and it must be an extreme case where an employer can ignore that possibility and still be considered to have acted reasonably. At all events, the nature of the test is essentially whether the conclusion could reasonably be drawn by an employer that a consultation, if provided, would have provided more information to the employer rather than whether it would have provided fair treatment to the employee. Hugh Collins has accurately described this as an economic efficiency model of procedural fairness.[9]

### *(b) The reasonable investigation of alternative employment*

As a matter of good industrial practice,[10] management should also make reasonable efforts to look for alternative employment for employees before making them redundant. At an early stage the NIRC in *Vokes Ltd v Bear*[11] found that a redundancy was unfair on the grounds that the employer had failed to investigate whether there were job vacancies within the group which might have been offered to the employee as an alternative to being made redundant. As the NIRC put it:

> 'The employer had not yet done that which in all fairness and reason he should do, namely to make the obvious attempt to see if Mr Bear could be placed somewhere else in this large group.'

In *Modern Injection Moulds Ltd v Price*[12] the EAT, per Mr Justice Phillips, adopted the statement of the law in *Vokes Ltd v Bear*, adding to it the following:

> 'In our judgment it can be said that in as much as there is this obligation on the part of the employers to try to find suitable alternative employment

8 [1993] IRLR 372.
9 See H Collins *Justice in Dismissal* (Clarendon Press, Oxford, 1993) p 110.
10 See eg *Williams v Compair Maxam Ltd* [1982] ICR 156, [1982] IRLR 83, EAT.
11 [1974] ICR 1, [1973] IRLR 363, NIRC.
12 [1976] ICR 370, [1976] IRLR 172, EAT.

within the firm, it must follow that if they are in a position pursuant to their obligation to make an offer to the employee of suitable alternative employment they must give him sufficient information on the basis of which the employee can make a realistic decision whether to take the new job.'

Quite clearly neither *Vokes Ltd v Bear* nor *Modern Injection Moulds* stood for the proposition that there was a duty to find alternative employment.[13] The employer's duty under s 98(4) was to take reasonable steps to try to find alternative employment before dismissal.[14] Here there is an important distinction to be drawn between a failure of investigation and the exercise of discretion once a reasonable investigation had occurred.

Thus, if the employer makes no effort at all to ascertain the possibility of alternative employment, that ground alone could justify a tribunal decision that he acted unfairly in dismissing that employee for redundancy. For example in *Thomas & Betts Manufacturing Ltd v Harding*[15] the Court of Appeal rejected the employer's argument that the tribunal's investigation of possibilities for alternative employment must be limited to the 'section of the business' in which the individual was employed. The Court also indicated that tribunals should have the discretion to take into account the possibility that it might be reasonable for the employer to 'bump', ie dismiss, another employee to provide alternative employment for the redundant employee.

And in *Avonmouth Construction Co Ltd v Shipway*[16] the EAT stated that implicit in the duty to look for alternative employment in a redundancy situation is the responsibility on the employer to give careful consideration to the possibility of offering the employee another job, including a possible demotion. This was a case where another, subordinate, job was actually available and the employer's reasons for not offering it to the employee were not accepted as reasonable by the industrial tribunal.

The court's statements on the latter issue were made in a case where the employer had made no effort to justify his failure to offer alternative employment. Assuming, however, that the employer has made some effort, the standard by which his efforts will be measured would be that of the reasonable employer, subject to the range of reasonable employer responses criterion.[17] Moreover, assuming that a vacancy is found, the employer has some discretion in deciding whether or not the redundant employee is suitable for the vacant position.[18] Furthermore, where the

13 *Brush Electrical Machines Ltd v Guest* (1976) EAT 382/76.

14 See *P v Nottinghamshire County Council* [1992] IRLR 362, CA; see Watt [1993] ILJ 44.

15 [1980] IRLR 255, CA.

16 [1979] IRLR 14, EAT.

17 *Green v A & I Fraser (Wholesale Fish Merchants) Ltd* [1985] IRLR 55, EAT.

18 See eg *Wood v Coverage Care Ltd* [1996] IRLR 264 (where employee had a spent conviction).

employer has some justification for the decision not to displace another employee, an industrial tribunal might not be allowed the discretion to find the dismissal for redundancy unfair on the ground that the effort was insufficient. For example, in *MDH Ltd v Sussex*[19] the EAT held that a tribunal had erred in law when it found that a redundancy dismissal was unfair because the employer had failed to look for alternative job opportunities in other companies in the same corporate group.[20]

Moreover, in *Barratt Construction Ltd v Dalrymple*,[1] the EAT overturned an industrial tribunal decision that a dismissal was unfair because the employer had only investigated the possibilities of similar alternative employment in the company and not considered the possibility of offering employment in a subordinate post to the employee. The EAT considered that it was not open to an industrial tribunal to speculate as to what further steps the employer ought to take and to draw an inference adverse to the employer because he had failed to take them.

### *(c) Unreasonable methods of selection*

The test of whether an employer acted reasonably in selecting one employee rather than another under s 98(4) has proved to be a particularly troublesome one for the courts. On the one hand they have accepted that an industrial tribunal would not be exercising its function under s 98(4), to act as an industrial jury if it defers entirely to an employer's discretion.[2] Thus, on occasion, the EAT has suggested that industrial tribunals should ensure that the criteria used by the employer are reasonable criteria for selection.[3] On the other hand, the courts have long been concerned that the residual test in s 98(4) should not be used by tribunals to apply too strict a test to an employer's decision to select employees for redundancy once the hurdle of a s 105 has been successfully overcome.[4]

Indeed, in Scotland the EAT has, on more than one occasion, suggested that:

> '... where the reason for dismissal is redundancy and that dismissal has survived the tests prescribed in [s 105] it will in most cases be extremely

19 [1986] IRLR 123, EAT.

20 See too *Huddersfield Parcels Ltd v Sykes* [1981] IRLR 115, EAT, which drew attention to the difficulties to the employer of adopting the bumping practice; *Tocher v General Motors Scotland Ltd* [1981] IRLR 55, EAT (on the effects of EPCA, s 140 on a bumping agreement); *Bowaters Containers Ltd v McCormack* [1980] IRLR 50, EAT, which indicated that an employer could not be expected to offer alternative work where it would contravene an agreement with the union.

1 [1984] IRLR 385, EAT.

2 *Kelly v Upholstery and Cabinet Works (Amesbury) Ltd* [1977] IRLR 91, EAT.

3 *Williams v Compair Maxam Ltd* [1982] ICR 156, [1982] IRLR 83, EAT.

4 *Atkinson v George Lindsay & Co* [1980] IRLR 196, Ct of Sess.

difficult for any tribunal to hold that in dismissing the particular individual, his employers acted unreasonably in the sense prescribed by [s 98(4)].'[5]

Underlying this view in part is the fact that where the parties have selected employees for dismissal in accordance with an agreed procedure, unless the procedure itself is unfair, it is reasonable for the employer to follow that procedure and it would be unreasonable for a tribunal to interpose other procedures than those which were agreed between management and unions.[6] Furthermore, the judiciary have indicated their awareness in redundancy selection cases that an employee has already received a redundancy payment.[7]

The basic test of selection as the EAT stated in *N C Watling & Co Ltd v Richardson* is the 'range of reasonable employer responses' test in which it has to be recognised that there are circumstances where more than one course of action may be reasonable.[8] This is essentially a non-interventionist standard applied by the judiciary.

However, as the EAT also pointed out, even under the range of the 'reasonable employer' test, there are at least two separate points upon which an employer's decision to dismiss can be found to be unreasonable. First, a tribunal would expect to be satisfied by an employer's evidence how the employee came to be dismissed, and who and what body, and in what circumstances, took the decision to dismiss him.[9] Clearly where an employer fails to come forward with evidence on the basis of selection and an indication of how the criteria were applied in practice, an industrial tribunal would be entitled to conclude that he acted unreasonably, assuming that the employee has raised a complaint about the selection process.[10]

Moreover, where an employer does come forward with some evidence on his criteria for selection and how they were applied, tribunals have on occasion asked management to indicate the factual basis for the criteria they applied. Thus in *Paine and Moore v Grundy (Teddington) Ltd*,[11] involving attendance records as a criteria, the EAT said:

'In general terms, if employers are going to rely upon what we will describe briefly as an "attendance record criterion" in redundancy cases, we think that it is desirable that they should seek to ascertain the reasons for the absences which made up the attendance record of the particular employees concerned and, for instance, if an employee happens still to be absent at the time that the redundancies have to be put into effect, that they should try to find out when that employee is likely to return to work. We think that

5 Ibid.
6 *Forman Construction Ltd v Kelly* [1977] IRLR 468, EAT.
7 *O'Hare v Rotaprint Ltd* [1980] ICR 94, [1980] IRLR 47, EAT.
8 [1978] ICR 1049, [1978] IRLR 255, EAT.
9 *Bristol Channel Ship Repairers Ltd v O'Keefe* [1977] 2 All ER 258, [1978] ICR 691.
10 *Cox v Wildt Mellor Bromley Ltd* [1978] ICR 736, [1978] IRLR 157.
11 [1981] IRLR 267, EAT.

> this is merely a particular application of the much more general principle of industrial relations that employers should do all that is reasonable to ensure that they have in their possession as full information as is reasonable about their employees and the relevant situation before coming to any decision, for instance, to dismiss on the grounds of redundancy.'[12]

Yet industrial tribunals have also been told that they must not impose too high a standard of proof upon the employer to show that his criteria have been met. Thus in *Buchanan v Tilcon Ltd*[13] an industrial tribunal insisted that the employers prove the accuracy of the information upon which they acted by providing direct evidence of the employee's relatively high absence rate. The EAT reversed this decision pointing out that where the employee's only complaint was that of unfair selection for redundancy and no other complaints were made, all the employers have to prove is that their method of selection was fair in general terms and that it was applied reasonably in the case of the employee. In doing so it was reasonable to call witnesses of reasonable seniority to explain the circumstances in which the dismissal was brought about. Once this had been done and there was no question of the manager acting unjustly and there was no reason to question the reliability of the company's information there was no need for him to prove the accuracy of the information by direct evidence.[14] Moreover, in *British Aerospace plc v Green*,[15] a large-scale redundancy of 530 employees, the Court of Appeal was unwilling to allow discovery of documents relating to employees other than those selected while the purpose was to determine whether there were any faults in selection. On the other hand, in *FDR Ltd v Holloway*,[16] the EAT was prepared to allow a discovery order of information of the eight employees not selected for redundancy, where there was an issue raised about the fairness of the selection because of the shorter service and poor record of one of the retained employees.

12 [1984] IRLR 385, EAT; cf *Boulton & Paul Ltd v Arnold* [1994] IRLR 532, EAT (where employer failed to distinguish between authorised and unauthorised absence); see too *MDH Ltd v Sussex* [1986] IRLR 123, EAT.

13 [1983] IRLR 417.

14 See too *Eaton v King* [1995] IRLR 75 (in which an industrial tribunal was revised by the EAT on appeal for finding an unfair redundancy dismissal where the marks of all employees were not given out and the manager who gave evidence before the industrial tribunal had not carried out the assessments and could not obtain discrepancies (reversed on other grounds by the CS *King v Eaton Ltd* [1996] IRLR 199.) *Clyde Pipeworks Ltd v Foster* [1978] IRLR 313, EAT.

15 [1995] IRLR 433, CA.

16 [1995] IRLR 400, EAT.

### *(d) Unreasonable criteria for selection*

Where the employer's criteria are manifestly unreasonable, industrial tribunals have a discretion to find a dismissal for redundancy unfair on that ground alone. For they can justify their decision on the basis that the employer's criteria were outside the range of criteria adopted by reasonable employers. For example, in *N C Watling & Co Ltd v Richardson*[17] the employer, an electrical contractor, had a largely unrestricted freedom who among the electricians to retain and who to let go when contracts expired. Nevertheless where the employer chose to retain an employee of only a half day's work over another employee of more than ten months' service claiming that the former was more suitable for deployment, the tribunal was entitled to decide that the employer's basis for selection was unreasonable. And in *Greig v Sir Alfred McAlpine & Son (Northern) Ltd* an industrial tribunal found a dismissal unfair because of a failure by the company to show that it used an objective system of assessment in selection. The method of selection including service, performance, and attendance was not made on the basis of company productivity records and the chargehand who applied the criteria testified that he had relied solely on management's skill and judgment.[18]

This principle was endorsed in *Williams v Compair Maxam Ltd*[19] in which an industrial tribunal had found it reasonable for the employer to select on the basis of one manager's view of which employees it would be best to retain in the interests of the company in the long run. The EAT overturned the tribunal's decision stating:

> 'The so-called criteria in this case lack any real objective element; the retention of those who, in the opinion of the managers concerned, would be able to keep the company viable. Such a criterion is entirely subjective and, as Mr Hennessy in his evidence accepted, was applied subjectively. The purpose of having, so far as possible, objective criteria is to ensure that redundancy is not used as a pretext for getting rid of employees who some manager wishes to get rid of for quite other reasons, eg for union activities or by reason of personal dislike. The danger of purely subjective selection is illustrated in this very case. It was common ground that the relations between Mr Hennessy and one of the applicants, Mr H Williams, were not good. Mr Hennessy accepted in evidence that he did not care for Mr H Williams and thought him a bit belligerent. They did not 'pass the time of day'. Except in cases where the criteria can be applied automatically (eg 'last in - first out'), in any selection for redundancy elements of personal judgment are bound to be required thereby involving the risk of judgment being clouded by personal animosity. Unless some objective criteria are

17 [1978] ICR 1049, [1978] IRLR 255, EAT.
18 [1979] IRLR 372, IT.
19 [1982] ICR 156, [1982] IRLR 83, EAT.

included, it is impossible to demonstrate to an employee like Mr H Williams who is not on good terms with the person making the selection that the choice was not determined by personal likes and dislikes alone: we would also have thought it was extremely difficult for an industrial tribunal to be satisfied on the point.

The majority of the industrial tribunal expressed surprise at the lack of established criteria for selection, but said that it was "a considerable factor" in their decision that even if criteria had been laid down the same result might have applied. This passage is the one which gives rise to doubt whether the majority did not misdirect itself in law. The industrial tribunal had to be satisfied that the applicants before them had been fairly selected: mere speculation as to whether they would have been selected had consultation taken place and criteria been agreed cannot constitute grounds sufficient to "satisfy" the industrial tribunal as required by s 98(4).'

The EAT then recommended as a matter of good industrial relations practice that whether or not an agreement as to the criteria to be adopted has been negotiated with the union, the employer should seek to establish criteria for selection which so far as possible do not depend solely upon the opinion of the person making the selection but can be objectively checked against such things as attendance record, efficiency at the job, experience, or length of service. It also recommended that the employer should seek to ensure that the selection is made fairly in accordance with these criteria and consider any representations the union has to make as to such selection.

Of course, the recommendations of *Compair Maxam*[20] are themselves only guidelines to tribunal discretion. The evaluation of criteria for selection will be left to the discretion of the industrial tribunal. The extent to which they apply in a given case will depend upon the circumstances. For example in a case where management simply follow criteria established in an agreed redundancy procedure, the *Compair Maxam* guideline may not be appropriate.[1]

Further, it is clearly the case that purely objective criteria such as 'last in - first out' are not always required.[2] In the exercise of their discretion under s 98(4), tribunals have on occasion approved criteria of a subjective kind.[3]

Moreover, the tribunals do have discretion should they choose to exercise it, to apply a reasonable employer test to the criteria for selection

20 [1982] ICR 156, [1982] IRLR 83, EAT.
1 See eg *Mehmi v Sterling Metals Ltd* PA/501/83.
2 See eg *Corning Ltd v Stubbs* (1981) EAT 569/80: '. . . we do not think that the decision in *Bessenden Properties Ltd v Corness* establishes the proposition that in all circumstances without exception, length of service must be one of the criteria by which the selection for redundancy is judged'. See too *Rolls-Royce Motors Ltd v Dewhurst* [1985] ICR 869, [1985] IRLR 184, EAT.
3 See eg *Cruickshank v Hobbs* [1977] ICR 725, EAT.

and their application. This discretion has been exercised inter alia in cases concerning the scope of the unit of selection chosen by the employer.[4]

In *Thomas and Betts Manufacturing Co Ltd v Harding*[5] the EAT rejected the employer's argument that where a redundancy situation occurs in one section of a business, the employer when making his selection ought to consider only that section in which redundancies have been established and ought not to look to see whether a place can be found for the redundant employee in some other section of the business. There was no rule of law, said the EAT, which limits the area where an industrial tribunal may look or says where a reasonable employer ought reasonably to have looked. This was approved by the Court of Appeal, which said that s 59 does not operate to limit s 98(4), so that it could not be said that selection must be limited to employees doing the same kind of work or in positions similar to that of the employee claiming compensation.

### *Reasonable timing, economic necessity and s 98(4)*

A second substantive head upon which the reasonableness of an employer's decision to dismiss for redundancy has been attacked has been the justification for the redundancy, either in terms of its timing or its economic necessity. Thus some redundancies have been held to be unreasonably premature under s 98(4)[6] whereas others have been held to be unwarranted by the prevailing economic conditions.[7]

However, in *Moon v Homeworthy Furniture (Northern) Ltd*[8] the EAT called this line of decisions into question. In *Moon*'s case, the employer had decided to shut down the factory following a series of disputes with the trade unions. The applicant complained that the employer's decision to close the factory was unfair because the business was still economically viable. The tribunal was reluctant to apply s 98(4) to challenge the creation of a redundancy and stating the following. The EAT agreed:

> 'The employees . . . were and are seeking to use the industrial tribunal and the Employment Appeal Tribunal as a platform for the ventilation of an industrial dispute. The Appeal Tribunal is unanimously of the opinion that if that is what this matter is all about it must be stifled at birth . . . the decision of the industrial tribunal was right and there could not and cannot be any investigation into the rights and wrongs of the declared redundancy.'

4 See eg *Thomas and Betts Manufacturing Co Ltd v Harding* [1980] IRLR 255, CA; *Calvert v Allisons (Gravel Pits) Ltd* [1975] IRLR 71.

5 [1978] IRLR 213, EAT. But see *Barratt Construction Ltd v Dalrymple* [1984] IRLR 385, EAT; *Babar Indian Restaurant v Rawat* [1985] IRLR 57, EAT.

6 See eg *Costello v United Asphalt Co Ltd* [1975] IRLR 194; *Tomson v Fraser Pearce Ltd* [1975] IRLR 54; *Hammond-Scott v Elizabeth Arden Ltd* [1976] IRLR 166.

7 See eg *Allwood v William Hill (North East)* [1974] IRLR 258.

8 [1977] ICR 117, [1976] IRLR 298 at 299.

This view was reaffirmed by the Court of Appeal in *James W Cook & Co (Wivenhoe) Ltd v Tipper*[9] where it stated that:

> 'it was not open to the court to investigate the commercial and economic reasons which prompted the closure. It may be that the court should have this power, but it does not have [it] at present.'

While industrial tribunals are not allowed to second-guess the employer's commercial judgment, particularly in the case of closures, they do retain the power to ensure that the employer acts reasonably regarding the financial position of the company as warranting redundancy. Thus in *Orr v Vaughan*[10] where an employer accepted the recommendation of a bookkeeper without further examination of the evidence, the EAT agreed with the tribunal's decision that the employer acted unreasonably in deciding to close down a beauty salon without a reasonable investigation of the available information. And in *Ladbroke Courage Holidays Ltd v Asten*[11] the employer's failure to provide evidence of economic necessity, including evidence of profits and losses, was a factor in the finding of unfair redundancy.

9 [1990] ICR 716, [1990] IRLR 386.
10 [1981] IRLR 63, EAT.
11 [1981] IRLR 59, EAT.

CHAPTER 11

# Reorganisation in the context of takeovers and transfers[1]

Takeovers and mergers, regardless of their legal form, normally involve a change in management structure and the introduction of a new management team to run the employing organisation. However, under UK law it is the legal form of the takeover which determines whether or not a change is viewed in legal terms as a change of employer.

At common law, where a takeover takes the form of a purchase of shares there is no change in the legal identity of the employer. The new management group step into the shoes of their predecessors much as if there had been an internal succession.

Where, however, the takeover takes the form of a sale or transfer of the business as a going concern, that is to say where the purchaser buys the assets *and goodwill* of the company outright, and assumes management, there is a break in continuity at common law. The employment contract is terminated. At this point there is applied 'the fundamental principle of common law that a free citizen in the exercise of his freedom is entitled to choose the employer whom he promised to serve, so that this right to his services cannot be transferred from one employer to another without his assent.'[2]

Statute law intervenes to alter the common law rule in two respects. First, the Employment Rights Act 1996 preserves continuity of employment for the purposes of eligibility for statutory employment protection[3] as well as for the purpose of calculating a redundancy payment.[4]

1 See McMullen *Business Transfers and Employee Rights* (2nd edn, 1992) for a comprehensive study of the subject.
2 *Nokes v Doncaster Amalgamated Collieries Ltd* [1940] AC 1014, [1940] 3 All ER 549, HL.
3 ERA, ss 210-219. See discussion, Ch 7.
4 ERA, s 162. See Ch 10.

Second, in the case of a 'relevant transfer', that is a transfer[5] of an undertaking[6] as a going concern and not merely a sale of the assets,[7] the Transfer of Undertakings (Protection of Employment) Regulations 1981, provide that employees' contracts which would otherwise have been terminated by the sale of the business at common law instead undergo a statutory novation and become contracts of employment with the new employer.[8]

The intention of the regulation, as well as the directive which it implements (Acquired Rights Directive EEC Council Directive No 77/187 EEC No 77/187), is to provide the safeguard to the employees of the transferor firm that they may enter into their relationship with the transferee employer with all or almost all their individual and collective rights, powers, duties and obligations vis-à-vis their former employer, in place.[9]

## WHAT IS A RELEVANT TRANSFER?

The directive is meant to apply to a wide variety of transfers including those between non-commercial ventures[10] and those involving the initial contracting out of services or part of an operation from one employer (public or private) to another,[11] as long as the business has retained its identity and the operation is continued.[12]

It does not matter that the transferor retains ownership of the assets used, or that the service is performed exclusively for the transferor, or that the service is performed for a fixed fee and hence the contractor's risk of loss

5 In deciding as a question of fact whether or not there is a business transfer, the facts as looked at are: has there been a transfer of goodwill, an acquisite of customers, work in progress along with physical assets? A transfer is not restricted to a sale, it can include a transfer of a lease or other disposition (*P Bork International A/S v Foreningen af Arbejdsledere i Danmark*: 101/87 [1990] 3 CMLR 701, [1989] IRLR 41, ECJ). *Lands-organisationen i Danmark v Ny Molle Kro*: 287/86 [1989] ICR 330, [1989] IRLR 37, ECJ; *Foreningen af Arbejdsledere i Danmark v Daddy's Dance Hall A/S*: 324/86 [1988] ECR 739, [1988] IRLR 315, ECJ. It can also extend to a series of two or more transactions between the parties, reg 3(4).

6 The undertaking does not have to be a commercial venture (reg 2 as amended by the 1993 Act).

7 *Kenmir Ltd v Frizzell* [1968] 1 All ER 414, [1968] ITR 159, DC; *Lloyd v Brassey* [1969] 2 QB 98, [1969] 1 All ER 382, CA; *Melon v Hector Powe Ltd* [1981] ICR 43, [1980] IRLR 477, HL; *Woodhouse v Peter Brotherhood Ltd* [1972] 1 All ER 1047, [1972] ICR 186; *Premier Motors (Medway) Ltd v Total Oil Great Britain Ltd* [1984] ICR 58, [1983] IRLR 471, EAT.

8 But see now *Katsikas v Konstantinidis*: C-132/91 [1993] IRLR 179, ECJ.

9 See eg *Wendelboe v LJ Music ApS*: 19/83 [1985] ECR 457, [1986] 1 CMLR 476, ECJ.

10 See eg *Dr Sophie Redmond Stichting v Bartol*: C-29/91 [1992] IRLR 366, ECJ.

11 *Rask and Christensen v ISS Kantine service AS*: C-209/91 [1993] IRLR 133, ECJ.

12 Ibid.

is nil as long as a stable economic operation continues. In *Schmidt*,[13] a case of a 'first generation' contracting out of a cleaning contract, the ECJ held that for the directive to be applicable, the transfer must relate to a 'stable economic entity' and a transfer of assets was not necessary where a specific activity of the transferor, performed by a dedicated employee, had been taken over by the transferee.[14] In *Suzen*,[15] however, a 'second generation' case, the ECJ made it plain that while a transfer of assets may not be essential, because it is normally only one of a number of factors which must be assessed to determine whether the conditions for a transfer of an 'entity' are met,[16] if there is no transfer of assets and the activity is labour intensive,[17] a further factor to be taken into account is whether or not a 'major part of the employees' were taken over by the transferee employer. The concept of an 'entity' refers to an organised grouping of persons and assets facilitating an activity[18] and could not be reduced merely to an activity consisting of a mere service contract by itself.[19] Shortly afterwards, in *Brintel*[20], a case where a contract for a helicopter service was lost by Brintel to KLM, no Brintel personnel were hired, KLM supplied their own helicopters and the only assets transferred were the landing rights on the oil platforms and airstrips, the Court of Appeal held that there could be no relevant transfer. Following the ECJ's clarification of the law in *Suzen*, the Court of Appeal said that the test must distinguish between two situations: (i) labour-intensive operations which, if they continue with substantially the same staff after the transfer, allow a court to conclude that the operation has retained its identity; and (ii) other types of operation in which the *Spijkers*[1] multi-factor test applies.

In *ECM Vehicles (Delivery Service) Ltd v Cox*,[2] however, the EAT was prepared to find that where an undertaking with an identifiable operation consisting of a delivery service, consisting of 19 dedicated drivers and a few administrative staff lost its contract to a second employer, the operation could transfer even if the employer did not take on any of the workforce of the transferor employer, particularly where the transferee employer's

13 *Schmidt v Spar - und Leihkasse der fruheren Amter Bordesholm, Kiel und Cronshagen* [1994] IRLR 302, ECJ.

14 Reg 3(4)(b) now provides that a transfer of an undertaking or part of one may take place whether or not any property is transferred to the transferee by the transferor.

15 *Suzen v Zehnacker Gebaudereinigung Gmbh Krankenhausservice* [1997] IRLR 255, ECJ; see *Davies* [1997] ILJ 190.

16 For the full list see eg *Spijkers v Gebroeders Benedik Abatoir CV* [1986] ECR 1119, ECJ.

17 Or transfer of use of assets.

18 An activity cannot be limited to a single works contract (para 13).

19 The ECJ cited to *Rygaard* [1996] IRLR 51, ECJ.

20 [1997 IRLR 361.

1 [1986] ECR 1119, EAT.

2 [1998] IRLR 416, EAT.

motives were to avoid the effects of the transfer regulation. The EAT reasoned that the key point in the *Suzen* decision was that Suzen was an employee of the contract cleaner which had the cleaning contract with the local authority and was not an employee dedicated to that operation.

The case law is thus not altogether clear on the relationship between contracting-out and transfers and awaits further judicial or legislative clarification.[3] In principle, however, the test of a relevant transfer should apply at the time of the transfer and not be dependent upon the employer's discretion afterwards.

At all events, if the transfer meets the test of maintaining the 'entity' or identifiable operation test, it does not matter whether it is a first or a second generation contracting out of an activity. There is no need under the Directive for there to be a direct contractual relationship between the transferor and the transferee; the transfer may take place in two stages through the intermediary of a third party such as the owner or a person putting up the capital.[4]

Reg 3(4)(a) as amended provides that a transfer of an undertaking or part of one may be 'effected by a series of two or more transactions.' This effectively legislates into British law the decision of the ECJ that the Directive also applies to operations which are interrupted by a change of employer and then resumed. For example in *Bork*[5] a factory lease was terminated and all workers were dismissed. The purchasers of the freehold undertaking took on more than half the previous employees without any negotiations with the original employers. The ECJ held that this was nevertheless a transfer in the meaning of the directive from the lessee to the new freehold owner.

Moreover, where an employer awards a contract of an operation to a second contractor having terminated the contract with the first contractor, and the employees of the operation are hired by the second contractor, the transfer is one to which the Directive applies. This is so because *the operation* though interrupted *has been resumed.*[6]

3 The Commission has made proposals for amendments to the Aquired Rights Directive Com (94) 300 final.

4 *Suzen* [1997] IRLR 255 at para 12; see too *Merckx v Ford Motors Co Belgium SA* [1996] IRLR 467, ECJ.

5 *P Bork International A/S v Foreningen af Arbejdsledere i Danmark*: 101/87 [1988] ECR 3057, [1989] IRLR 41, ECJ; see too *Daddy's Dance Hall*: 324/86 [1988] IRLR 315, ECJ (where the grant of a second lease by lessor was held to be in effect a transfer from the first lessee to second lessee).

6 See *Rask* op cit; *Ny Molle Kro*: 287/86 [1989] ICR 330 where the termination of a tavern lease by the landlord in the slack season and the resumption of the tavern business by him at a later date was held to be a transfer between the lessee and the landlord. See too *Kenny v South Manchester College* [1993] IRLR 265, EAT.

## WHAT IS THE EFFECT OF A 'TRANSFER'?

As reg 5(1) states:

> 'A relevant transfer shall not operate so as to terminate the contract of employment of any person employed by the transferor . . . but any such contract . . . shall have effect after the transfer as if originally made between the person so employed and the transferee.'

Regulation 5(1) incorporates the principle of the automatic transfer of employment contracts. The transfer occurs whether or not the employer complies with the formalities.[7]

At the individual level, reg 5(2)(a) ensures that 'all the transferor's rights, powers, duties and liabilities *under or in connection with any such contract* shall be transferred . . . to the transferee'. This means that, assuming a relevant transfer of the business, the transferee employer is required to take on all contractual obligations, apart from those rights under an occupational pension scheme (reg 7).[8] Moreover, where statutory obligations arise in connection with the contract, such as unfair dismissal, redundancy, national insurance, and liabilities for negligence, these too are transferred under reg 5(2).[9]

At the collective level, reg 6 of the Transfer Regulations provide that the collective agreement made by the transferring employer in respect of any employer whose contract has been preserved by reg 5 shall continue to have effect as between the trade union and the transferred employee. Regulation 9 provides that recognition of the trade union is transferred from the transferor to the transferee.[10] Finally, regs 10 and 11 place certain obligations upon the transferring employer to inform to and consult with recognised trade union representatives in respect of the transfer. Under reg 10 the obligation to consult has been amended by TURER to extend to a duty to consult with a view to reaching agreement. This at the very least requires the employer to go beyond the mere disclosure of information and may require some evidence of attempting to reach a consensus or

7 See *Rotsart de Hertaing v J Benoitt SA* [1997] IRLR 127, ECJ.

8 Reg 7 has been amended by TURER 1993, s 33 which narrows the pension exception so that it applies only to those provisions of occupational schemes which relate only to old age, invalidity and survivor's benefits (reg 7(1) and (2)). See *Adams v Lancashire County Council and BET Catering Services Ltd* [1997] IRLR 436, CA (transferee employers are not obliged to provide comparable occupation schemes to employees who transfer but must protect accrued pension rights in respect of periods of service occurring prior to the transfer).

9 Certain liabilities, such as criminal liabilities (rule 5(4)), vicarious liability to third parties and liability for a failure to consult with trade unions over redundancies, are cut off by the transfer.

10 This is not now legally binding but may become so if the Labour Government enacts its proposals to introduce a legal recognition procedure in 'Fairness at Work'.

compromise. Reg 11 has been changed to provide slightly stiffer penalties.[11] The maximum penalty for non-compliance has been increased from two weeks' to four weeks' pay for each employee and there are no deductions permitted for any compensation paid to employees for a failure to consult on redundancies.[12]

Furthermore, reg 6 provides specifically for the transfer of the collective rights of employees where there is in existence a collective agreement. Since collective agreements are not normally legally enforceable in the UK, however, the only rights under collective agreements that will be preserved are those which can be incorporated in individual contracts and transferred under reg 5(2). If the term of a collective agreement is incorporated into the contract of employment then it can continue as an obligation of the transferee employer even if he or she derecognises the union and withdraws from the collective agreement.[13]

## WORKFORCE REORGANISATIONS AND TUPE

As part of its safeguard of the contractual position, the Transfer Regulations also regulate attempts at workforce reorganisation both before and after the transfer. Thus they provide that the purchasing employer cannot escape liability by insisting as a condition of the transfer that the selling employer restructure the workforce to his design prior to the transfer.

Regulation 5(2)(b) provides that anything done before the transfer is completed by or in relation to the transferor in respect of that contract or a person employed in that undertaking or part shall be deemed to have been done by or in relation to the transferee. The main safeguard underlying the rule in reg 5(2)(b) is found in reg 8(1) which provides that where either *before or after* a relevant transfer any employee of the transferor or transferee is dismissed, the employee shall be treated as automatically unfairly dismissed if the transfer or a reason connected with it is the reason or principal reason for his dismissal. Consequently if a transferee employer insists as a condition of the transfer that the transferor employer dismisses employees prior to the transfer, the transferee employer will normally be held responsible for the dismissal.

Regulation 5(3) provides that a person employed in an undertaking for the purposes of reg 5(1) and 5(2) is 'a person so employed *immediately before* the transfer . . .' At one point, the regulation was interpreted to mean that employees dismissed before the transfer were the responsibility of the transferor employer. The Court of Appeal in *Secretary of State for*

11 See amendment introduced by s 33 of TURER.
12 Ibid.
13 See *Whent v Cartlidge* [1997] IRLR 153, EAT; see Ch 5.

*Employment v Spence*[14] decided that this regulation should be interpreted literally to mean those employed at the moment of transfer. Hence in *Spence*, where employees were dismissed three hours before the sale of the business, the employees' rights were not transferred to the transferee employer, but remained with the transferor employer who had become insolvent.

The Court of Appeal chose not to interpret the regulation purposively in the light of Article 3(1) of the Acquired Rights Directive which provides that:

> 'The transferor's rights and obligations arising from a contract of employment or from an employment relationship existing *on the date* of a transfer within the meaning of Article 1(1) shall by reason of such transfer be transferred to the transferee.' (emphasis added)

Instead, the court interpreted this to mean that as long as the employees are not employed in the undertaking at the time of the transfer, they are not within the scope of protection envisaged by the directive. They were fortified in this view by the opinions of Advocate-General Sir Gordon Slynn in several ECJ decisions.[15]

However, in *Litster v Forth Dry Dock and Engineering Co Ltd*[16] the House of Lords made it clear that this was a misinterpretation of the purpose of the EC directive upon which the Regulations were based. The directive clearly indicated that the Council of Ministers had directed that on a relevant transfer the benefit and burden of contracts of employment should devolve upon the transferee employer and that the transfer should not itself be grounds for dismissal. The 1981 Regulations approved for the purpose of implementing the directive had not achieved this because they provided only that the rights and liabilities of employees employed in the undertaking immediately before the transfer were transferred (reg 5(3)). Since the regulations failed to give effect to the directive and since UK courts were under a duty to give a purposive construction to such regulations, the regulations were to be read as if they applied to employees employed immediately before the transfer *or those who would have been* employed had they not been unfairly dismissed by the transferor before the transfer for a reason connected with the transfer.[17]

As a consequence, where an employee is dismissed for a reason connected with the transfer whether by the transferee employer after the transfer or by the transferor before the transfer, then under reg 8(1) the

14 [1987] QB 179, [1986] 3 All ER 616, CA.
15 Eg *Wendelboe v L J Music Ap S*: 19/83 [1985] ECR 457, [1986] 1 CMLR 476, ECJ; *Mikkelsen v Danmols Inventar A/S*: 105/84 [1985] ECR 2639, [1986] 1 CMLR 316, ECJ.
16 [1989] ICR 341, [1989] IRLR 161, HL.
17 Ibid.

contracts continue and the transferee employer will be responsible for the automatically unfair dismissal.[18] Where, however, an employee is dismissed for a reason not linked to the transfer, such as a dismissal for capacity or conduct or redundancy then it will escape the automatic unfairness rule of reg 8(1) but it may fit within reg 8(2), which provides that where an employee is dismissed, whether before or after the transfer, for an 'economic, technical or organisational' reason entailing changes in the workforce there is no automatic unfairness. Instead, the employer can justify it as having been for a substantial reason for dismissing that employee from the position which that employee held. In order for the dismissal to fall within reg 8(2), however, the employer must be able to show that the reason for the dismissal fits within the definition of an economic, technical or organisational reason, eg redundancy or reorganisation.[19] If the reason is an economic one, it must, on the balance of authority, be related to the actual conduct of the business, eg redundancy and not merely a precondition of the sale insisted upon by the purchaser.[20]

Moreover, the employer must be able to show that the reason involved *a change in the workforce*. For example in *Berriman v Delabole Slate Ltd*[1] the company gave the employee an ultimatum to accept a reduced rate of pay because it wished to standardise rates of pay between new and existing employees.

The Court of Appeal held that Mr Berriman's resignation in response to the ultimatum was a constructive dismissal and automatically unfair under reg 8(1). The employer's argument that the dismissal was a reg 8(2) reason could not be accepted because a change in rates of pay by itself was not a change in the workforce. To be a reason entailing a change in the workforce, the Court stated there must be a change either in the 'overall numbers or the functions of the employees looked at as a whole . . .' The Court's view was that the word 'workforce' denotes the whole body of employees as an entity - its 'strength' or 'establishment'. So that if one employee is dismissed and another is engaged in his place, there is no change in the workforce.

On the other hand, if there is a change in the functions of the employees, that is to say in the jobs that they do, that could be a 'change in the

18 See *Wilson v St Helens Borough Council*; *Meade v British Fuels* [1997] IRLR 505, CA.

19 See eg *Gorictree Ltd v Jenkinson* [1985] ICR 51, [1984] IRLR 391, EAT; *Anderson v Dalkeith Engineering Ltd* [1985] ICR 66, [1984] IRLR 429 EAT.

20 See *Wilson v St Helens Borough Council*; *Meade & Baxendale v British Fuels Ltd* [1997] IRLR 505, CA. (Where it was held that the employers had effectively varied the terms and conditions of employees following a transfer when they had dismissed and offered the new terms for an ETO.) *Wheeler v John Golding Group of Companies Ltd* [1987] IRLR 211, EAT; *Gateway Hotels Ltd v Stewart* [1988] IRLR 287, EAT; but see *Anderson* (above).

1 [1985] ICR 546, [1985] IRLR 305, CA.

workforce' even if there is no change in the identity or total number of the workforce. For example in *Crawford v Swinton Insurance Brokers Ltd*[2] a clerk-typist was ordered by the transferee employer to change to a job as an insurance salesman. This was a change in the workforce in the meaning of reg 8(2) because there was one less clerk typist and one more insurance salesman. As long as the reason for dismissal falls within reg 8(2), it is not automatically unfair nor is it automatically fair. Instead it is deemed to be for some other substantial reason under s 98(1) and then subjected to the same test of 'reasonableness' under ERA, s 98(4)[3] as is applied to dismissals for either redundancy[4] or reorganisation.[5]

Where a dismissal, whether intentional or constructive, falls outside reg 8(2), it can be automatically unfair under reg 8(1). This would apply to any change in terms and conditions caused by a reorganisation including 'a substantial change in working conditions to the detriment of the employee' (reg 5(5)) which fell short of changing the job content or ending the job of the employee.

The effect of the transfer regulations is that a reorganisation of new terms which does not produce a change in the workforce will, if it results in a constructive dismissal, also result in unfair dismissal compensation for employees who refuse to accept it. This means that after a transfer it is legally more difficult to reorganise terms and conditions than in a take-over based on a transfer of shares - or in reorganisation in a situation of continuous employment. As the Court of Appeal in *Berriman* pointed out:

> 'It was far from clear that there was a clear statutory intention to ensure that a transferee company can insist on equating the terms and conditions of the employees of the transfer undertaking to those of its existing employees notwithstanding that such alteration may constitute a detriment to the transferred employees. The purpose of the EEC Directive which required the Regulations was "the safeguarding of employees' rights in the event of transfers" and among the most crucial rights of employees are their existing terms of service.'[6]

The regulation's concern to safeguard existing employee rights in the event of a transfer, however, is not without an accompanying commercial motive; it facilitates such transfers by providing a clear disposition of employee rights as between transferor and transferee employer. Thus once the transfer is complete, the transferor employer has no further

2 [1990] ICR 85, [1990] IRLR 42, EAT.
3 Regulation 8(2)(b); see eg *McGrath v Rank Leisure Ltd* [1985] ICR 527, [1985] IRLR 323, EAT.
4 See Ch 9.
5 See Ch 11.
6 [1985] IRLR 305, CA.

responsibility to employees whatever subsequently happens under the new employer. As the ECJ stated in *Berg*:[7]

> 'After the date of the transfer and by virtue of the transfer alone, the transferor is discharged from all his obligations.'

This rule is sufficiently clear to provide the starting point for negotiations between transferor and transferee employer over the terms of the transfer. However, the difficulties of harmonising the terms of employment of the newly transferred employees with those of existing employees are not easily resolved, and may actually deter transfers in extreme cases.

Contracting out of the protections is restricted by reg 12. Moreover, to avoid an unfair dismissal under reg 8(1) the harmonisation must involve a genuine change in the number or functions of the workforce, neither of which may have been originally intended by the transferee employer.

7 *Berg and Busschers v Besselsen*: 144, 145/87 [1989] 3 CMLR 817, [1989] IRLR 447, ECJ.

CHAPTER 12

# Management reorganisations and workers' rights: a summary of the current position

## INTRODUCTION

Management decisions to reorganise workforces in response to product market conditions, either by the introduction of new technology or owing to cost-cutting plans, often entail considerable changes in employees' terms and conditions of employment. In some cases employees actually benefit from such reorganisations, individually by being upgraded or generally by the improved position of the firm. There are also cases, however, where reorganisations result in de-skilling, downgrading and less favourable conditions for employees.[1] Conceptually, the issue is not dissimilar to redundancy. Reorganisations are designed to improve the position of the majority of the workforce and the company as a whole but this improvement occurs at the expense of a minority. Through no fault of their own, some employees must accept a worsening of terms and conditions even if they do not actually lose their job in the legal sense.

The introduction of new technology and other forms of workforce reorganisation is an issue specifically dealt with in collective agreements, often by provision for prior consultation and income protection for employees adversely affected by such change.[2] This reflects good managerial practice. To what extent does legislation promote it?

The current legislative structure, as a result of amendments introduced by TURER 1993, makes some provision for collective consultations prior to certain workforce reorganisations. Nevertheless, in the UK, unlike other member states in the EEC,[3] in many cases the issue is left to be dealt with at the margins of existing employment protection statutes and within the framework of the contract of employment.

1 See eg Labour Research Department/Bargaining Reports, September/October 1982.
2 Ibid.
3 *ILO Worker Participation in Decisions within Undertakings* (1981).

Let us review the current legal structure to remind ourselves precisely how workforce reorganisations are dealt with under UK law. Such an examination, we shall see, throws considerable light on the balance struck by existing legal rights and duties between autonomy for management decisions and the protection of workers' rights.

## (i) The new collective legal framework for change

In the case of management reorganisations of whatever type which produce dismissals the direct legislative support to trade unions as employee representatives is provided by two specific statutes.[4] The obligation placed upon employers to inform and consult with recognised trade unions over redundancies applies when it is proposed that an employee is to be dismissed as redundant (Ch 15). Since 1993, the definition of 'redundancy' requiring such consultation in s 195 of TULR (C)A has been widened by TURER 1993, s 34, to extend to all dismissals 'for a reason not related to the individual concerned or for a number of reasons all of which are not so related': in effect all economic dismissals. Moreover the obligation to consult has been redefined to require 'consultation with a view to reaching agreements and a failure by the employer to comply with the consultation requirement can result in a protective award for all employees affected. Finally, the employer must now consult specifically about ways of

'(a) avoiding the dismissals,
'(b) reducing the numbers of employees to be dismissed, and
'(c) mitigating the consequences of the dismissals.'[5]

Secondly, in the special case of a transfer of the business under the Transfer of Undertaking (Protection of Employment) Regulations 1981 consultation is required in respect of the transfer again 'with a view to seeking their agreement to measures to be taken.' Such cases are becoming an increasing proportion of workforce reorganisatons, with the wider definition of 'transfer' introduced by TURER 1993.[6]

As a consequence, within trade union sectors there may well now be in place a new 'collective' legal framework for the introduction of change, such as technological change, and consequent workforce reorganisation.[7]

4 In addition, s 1 of the Employment Act 1982 requires that companies employing more than 250 employees must include in company directors' reports to shareholders action taken 'to introduce, maintain or develop arrangements' aimed at promoting various forms of 'employee involvement'. However, this is a reporting provision only; it does not require companies to adopt any particular form of involvement or consultation.

5 See TULR(C) A 1992, ss 188-90, amended by TURER 1993, s 34.

6 See Ch 10.

7 However, see too the development of 'derecognition' reorganisations, Ch 15.

It remains to be seen how this new legislative framework will be applied by trade unions, other employee representatives and employers in practice. At all events, it is only one tier of the law of workforce reorganisations. Accompanying it is an extensive body of individual employment law which is relevant, ie the law of the employment contract, redundancy payments and unfair dismissal.

## (ii) Individual employment contracts and work reorganisations

Management decisions to introduce technological change and change in pay or hours are legally assessed by the effect of those decisions upon the individual employee's contractual terms and conditions of employment. If the employer has contractual authority for the change then, in legal terms, the employee is in no position to refuse it.[8] Subject to the limits of the implied term of trust and confidence,[9] and a possible health and safety objection[10] the employer may insist upon the change even to the point of dismissal for refusal to accept it. On the other hand, if the change lies outside the contractual authority of the employer an insistence upon the change by the employer would constitute a breach of contract entitling the employee either to sue in the ordinary courts for breach of contract or to resign and claim constructive dismissal.[11]

### *Contractual authority for a change: flexibility and mobility terms*

As we have seen in Chapters 3 and 4, however, the line between contractual authority and non-contractual insistence is not altogether clear. In the first place, the employer may have reserved a contractual discretion to introduce changes in hours, work or place of work through the use of express flexibility clauses. Second, there is the possibility that a degree of flexibility may be *implied* into an employee's contract of employment providing contractual authority for the reorganisation.

For example, in *Cresswell v Board of Inland Revenue*[12] a group of tax officers brought an action against the Inland Revenue for refusing to pay them unless they worked a new computerised system for administering PAYE. They were told that the employer had not broken the contract since there was an implied contractual duty on the part of employees to adapt

8 If the policy change is introduced for a legitimate purpose eg a no smoking policy, and no implied term is breached, then the employer's act is not repudiatory: see *Dryden v Greater Glasgow Health Board* [1992] IRLR 469, EAT.
9 *United Bank Ltd v Akhtar* [1989] IRLR 507, EAT.
10 See s 100 of ERA 1996.
11 See eg *Alcan Extrusions v Yates* [1996] IRLR 327 noted 1997 ILJ 252.
12 [1984] ICR 508, [1984] IRLR 190.

themselves to new methods and techniques. The court held that as long as the job functions remained the same, ie tax officers working on the PAYE system, and it was simply a question of doing the same job in a different way, eg computerised information handling rather than manual information handling, the employer could require the employee to adapt to the new method. The court did add that, in a proper case, the employer might be required to provide training or re-training. It also set two outer limits to the employer's contractual discretion to change working conditions. First, the employer could not ask employee's to do work that they were not contractually employed to do. Thus, if an employee, under his or her contract, was employed as a specialised gas fitter he could not be asked to do general plumbing; if, on the other hand, he had been trained as a general plumber - even if he had worked as a specialist gas fitter for 25 years - he still could be asked to do general plumbing.[13] The second limit was that whilst employees must be expected to adapt to new methods and techniques introduced in the course of employment, where the new techniques involved the acquisition of such esoteric skills that it would not be reasonable to expect the employee to acquire them the employer must provide adequate training. Whether this point had been reached was a question of fact.[14]

The consequences of this judicial view that employers have implied contractual powers to unilaterally impose a change of working methods are profound. Not only is the employer entitled to deduct pay for resistance as in *Cresswell* but where employees choose to resign in the face of the employer's insistence, they may well fail in a claim of constructive dismissal.

In *Cresswell*'s case the employees were resisting the change as part of a campaign to insist that the new system should be covered by a collective agreement - eventually the Inland Revenue negotiated a wide-ranging collective agreement covering all staff and stressing methods of avoiding redundancies.

### Collective agreements and reorganisations

Even where collective agreements are in place they can only modify the individual contractual position to a limited extent; they do not necessarily have effect as legally binding terms.

As we have seen in Chapter 5, collective agreements are rarely, if ever, directly enforceable between unions and employers. On the other hand, if employees can show that the contents of a collective agreement have been incorporated into their contracts of employment, a change in working

13 See eg *Murphy v Epsom College* [1984] IRLR 271, CA.
14 See eg *MacPherson v London Borough of Lambeth* [1988] IRLR 470.

conditions which modifies collective arrangements could be a breach of their contracts of employment.[15]

Where a collective agreement provides that there should be collective consultation between employer and trade union representatives, such a collective provision is normally inappropriate for incorporation in the contract of employment because it is viewed as creating rights and obligations solely between the trade union and employer. Where the collective agreement provides for an individual right to consultation, however, there may be a ground for enforcement under the contract of employment though in such cases enforcement is not always assured.[16] Moreover, since the right is only procedural, the employee may obtain the interview but no substantively satisfactory result.

In cases where the employees enforce substantive rights,[17] as well, the victory may be short-lived. An employer is bound by collectively agreed pay rates or pay schemes only as long as the individual contract of employment remains in effect. If the employer terminates the employment contract upon giving due notice to the individual employee and offers a new contract on revised terms, the employee has no recourse in contract though there may be a claim of unfair dismissal and/or redundancy. How are such claims treated under redundancy and unfair dismissal law?

### (iii) Reorganisations and redundancy payments

In cases of technological reorganisation, if new contracts are issued, the claim for redundancy will only be successful if an employees' 'job' has disappeared, that is to say that the employer's requirements to do work of a particular kind have ceased or diminished. At one stage, the judges held in defining 'work of a particular kind', that the statutory language did not refer to the work the employee was actually doing, but to the way the employee's work was defined by the contract of employment. Hence if the employer had given the employee a wide job description or had included an express job flexibility clause in the employee's contract or there was an implied flexibility obligation in the contract, the courts would define the employees' 'work' to be the tasks which they could be required to perform under their contract of employment.[18]

15 *Robertson v British Gas Corpn* [1983] ICR 351, [1983] IRLR 302, CA. See Leighton [1983] ILJ 115; *Rigby v Ferodo Ltd* [1988] ICR 29, [1987] IRLR 516, HL; *Burdett-Coutts v Hertfordshire County Council* [1984] IRLR 91. See *Anderson v Pringle of Scotland* discussed in Ch 5.

16 *British Leyland UK Ltd v McQuilken* [1978] IRLR 245, EAT; see discussion in Ch 5.

17 See eg *Hughes v London Borough of Southwark* [1988] IRLR 55.

18 *Sutcliffe v Hawker Siddeley Aviation Ltd* [1973] ICR 560, [1973] IRLR 304; see discussion in Chs 3 and 4. The employer must actually rely upon the flexibility clause in a reorganisation. See eg *Curling v Securicor Ltd* [1992] IRLR 549, EAT.

In recent years, the courts have begun to view the statutory phrase rather more independently of its contractual foundation. 'Work of a particular kind' has been held to refer to work actually done and the contract's provision for further possibilities has been viewed as only a guideline.[18a]

On the other hand changes to the kind of work can be sufficient in scale to produce a change in the contractual nature of the work. For example in *Murphy v Epsom College*[19] a plumber, replaced by a heating engineer when a modern system of central heating was installed, was nevertheless held to be redundant under the Act because the nature of the work had changed. This result also presupposes that there has been no suitable alternative work offered which has been unreasonably refused.[20] Moreover, the change must occur in the kind of work; it is not enough simply to have a reorganisation of hours of work, however repudiatory of the original contractual arrangement.[1]

The net effect of these decisions is to create considerable scope for managerial reorganisations of terms and conditions of jobs which fall short of the technical definition of redundancy. As Lord Denning remarked in *Johnson's* case:

> 'an employer is entitled to reorganise his business so as to improve its efficiency and in so doing to propose to his staff a change in the terms and conditions of their employments: and to dispense with their services if they do not agree. Such a change does not automatically give the staff a right to redundancy payments. It only does so if the change in the terms and conditions is due to a redundancy situation.'[2]

One consequence of these legal decisions is that employees resigning because of the denial of their contractual expectations and their refusal to accept new terms may be constructively dismissed but may nevertheless be denied a redundancy payment because the reason for dismissal is not redundancy.

## (iv) Reorganisations and unfair dismissal

In cases of dismissals arising from reorganisations owing to new technology the main statutory safeguard for employees is the law of unfair dismissal.

18a See p 179 supra.
19 [1985] ICR 80, [1984] IRLR 271, CA.
20 See Ch 8; see also *Dacorum Borough Council v Eldridge and Townsend* 18.5.90 EAT 606/89 IRLIB 21.8.90.
1 *Johnson v Nottinghamshire Combined Police Authority* [1974] ICR 170, [1974] IRLR 20, CA.
2 [1974] ICR 170, [1974] IRLR 20, CA.

Where, in the course of a workforce reorganisation, an employer either unilaterally insists on a change in an employee's contractual terms and conditions and a constructive dismissal results, or uses the technique of dismissing employees with proper contractual notice, offering contracts on new terms, an employee has a potential claim for unfair dismissal. In such cases, employers often claim that the dismissal was for 'some other substantial reason' under ERA, s 98(1)(b) and that it was reasonable in the circumstances under ERA, s 98(4).

The EAT first gave its unreserved support to the notion that such dismissals could qualify as 'some other substantial reason' in *Ellis v Brighton Co-operative Society Ltd*.[3] In that case a reorganisation of the business which had been agreed with the trade union[4] involved a change in the working week of Mr Ellis, a foreman - from a basic work week of 48 hours, to one averaging 58 hours. Moreover, he was to assume more onerous duties. Contractually he had no obligation to go along with the new duties because, as a non-member of the union, he was not bound by the change. Nevertheless, the EAT considered that his refusal amounted to grounds for dismissal for 'some other substantial reason' and that the employers had acted reasonably in the circumstances.

At one point, in *Evans v Elemeta Holdings Ltd*, the EAT appeared to suggest that the test of reasonableness could be posed in terms of the reasonableness of the change from the employee's point of view. It stated:

> '. . . the question under s 98(4) is whether the employee's conduct was reasonable. But, as the industrial tribunal recognised, that question necessarily required the industrial tribunal to find whether it was reasonable for Mr Evans to decline the new terms of the contract. If it was reasonable for him to decline these terms, then obviously it would have been unreasonable for the employers to dismiss him for such refusal.'[5]

In *Chubb Fire Security Ltd v Harper*,[6] however, the EAT, Balcombe J presiding, reminded that the test under s 98(4) was essentially whether the employer acted reasonably in dismissing the employee for refusing to enter into the new contract and could not be examined solely from the employee's point of view. Then in *Richmond Precision Engineering Ltd v Pearce*,[7] the EAT held that while the test is whether the terms offered

3 [1976] IRLR 419, EAT.

4 See too *Catamaran Cruisers Ltd v Williams* [1994] IRLR 386, EAT (in which it was stressed that the trade union's and other employees' reactions to the changes were factors to be taken into account).

5 [1982] IRLR 143 at 145, EAT.

6 [1983] IRLR 311 at 313, EAT. See too *Catamaran Cruisers Ltd v Williams* [1994] IRLR 386, EAT

7 [1985] IRLR 179, EAT. See too *St John of God (Care Services) Ltd v Brooks* [1992] IRLR 546, EAT (in which the point was made that strictly speaking the test was the reasonableness of the employer's decision to dismiss in response to employee's refusal to accept the offer).

are ones which a reasonable employer would offer in the circumstances, to find an offer unreasonable a tribunal must be able to say that the offer was outside the range of offers that was reasonable in all the circumstances.

The range of reasonableness responses test gives considerable discretion to employers to reorganise terms and conditions of work without incurring the costs of an unfair dismissal. However, as we shall see, it does set certain limits, both procedural and substantive to the scope for employers to impose new and less attractive contractual terms upon employees as a consequence of a reorganisation.

## The business need for the reorganisation

What is clearly not part of the tribunals' remit under s 98(4) however, is to second-guess the business judgment of the employer.

In *Ellis* the EAT appeared to suggest that before an employer could reasonably impose a change in contractual terms as a result of a reorganisation there would have to be a finding that the reorganisation was prompted by business necessity. Indeed the standard applied by *Ellis* was that 'the reorganisation if not done would bring the business to a standstill'. However, in the *Hollister v National Farmers' Union* case the Court of Appeal made it clear that the standard implied by *Ellis* that the reorganisation if not done would 'bring the business to a standstill' was not a fixed and immutable requirement. It was enough for the tribunal to find that there was a sound, good business reason for the reorganisation.[8] And indeed, in subsequent cases, the EAT formulated this test in increasingly less stringent terms. In *Genower v Ealing, Hammersmith and Hounslow Area Health Authority*[9] it was: 'there would be some serious effect upon the business'. In *Bowater Containers Ltd v McCormack*, for example, it was enough that the reorganisation was 'beneficial to the running of the company'.[10] In *Banerjee v City and East London Area Health Authority*, moreover, it was sufficient to show that there were 'discernible advantages to the organisation'.[11] In these cases, the Court of Appeal and the Appeal Tribunal appeared to be moving towards a formulation that limited the role for industrial tribunals to examine the employer's motivation for the reorganisation under s 98(4).

There is, however, a need for the employer to show that there was *some* factual basis to his assertion that there was a need for the reorganisation; a belief however genuine will not be adequate if it is unaccompanied by

8 [1979] IRLR 238 at 280, CA.
9 [1980] IRLR 297, EAT.
10 [1980] IRLR 50, EAT
11 [1979] IRLR 147, EAT.

some evidence of the grounds for that belief. For example, in *Humphreys and Glasgow Ltd v Broom and Holt*,[12] the EAT upheld an industrial tribunal which found that an employer who increased working hours from 37 to 40 a week without an increase in pay and without compensation, arguing that there was a need to cut overheads had failed to show any evidence of the need. There was no indication of pressure from the parent company to reduce costs or improve losses; nor was there any other evidence of pressing financial need.[13]

Moreover, in *Ladbroke Courage Holidays Ltd v Asten*[14] the EAT indicated that an employer relying on business reorganisation as a reason for dismissal had to produce some evidence of the reorganisation as well as the need for economies. And in *Orr v Vaughan*[15] the EAT was willing to uphold an industrial tribunal that found that an employer had not made reasonable inquiry to ascertain the financial position.

However, this safeguard is a minimalist obligation for the employer. It does not provide a platform for tribunals to question the business judgment of the employer.

## Procedure and reorganisations

Reorganisation often calls for some form of collective consultation with employees as well as individual consultation prior to a decision to dismiss being taken. The House of Lords decision in *Polkey v A E Dayton Services Ltd*[16] suggests that the procedural aspects of any proposed reorganisation will be looked at quite closely. Certainly where the employer's procedure was outside the range of reasonable employer responses, a tribunal could find a reorganisation dismissal unfair on that ground. For example, a tribunal could decide that it was unreasonable for an employer to stop short at collective consultations with employee representatives without dealing directly with the employee as an individual, or that it was unreasonable for an employer in the course of consultation to omit to make an attempt to demonstrate to the employee the need for the reorganisation and answer the employee's representations, or that it was unreasonable for an employer not to use consultation to investigate whether or not it is possible to make

12 [1989] IRLIB 369, EAT.

13 If external pressure for change from insurers, creditors or customers, can be shown, there is still a need to show that the employer's response was reasonable. See eg *Dobie v Burns International Security Services UK Ltd* [1984] IRLR 329, CA.

14 [1981] IRLR 59; see also *Robinson v British Island Airways Ltd* [1978] ICR 304, [1977] IRLR 477 which talked of 'a genuine reorganisation' as a condition to s 91(1)(b) - but see discussion in Ch 4.

15 [1981] IRLR 63, EAT; but see too *Banerjee v City and East London Area Health Authority* [1979] IRLR 147, EAT.

16 [1988] AC 344, [1988] ICR 142, HL.

an exception for the employee rather than forcing him into a collective change without any such investigation.[17] For as we have seen, under s 98(4) the procedural element of the reasonableness test is viewed more in terms of assuring that the employer receives all relevant information than that fairness is observed for its own sake.

Thus where, as in *Humphreys and Glasgow Ltd*[18] the employers indicated that they did not engage in prior consultation because it was too difficult and lengthy, it was open to the industrial tribunal to find the failure to consult as outside the range of reasonable employer responses.

On the other hand, where, as in *Ellis v Brighton Co-operative Society Ltd*,[19] the employer had taken the precaution of agreeing the reorganisation with trade union representatives, this went a long way to establish the employer's reasonableness procedurally.

## Reasonable means

As we have seen, if the range of reasonable responses test allows employers a wide margin within which to take reorganisation decisions, the industrial tribunals are able to ask themselves, given the need for a reorganisation, was this particular reorganisation effected in a reasonable way?

In *Kent County Council v Gilham*,[20] for example, an industrial tribunal considered it extremely important in weighing the reasonableness of an employer's decision to dismiss an employee that the employer, a local authority, had broken a term of a collective agreement incorporated into the employee's contract of employment. Consequently even though the tribunal accepted the substantial reason for economies to be introduced, they were convinced that the decision to dismiss employees on the basis of abrogated agreements was unreasonable. As they put it:

> 'We do not propose to put forward our solution (that is to say what the county council could otherwise have done). We do not have one, but we do feel that reasonable councils could not act in this way. There is the matter of their word to an agreement and there are far greater implications, we have seen. We regret that they have approached matters by this means.'

On appeal it was argued that the tribunal had treated the issue of the collective agreement as a 'sacred cow', taking the position that any breach of the collective agreement was automatically unfair and rendered the dismissal in the circumstances unreasonable. The EAT, however, accepted

17 See also *Martin v Automobile Proprietary Ltd* [1979] IRLR 64, EAT.

18 [1989] IRLIB 369, EAT.

19 [1976] IRLR 419, EAT. See too *Catamaran Cruisers Ltd v Williams* [1994] IRLR 386, EAT.

20 [1983] IRLR 353, EAT.

that the industrial tribunal had acted within its jurisdiction balancing a number of factors in reaching its decision and had neither misdirected itself nor come to a perverse decision.

In *Evans v Elemeta Holdings Ltd*[1] an employer sought to change the provisions of his employee's contracts from voluntary overtime, paid at a higher rate after the first five hours to a position where all overtime was to be unrewarded by a premium and unlimited in extent except on Saturdays. Mr Evans refused to accept the new terms because the obligation to work compulsory unpaid overtime was so open-ended. The EAT overturned the industrial tribunal's finding of fair dismissal indicating that the industrial tribunal had to address itself more carefully to the question of the reasonableness of the change in terms introduced by the employer, especially the need for the employer to present some evidence of the need for the particular type of change in the contractual provisions. As the EAT put it:

> 'If it had been shown in this case that there was some immediate need for the employer to increase the overtime work or to require mandatory overtime as opposed to voluntary overtime, that might have fundamentally altered the position.'

This serves to remind that the net result of the range of reasonable employer responses test is to create a situation in which rights, including contractual rights for employees, can be set aside in order to satisfy the business needs of employers.

Not only external pressures,[2] but also the exercise of business judgment,[3] can be used to justify decreases in pay or the introduction of less advantageous terms. *Gilham*'s case[4] turned on a question of fact. Other tribunals dealing with the same set of facts have found the employer's decision to dismiss to be fair.

## CONCLUSIONS

Current judicial and legislative views of rights of employees in the course of reorganisation operate to undermine the protective purpose of the legislation and create insecurity for employees in respect of their job rights generally.

1 [1982] ICR 323, [1982] IRLR 143, EAT.
2 *Industrial Rubber Products v Gillon* [1977] IRLR 389, EAT. But see *Dobie v Burns International Security Services UK Ltd* [1984] IRLR 329, CA (the external pressure must be treated reasonably).
3 *MacPherson v London Borough of Lambeth* [1988] IRLR 470.
4 [1983] IRLR 353, EAT.

The underlying motivation for this interpretation of the statute has long been plain. In *RS Components Ltd v Irwin* the NIRC made it clear that they were concerned about the possibility that technical progress might be inhibited by employees' exercise of their legal rights. As the NIRC put it:

> 'It would be unfortunate for the development of industry if an employer was unable to meet such a situation without infringing or risking infringement of rights conferred by unfair dismissal provision.'[5]

However, this approach does not do justice to the point that some form of compensation for employees who suffer a reduction in contractual terms and benefits as a result of a reorganisation might help to facilitate such changes. In other words this form of 'social regulation' may be more effective managerially than 'deregulation', as well as being fairer to the employees concerned. A way forward might be to require payments for economic dismissal as defined in TULR(C)A s 195, as amended by TURER 1993 s 34. After all, the reduction in the terms and conditions of such individuals is the cost which provides the benefit for the remainder of employees and the firm.

It would have been possible to draft the statute to ensure that the contract and collective agreement established minimum rights for employees rather than allowing the statutory test of fairness to undermine contractual rights. However, this would have required a greater willingness to ensure that 'collective rights' were integrated into 'individual rights'.[6] It would have also meant subordinating the value of autonomy of managers to the value of protection of workers.

It is true that as a result of *Polkey* there is a fairly stiff requirement of procedural reasonableness for employers when reorganising their businesses. However, this requirement is expressed as a legal norm only in the form of an element of the 'some other substantial reason' test. There is a case, both from the point of view of spreading an enlightened employer approach to managing change and fairness to employees, to create a duty to inform and consult both individuals and their representatives in cases where changes are introduced to terms and conditions of employment. The recent amendments by TURER 1993 to the redundancy and transfer of undertaking consultation provisions appear to have taken the legal framework partly in that direction in terms of imposing a collective

5 [1974] 1 All ER 41, [1973] IRLR 239, NIRC.

6 See discussion in Anderman 'Labour Law in Sweden: A Comment' in Neal (ed), *Law and the Weaker Party* Vol I Professional Books, see too Wedderburn 'The Italian Workers' Statute: Some British Reflections' (1990) ILJ 154; Wedderburn 'Interrogability, Collective Agreements, and Community Law' (1992) ILJ 245. See now the treatment of collective agreements in the proposed enforcement procedure for legal recognition in 'Fairness at Work'.

information and consultation requirement for an increasingly wider range of reorganisations. This brings us closer to the legal models employed in other member states.

It also places the UK in a better position to conform to the requirements of the EC Directive on Works Councils, as well as those of the Fifth Company Law Directive and the European Company Statute, should the latter two one day be approved.[7]

To move to a wider statutory duty upon employers to consult before making changes in terms and conditions, however, may entail more than a simple statutory amendment. It requires a change in the structure of collective representation for employees. The system of 'single channel' collective representation which characterises the redundancy transfer of undertaking consultation provisions introduced in the 1970s[8] has to be reconciled with the EC structures which are employee-based rather than trade-union-based. These employee-based structures such as works councils do not preclude trade union representatives obtaining de facto control but they do require elections by all employees whether trade union members or not. In other words, the concept of social rights under EC law will involve not only a new legal regulation of managerial prerogative; it will also create a new legal framework for collective employee representation.[9]

7 See Docksey 'Information and Consultation of Employees' [1986] MLR 281; Wedderburn *The Social Charter, European Company and Employment Rights: An Outline Agenda* (1990) IER; Hall 'Beyond the EC Works Council Directive' [1992] BJIR 547.

8 See Ch 16.

9 See discussion in Ch 16.

# CHAPTER 13
# Sex discrimination

## LEGISLATION AGAINST DISCRIMINATION IN EMPLOYMENT

Sex discrimination has long been endemic in employment, yet discrimination legislation is of relatively recent origin. The Equal Pay Act was enacted in 1970 and came into effect in 1975; the Sex Discrimination Act was enacted in 1975. These laws have been amended frequently in the ensuing years, but there is little evidence that they have had a major impact on patterns of discrimination - sex discrimination and unequal pay persist.[1] Women continue to be disadvantaged in terms of disproportionately low representation in the better paid, higher status jobs and in the access routes to those jobs - education, vocational training and the hiring process.

To suppose that legislation by itself can end discrimination at work is a triumph of hope over experience. The reality is that there are limits to the extent to which legislation as such can alter the social structures underpinning features of working life. The real potential of labour legislation is more limited, ie to eliminate the more blatant acts of discrimination at work.[2] Any more radical change is dependent upon a basic change in social attitudes towards women's roles in the home and in the labour market.[3]

Nevertheless, it is possible for legislators to take a more or less robust view of the use of legislation to produce social change.

1 See eg J Martin and C Roberts *Women and Employment: A Lifetime Perspective* (1984) Ch 3; C Craig, E Garnsey and J Rubery *Payment Structures and Smaller Firms* DE Research Paper 48, 1985, p 99.

2 Much of this perspective applies equally to the Race Relations Act 1976, which has a similar definition of discrimination and remedies. There are differences in the definition of discrimination in the Disability Discrimination Act 1995.

3 B Chaplin and P Sloane *Tackling Discrimination at the Workplace* (1982) p 132; M Snell, P Glucklich and M Poval *Equal Pay and Opportunities* (1981) p 97.

Legislators respond to the social pressures to deal with the 'problems' of discrimination by producing legislation which creates rights for those who are targets of discrimination (a process which itself provides an initial reassurance to those individuals that something has been done).

One major issue raised by discrimination legislation is to what extent will it be used to redress the historic and current imbalance of advantage by giving preferential treatment to disadvantaged groups? Any effort to redress existing imbalance will inevitably create a disadvantage to those groups which currently enjoy the higher paid, higher status jobs. To what extent may such groups invoke the principle of equal treatment itself to limit preferential measures to redress historic imbalances? The argument is often made that to reconcile these two factors, anti-discrimination laws should be limited to removing the barriers to *access* and concentrate on creating equality of opportunity rather than extending to measures which operate to ensure equality of *outcome* or representation, such as quota systems.

This is true of anti-discrimination legislation generally. In the application of such legislation to employment, there is a further balance that must be struck: the trade off between reducing discrimination and increasing the limits to employer prerogatives and freedom of enterprise.

Thus, in shaping the content of the legislation, the concern of legislators is not to remove discrimination in employment at all costs. There is in their minds a trade-off between the desirability of helping women (say) to achieve greater equality of treatment and opportunity and the effect of social regulation on industry. A similar, but by no means identical, trade-off is apparent in the approach of the judiciary to the interpretation of the legislation; judges often tend to strike their own balance between the two different sets of values in this sphere. As Browne-Wilkinson J (as he then was) put it in *Steel*, 'the comparative importance of eliminating discriminatory practices on the one hand: as against, for example, the profitability of a business on the other.'[4]

A legal analysis of discrimination legislation therefore requires not only an understanding of the precise form of the legislation as the expression of legislative policy,[5] but also the experience of the process of judicial interpretation, and in particular the extent to which the judiciary have been willing to interpret legislation to intervene in managerial decisions in the interests of producing social change. The role of the judiciary cannot be regarded as one of passively providing a literal interpretation of legislation,

4 *Steel v Union of Post Office Workers* [1978] 2 All ER 504, [1977] IRLR 288, EAT.

5 In this field of employment law, unlike other employment protections such as unfair dismissals and redundancy, legislation is relatively free of contractual principles; apart from the remedies for acts of discrimination which are tort based, the statutory principles are free-standing owing less to common law principles than other forms of employment protection.

since legislation is almost always drafted using language which is capable of more than one interpretation.

In engaging in this study of legislative drafting and judicial interpretation of statute law, we have a ready-made basis of comparison between UK law and EC law. As we have seen, however, the point of studying EC law alongside UK law is not solely to compare styles and substantive decisions for the sake of showing contrasts; for UK law since 1972 has been *subject to* EC law.[6]

In *Shields v E Coomes (Holdings) Ltd*[7] the Court of Appeal stated that 'the Equal Pay Act and the Sex Discrimination Act formed two complementary parts of a single *comprehensive* code directed against sex discrimination'. However, the Equal Pay and Sex Discrimination Acts themselves must be interpreted to give effect to EC law directives as well as Article 119 of the Treaty.

Article 119, being sufficiently clear and precise, has been held to be directly applicable in the UK, constituting an independent source of legal rights to individuals against the discriminatory acts of public authorities[8] or private persons, including employers. It may be relied upon by a litigant before a national court in order to persuade that court to depart from any national legislation including provisions resulting from collective agreements.[9] Indeed the national court must apply the provisions of Community law in full, disapplying where necessary any contrary provision of national legislation without waiting for the removal of that provision by legislative means or by any other constitutional process.[10]

In contrast, Council directives are generally only directly applicable to public authorities (or organs of the state)[11] and not to private employers.[12] In the case of questions arising under the Equal Pay Directive this creates no difficulties since it is co-extensive with Article 119.[13] However, it does mean that the Equal Treatment Directive 76/207/EEC[14] is directly effective

6 European Communities Act 1972, s 2(4).

7 [1978] ICR 1159, [1978] IRLR 263, CA.

8 *Foster v British Gas plc*: C-188/89 [1991] ICR 84, [1990] IRLR 353, ECJ.

9 *Defrenne v SABENA*: 43/75 [1981] 1 All ER 122n, [1976] ECR 455; *Kowalska v Freie und Hansestadt Hamburg*: C-33/89 [1990] IRLR 447; *Nimz v Freie und Hansestadt Hamburg*: C-184/89 [1991] IRLR 222, ECJ.

10 *Simmenthal*: 106/77 [1978] ECR 629.

11 *Foster v British Gas plc* [1991] ICR 84, [1990] IRLR 353, ECJ.

12 *Marshall v Southampton and South West Hampshire Area Health Authority (Teaching)*: 152/84 [1986] ICR 335, [1986] IRLR 140.

13 See eg *Jenkins v Kingsgate (Clothing Productions) Ltd*: 96/80 [1981] ICR 592, [1981] IRLR 228, ECJ.

14 76/207/EEC and other directives, eg social security 79/7/EEC; occupational social security scheme 86/378/EEC.

in the UK only vertically, ie only against 'organs of the state' public authorities in the widest sense.[15]

In addition to direct effect, a directive can also be relied on 'indirectly' to interpret national law and, in particular, national provisions intended to implement the Community text.

As the ECJ stated, in *Von Colson*:[16]

> 'In applying national law and particularly those provisions of national law specially introduced to give effect to a Directive, the National Court is bound to interpret its national law in the light of the text and of the aim of the Directive to reach the result envisaged by Article 189(3) of the Treaty.'

In such a case, however, it must be 'possible' for the national courts to interpret the legislation in this way.

In *Duke v GEC Reliance Ltd* the House of Lords held that the Equal Treatment Directive could not be applied to the interpretation of the Sex Discrimination Act since that Act was not enacted to give effect to Community obligations.[17] In *Marleasing SA v La Comercial Internacional de Alimentacion SA*, however, the ECJ held that 'in applying national law, whether the national law pre-dates or post-dates the Directive, the national court interpreting the national law is obliged to do everything possible in view of the wording and objectives of the Directive to achieve the result laid down by it and thereby comply with Article 189(3) of the Treaty'.[18] In *Webb v EMO Air Cargo UK Ltd*,[19] as mentioned, the House of Lords accepted that the timing of the national legislation was no longer an issue under EC law. However it added two conditions: (i) that the purposive interpretation could be given without distorting the meaning of the domestic legislation, and (ii) it must be 'possible' to give the domestic law such an interpretation.

In the event, the relevant code of law regulating discrimination in the UK today consists of the domestic Equal Pay Act and the Sex Discrimination Act *read in the light of EC sources*. The scheme of this chapter is to examine the Sex Discrimination Act in the light of relevant EC law, illustrating how in fact EC law has already modified UK legislation

15 *Marshall v Southampton and South West Hampshire Area Health Authority (Teaching)*: 152/84 [1986] ICR 335, [1986] IRLR 140, ECJ.

16 *Von Colson*: 14/83 [1984] ECR 1891; see too *Murphy* 157/86 [1988] ICR 445, [1988] IRLR 267, *Officier van Justitie Kolpinghuis Nijmegen BV* [1987] ECR 3969.

17 [1988] ICR 339, [1988] IRLR 118, HL; see too *Finnegan v Clowney Youth Training Programme Ltd* [1990] ICR 462, [1990] IRLR 299, HL.

18 *Marleasing SA v La Comercial Internacional de Alimentacion SA*: C-106/89 [1990] ECR I-4135.

19 [1992] 4 All ER 929, [1993] IRLR 27, HL.

and assessing how further modifications could occur.[20] In the next chapter, we shall look at the Equal Pay Act in a similar way.

## THE SCOPE OF THE SEX DISCRIMINATION ACT

The Sex Discrimination Act establishes a wide-ranging prohibition of discrimination in employment and makes it available to a large group of workers. Not only are 'employees' covered, but also those employed under a contract for services, eg 'a contract personally to execute any work or labour' (SDA, s 82 ) and 'contract workers', working under a labour supply contract (SDA, s 9).[1] Furthermore, there is no requirement of a period of continuous service or minimum hours of work per week to qualify to bring a claim under the Act.

The prohibition against discrimination in the SDA applies to a wide range of specific decisions by the employer taken vicariously or personally[2] in relation to work. In the first place, the Act prohibits an employer from discriminating in the arrangements made for determining who shall be offered employment (SDA, s 6(1)(a); cf Art 3, para 1, ETD). This applies to the recruitment process[3] and the interview itself.[4] Moreover, both discriminatory advertising (SDA, s 38) and a discriminatory refusal to offer employment (SDA, s 6(1)(c)) are illegal. This applies to selection for new jobs consequent upon a reorganisation.[5] The Act also prohibits discriminatory decisions in respect of access to opportunities for promotion, transfer or training (SDA, s 6(2)(a); cf Art 4, ETD).[6]

In the case of training where there is evidence of under-representation of one sex in a particular type of work, the employer can place

20 See further: Fredman, *Women and the law* (1997, OUP). Ellis *European Community, Sex Equality Law* (1991), Preschal and Burrows *Gender Discrimination Law of the European Community* (1990); McCrudden *Women Employment and European Equality Law* (1987); Shaw 'European Community Judicial Method' [1990] ILJ 232.

1 See Ch 7, supra; but see *Mirror Group Newspapers Ltd v Gunning* [1986] ICR 145, [1986] IRLR 27, CA; (dominant purpose not to execute personal work); workers mainly working abroad are excluded, SDA, s 10(1); *Haughton v Olau Line (UK) Ltd* [1986] ICR 357, [1986] IRLR 465, CA; *Deria v General Council of British Shipping* [1986] ICR 172, [1986] IRLR 108, CA.

2 Moreover, employers are both personally and vicariously liable (SDA, s 41). Any other person who knowingly aids an act of discrimination is liable. There is an exclusion for household employers, but no longer for small employers, following the ECJ decision that the small firm exemption contravened the Equal Treatment Directive 76/207 EEC.

3 See eg *Brennan v JH Dewhurst Ltd* [1984] ICR 52, [1983] IRLR 357.

4 *Saunders v Richmond-upon-Thames London Borough Council* [1978] ICR 75, [1977] IRLR 362, EAT; *Simon v Brimham Associates* [1987] ICR 596, [1987] IRLR 307, CA.

5 *Timex Corpn v Hodgson* [1982] ICR 63, [1981] IRLR 530, EAT.

6 *Watches of Switzerland v Savell* [1983] IRLR 141, EAT; *Perera v Civil Service Commission (No 2)* [1983] ICR 428, CA.

advertisements or otherwise encourage individuals of one sex to apply for jobs. He may also provide employees of one sex only with training facilities without being discriminatory. Otherwise the Act, however, does not adopt 'positive action' in the sense of allowing employers to compensate for past discrimination by positive discrimination in selection at job interviews, setting out minimum quotas for one sex or guaranteeing jobs at the end of special course.[7]

The Act makes it illegal for employers to discriminate in respect of access to benefits, facilities and services (SDA, s 6(6)). The Act also makes discriminatory dismissals unlawful[8] as well as other detriments such as sexual harassment.[9] In both cases there is an overlap with the unfair dismissals provisions of the EPCA.

Section 6 of the SDA 1986, as amended by TURER 1993 s 32, gives persons a right to have discriminatory terms of collective agreements and employer's rules declared void.[10]

Finally, the Act gives a separate right to workers to complain of unfair treatment as a consequence of bringing proceedings or giving evidence or information in connection with proceedings brought under the Act.[11]

The main omissions in the Sex Discrimination Act are:[12]

(i) contractual *money* benefits for employees (these are left to be regulated by the Equal Pay Act);
(ii) genuine occupational qualifications;[13]
(iii) provisions in respect of death and retirement;[14]
(iv) pregnancy.[15]

7 See McCrudden, 'Rethinking Positive Action' [1986] ILJ 219; McCrudden (ed) *Women, Employment and European Equality Law* (1987); see also Lewis 'Genuine Occupational Qualifications and Reverse Discrimination' [1991] ILJ 67.

8 *Webb v EMO Air Cargo (UK) Ltd* [1993] IRLR 27, HL, Art 5, para 1, ETD 'working condition' including dismissals.

9 See eg *Bracebridge Engineering Ltd v Darby* [1990] IRLR 3, EAT.

10 See Fitzpatrick B 'The Sex Discrimination Act' [1986] MLR 934.

11 SDA, s 4.

12 In addition, acts chosen under a statutory authority and certain groups of workers such as police and ministers of religion, SDA, s 51; *Hampson v Department of Education and Science* [1990] ICR 511, [1990] IRLR 302, HL; *General Medical Council v Goba* [1988] ICR 885, [1988] IRLR 425, EAT; *Page v Freight Hire (Tank Haulage) Ltd* [1981] ICR 299, [1981] IRLR 13, EAT.

13 SDA, s 7; *Tottenham Green Under-Fives Centre v Marshall* [1989] ICR 214, [1989] IRLR 147, EAT; *Lambeth London Borough Council v Commission for Racial Equality* [1990] ICR 768, [1990] IRLR 231, CA; *Etam plc v Rowan* [1989] IRLR 150, EAT. See Lewis [1991] ILJ 67; see amendments in Sex Discrimination Act 1986.

14 Now defined narrowly following *Marshall*'s case: 152/84 [1986] ECR 723, ECJ, to apply only to the determination of pensionable age for the purpose of granting state social security schemes for old age and retirement.

15 SDA s 2(2).

To indicate the range of employer decisions and collective agreements which are covered by the Sex Discrimination Act, however, is to present only part of the regulatory picture. We must try to understand more precisely how the legislation places limits upon employer decisions. Central to this question is the issue of how the statute defines discrimination and how that definition has been interpreted. An analysis of this issue helps us to discern the precise demarcation line drawn between workers' rights and management discretion. In analysing anti-discrimination legislation, the way the balance is struck can be discerned by analysing the judicial interpretation of the three main concepts of discrimination: direct discrimination, indirect discrimination and positive discrimination.[16]

## THE DEFINITION OF DISCRIMINATION

Under the Sex Discrimination Act and Race Relations Act, discrimination may be either direct, indirect or positive.[17] Direct discrimination consists of treating another individual less favourably on grounds of sex (or race), and the main issue presented is whether the less favourable treatment has been *caused* by reasons of sex (or race) as opposed to some other, sex (or race)-neutral business reason. Indirect discrimination is a more complex prohibition consisting of treatment in the form of a requirement or condition which appears to be applied neutrally to both sexes (or races) but in fact has the result that a considerably smaller proportion of persons in one sex (or race) can comply with it. In such a case the central issue is whether the employer can *justify* such discrimination. Finally, positive discrimination consists of the extent to which legislation allows preferential treatment to disadvantaged groups to redress existing imbalances.

### Direct discrimination

The Sex Discrimination Act, s 1(1)(a) defines direct discrimination as where a person *on the ground of her sex* treats a woman less favourably

16 There is a further test of victimisation, ie where a person is subjected to less favourable treatment for bringing a claim or giving evidence in proceedings or making allegations in good faith against a discriminator: SDA, s 4; RRA, s 2.

17 Much of the following discussion of direct and indirect sex discrimination is applicable to the law of racial discrimination, though the numbers of the sections of the Acts may differ. Indeed as we shall see, precedents from both laws are used interchangeably in legal argument. It is possible that the higher standards of sex discrimination law promoted by EC law may actually filter through to British race discrimination law.

than he treats or would treat a man.[18] This gives rise to two separate but related issues: (i) whether the treatment is less favourable than the treatment given to the opposite sex (the 'comparison element'), and (ii) whether the less favourable treatment is on the grounds of sex (the 'causation element').

## On the grounds of sex

The phrase 'on the grounds of her sex' clearly calls for a test of causation. If an employer can show that the discriminatory treatment is caused by a factor other than sex it will clearly not be caught by the Act. What is not entirely clear from the language of the statute, however, is whether the words 'on the ground of' refers to the employer's reasons in the sense of subjective intentions or the factual basis for the employer's decision.

In *Birmingham City Council v Equal Opportunities Commission*,[19] a case where the council continued an earlier practice of providing more grammar school places to boys than girls, the House of Lords held that the issue was whether the girls were *in fact* placed at a disadvantage as a result of the treatment rather than whether the council intended to place them at a disadvantage. As Lord Goff of Chieveley put it:

> 'There is discrimination under the statute if there is less favourable treatment on the grounds of sex, in other words if the relevant girl or girls would have received the same treatment as the boys *but for* their sex.'

The employer's motive or reason for the discriminatory policy 'can in no way affect or alter the facts that *a policy was implemented*' which was discriminatory (italics mine).

In *James v Eastleigh Borough Council*,[20] a case where a man of 61 was denied free swimming facilities in accordance with a Council policy of limiting free swimming to persons of retirement age 60 for women and 65 for men, the House of Lords[1] adopted the objective, 'but for' test set out in *Birmingham City Council v EOC*.[2]

Lord Goff of Chieveley stated:

> 'I do not read the words on the ground of sex as necessarily referring only to the reason why the defendant acted as he did but embracing cases in which

18 SDA, s 3(1) provides that a person discriminates against a married person of either sex if on the grounds of marital status he treats that person less favourably than he treats a single person; s 5(3) states that a comparison of the cases of persons of different sex or marital status under s 1(1) or 3(1) must be such that the relevant circumstances in the one case are the same, or not materially different, as the other. See eg *Bullock v Alice Ottley School* [1991] ICR 838, [1991] IRLR 324, EAT.

19 [1989] AC 1155, [1989] IRLR 173, HL.

20 [1989] ICR 423, [1989] IRLR 318, CA.

1 [1990] ICR 554, [1990] IRLR 288, HL.

2 [1989] AC 1155, [1989] IRLR 173, HL. See Watt [1998] ILJ 121.

a gender-based criterion is the basis upon which the complainant has been selected for the relevant treatment. There may be cases where the defendant's reasons for his action may bring the case within the subsection as when the defendant is motivated by an animus against persons of the complainant's sex or otherwise selects the complainant for the relevant treatment because of his or her sex. But it does not follow that the words 'on the ground of sex' refer only to cases where the defendant's reason for his action is the sex of the complainant.'

He added the following:

'However, taking the case of direct discrimination under section 1(1)(a) of the Act, I incline to the opinion that, if it were necessary to identify the requisite intention of the defendant, that intention is simply an intention to perform the relevant act of less favourable treatment . . . [An act of discrimination] is not saved from constituting unlawful discrimination by the fact that the defendant acted from a benign motive . . .'

In *James*'s case the reason for the rule giving free swimming lessons to those of pensionable age was to assist pensioners whose resources would be likely to be reduced by retirement. However, its effect was that men of 60-64 had to pay and women in the same age group did not.

The effect of these two House of Lords decisions is to ensure that in cases of direct discrimination the test provided by the statutory criterion 'the ground of sex' is an objective causative test; was the criterion used by the employer for the rule or decision gender-based or based on some other ground? The employer's motive will generally not be relevant as a defence to the issue of liability[3] although it may resurface in questions of compensation.

At the same time, however, the test of causation provided by the 'but for' test is fairly rigorous. It appears to require not merely that discrimination should be a ground for the less favourable treatment[4] but that it should be an 'effective' ground.[5] This opens up to employers a line of defence based upon a causation argument, that their criterion was not gender-based but based upon some other factor.[6] It also opens to judicial

3 See eg *Bullock v Alice Ottley School* [1991] ICR 838, [1991] IRLR 324, EAT.

4 See eg *Owen and Briggs v James* [1982] ICR 618, [1982] IRLR 502, CA.

5 In *O'Neill v Governors of St Thomas More RCVA Upper School* [1996] IRLR 372, EAT Mummery J suggested that the basic question in the 'causation test' is 'what out of the whole complex of facts before the tribunal, is the "effective and predominant cause" ...'. The 'event or factor... need not be the only or even the main cause of the result complained of... It is enough if it is an effective cause' (at p 376).

6 Apart from the causation issue, there is no general 'justification' escape from liability in the case of direct discrimination. In *Dekker* [1991] IRLR 27, ECJ the ECJ made it plain that the only defences to prima facie unlawful direct discrimination were those set out in Article 2 of the Equal Treatment Directive. Similarly, under UK law, the 'justifications' for direct discrimination are the Genuine Vocational Qualifications set out in the discrimination statutes, and the possibilities for positive action in the case of vocational qualifications.

discretion, or more accurately tribunal discretion, the issue of which of several factors was the decisive factor. For example, in *Bullock v Alice Ottley School*,[7] an employer had different retiring ages for teaching and domestic staff (60) and gardeners and maintenance staff (65). The former were predominantly female while the latter were all male. When a female domestic worker was to forced to retire at 60 complained that such a result was an act of sex discrimination, the Court of Appeal disagreed. The true 'cause' of the different retiring rules was the employer's need to overcome difficulties in recruiting to the maintenance and gardening grades. The outcome of this causation test was reinforced by the 'comparison' element, ie the Court of Appeal's decision that the retirement ages could not be viewed as less favourable to women because a man in the same job would have been treated in the same way.

## PREGNANCY AND DIRECT DISCRIMINATION

In the context of pregnancy dismissals, the UK Courts, led by the decisions of the ECJ have had to curb their inclinations to import into the causation test an economic defence for employers based on a comparison element.

In *Dekker v Stichting Vormingscentrum voor Jong Volwassenen (VJV-Centrum) Plus*[8] an applicant for a post of training instructor in a youth centre was rejected for a post when she informed the employer that she was pregnant. The employer gave as his reason that the insurer would not reimburse the sickness payments which the employer would have to pay to Mrs Dekker during her maternity leave because she was pregnant at the time of her application. The ECJ held, however, that a refusal by the employer to employ a woman because of the possible adverse consequences for him of employing a pregnant woman was direct discrimination on grounds of sex in direct contravention of Articles 2(1) and 3(1) of the Equal Treatment Directive, because the refusal to employ because of the financial consequences of absence connected with the pregnancy was based principally on grounds of the pregnancy rather than principally on grounds of the financial consequences.[9]

Initially, the House of Lords in *Webb v EMO Air (UK) Ltd Cargo*[10] were minded to uphold an industrial tribunals' decision that the dismissal of a

7 [1992] IRLR 564, CA.
8 C-177/88: [1990] ECR I-3941, [1991] IRLR 27, ECJ; See Hare 'Pregnancy and Sex Discrimination' [1991] ILJ 124; see too Asscker Von K [1991] ILJ 152.
9 Section 99 of the Employment Rights Act 1996 now makes a dismissal on grounds of pregnancy or child birth automatically unfair. However s 99 also contains a causation test; it requires that the reason (or ... the principal reason) for her dismissal is that she is pregnant or any other reason connected with her pregnancy.
10 [1993] IRLR 27, HL.

pregnant woman, who had been hired as the replacement for another employee on maternity leave, was not on grounds of sex but on the grounds of the consequence of her non-availability for work at the critical time she was needed by the employer. However, in the light of *Dekker* the House of Lords referred the issue to the ECJ.

The ECJ held that a dismissal of a woman on grounds of pregnancy constitutes direct discrimination on grounds of sex, rejecting as a possible alternative 'cause' the firm's need for the employee to be at work during the period of maternity, however 'essential' it might be 'to the proper functioning of the undertaking.' It reasoned that any other interpretation would undermine the protective provisions of the ETD during the period beginning from women's pregnancy to the end of their maternity leave.[11] In effect, during that period a dismissal for pregnancy is per se directly discriminatory. When *Webb* returned to the House of Lords the Law Lords acknowledged that it was necessary to interpret the test of direct discrimination in the 1975 Act to fit within the terms of the ECJ's ruling, per Lord Keith, '...the only way to do so is to hold that, in a case where a woman is engaged for an indefinite period, the fact that the reason why she will be temporarily unavailable for work at a time when her knowledge and her services will be particularly required is pregnancy is a circumstance relevant to her case, being a circumstance which could not be present in the case of a hypothetical male,[12] ie in such cases the comparative element is not relevant.

## LESS FAVOURABLE TREATMENT

To show less favourable treatment it is enough to show that there has been a loss of a chance of something reasonably considered to be of value.[13]

Less favourable treatment, however, presupposes a basis for comparison, in the sense that the unfavourable treatment must not only be unfavourable but *more* unfavourable that the treatment given to members of the opposite sex. Moreover, the comparison must be made between cases 'where the relevant circumstances are the same; or not materially different' (SDA, s 5(3)).

11 [1994] IRLR 482, ECJ, at 494. In *Webb* as in *Dekker*, the employer had to bear the replacement costs.

12 *Webb v EMO Air Cargo (UK) Ltd (No 2)* [1995] IRLR 645, HL. The decision of the House of Lords in *Webb* also suggests that the fact that the employee's contract was one for and indefinite term is an important qualification. In cases of fixed-term contracts, there may be more room for a comparability test which would in effect give greater recognition to the employer's economic needs. Both factors are circumstances which are relevant under s 1(1)(a) and 5(3) of the SDA, which allow them to be construed in accordance with Articles 2(1) and 5(1) of the ETD.

13 *Birmingham City Council v Equal Opportunities Commission* [1989] AC 1155, [1989] IRLR 173, HL.

This too opens an important line of defence for employers. The argument can be made that a male in circumstances comparable to those of the female would have been treated in the same way.[14] Thus, in *Webb*, the ECJ expressly left open the possibility that after the protected period other causes could supervene, ie even pregnancy related illness could be treated as ordinary illness subject to the comparison test, and if the circumstances were right constitute a non-discriminatory cause of dismissal. For example, in *Hertz v Aldi Marked K/S*,[15] a part-time cashier and saleswoman who returned to work after maternity leave was dismissed after 18 months because she had been off work repeatedly for more than 100 days in a 12-month period owing to a pregnancy-related illness. The ECJ held that a dismissal of a female worker because of her pregnancy during maternity leave, stipulated under national law, constitutes direct discrimination on grounds of sex in the same way as a refusal to recruit a pregnant woman. However, in a case of dismissal for pregnancy-related illness which occurs after maternity leave there is no reason to distinguish between pregnancy and any other illness since female and male workers are equally exposed to the risks of illness. The only issue at that stage is whether the treatment of illness generally is on the same conditions for men and women. After the 'protected period' the comparability issue can be given greater weight.[16]

The effect of the comparison element in the test of direct discrimination is to give greater weight to market forces and managerial discretion in the judicial decision whether a particular form of treatment is on grounds of sex. We can see this in two fields in particular.

## Employer dress and appearance rules

Employers frequently regulate employees' dress and appearance using rules in employees handbooks which are backed up by disciplinary rules and procedures and often incorporated in employees' contracts of employment. The rules relate to the needs of the enterprise ranging from the more objective operational needs such as the need to regulate personal hygiene and hair covering in food production and use of safety equipment, to the more discretionary corporate imaging programmes which require uniforms or restrictions on hair style. In so far as employer appearance 'codes' impose different rules upon men and women and reinforce sexual

14 An argument to this effect was lost in *Porcelli v Strathclyde Regional Council* [1986] ICR 564, Ct of Sess but succeeded in an early case of pregnancy dismissal *Hayes v Malleable Working Men's Club and Institute* [1985] ICR 703, EAT.

15 C-179/88 [1990] ECR I-3979 [1991] IRLR 31, ECJ.

16 See eg *British Telecommunications plc v Roberts* [1996] IRLR 601, EAT where a employer's refusal to allow a request to jobshare after maternity leave could not be viewed as automatically direct discrimination.

stereotypes, they may be limited by the equal treatment requirements of the Sex Discrimination Act. Much depends upon whether the treatment of employees by employers fits into the range of conduct proscribed by the statute. Thus, an employee may argue successfully that a particular rule which differentiates between men and women constitutes a detriment because it imposes an uncomfortable form of attire or restricts his or her hair length outside of working life. To prove discrimination, however, the employee must also show that the rule is a form of sex discrimination because it shows that the rule is less favourable to one sex by comparison to the other.

A prototypical case was *Schmidt v Austicks Bookshops Ltd*[17], in which a female employee complained that the requirement that she may not wear trousers at work was discriminatory on grounds of sex. The EAT held, however, that since men and women were both subject to rules restricting their appearance and apparel even though the rules were not identical, they were treated alike in the meaning of the statute and there was no discrimination. The Court signalled an early concern with the potential intrusiveness of discrimination legislation when it stated: 'An employer is entitled to a large measure of discretion in controlling the image of his establishment , including the appearance of staff, especially when those staff, as a result of their duties, come into contact with the public.'

In *Burrett v West Birmingham Health Authority*,[18] a female nurse was required to wear a cap as part of her uniform; there was no such requirement for men. The EAT was prepared to hold that this was not less favourable treatment because the requirement to wear a uniform applied equally to men. Moreover, when the woman was disciplined for a refusal to conform, the disciplinary sanction was not discriminatory because a man who refused to abide by the employer's rules relating to uniforms would also have been similarly treated.

In *Smith v Safeway plc*[19] a case concerning a rule that men could not have long hair, the Court of Appeal held that appearance codes do not have to be identical for men and women and that the effect of the code must be viewed overall and not on an item by item basis. One item by itself could be enough but the effect must be considered in the context of the code as a whole. Moreover, it could not accept that employer policies which mirrored conventional differences between the sexes were necessarily irreconcilable with the discrimination laws. Treatment is not less favourable if appearance codes even-handedly applied conventional

17 [1977] IRLR 360, EAT.
18 [1994] IRLR 7, EAT.
19 [1996] IRLR 456, CA.

standards to men and women.[20] It indicated its reluctance in the name of equality to make employers into involuntary agents to establish rules which created freedom from sexual stereotypes.

## Sexual and racial harassment at work

Sexual and racial harassment by fellow employees can come within the scope of unlawful discrimination under both Acts only if the employee can show that the alleged harassing conduct (i) is a detriment under s 6(2)(b),[1] and (ii) constitutes less favourable treatment on grounds of sex or race. To show that the harassing treatment was on grounds of sex or race requires evidence of treatment which was less favourable than that to which a man or another race would have been subjected. In *Strathclyde Regional Council v Porcelli*[2] the Court of Session suggested that there was a category of harassment which is so sexually or racially specific that the causation test is satisfied without the need to find a comparator.[3] Thus, in *Porcelli*, a case where a woman had been subjected to persistent insults, obscenities and unwanted physical conduct, the Court held that if the unfavourable treatment to which the woman was subjected includes significant sexual language to which a man would not be vulnerable, the treatment can be viewed as on the grounds of her sex within the meaning of the Act.[4]

In other cases, however, the need to show a comparatively worse form of treatment has operated to reduce the scope of the application discrimination legislation to cases of sexual or racial harassment. In

20 The Court of Appeal was not persuaded by the decision of the EAT that the hair length restriction was not evenhanded because it applied only to men and away from work as well as at work. At a technical level, it rested its case on the point that that this was not enough to show that the IT's decision based on *Schmidt* was perverse.

1 This threshold test is not particularly severe in sexual harassment cases. It does not require a persistent course of harassment; one act of verbal abuse can be sufficient if it is serious enough in the circumstances. Moreover, in such cases, the test of detriment is weighted towards the subjective, consisting of 'unwanted conduct of a sexual nature,' reflecting the EC Recommendation and Code of Practice on sexual harassment. In racial harassment cases, however, the courts have injected a stiffer, more objective, test of detriment. In *De Souza v Automobile Association* ([1986] IRLR 103, CA) the Court of Appeal stated that a racial insult by itself is not 'enough, even if that insult caused him or her distress.' The conduct must be such 'that a reasonable worker would or might take the view that he had been thereby disadvantaged in the circumstances in which he had thereafter to work.'

2 [1986] IRLR 134.

3 See eg *British Telecom v Williams plc* [1997] IRLR 668, EAT.

4 See too *Burton v De Vere Hotels* [1996] IRLR 596; *British Telecommunications v Williams*, in which the EAT reiterated that 'because the conduct which constitutes sexual harassment is itself gender specific, there is no necessity to look for a male comparator' [1997] IRLR 668 at 669.

*Stewart v Cleveland Guest (Engineering) Ltd*,[5] for example, the complainant found the display of nude women in calendars offensive but the tribunal found that they were 'neutral' in the sense that a man might have found the display as offensive as the applicant.[6] Similarly, in *Balgobin v London Borough of Tower Hamlets*,[7] the fact that the complainant was required to go back to work with the alleged harasser after an employer investigation was inconclusive was not discriminatory because a man would have had to accept the same personnel decision. In *British Telecommunications v Williams*,[8] the EAT reversed on appeal an industrial tribunal finding of sexual harassment that a reasonable person in the female applicant's position could regard an appraisal interview with a male manager to be offensive and sexually intimidating because of its excessive length, the physical proximity of the man, and the fact that the manager was unaccompanied by a woman manager inter alia because in law and practice it could not accept that an interview by a male manager with a female employee could be viewed as sexually intimidating merely because there was no woman present, and the interview took place in an enclosed space. In this field, the comparison element so reduces the scope of sexual or racial harassment within the discrimination laws that there is a strong case for specific legislation to provide adequate protection.[9]

## Sexual orientation and direct discrimination

In recent years courts have begun to explore whether the concept of discrimination on grounds of sex extends to discrimination on grounds of sexual orientation. In *P v S and Cornwall County Council*,[9a] the ECJ held that the provisions of the Equal Treatment Directive prohibiting discrimination between men and women were simply the expression of the principle of equality and that this could apply to discrimination based on the worker's gender reassignment, ie transsexuality. In *Grant v South-West Trains*,[9b] however, the ECJ held that 'Community Law as it stands at present does not cover discrimination based on sexual orientation' although the case itself was one of a travel concession falling under art 119. In *Smith v Gardner Merchant*,[9c] an individual with less than two years' service

5 [1994] IRLR 440, EAT.
6 The neutrality finding might possibly have been influenced by the fact that a delegation of women employees had informed management that they were not particularly bothered by the particular calendars in question.
7 [1987] IRLR 401, EAT.
8 [1997] IRLR 668, EAT.
9 See eg Dine and Watt (1995) MLR 343.
9a [1996] IRLR 347, ECJ.
9b [1998] IRLR 206, ECJ.
9c [1998] IRLR 510, CA.

claimed that he was discriminated against under the Sex Discrimination Act and the Equal Treatment Directive both on grounds of homosexuality and harassment for homosexuality. The Court of Appeal reaffirmed that the basic test of discrimination on grounds of sex under either statutes did not extend to discrimination based on sexual orientation. This part of the Appeal Court's decision held that the views of the ECJ in *Grant* under art 119 extended as well to cases falling under the Equal Treatment Directive.[9d] Support for this proposition could also be gathered from the proposal for the insertion of art 6a in the Treaty of Amsterdam which will allow the Commission, after receiving the necessary authorisation, 'to take appropriate action to eliminate ... discrimination based on sexual orientation'.

Yet the Court of Appeal in *Smith's* case also made the point that the issue of harassment for homosexuality under the Sex Discrimination Act could arise as long as the comparator test, based both on ss 1(1)(a) and 5(3), was carefully applied. These provisions required a comparison of the treatment meted out to a member of the opposite sex in circumstances which were roughly similar. In the context of harassment of a male homosexual, therefore, the correct test was whether the same treatment would have been given to a female homosexual. Similarly, in the case of discrimination generally, '... if an employer were willing to employ lesbians but not male homosexuals, that would be discrimination on grounds of sex.'[9e] Finally, in the case of transsexuals, as in *P's* case, it is the difference of treatment based on the change of sex which brings it into the category of discrimination based on sex. In these three cases, the illegal discrimination is based on less favourable treatment to persons of the opposite sex rather then because of their gender orientation.

## Indirect discrimination

If a woman is unable to show that she was subjected to discriminatory treatment because of her sex, that eliminates a claim of direct discrimination under s 1(1)(a). However, action taken by employers on grounds which are neutral as between men and women can nevertheless be discriminatory if in fact it has a disparate impact upon one sex or the other. Following the pattern of US law[10] the statute prohibits management requirements or conditions which are neutral in form but which are discriminatory in operation by putting one sex at a disadvantage. In such

9d See too decision of Lightman J in *R v Secretary of State, ex p Perkins (No 2)* [1998] IRLR 508, HC.

9e See remarks of Brown LJ in *R v Secretary of State for Defence, ex p Smith* [1995] IRLR 585, HC.

10 See eg *Griggs v Duke Power Co* 401 US 424 (1971).

a case however, there is a defence of justification allowed, ie that the discriminatory pattern is justifiable[11] irrespective of the sex of the person to whom it is applied (SDA, s 1(1)(b)(3)).

Indirect discrimination is defined by the SDA as applying to a woman a *requirement or condition* equally as to a man but: (i) which is such that the proportion of women (or men) who can comply with it is considerably smaller than the proportion of men who can comply with it, and (ii) it is to her detriment because she cannot comply with it.

Let us examine each element in turn.

## Requirement or condition

The statutory phrase 'requirement or condition' has been interpreted to require the plaintiff to convince the industrial tribunal that there was in fact a rule or practice followed by the employer which so restricts access to employment or a benefit of employment that it constitutes a virtual condition for that job or related benefit. For example in *Jones v University of Manchester*[12] the industrial tribunal found as a matter of fact that an advertisement of a vacancy for graduates aged between 27 and 35 was an absolute bar to the 46-year old applicant despite the employer's claim that it was only a preference. Similarly in *Home Office v Holmes*[13] the refusal to allow the employee to transfer to part-time work could be tested for its discriminatory effect because the obligation to work full-time was a requirement or condition. Further, in *Clarke v Eley (IMI) Kynoch Ltd*[14] a jointly agreed selection procedure for redundancy which stipulated that 'part-timers first' was the rule for selection met the test for requirement and condition and could be looked at to determine disproportionate impact and justification. In both cases, the EAT emphasised that this crucial statutory precondition should not be given a restrictive interpretation.

Where, however, the alleged discrimination consists of a selection or promotion procedure which provides several criteria upon which applicants are to be assessed, only one of which is indirectly discriminatory, it is not clear that UK courts will recognise the procedure as imposing a *requirement or condition* as required by s 1(2)(ii). It was successfully argued in *Watches of Switzerland v Savell*,[15] a sex discrimination case, that

11 As Townshend-Smith reminds us, in *Griggs* the term used was 'business necessity' but Parliament rejected this in favour of 'justifiable'. Sex Discimination in Employment (1989) p 22.

12 [1993] IRLR 218, CA. See too *Price v Civil Service Commission* (between 17 and 28 years of age).

13 [1984] ICR 678, [1984] IRLR 299.

14 [1983] ICR 165, [1982] IRLR 482. Ibid.

15 [1983] IRLR 141, EAT (claim defeated on other grounds).

the need to satisfy the criteria in the procedure is itself a condition or requirement under the Act. However, in *Perera v Civil Service Commission (No 2)*[16] a solicitor rejected for the post of Legal Assistant alleged that a procedure requiring an assessment of candidates for the post on the basis of a set of factors which included 'experience in the United Kingdom' was indirectly racially discriminatory. The Court of Appeal held that the procedure as such could not be viewed as indirectly discriminatory because the factors to which the interviewing board was to have regard were not requirements or conditions, since no one factor itself was an absolute bar to selection. In *Meer v London Borough of Tower Hamlets*,[17] another case under the Race Relations Act, the Court of Appeal held that even though one of twelve selection criteria for Borough Solicitor, 'experienced in Tower Hamlets', was discriminatory, the selection process was not a *requirement* for the purpose of s 1(1) of the Act since it was not in *itself* a 'must' for appointment.

In *Meer*, Balcombe LJ thought that there were strong arguments that the 'absolute bar' view in *Perera* may not be consistent with the object of the legislation, though he considered it to be binding precedent. Rubenstein has suggested that it could be a derogation from the provisions of the EC Equal Treatment Directive and is susceptible to attack on that account which, as interpreted in *Bilka-Kaufhaus*, requires an employer to justify any 'practice' which 'in fact affects more women than men'. He suggests that 'any policy or practice which is used as grounds for decision-making falls within the potential scope of the protection provided by the Directive'.[18] In *Enderby v Frenchay Health Authority*[19] the ECJ held that a statistically demonstrable difference in pay between two jobs of equal value, one predominantly performed by women and the other exclusively by men was enough to meet the prima facie test of an indirect indiscriminatory pay practice, shifting the burden to employers to show objective justification.

In *Falkirk Council v Whyte*[20] the EAT sitting in Scotland confirmed that a criterion for selection stated as a desirable qualification rather than an absolute bar could be viewed as a requirement or condition under the SDA in view of the fact that the ETD had direct effect in the case of public employers.

In so far as *Perera* continues to be followed in the private sector in construing the term requirement or condition, it provides a full defence

16 [1983] ICR 428, [1983] IRLR 166, CA.
17 [1988] IRLR 399, CA. See too *Brook v London Borough of Haringey* [1992] IRLR 478, EAT.
18 M Rubenstein 'The Equal Treatment Directive and UK Law' in McCrudden (ed) *Employment & European Equality Law* (1988) Eclipse, at p 84.
19 [1993] IRLR 591, ECJ.
20 [1997] IRLR 560, EAT.

against indirect discrimination which is far more formalistic than the test of justification.[1] It is also open to the criticism that it is a defence which can be designed into procedures by employers as well as making it more difficult to apply the legal norms to existing discretionary recruitment procedures. It therefore operates as a limit upon the reach of the statute allowing considerable discretion to management decisions as to the application of criteria to candidates for selection or promotion. It means that such decisions can be tested if at all only under the test of direct discrimination.

Under Article 119, and to the extent that the ETD has direct effect upon public employers, in contrast, it is enough for the plaintiff to show that there is a discriminatory pay practice, ie that arrangements such as collective agreements and job evaluation systems and presumably procedures, whatever their form, have an adverse impact on women and hence require justification to avoid a finding of discrimination.[2] In so far as individuals find their claims prevented by the first hurdle in the SDA, they may choose to bring a claim directly under article 119.

## Disproportionate impact of a requirement or condition

The second condition necessary to establish indirect discrimination is that a 'considerably smaller' proportion of individuals of a particular sex can comply with the requirement or conditions. The difficulty here for the plaintiff is to choose the right comparators with which to compare herself. SDA, s 5(3) stipulates that comparisons must be made with persons in circumstances which are 'not materially different'. This issue is one of fact for tribunals to decide, subject only to appeal on grounds of perversity or some other error or law.[3]

The test as suggested by Ralph Gibson LJ in *Jones v University of Manchester*,[4] requires at the outset a definition of 'the relevant total.' This he defined as the 'number of men and women to whom ...the employer... applies or would apply the requirement'. For example, in *Jones v University of Manchester*, a post of careers advisor was advertised with the conditions 'graduate preferred 27-35, with relevant experience.' Jones applied and, though qualified in terms of experience, was not shortlisted because of her age, 46. The industrial tribunal found that the requirement

1 See eg *Bhudi v EMI Refiners Ltd* [1994] IRLR 204, EAT.
2 See eg *Bilka-Kaufhaus v Weber von Hartz*: 170/84 [1987] ICR 110, [1986] IRLR 317, ECJ; *Danfoss*: 109/88 [1991] ICR 74, [1989] IRLR 532, ECJ.
3 *Kidd v DRG (UK) Ltd* [1985] ICR 405, [1985] IRLR 190, EAT; *Greater Manchester Police Authority v Lea* [1990] IRLR 372, EAT.
4 [1993] IRLR 218, CA.

was indirectly discriminatory because the proportion of women mature graduates was smaller than the proportion of male mature graduates. The Court of Appeal agreed with the EAT that the IT had taken the wrong pool for comparison. It held that the appropriate pool was all graduates with relevant qualifications and not merely mature graduates. In the event, the proportions of male and female graduates who could meet the requirement were less dramatically different. Similarly, in *R v Secretary of State, ex p EOC*,[5] the House of Lords held that in analysing the exclusion of those employees working fewer than 16 hours per week, or in some instances 8 hours per week, from the main employment protections, the relevant pool was the working population as a whole.

In ascertaining the relevant group for comparison, the appropriate pool has also been viewed as all those men and women with the qualifications for the post excluding the requirement or condition complained of.[6] For example in *Price v Civil Service Commission*[7] the employer argued that an upper age limit of 28 for applications to join the executive grade of the Civil Service should be viewed as it applied to men and women in the population at large. The EAT rejected this basis of comparison insisting that the correct pool of people to look at were those qualified to apply for the job and since in that group there were fewer women who were able to seek such employment, a disproportionate impact was shown.

Once the relevant pool is established, the next step is to determine whether the proportion of women who cannot comply is significantly greater than the proportion of men who cannot comply with the condition. In *R v Secretary of State for Education, ex p Schaffter*,[8] Schiemann J suggested that the subsection could be applied in three stages: first you must establish the proportion of all women who can comply with the requirement; second, the proportion of all men who can comply with the requirement and third compare both proportions and determine which is considerably smaller than the other.[9]

In *Jones v University of Manchester*[10] Lord Justice Ralph Gibson pointed out that the relevant total was not the *number* of men and women who can comply with the requirement or condition but the number of men and women who can comply with the condition *as a proportion* of the number of men and women to whom the requirement is or would be

5 [1994] IRLR 176, HL.
6 See too *Jones v Chief Adjudication Officer* [1990] IRLR 533, CA, for a more complex formula.
7 [1978] ICR 27, [1977] IRLR 291, EAT; see too *Clarke v Eley (IMI) Kynoch Ltd* [1982] IRLR 482.
8 [1987] IRLR 53, EAT.
9 *Jones v University of Manchester* [1993] IRLR 218, CA.
10 [1993] IRLR 218, CA.

applied. In that case, for example, the total number of young graduates who could comply with the 24 to 37 age requirement was 175,748. Of these 103,731, or 59%, were men and 72,017, or 41%, were women. To satisfy the requirement of the section the industrial tribunal would have needed to compare those proportions to determine whether the proportion of women in the group that can comply is considerably smaller than the proportion of men in that group. In *R v Secretary of State for Employment, ex p Seymour-Smith*,[11] the Court of Appeal made it clear that while the difference between the proportions must be more than de minimis, the weight to be attached to the word 'considerable' should not be exaggerated bearing in mind that Article 2 of the ETD required that 'there shall be no discrimination whatsoever on ground of sex.' The case concerned the effect of the two-year qualifying period for bringing a complaint of dismissal and accepted the statistical evidence establishing that a lower proportion of women could comply with this condition.

Yet there remains a lack of legal certainty because of tribunal discretion. In *R v Seymour-Smith*, the proportion of women who could comply with the requirement of two year's continuous service was 90% of the proportion of men and this was significantly smaller.[12] Yet in *Staffordshire County Council v Black*,[13] the EAT was prepared to agree with the industrial tribunal's assessment that where 89.5% of the women and 97% of the men could comply with the requirement of working full time, the difference was not considerably smaller.

### Detriment

The applicant must also show that the discriminatory requirement or condition is to her detriment because she 'cannot comply with it'.[14] At first sight, this appears to be relatively easy to establish in discrimination cases. For as Brandon LJ in *Ministry of Defence v Jeremiah*[15] viewed 'detriment',

11 [1995] IRLR 464, CA. Referred to HL: [1997] IRLR 315, HL.

12 See too *London Underground Ltd (No 2) v Edwards* [1997] IRLR 157, EAT where the proportion of female train operators who could comply with new rostering arrangements 95% (20 out of 21) was held to be considerably lower than the 100% of men; moreover, in *Greater Manchester Police Authority v Lea* the discrepancy between the proportions of men and women who could comply with the condition had been reduced to 99.4% and 95.3% respectively (upheld by EAT) [1990] IRLR 372, EAT 4 [1995] IRLR 234, EAT.

13 [1995] IRLR 234, EAT.

14 See eg *Mandla v Dowell Lee* [1983] IRLR 209, HL; *Turner v Labour Party* [1987] IRLR 101, EAT; *Clarke v Eley (IMI) Kynoch Ltd* [1983] ICR 165, [1982] IRLR 482, EAT; *Steel v Union of Post Office Workers* [1978] ICR 181, [1977] IRLR 288, EAT.

15 [1980] QB 87, [1980] ICR 13, CA.

it meant little more than 'putting under a disadvantage'.[16] Yet in employment cases it is a condition of the statute which can be interpreted restrictively. For it is necessary to establish that the detriment occurs in relation to the employment. For example in *De Souza v Automobile Association*[17] the EAT considered that a prejudicial statement by one manager to another to 'get your typing done by the wog' was not to the disadvantage of the plaintiff *in relation to her employment.*

The Court of Appeal did not allow the appeal. It agreed that the detriment could not consist of racial insults reported second-hand. A detriment had to be one in which 'the reasonable employee could justifiably complain about his or her working conditions or environment'.[18]

On the other hand, in *Bracebridge Engineering Ltd v Darby*[19] the EAT held that an industrial tribunal was able to find that a single act of sexual harassment was a detriment within the meaning of SDA, s 6(2)(b). The respondent, an employee of 13 years, had been grabbed by her charge-hand, taken into the works management office and sexually assaulted. This conduct clearly fell within 'the context of her employment' under SDA, s 6(2)(b) since the harassers were part of the supervisory structure.

### *Justification*

In the case of indirect discrimination, unlike direct, employers have the potential defence that the discriminatory requirement or condition is 'justifiable irrespective of the sex of the person to whom it is applied' (SDA, s 1(1)(b)(3)). The way this defence has been interpreted by the courts is a good indication of the balance that is struck between the values of 'eliminating discriminatory practices on the one hand' and 'the profitability of the business on the other'.[20]

At an early stage in *Steel v Union of Post Office Workers*,[1] a practice of allocating postal rounds in accordance with the accumulated seniority of

16 *Meer v London Borough of Tower Hamlets* [1988] IRLR 399, CA.
17 [1986] ICR 514, [1986] IRLR 103, CA.
18 Ibid.
19 [1990] IRLR 3, EAT; see also *Enterprise Glass Co Ltd v Miles* [1990] ICR 787 (managers deficient in procedure); *Porcelli v Strathclyde Regional Council* [1986] IRLR 134, [1986] ICR 564, Ct of Sess (harassment itself the detriment). See *Balgobin v Tower Hamlets London Borough Council* [1987] ICR 829, [1987] IRLR 401 for an example of the employer's defence under s 41(3). See too *Wadman v Carpenter Farrer Partnership* [1993] IRLR 374, EAT.
20 Browne-Wilkinson in *Steel v Union of Post Office Workers* [1978] 2 All ER 504, [1977] IRLR 288, EAT.
1 Ibid.

established full-time workers was shown to be discriminatory against women workers because they were ineligible for established full-time work prior to 1976.

The EAT stated that the role of the industrial tribunal was 'to weigh up the needs of the enterprise against the discriminatory effect of the requirement or condition'. It also provided a structure to guide tribunals in balancing these factors.

The EAT first applied the standard of business necessity to the employer's rule or condition, ie to be justified the discriminatory practice had to be necessary rather than merely convenient. It then added the further requirement that in judging necessity it was 'relevant to consider whether the employer can find some other and non-discriminatory method of achieving this objective'.

In later race relations cases, there was a progressive weakening of this objective test by more subjective standards. In *Singh's*[2] case the test was one of 'reasonable necessity'. In *Panesar*[3] it became 'right and proper in the circumstances'. In *Ojutiku*[4] Stephenson LJ held that the party applying the discriminatory condition must prove it to be justifiable in all the circumstances on balancing its discriminatory effect against the discriminator's need for it.[5] .

In *Bilka-Kaufhaus*[6] the European Court of Justice introduced a stricter test of justification for indirect discrimination under Article 119. In *Bilka* the employer, a major department store chain, preferred full-time employees to part-time employees and allowed part-time employees to qualify for its supplementary occupational pension scheme only after 15 years of full-time working. The female applicant had worked 15 years as a sales assistant but had only worked 11 years full-time.

The ECJ held that the department store's exclusion of part-time employees from the occupational pension scheme infringed Article 119 where the exclusion affected a far greater number of women than men, unless the undertaking shows that 'the exclusion is based on objectively justified factors, unrelated to any discrimination on the grounds of sex'. This entailed a finding that occupational pension schemes fell within the concept of pay in Article 119. It is also confirmed that indirect, as well as direct discrimination, was covered by Article 119.[7] Moreover, the ECJ further held that the test of objective justification on economic grounds

2 *Singh v Rowntree MacKintosh* [1979] ICR 554, [1979] IRLR 199, EAT.
3 *Panesar v Nestlé Co Ltd* [1980] ICR 144n, [1980] IRLR 64, CA.
4 *Ojutiku v Manpower Services Commission* [1982] ICR 661, CA.
5 See discussion in Townshend-Smith *Sex Discrimination in Employment* (1989) p 81.
6 *Bilka-Kaufhaus GmbH v Weber von Hartz*: 170/84 [1987] ICR 110, [1986] IRLR 317, ECJ.
7 The ECJ affirmed the decision of *Jenkins v Kingsgate (Clothing Productions) Ltd*: 96/80 [1981] ICR 592, [1981] IRLR 228.

included two elements. First, there must be a finding by the national court that the practice corresponds to a real need on the part of the undertaking.[8] Second, it must be 'appropriate' with a view to achieving the objective in question and 'necessary' to that end. This second requirement suggested that if it could be shown that the employer could achieve the same objective by a less drastic means, then the requirement would not be objectively justified.

The purpose of the decision was only to insist upon a properly objective test of the employer's view of the economic needs of the business. It did not place close limits upon the employer's choice of business objective.[9] Nor did it suggest the introduction of other values, such as family responsibilities, to be weighed in the balance. In its third holding, the European Court stated that:

> 'Article 119 does not have the effect of requiring an employer to organise its occupational pension scheme in such a manner as to take into account the particular difficulties faced by persons with family responsibilities in meeting the conditions for entitlement to such a pension.'[10]

Though *Bilka* was an equal pay case brought under Article 119, it was directly relevant to the test of justification of indirect discrimination under the Equal Treatment Directive and the UK Sex Discrimination Act. This latter point was underlined in the House of Lords decision in *Rainey v Greater Glasgow Health Board*[11] in which Lord Keith stated in obiter:

> 'there would not appear to be any material distinction in principle between the need to demonstrate objectively justified grounds of difference for the purpose of s 1(3) [of the Equal Pay Act] and the need to justify a requirement or condition under s 1(1)(b)(ii) of the Sex Discrimination Act 1975.'

In *Rainey*, however, Lord Keith made no explicit reference to the two-part test of justification in *Bilka*. He was more concerned to establish that economic and administrative grounds could be considered in the test of objective justification.

In *Hampson v Department of Education and Science*[12] the Court of Appeal held that the test of justifiability under RRA, s 1(1)(b)(ii) requires

8 See eg *Nimz v Freie und Hansestadt Hamburg*: C-184/89 [1991] ECR 1-297, [1991] IRLR 222, ECJ; *Rinner-Kuhn v FWW Spezial-Gebaudereinigung GmbH & Co KG*: 171/85 [1989] IRLR 493, ECJ; *Botel*: C-360/90 [1992] IRLR 423, ECJ.

9 See discussion in Ch 13.

10 See now Third Social Action Programme 1991-95 Com 90 final Brussels 6 November 1990 Szyszczak 1991 ILJ 156.

11 [1987] ICR 129, [1987] IRLR 26 at 31, HL.

12 [1989] ICR 179, [1989] IRLR 69. In *Webb v EMO Air Cargo (UK) Ltd* [1992] 4 All ER 929, [1993] IRLR 27, HL, the House of Lords stated that the test of what is justifiable formulated by Balcombe LJ in *Hampson* must be regarded as the appropriate one and as superseding that expressed by Eveleigh LJ in *Ojutiku*.

an objective balance to be struck between the discriminatory effect of the requirement or condition and the reasonable needs of the person who applied it. Balcombe LJ claimed that he could see no significant difference between the test he had formulated and that adopted by the House of Lords in *Rainey*:

> '. . . it is obviously desirable that the test of justifiability applied in all three closely related fields should be consistent with each other.'

However, there are important differences between the test of *Hampson* and that in *Rainey* based on *Bilka*. One difference is the test of the employer's reason. In *Bilka* the condition must correspond to a real need of the enterprise, ie a test of genuine necessity based on objective grounds. In *Hampson,* the requirement was that of reasonable necessity.

A second difference is the explicit requirement in *Bilka* that the measures chosen must be 'appropriate and necessary with a view to achieving the objectives pursued'. This is essentially a 'proportionality' test - one of the general principles of the Community legal order[13] and one which allows the adjudicating tribunal to ask whether the exclusion was not too wide in view of the objective. It is not entirely clear that the balancing test in *Hampson* includes the proportionality test in *Bilka*.

The approach of the German Federal Labour Court in deciding *Bilka* after the reference to the ECJ offers a good illustration of how such criteria can be applied in a 'structured' way. In *Bilka*[14] the finding of the Labour Court that Ms Weber was a victim of unjustified indirect discrimination as a part-timer excluded from an occupational pension was based on a careful application of the points set out by the ECJ.

First, the Court found the employer had failed to establish that the objective sought by the company corresponded to a real need of the undertaking for full-time workers. The company's arguments that part-timers caused organisational problems such as refusing to work on Saturdays and involved higher labour costs, was not substantiated by the personnel management literature and any extra costs or organisational problems were more than compensated by the chance to have staff cover the longer opening hours of department stores.

The Court found, secondly, that even if it was necessary to encourage work on Saturdays, it was unclear how Bilka's pension policy was appropriate for such a purpose. The pension scheme did not differentiate between Saturday workers and part-time workers, nor did it make it

13 *Johnston v Chief Constable of the Royal Ulster Constabulary*: 222/84 [1987] ICR 83, [1986] IRLR 263, ECJ.
14 [1986] ECR 1607 discussed in Preschal and Burrows (1990) pp 260-261.

possible for part-time workers to qualify for a pension by accepting work on Saturday.[15]

Finally, when the employer argued that the costs of giving pensions to part-timers on a retroactive basis were prohibitive, the court dismissed the argument by stating that the interest of Ms Weber in not being discriminated against must be given precedence over the interests of the employer concerning the size of the pension reserve.

Under the proportionality test the justification defence can be defeated if the plaintiff can point to an alternative formulation of the condition which would allow the purposes of the business to be pursued with a less discriminatory effect. For example in *Steel* the women could be given full-time credit for part-time work done before they were eligible for full-time work or in *Bilka* itself the qualifying periods could be shorter. The balancing test of *Hampson* has fewer guidelines to discretion and is therefore more unpredictable in its outcome. One has only to compare for example *Jones v University of Manchester*[16] where discriminatory effect was taken seriously, with *Bullock v Alice Ottley School*[17] where it was virtually ignored. It would seem to be singularly inappropriate as a legislative standard for an issue of fact for tribunals, unless the judiciary can build in a more reassuring set of limits to judicial discretion in its application.[18]

Initially in *Webb v EMO Air Cargo (UK) Ltd*[19] the House of Lords described the *Hampson* test as the correct test for indirect discrimination. In *R v Secretary of State for Employment, ex p EOC*,[20] however, the Law Lords applied a proportionality test to the Government's claim that the eight- and sixteen-hour qualification for employment protection legislation was designed to encourage employers to hire more workers on a part-time basis than they might otherwise have done. The Court accepted that the goal was legitimate, there was a failure to show that the condition was an appropriate means of achieving that goal. As we shall see in the next chapter, the proportionality test of EC law itself contains considerable deference to employer and legislative objectives.

Even the *Hampson* test requires as a minimum objective test that a nexus be established between the need of the employer and the condition which was imposed.

15 Cf the industrial tribunal's finding on appropriateness in *Greater Manchester Police Authority v Lea* [1990] IRLR 372.

16 [1993] IRLR 218 at 223.

17 [1993] ICR 138, [1992] IRLR 564, CA.

18 Rubenstein, M 'The Equal Treatment Directive and UK Law' in McCrudden *Women, Employment and European Equality Law* Eclipse (1987).

19 [1992] 4 All ER 929, HL.

20 [1994] IRLR 176, HL.

In *Greater Manchester Police Authority v Lea*[1] the EAT held that where the police authority failed to show a *relevant* need on the part of the police authority to impose a condition preventing applications from those who were in receipt of occupational pensions or who had accepted voluntary redundancy or early retirement, it could not justify the condition. It was not enough to show that the authority wished to pursue the policy of helping the unemployed; a policy which was generally laudable. If the condition did not promote the purpose of the undertaking there could be no justification.

## Positive discrimination

Positive action in favour of one sex or race would appear to amount to preferential treatment which itself could be viewed as directly discriminatory under sex and race legislation. If, however, no preferential treatment is given to the group disadvantaged by a long period of past discrimination, movement towards equality of outcome will be an exceedingly lengthy process possibly stretching over generations. Hence discrimination statutes often acknowledge this by providing that certain forms of preferential treatment are lawful. However, the scope of the provision for positive action can vary considerably. For example in the SDA 1975, s 47 provides the rather limited exception that the employer may discriminate in favour of one sex in vocational training where it appears that in the previous 12 months no person of that sex was employed in the work in question in the country or the number so employed was comparatively small. In the Equal Treatment Directive, in contrast, the exception for positive action is expressed in wider terms. Article 2(4) states that the Directive shall be without prejudice to measures to promote equal opportunities for men and women in particular by removing existing inequalities which affect women's opportunities in the areas referred to in Article 1(1), ie access to employment, including promotion, and working conditions as well as vocational training. This wider statutory formulation is open to varying interpretations. It can clearly apply to removing barriers to equal opportunity including education and vocational training. To what extent however, can it apply to questions of ensuring a redress of inequality of outcomes of hiring and promotion processes? In *Kalanke v Freie Hansestadt Bremen*,[2] a woman and a man were found to be equally qualified for the position of section manager in the parks section of the city. The Land had a law which provided that in case of a tie between

1 [1990] IRLR 372, EAT.
2 [1995] IRLR 660, ECJ.

candidates of different sexes, preference should automatically be given to the woman, if women were 'under-represented' in the sense of constituting less than 50% of the relevant pay bracket of the relevant work group. The ECJ acknowledged that Article 2(4) was specifically and exclusively designed to allow measures which although discriminatory in appearance, were in fact intended to eliminate or reduce actual instances of inequality which may exist in the reality of social life. It thus permitted national measures relating to access to employment including promotion, which gave a specific advantage to women with a view to improving their ability to compete on the labour market and to pursue a career on an equal footing with men.[3] The Court held however that a national rule which automatically guaranteed women absolute and unconditional priority for appointment or promotion in sectors where they were under-represented when shortlisted and candidates of both sexes were equally qualified, exceeded the limits of the exception in Article 2(4).

In the later case of *Marschall v Land Nordrhein-Westfalen*,[4] the legislation was less automatic in effect. It provided that 'where there were fewer women than men in a particular higher post in a career bracket, women are to be given priority for promotion in the event of equal suitability, competence, and professional performance, unless reasons specific to an individual [male] candidate tilt the balance in his favour.' Marschall was a schoolteacher who applied for promotion to a higher position and was told that a woman was appointed owing to the operation of this rule. His case to the German court that the law was incompatible with Article 2(4) was referred to the ECJ. The ECJ held that legislation providing for preferential treatment for women in cases of equally qualified candidates in sectors where women are under-represented may fall within the exception of Article 2(4) it contains a savings clause in the case where reasons specific to the male tilt the balance in his favour. Such a rule, unlike the rule in *Kalanke*, did not guarantee absolute and unconditional priority for women and therefore fell within Article 2(4). An important ground for this decision to widen the basis for positive discrimination was the Court's acceptance of a need to reconcile equal treatment with the *existing* prejudice against women. As the ECJ stated, 'As the Land and several governments have pointed out, it appears that even where male and female candidates are equally qualified, male candidates tend to be promoted in preference to female candidates, particularly because of prejudices and stereotypes concerning the role and capacities of women in working life...For these reasons, the mere fact that a male candidate and a female candidate are equally qualified does not mean they have the same chances.'

3 Ibid at paras 18-19.
4 [1998] IRLR 39.

In so far as a practice of existing discrimination is evident, positive discrimination need not be limited solely to the removal of barriers to qualification for women in education and vocational training; it can also extend to suitably drafted measures designed to accelerate equality of representation. Nevertheless, the proponents of the amendment to Article 119 in the draft Amsterdam Treaty have been well advised to advocate the insertion of the following rule in the Treaty: 'With a view to ensuring full equality in practice between men and women in working life, the principle of equal treatment shall not prevent any Member State from maintaining or adopting measures providing for specific advantages to make it easier for the under-represented sex to pursue a vocational activity or to prevent or compensate for disadvantages in professional careers.'

## PROVING DISCRIMINATION

In principle, the burden of proof of discrimination is placed upon the party alleging discrimination. Employers bear the burden of proof only where they seek to establish a defence. Nevertheless, in discrimination cases the judiciary have allowed an inference to be drawn where the circumstances are consistent with the possibility of discrimination taking place which makes allowances for the difficulties of complainants having access to affirmative evidence. In two 1981 cases, the EAT[5] urged that in cases of sex discrimination and race discrimination it was important to recognise that a person who claims that he or she has been a victim of unlawful discrimination will almost always face great difficulties in proving the case because (a) the alleged discriminator is most unlikely to admit the discrimination, and (b) the discrimination can often result from a wish to preserve an existing pattern of employment which works well rather than a deliberate wish to exclude the complainant as an individual.

In *Baker v Cornwall County Council*[6] the Court of Appeal endorsed this approach by holding that if discrimination takes place in circumstances which are consistent with the treatment being based on grounds of sex or race, the industrial tribunal should be prepared to draw the inference that the discrimination was on such grounds unless the alleged discriminator can satisfy the tribunal that there was some other innocent explanation. In effect the Court of Appeal was saying that if the complainant could present an adequate prima facie case, then the burden of proof (not simply the burden of producing evidence) shifts to the defendant. In *Baker*, the

5 *Khanna v Ministry of Defence* [1981] ICR 653, [1981] IRLR 331, EAT; *Chattopadhyay v Headmaster of Holloway School* [1982] ICR 132, [1981] IRLR 487, EAT.

6 [1990] ICR 452, [1990] IRLR 194, CA.

prima facie case consisted of Mrs Baker's success in being the only one qualifying for a post when it was first advertised and not being given the job when the vacancy was re-advertised.

Moreover, in *North West Thames Regional Health Authority v Noone*[7] the Court of Appeal stated that where there is a finding that a black candidate has not been selected in spite of having superior qualifications and there is an inadequate or unsatisfactory explanation by the employer for the discrimination, then usually the legitimate inference will be that the discrimination was on racial grounds.

In *Dornan v Belfast City Council*[8] the Northern Ireland Court of Appeal held that a prima facie case was established when the complainant had shown that (a) she was *better* qualified than the successful candidate, and (b) the unsuccessful candidate was a woman and the successful candidate was a man. Once a prima facie case was made out, the evidential burden shifted to the employer to disapprove such discrimination by providing a clear and specific explanation to the satisfaction of the tribunal.

Another way of establishing a prima facie case is by the use of a statistical inference of discrimination. In *West Midlands Passenger Transport Executive v Singh*[9] the Court of Appeal indicated that:

> '... evidence that a particular employer has or has not appointed any or many coloured applicants in the past is ... material to the question whether he has discriminated on racial grounds against a particular complainant.'

Since discrimination involved an individual not being treated on his own merits but as receiving unfavourable treatment because he was a member of a particular group, statistical evidence might establish a discernible pattern which might give rise to an inference of discrimination against the group. For if a practice were being operated against a group, unless the employer could give a satisfactory explanation, it was reasonable to infer that the complainant as a member of the group had himself been treated less favourably on the grounds of race.

*Singh*'s case also suggested a wider criterion of relevance and necessity in the discovery procedure available. The difficulties faced by complainants to meet their burden of proof were acknowledged in the Sex Discrimination Act by the provision of two procedures. The first is a questionnaire procedure which allows the complainant to serve a notice on a potential or actual respondent within 21 days of the commencement

7 [1988] ICR 813, [1988] IRLR 195, CA. See also *King v Great Britain-China Centre* [1992] ICR 516, [1991] IRLR 513, CA.

8 [1990] IRLR 179, NICA, but see *British Gas plc v Sharma* [1991] ICR 19, [1991] IRLR 101, EAT.

9 [1988] ICR 614, [1988] IRLR 186, CA.

of proceedings questioning the respondent on his reasons for doing any relevant act or on any other relevant matter. The question and reply are admissible in evidence and a failure to reply or evasiveness entitle the tribunal to draw an inference of discrimination, though few do so apart from in exceptional circumstances.[10]

The rather more substantial procedure is the discovery procedure which has been described as 'specifically designed to offset the prohibitive disadvantage which the complainant would otherwise suffer'.[11] It is guided by principles set out by the House of Lords in *Nasse and Vyas*,[12] ie that:

(i) discovery is essential to a fair decision because the necessary information to prove discrimination is normally in the possession of respondents;
(ii) confidentiality is a factor to be considered but not a reason for refusing discovery; the necessity of disclosure should not preclude close attention to the possibility of preserving confidentiality of irrelevant information;
(iii) the test for courts and tribunals is the necessity of discovery for fairly disposing of the proceedings or for saving costs.

Employers can plead that discovery requests are oppressive where they require the presentation of material not readily available and requiring great expense, or excessively difficult to obtain, or if the process will add greatly to the length and costs of the hearing.[13] So the test is threefold: is the material relevant? Is the material necessary for fairly disposing of the case? Is its production not oppressive?

## ENFORCEMENT AND REMEDIES

The classic feature of discrimination legislation is that individuals are hurt by a collective practice. An effective type of remedy would be one directly aimed at the collective practice. The Sex Discrimination Act however does not incorporate such a remedy in its armoury of enforcement measures.

10 But see now *Carrington v Helix Lighting Ltd* [1990] ICR 125, [1990] IRLR 6, EAT. No duty on employers to provide details of the ethnic composition of their workforce if not already available to them.
11 *British Library v Palyza* [1984] ICR 504 at 507.
12 *Science Research Council v Nassé* [1979] ICR 921, [1979] IRLR 465; *Leyland Cars v Vyas* [1979] ICR 921, [1979] IRLR 465.
13 *West Midlands Passenger Transport Executive v Singh* [1988] 2 All ER 873, CA.

Instead, it provides three types of remedy for individual workers who bring a complaint within the relevant time limit.[14] In addition to the remedy of a declaration of rights,[15] the Act provides for a remedy of compensation of an amount corresponding to any damages in like manner as any other claim in tort.[16] Finally, the Act provides the remedy of a recommendation for action by the employer to remove the discrimination.[17] The legislation makes it plain that court orders have no place in the armoury of enforcement measures for individual claims. The recommendation for action is clearly that and not an order. If employers fail to observe such recommendations unreasonably there may be an added element of compensation, but not above the statutory limit for compensation.

Under UK law an action recommendation does not include the power to make a recommendation as to payment of remuneration.[18] Under EC law there could be a different result. In *Kowalska v Freie und Hansestadt Hamburg*[19] the ECJ held that the clauses of a collective agreement which excluded part-time workers from a right to severance payments were in breach of Article 119 unless the employer could show objective justification. It was not enough, however, merely to declare the term void as German law provided, it was necessary to award benefits which were proportionate to their hours of work.[20] Moreover, UK courts are obliged by the principle of direct effect to do everything in their power to provide effective remedies.[1]

14 Normally three months from the time the act was done (s 76(1)); or a deliberate omission (s 76(6)(c)); or the end of a continuing act (s 76(6)(b)). The tribunals have discretion to consider out of time complaints on equitable grounds (s 76(5)).
15 SDA, s 65(1)(a).
16 SDA, s 65(1)(c).
17 SDA, s 65(1)(c).
18 *Prestcold Ltd v Irvine* [1981] ICR 777, [1981] IRLR 281, CA.
19 C-33/89 [1990] ECR I-2591, [1990] IRLR 447. See *Defrenne v SABENA*: 43/75 [1981] 1 All ER 122n, [1976] ECR 455 in which the ECJ indicated that an adjustment of unequal pay and conditions should be 'upwards'. See *Fitzpatrick* case note [1991] MLR 271 at 276 arguing the relevance of Article 117/EEC and the third recital of the preamble of the Treaty of Rome for the principle of upwards equalisation. See Reiland 'Sex Discrimination in Collective Agreements' [1991] ILJ 79; Nielson and Szyczak *Social Policy in the EEC*.
20 See now s 25 of TURER giving individuals a right to complain of discriminatory terms in collective agreement with a remedy of a declaration that the term is void.
1 See eg Fitzpatrick 'The Sex Discrimination Act 1986' [1987] 50 MLR 934.

## Compensation for discrimination

In calculating the amount of compensation for direct sex discrimination, tort principles normally apply.[2] In cases where individuals have missed out on an opportunity for selection, the measure of damages must take into account the fact that what has been lost as a result of the discrimination is the loss of an opportunity to compete as opposed to the loss of the job itself.

Injury to feelings is an important head of damages.[3] At an earlier stage a figure of £3,000 was regarded as the top end of the range but with the removal of the maximum limit to compensation generally, a figure of £21,000 was found acceptable in *Armitage, Marsden and HM Prison Service*,[4] because the effect of discrimination went to thwarted long-term ambitions as opposed to a more concrete pattern of harassment. In cases where the defendant has acted maliciously or insultingly or oppressively, the plaintiff can ask for aggravated damages.[5] Exemplary damages are rare in such cases.[6]

In cases of discriminatory dismissals, the measure of damages is the financial loss caused by the dismissal usually broken down into: (a) the loss incurred up to the date of the tribunal hearing, and (b) the loss which may be expected to arise out of either future unemployment or a job which pays less and/or offers fewer fringe benefits.

In *Marshall v Southampton and South-West Hampshire Area Health Authority (No 2)*,[7] the ECJ ruled that (i) damages for discriminatory dismissals may not be subject to an upper limit fixed *a priori* or excluding interest for delayed payment, and (ii) Article 6 of the ETD is directly effective vertically to set aside a national law imposing limits on compensation. Regulations have since been promulgated to remove such

2 In the case of vicarious liablity of employers for sex and racial harassment there is a wider test of scope of employment. See eg *Tower Boot Co Ltd v Jones* [1995] IRLR 529, EAT; see too *Chessington World of Adventures v Reed* [1997] IRLR 556, EAT; *Burton v De Vere Hotels* [1996] IRLR 596, EAT.

3 See *Alexander v Home Office* [1988] ICR 685, [1988] IRLR 190, CA. See too *Sharifi v Strathclyde Regional Council* [1992] IRLR 259, EAT (£500 at or near the minimum); *Deane v Ealing London Borough Council* [1993] ICR 329.

4 [1997] IRLR 162, EAT. See eg *Chaplin v Hicks* [1911] 2 KB 786, CA.

5 See *Skyrail Oceanic Ltd v Coleman* [1981] ICR 864, [1981] IRLR 398, CA; *Deane* ibid.

6 Ibid; see now *Deane v Ealing London Borough Council* [1993] ICR 329, [1993] IRLR 209, EAT, see also *North West Thames Regional Health Authority v Noone* [1988] ICR 813, [1988] IRLR 195, CA. *Alexander v Home Office* [1988] 2 All ER 118, [1988] IRLR 190, CA; *Bradford City Metropolitan Council v Arora* [1991] 2 QB 507, [1991] IRLR 165, CA; Phang [1991] ILJ 139.

7 [1991] ICR 136, [1990] IRLR 481.

limits from the Sex Discrimination Act[8] along with the former provision that there could be no compensation for unintentional indirect discrimination.[9] Recent complaints against the Ministry of Defence by service women dismissed for pregnancy brought under the new rules have resulted in compensation of more than £300,000.[10]

As mentioned, the Sex Discrimination Act does not include a collective remedy. The device of the class action - a feature of the US rules of Federal Procedure - has been eschewed, despite the potential in such actions to combine individual claims into actions with a scale of liability for organisations which can bring about widespread changes in policy. Instead, a 'softly–softly' approach has been taken to the collective aspects of discrimination issues. An enforcement agency has been created, the Equal Opportunities Commission, to assist individual claimants who need financial and legal help with their claims. In recent years, the EOC has also directly used judicial review to achieve results. In *Birmingham City Council v* EOC,[11] the Commission succeeded in establishing that the Council was in breach of the Act in failing to provide an equal number of grammar school places for girls as for boys. In *R v Secretary of State for Employment, ex p EOC*,[12] the House of Lords held that the EOC could challenge the qualifying conditions placed on part-timers for claims for redundancy payments and unfair dismissals. In addition, it has power to engage in formal investigation of wider issues of discrimination - to issue non-discrimination notices and enforce them (SDA, ss 67-70). Moreover there are powers to act against discriminatory advertisements (SDA, s 72) and to obtain injunctions to stop persistent discrimination (SDA, s 7).

There is an obligation to inform accused persons, and offer a hearing with a representative. But there is also a power to compel the disclosure of information, backed by the sanctions available to summon witnesses in the ordinary courts.

The real potential of the enforcement agency to bring about change in the short term lies with its powers to conduct formal investigations and bring enforcement proceedings in specific areas of discriminatory advertising, instructions and pressure to discriminate and persistent discrimination. The power to conduct formal investigations is wide (SDA, s 57). These investigations can either take a general form, for example the provision of equal opportunities in entry to training courses in the accountancy profession, or they can be accusatory in form - for example

8 Sex Discrimination and Equal Pay (Remedies) Regulations 1993, SI 1993 No 2798.
9 SI 1996 No 438.
10 See eg *Ministry of Defence v Cannock* [1994] IRLR 509, EAT; *Ministry of Defence v Hunt* [1996] IRLR 139, EAT.
11 [1989] IRLR 173, HL.
12 [1995] 1 AC 1, HL. See discussion Ch 7.

investigations of actions of a particular named employer. In the latter case the formal investigation must proceed on the basis of terms of reference drawn up by the Commission or the Secretary of State which must include the belief held by the Commissioner as to the unlawful acts which may have been committed.

As the House of Lords has held, however, the terms of reference for a named accusatory investigation must disclose at least 'a suspicion that there may have been an act by the person named of racial discrimination of the kind that it is proposed to investigate'[13] or 'some grounds for so suspecting'[14] even if the grounds were tenuous at that stage. These interpretations have meant that despite the wealth of the formal legislative powers of the Commissions, they cannot engage in *inspection* at their own initiative. As Lacey has pointed out, 'the judgments are dominated by the legal perspective of the CRE primarily fulfilling a policing and accusation function' rather than the wider statutory aims of good relations and equality of opportunity.[15] Moreover, the procedural steps in the accusation procedures have proven to be a fertile source for delaying tactics by the legal advisers of accused companies.

These enforcement agencies have been more successful in pursuing their educational role. They help to promote research, keep the law under review, suggest proposals for amendments and issue Codes of Practice.

The codes have been used to elaborate on the nature of the practices which have been made unlawful. They also contain recommendations for action on employers to prevent discrimination, such as wider notification of vacancies, promotion and training opportunities; the monitoring of selection tests; the regular re-examination of GOQs to see whether they continue to be necessary; emphasis on the need for active support from higher management and the importance of positive action. However, the codes are not directly binding in law, though they can be taken into account by tribunals where they are relevant to an issue in a case (SDA 1975, s 56A(10)). The beneficial effects of the codes are likely to be felt in the long term.

There is little doubt that the legislation overall has had a relatively limited effect on discrimination. It could be argued that even if many of the specific recommendations for strengthening the legislation were adopted, there would still be difficulties in making inroads into the structural features of discrimination in society. Nonetheless, there is a difference between producing legislation close to the edges of legislative

13 *Hillingdon London Borough Council v Commission for Racial Equality* [1982] AC 779 at 791, HL.
14 *Re Prestige Group plc* [1984] ICR 473 at 481, HL.
15 Lacey (1985) 14 ILJ 64 at 66.

possibility and producing legislation which falls short of the potential of what *legislation* can do. It is on that criterion that existing discrimination law is found wanting.

The major and ineluctable impetus to change in the legislation appears to be the ongoing need to adjust to the changing requirements of Article 119 as interpreted by the ECJ.

# CHAPTER 14
# Equal pay

## INTRODUCTION: THE EQUAL PAY CLAIM

The average pay of men and women in private industry and in public sector employment is unequal. Average hourly female earnings are about 79% of male earnings. Weekly earnings of full-time manual women workers amount to just over 72% of the weekly earnings of full-time manual men. The extra overtime worked predominantly by men accounts for less than one-third of the difference.

The main reason for the difference in pay between men and women is that men and women work mainly in different jobs with different rates of pay and jobs which are predominantly women's jobs are traditionally paid at lower levels.[1]

Management and collective bargaining have helped both to originate and perpetuate the development of these sectors of lower paid work for females and higher paid work for males. Job evaluation and job classification schemes have historically either openly discriminated against women's work by setting separate pay rates for men and women or more subtly discriminated by giving different weights to the factors which predominate in female work. Along with the prejudice which underlies the lower valuation of women's work is the real difference in labour market behaviour of women workers owing to their greater share of responsibility for child rearing.[2]

This area became ripe for reform in the late 1960s in part because of the pressure generated from international sources: the ILO convention on equal pay for equal value affected policy preparation even though Britain

1 See Fredman *Women and the Law* (Clarendon Press, Oxford, 1997); Rubenstein 'The Equal Treatment Directive and UK Law' in McCrudden (ed) *Women, Employment and European Equality Law* (1987).

2 See Szyszczak 'The Equal Pay Directive and UK Law' in McCrudden (ed) *Women, Employment and European Equality Law* (1987).

did not ratify it until 1971. Moreover, Article 119 of the Treaty of Rome was influential even though Britain did not enter the Common Market until 1973. However, domestic pressures were also compelling. In the late 1960s, reacting to a well publicised sewing trim machinists strike at Fords, the Labour government produced a new law on equal pay in 1970, to come into effect in 1975.[3]

The 1970 Act contained two main methods to achieve equality of pay and other terms and conditions between men and women. One was to deal directly with collective agreements and pay structures to remove their discriminatory provisions. The Act provided a procedure for referring collective agreements or pay structures to the Central Arbitration Committee (CAC). If the agreement or pay structure was discriminatory on its face, eg by setting separate male and female rates, the CAC could raise the female rates to the lowest male rate. If the discrimination took a more subtle form, however, it could not be dealt with by this provision.[4] With so much pay inequality residing in pay structures, whether established by collective agreement or by managerial pay systems, the logical approach to legislation would have been to attempt to achieve equal pay by a method which emphasised action directed towards collective agreements or pay structures as collective entities. However, logic and policy do not always coincide and the 'collective route' chosen in the statute was too narrow to have any real impact on pay inequality.

The second method, which is the primary approach now used, was to allow individuals[5] to make an equal pay claim to industrial tribunals. First, the Act provided that where men and women were employed on 'like work' in the same employment, an employee could claim that there was an inequality in the terms and conditions of their contracts of employment (Equal Pay Act, s 1(2)(a)). The 1970 Act defined 'like work' very narrowly as consisting of the 'same work' or 'work of a broadly similar nature' (Equal Pay Act, s 1(4)). It made no effort to allow women to draw comparisons with men in jobs which were 'of equal value', following the principles of the ILO convention. In part, the draughtsmen assumed that the EC standard of equal work meant the 'same work'. Moreover, the line drawn reflected a legislative concern that too wide an individual claim might create too much disruption to established pay structures.[6]

3 Davies, P L 'European Equality Legislation, UK Legislative Policy and Industrial Relations' in McCrudden *Women, Employment and European Equality Law* Eclipse (1987) p 26.

4 See eg CAC Annual Report 1977; See also *R v Central Arbitration Committee, ex p Hy-Mac Ltd* [1979] IRLR 461. Davies, P L 'The Central Arbitration Committee and Equal Pay' [1980] CLP 165.

5 Ie 'employees' or those working under a contract personally to execute any work or labour: EPA, s 1(8).

6 See Davies, fn 3, p 27.

Along with the like work claim was a second claim, ie where men and women in the same employment were employed on work which was 'rated as equivalent', and there was an inequality of terms and conditions of their contracts of employment (Equal Pay Act, s 1(2)(b)). This claim applied only to those relatively rare cases where jobs were rated equivalent but pay structures were discriminatory. It allowed no challenge to discriminatory job evaluation systems which unfairly produced non-equivalent ratings for jobs.[7]

With Britain's entry to the Common Market, this rather limited approach to equalisation of pay soon had to be reformed. At the time, the scope of the equal pay principle under Article 119 was not fully appreciated in the UK. It was viewed initially as equal pay for the same work, a view fortified by a rather literal reading of the phrase *le même travail* in the official French text of the Treaty. However, in 1975 the EEC Council, concerned at the uneven progress in implementation of Article 119, adopted an Equal Pay Directive 75/117 which made it clear to member states that the principle of equal pay outlined in Article 119 of the Treaty (which they were obliged to implement) meant that there should be no discrimination in the pay and other terms and conditions of men and women in either the same work or in work of equal value, and that in particular where there was a job classification system used for determining pay it could not be discriminatory on grounds of sex (Article 1).

Although the ECJ itself initially viewed the directive as extending the Article by widening the definition of equal pay,[8] in *Jenkins v Kingsgate (Clothing Productions) Ltd*[9] it proclaimed that Article 1 of the Equal Pay Directive re-states the principle of equal pay set out in Article 119 of the Treaty, and it 'in no way alters the content or scope of the principle as defined in the Treaty'.[10]

The UK Government was slow to respond to the Equal Pay Directive and was the subject of infringement proceedings by the EC Commission before the ECJ.[11] In response, the UK Government enacted the Equal Pay (Amendment) Regulations 1983 which amended the 1970 Act, by providing that in addition to drawing comparisons with men in 'like work', women could draw upon men in the same employment in work of equal value as comparators.

The Equal Pay Act 1970, as modified by the Equal Pay (Amendment) Regulations 1983 now provides an entitlement for women to equal pay as well as other terms and conditions of employment in three circumstances:

7 One reason for this was the concern to avoid comparability pay claims motivated by grounds other than sex discrimination. See Davies, note 3, p 27.

8 *Defrenne v Sabena*: 43/75 [1981] 1 All ER 122n, [1976] ECR 455.

9 96/80: [1981] ECR 911, [1981] IRLR 228.

10 Ibid.

11 *EC Commission v United Kingdom*: 61/81 [1982] ICR 578, [1982] IRLR 333, ECJ.

(i) where they are able to show that their work is either the same or broadly similar (s 1(2)(a), s 1(4));
(ii) where their work is rated as equivalent under a job evaluation scheme (s 1(2)(b)); or
(iii) where their work is of equal value (s 1(2)(c)) as the work of a man, as long as that man is working in the same employment or in another establishment of the same employer or an associated employer where common terms and conditions of employment are observed.

In such cases, however, employers have a defence under s 1(3): they may show that the unequal pay was due to a material factor other than sex. If unlawful pay discrimination is proved the Act gives industrial tribunals the statutory power to deem a woman's contract to include a contractual term corresponding to that in a male comparator's contract (Equal Pay Act 1970, s 1(1), s 1(2)) and provides a claim for damages in respect of any contravention of the statutorily modified term, (Equal Pay Act, s 2(1)).[12]

A woman can choose to compare any term of her contract with that of a man, whether the term is one of pay or not, unless the term falls within one of the three main exclusions, ie contractual terms affected by protective legislation for women (s 6(1)(a)); contractual provisions connected with pregnancy or childbirth (s 6(1)(b)); and contractual provisions related to or connected with death and retirement (s 6(1A)(b)), or is a social security scheme or benefit directly settled by law.[13]

The provisions of the Equal Pay Act must now be read in conjunction with Article 119 and the Equal Pay Directive. For it is now settled law that Article 119 operates not only by impliedly amending the 1970 Act[14] but also by conferring a freestanding right independently of that Act[15] enforceable by industrial tribunals in cases which are not covered by the Act.

For the purpose of this chapter therefore we shall look at the essentials of the equal pay claim under UK law, as modified by Community law.

12 See eg *Sorbie v Trust Houses Forte Hotels Ltd* [1977] ICR 55, [1976] IRLR 371, EAT (the effect of an equality clause is to strike out the less favourable rate and substitute the higher rate). See too *Hayward v Cammell Laird Shipbuilders Ltd* [1988] AC 894, [1988] IRLR 257, HL.
13 *Defrenne v Belgium* 80/70 [1976] ECR 455 para. 7
14 *Pickstone v Freemans plc* [1988] ICR 697, [1988] IRLR 357, HL.
15 *Albion Shipping Agency v Arnold* [1982] ICR 22, [1981] IRLR 525, EAT.

## THE SCOPE OF 'PAY' UNDER THE EQUAL PAY ACT AND ARTICLE 119

The Equal Pay Act itself does not define pay but the ECJ has given it a wide interpretation making full use of the fact that under Article 119 'pay' includes not only 'the ordinary basic or minimum wage or salary' but also 'any other consideration, whether cash or kind, which the worker receives, directly or indirectly in respect of his employment from his employer.' In *Garland v British Rail Engineering Ltd*,[16] for example, special facilities for travel made available to employees upon retirement were held to be covered by Article 119. Pay was defined for the purposes of Article 119 as including 'any consideration, whether in cash or in kind, whether immediate or future, provided that the worker receives it albeit indirectly in respect of his employment from his employer.'

In *Barber v Guardian Royal Exchange*,[17] the ECJ decided that certain payments made after the termination of the employment relationship did not preclude them from constituting pay within the meaning of Article 119 of the Treaty. In that case, Mr Barber was dismissed for redundancy at the age of 52 and was not granted an immediate pension by the employer but only a pension deferred until he reached the age of 62. He complained that had he been a woman aged 52, he would have had an immediate pension as well as a redundancy payment since women who had been made redundant and had reached the age of 50 qualified for an immediate pension whereas men had to reach the age of 55.

The ECJ, after confirming that the concept of pay within the meaning of Article 119 comprises all benefits in cash or in kind, present or future, provided they are paid, albeit indirectly, by the employer to the worker in connection with his employment, held that voluntary or contracted out pensions were to be regarded as pay under Article 119 as opposed to occupational pensions under the Occupational Social Security Directive.[18] For unlike the benefits awarded by national statutory social security schemes, a pension paid under a contracted out scheme constitutes consideration paid by the employer to the worker in respect of his employment.

Since *Defrenne*[19] it had been thought that social security schemes, in particular retirement pensions, directly governed by legislation without any element of agreement within the undertaking and which were compulsorily applied to general categories of workers, fell outside the

16 12/81: [1982] ICR 420, [1982] IRLR 111, ECJ.

17 C-262/88: [1990] ICR 616, [1990] IRLR 240, ECJ.

18 Directive 86/378 on Equal Treatment in Occupational Social Security OJL 225/40 12.8.1986. *Barber* also held that Article 119 rendered nugatory certain exceptions in that Directive, see Ellis *European Community Sex Equality Law* pp 52-3.

19 *Defrenne v Belgium*: 80/70 [1976] ECR 455 para 7.

scope of Article 119. Moreover, in *Newstead v Department of Transport*[20] the ECJ held that contributions to a contracted out pension scheme, just like contributions to a statutory scheme, must be considered to fall outside Article 119 because they were matters of social security governed by Article 118. In effect *Newstead* viewed the voluntary retirement as tied to the statutory pension scheme.

However, in *Barber* the ECJ pointed out that a voluntary or contracted out pension was wholly or largely financed by the employer and therefore formed part of the consideration offered to workers by the employer. Even if the benefits which such schemes provided were in part a substitute for those of a general statutory scheme, they nevertheless were similar in function to the *Bilka* type supplementary pension schemes,[1] where affiliation to the statutory scheme was compulsory, and hence were pay falling within Article 119.

*Barber* thus confirmed the narrow interpretation of the exclusion in relation to death and retirement contained in Article 7(1)(a) and the link between employment terms and the exclusion of the Social Security Directive for social security given in *Marshall*'s case.[2] In *Marshall*'s case an employer's mandatory retiring age was classified as a 'working condition'. The ECJ held that it was contrary to Article 119 to impose an age condition which differs according to sex in respect of pensions paid under a contracted out scheme, even if the difference between the pensionable ages of men and women is based on a national statutory scheme. This marked the end of a line of cases such as *Newstead* which had given an unduly wide interpretation to the end phrase in Article 7(1)(a) 'and the possible consequences thereof for other benefits'.[3]

The ECJ later confirmed in *Bestuur van het Algemeen Burgerlijk Pensioen fonds v Beune*[4] that 'pay' in Article 119 applies to all pension benefits paid to a worker under the employment relationship. The ECJ in *Barber* held that its judgment was not to have retrospective effect apart from those who had already initiated proceedings. In *Teu Oeuer*[5] the ECJ

20 192/85: [1988] 1 All ER 129, [1988] IRLR 66, ECJ.

1 See eg *Bilka-Kaufhaus GmbH v Weber von Hartz*: 170/84 [1987] ICR 110, [1986] IRLR 317, ECJ.

2 *Marshall v Southampton and Southwest Hampshire Area Health Authority (Teaching)*: 152/84 [1986] QB 401, [1986] IRLR 140, ECJ; *Newstead v Department of Transport*: 192/85 [1988] ICR 332, [1988] IRLR 66, ECJ.

3 See eg *Burton v British Railways Board*: 19/81 [1982] ECR 555, [1982] 2 CMLR 136; *Thomas v Adjudication Officer and Secretary of State for Social Security* [1990] 3 CMLR 611, [1990] IRLR 436, CA.

4 [1995] IRLR 103, ECJ.

5 *Ten Oever v Stichting Bedrijfspensioen Fonds* [1993] IRLR 601, ECJ; see too *Coloroll Pensions Trustees Ltd v Russell* [1994] IRLR 586, ECJ; *Moroni v Firma Collo GmbH* [1994] IRLR 130, ECJ.

confirmed that Article 119 could only apply to benefits payable in relation to periods of service after the date of the *Barber* judgment.

In *Barber*, the ECJ also confirmed that compulsory redundancy payments in principle fell within Article 119 because they were a form of payment to which workers are entitled in respect of their employment relationship with a view to facilitating their adaptation to the new circumstances which are the result of this termination. It is in effect a form of deferred remuneration.[6] Ex gratia payments fell within pay under Article 119 because that article applies to advantages which employers grant to workers although they are not required to do so by contract. Moreover, the fact that redundancy payments were a statutory payment did not preclude them from falling within Article 119 because although they reflected considerations of social policy, they were benefits in the nature of pay which the employee was entitled to receive by reason of the existence of the employment relationship.[7]

One effect of the *Barber* decision was to widen the category of cases covered by Article 119/EEC and narrow that covered solely by 'working conditions' under the Equal Treatment Directive 76/207. In *Defrenne v SABENA*[8] the Court held that 'the fact that the fixing of certain conditions of employment may have pecuniary consequences is not sufficient to bring such conditions within the field of application of Article 119. In *Bilka* the Court held that conditions of access to an occupational pension scheme fell within Article 119. In *Burton v British Railways Board*,[9] however, the ECJ had held that the conditions of access to a voluntary redundancy scheme did not fall within Article 119; it fell under the Equal Treatment Directive.

The ECJ in *Barber* held that the imposed age condition for the voluntary pension fell within Article 119 (para 32), leaving in place its view in *Bilka* that Article 119 applies to working conditions with direct legal consequences. This distinction has since been upheld. In *Nimz*[9a], the semi-automatic reclassification rules for salary grades in a collective agreement were held to be 'pay' under Article 119 whereas in *Gerster*[9b] a system of seniority for civil servants was held to be too indirectly linked to fall under Article 119. In *Seymour-Smith*[9c] the Attorney-General recommended that the two-year service condition for unfair dismissal was not pay under

6 *Kowalska v Freie und Hansestadt Hamburg* :C-33/89 [1992] ICR 29, [1990] IRLR 447, *Garland v British Rail Engineering Ltd*: 12/81 [1983] 2 AC 751, [1982] 2 All ER 402. See too *McKechnie v UBM Building Supplies (Southern) Ltd* [1991] 2 CMLR 668, [1991] IRLR 283.

7 See now *Rankin v British Coal Corpn* [1993] IRLR 69, EAT.

8 149/77: [1978] ECR 1365, p 21.

9 19/81: [1982] ECR 555, ECJ.

9a [1991] ECR I-297 (para 10).

9b [1997] ECR I-5253 (para 21).

9c Case C-197/97, 14 August 1998.

Article 119 even though compensation for unfair dismissal might be. The ECJ judgment is awaited.

In *Vroege v NCIV Institut voor Volkshuisvesting Bv*[10] the ECJ reaffirmed *Bilka* but held that the retrospectiveness limits in the *Barber* judgment and the protocol to the Maastricht Treaty applies to benefits and not to rights of access to pension schemes. This right was qualified in *Fisscher v Voorhuis Hengelo Bv*[11] by the requirement that the employee must pay employee contributions and respect national time limits.

## EACH ELEMENT OF REMUNERATION

Finally, *Barber* confirmed that under Article 119 the principle of equal pay applied in respect of any term of the contract to 'each element of remuneration' and cannot be based on a comprehensive assessment of the consideration paid to workers. In *Hayward v Cammell Laird Shipbuilders Ltd*[12] the House of Lords held that under the Equal Pay Act, as amended, an employee can choose to compare any term of her contract (whether pay or otherwise) with her comparator and that it was not open to the employer to argue at this stage that the package of remuneration as a whole should be considered a 'term' of the contract.

Hence on this point UK law was in line with Article 119. What was less clear, however, was to what extent it was open to the employer to put forward the argument as a defence under s 1(3) of the Equal Pay Act, that the overall package of remuneration restored equality of pay. We shall return to this point later in this chapter.

### Choice of comparator

Under the Equal Pay Act a woman can choose any comparator she likes[13] provided that he is, or has been,[14] in the same employment or in another

10 [1994] IRLR 651, ECJ. Note that the retrospective effect of *Barber* goes back as far as 8 April 1976, the date of the ruling of the ECJ in *Defrenne v Sabena* [1976] ECR 455, ECJ, that Article 119 had direct effect.

11 [1994] IRLR 662, ECJ.

12 [1988] ICR 464, [1988] IRLR 257, HL.

13 See eg *Ainsworth v Glass Tubes and Components Ltd* [1977] ICR 347, [1977] IRLR 74, EAT; *Pickstone v Freemans plc* [1989] AC 66, [1988] 2 All ER 803, HL but see *Dance v Dorothy Perkins Ltd* [1978] ICR 760, EAT (the anomalous comparator). See also *McPherson v Rathgael Centre for Children and Young People* [1991] IRLR 206, NICA.

14 A predecessor in the same employment can be a comparator. See eg *Albion Shipping Agency v Arnold* [1982] ICR 22, [1981] IRLR 525, EAT. See too *Macarthys Ltd v Smith* [1980] ICR 672, [1980] IRLR 210, ECJ.

employment of the same employer, or an associated employer[15] where common terms and conditions are observed. Under Article 119, the limits to the scope for comparison are less clearly defined.[16]

In choosing a comparator from the same establishment, it is possible to cross traditional demarcation lines and compare salaried with manual jobs as well as jobs in different grades within each sector. For example, Julie Hayward was a canteen cook and chose to compare herself with skilled craftsmen such as painters, joiners, etc.[17]

Moreover, where there is no suitable individual in the same establishment, the comparison may be drawn with a man in another establishment[18] of the same employer, or an associated employer, provided that common terms and conditions are observed either generally or for employees of the relevant class (s 1(6)). In *Leverton v Clwyd County Council*,[19] a Local Authority nursery nurse, who had school holidays and worked only school hours, was successful in her claim to be compared with male clerical workers employed elsewhere by the Local Authority on the same set of salary scales based on collective agreement albeit at different grade points. The House of Lords held that s 1(6) which required that terms and conditions of employment in the two establishments must be broadly similar was satisfied since the section contemplated terms and conditions applicable to a wide range of employees whose individual terms varied greatly. It could not accept that it was appropriate to narrow down the focus to the terms and conditions of the complainant and her comparators under s 1(2)(b). Again, this did not preclude the employer bringing in the differences in terms and conditions as a defence under s 1(3). This would also suggest that a common pay structure imposed by management will also allow a cross-establishment equal pay claim.

The Court made the point that, 'The paradigm, though not the only example, of the common terms are conditions of employment governed by the same collective agreement.' In the case of separate collective agreements or pay and benefit structures in two or more establishments terms and conditions must be 'substantially comparable' or 'broadly similar' for a claim to fall within s 1(6).[20]

15 An associated employer is defined in s 1(6)(c) to be where 'one is a company of which the other (directly or indirectly) has control or if both are companies of which a third person (directly or indirectly) has control'.

16 See *Ellis* pp 62-4. See *British Coal Corpn v Smith* [1996] IRLR 404, HC ('sufficiently similar to allow comparison to be made' (at p 408)).

17 *Hayward v Cammell Laird Shipbuilders Ltd* [1988] ICR 464, [1988] IRLR 257, HL.

18 The choice of comparator has been further expanded by EEC law; in *Macarthys Ltd v Smith* [1980] ICR 672, [1980] IRLR 210, the ECJ held that a woman could compare herself with her predecessor.

19 [1989] AC 706, [1988] IRLR 239, CA.

20 See eg *British Coal Corpn v Smith* [1996] IRLR 404, HC.

## THE METHODS OF ACHIEVING EQUAL PAY

As mentioned, statute law makes available to individuals three separate methods of attempting to achieve equal pay.

### (i) Like work

First, under s 1(2)(a), there must be equality of pay if a woman is employed on like work with that of a man. Like work is defined by s 1(4) as work of the same or a broadly similar nature where the differences in terms and conditions of employment are not of practical importance in relation to terms and conditions of employment or a frequent occurrence.

In comparing two jobs to determine whether they are 'like', tribunals have been told to take a broad brush approach rather than to make a microscopic examination, and to avoid trivial distinctions. Thus in *Capper Pass Ltd v Lawton*[1] the EAT found that a canteen cook's work was comparable to that of a male assistant chef in the director's dining room. Where one person has greater responsibilities, such as responsibility for items of greater value as in *Eaton Ltd v Nuttall*[2] or has to move heavier material when deliveries are made, as in *Dance v Dorothy Perkins Ltd*[3] then whether this is contractual or simply part of the performance of the job duties, a claim that the work is 'like' work will be defeated. However, if the different duties are infrequently exercised in practice then these differences can be ignored. Thus in *Shields v E Coomes (Holdings) Ltd*[4] special security responsibilities were rarely exercised. Moreover, in *Dugdale v Kraft Foods Ltd*[5] the male employee was 'prepared to work night shifts' but in fact rarely did.

### (ii) Work rated as equivalent

Secondly, under s 1(2)(b), there must be equality of pay if a woman's work is rated as equivalent to a man's, ie if there has been a job evaluation study which has given them equal value in terms of the demands made upon the worker under effort, skill, decision (s 1(5))[5a]. Under this head, however, there can be no in depth investigation of the discriminatory nature of the job evaluation system: there must be a plain error on the face of the record

1 [1977] ICR 83, [1976] IRLR 366, EAT.
2 [1977] ICR 272, [1977] IRLR 71, EAT.
3 [1978] ICR 760, EAT. See too *Thomas v National Coal Board* [1987] IRLR 751, EAT.
4 [1978] ICR 1159, [1978] IRLR 263, CA
5 [1977] ICR 48, [1976] IRLR 368.
5a See *Springboard Sunderland v Robson* [1992] IRLR 261, EAT (equal value extends to the full results of a scheme including the conversion of points to pay grades).

eg in the values set for certain factors, or some other fundamental error, for the results of the study to be challenged.[6]

If a job evaluation scheme is insufficiently 'analytical' in the meaning of the section, it can be challenged as falling outside the definition. For example, in *Bromley v H & J Quick Ltd*[7] a group of consultants had used a method of ranking jobs based on job description to establish the position of the bench mark jobs. At no point were the jobs other than the bench mark jobs analysed in terms of the factors of effort, skill, decision responsibility, etc unless there happened to be an appeal against the grade allocated to a particular job. The Court of Appeal held that s 1(5) requires that the work of the woman and her comparator must have been analysed under the relevant headings. It was not sufficient for the bench mark jobs to be analysed if the jobs in question were not. However, this basis for challenge is fairly rarely of use.

On the other hand it is possible to claim under Community law that if a job classification system is used for determining pay, it must be based on the same criteria for both men and women and so drawn up as to exclude any discrimination on grounds of sex. This provision was aimed at indirect or disguised discrimination in such schemes.[8]

In *Rummler v Dato-Druck GmbH*[9] a female printer in Germany claimed that she was wrongfully classified under a job classification scheme based on a national collective agreement because the system gave undue weight to muscular effort. The German Labour Court referred the issue to the Court of Justice which held that not only must job classification schemes use the same criteria for men and women but that such schemes must be organised so that as a whole they do not in practice discriminate against one sex. Ms Rummler had argued that the directive outlawed any distinction in job evaluation systems based on muscular effort. The court held that such criteria were permissible as long as they were objectively measurable. However, if a job classification system as a whole was to be non-discriminatory such criteria had to be accompanied by other criteria 'in relation to which women had a particular aptitude'.[10] Moreover, the methods of evaluating criteria must not disadvantage a group of workers of one sex, since that would run the risk of indirect discrimination.

6 *Eaton Ltd v Nuttall* [1977] ICR 272, [1977] IRLR 71; *England v Bromley London Borough Council* [1978] ICR 1, EAT.

7 [1988] ICR 623, [1988] IRLR 249, CA. See too *Eaton Ltd v Nuttell* [1977] ICR 272 (the system must be capable of impartial application and not involve subjective judgments re the nature of the job).

8 See European Commission's Report to the Council on the Application of the Principle of Equal Pay for Men and Women COM (78) 711 pp 65-83.

9 237/85 [1986] ECR 2101, [1987] 3 CMLR 127, ECJ.

10 Ibid at 139.

### (iii) Equal value claims

The third basis for a claim is that of equal value. The equal value claim under the Equal Pay Act, s 1(2)(c) allows a woman to claim that she is employed on work which is in terms of the demands made upon her (for instance under such headings as effort, skill and decision) of equal value to that of a man in the same employment, etc. If read literally, it appears to be essentially a residual right, available only where a woman is employed on work which is neither 'like work' nor 'work rated as equivalent' (s 1(2)(c)).

In *Pickstone v Freemans plc*,[11] however, the House of Lords held that s 1(2)(c) could not be given a purely literal reading given that the scheme of the Treaty and directive required a woman to have an unqualified claim of equal value. In that case women warehouse operatives who brought an equal value claim comparing their work with a checker warehouse operative found that their employers could successfully argue right up to and including the Court of Appeal that the fact that there were men employed as warehouse operatives alongside the complainants meant that the women were employed in 'like work' with men and therefore, reading s 1(2)(c) literally, the equal value claim was not available to them.

The House of Lords decided however that, following the principle in *Von Colson*, to achieve the purpose of interpreting the statute consistent with Community law, it was necessary to read into the language of s 1(2)(c) an additional phrase that it was only where the woman *chose to compare herself with a particular man* that the equal value claim was unavailable if she had a like work or work rated as equivalent claim. This was a clear example of purposive interpretation by the House of Lords sitting as a European Court, widening the substantive base of the UK statute.

## EMPLOYERS' DEFENCES UNDER UK AND EC LAW

Even if an employee succeeds in establishing an equal pay claim under s 1(2)(a), (b) or (c), such a claim may nevertheless be rendered inoperable if the employer can establish either that:

(a) the variation is genuinely due to a material fact or, which is not the difference of sex[12] (s 1(3)); or

11 [1989] AC 66, [1988] IRLR 357, HL.

12 In the case of claims of like work or work rated as equivalent the material factor must be a difference between the man and woman's case; in the case of claims of equal value it may be a difference between the two cases.

(b) there is in existence a job evaluation scheme and there are no reasonable grounds for determining that the scheme was discriminatory (s 2A(2)).

Similarly, under Article 119, once an employee shows that she is receiving unequal pay for equal work, the employer can show on the balance of probabilities that the difference in pay was not based on sex.[13] In such a case, as we shall see, since the object of the exercise for the employer is to show that the pay difference is not discriminatory, it will be necessary for the employer to show that the pay difference is neither *directly* nor *indirectly* discriminatory.

## (a) The material factor defence

The scope of the material factor defence is an extremely important element in the demarcation line between worker protection and management decisions. If drawn too widely it can defeat the purpose of the legislation to move towards equal pay; if drawn too narrowly it could put employers in a difficult position financially to make up for past inequality. For the line drawn by individual litigation must inevitably force many employers to change existing systems of pay simply because differences based on discrimination inherited from past discriminatory pay systems cannot be justified on the grounds that the employer had no intention of discriminating on grounds of sex.[14] Hence, judicial sympathy for the predicament of the employer can lead to an assessment of material difference which makes undue allowance for historical factors in the assessment of market factors or collective bargaining structures as justifications.

Initially, this issue was not allowed to arise. The courts interpreted the language of what is now s1(3)(a) (which states that in like work and work related as equivalent cases, s1(3)(a) or (b), the factor *must* be 'a material difference between the woman's case and the man's) to exclude 'external' factors and apply only to differences in the 'personal' circumstances of the man and woman's case such as age, length of service, skill or productivity. Where a woman's replacement was paid more because of a change in market conditions, eg because he would not come unless he received higher pay, the court would not accept that 'extrinsic' factor as part of the defence.[15] On the other hand where the employer could show

13 See eg *Handels-og Kontorfunktionaerernes Forbund i Danmark v Dansk Arbejdsgiverforening (Danfoss)* [1989] IRLR 532, ECJ.

14 *Jenkins v Kingsgate (Clothing Productions) Ltd (No 2)* [1981] ICR 715, [1982] IRLR 388, EAT; *Snoxell v Vauxhall Motors Ltd* [1977] ICR 700, [1977] IRLR 123, EAT.

15 *Clay Cross (Quarry Services) v Fletcher* [1979] 1 All ER 474, [1978] IRLR 361, CA.

that after a reorganisation of work a more highly paid male worker had been 'red circled', that his pay level had been frozen at a higher personal rate until the pay rates for the new job had caught up, that difference in the 'personal equation' was material.[16]

In *Rainey v Greater Glasgow Health Board*,[17] however, the House of Lords held that a relevant difference for the purposes of s 1(3) may relate to circumstances other than the personal skill, experience or training of the complainant and her comparator. It held that, where there is no question of intentional sex discrimination - whether direct or indirect - a difference which is connected with objectively demonstrated economic factors affecting the efficient carrying on of the employer's business or official activity may be relevant. It added that this test would not preclude objective grounds of defence other than economic, such as administrative efficiency in the case of organisations not engaged in commerce or business.

*Rainey* was a case where the employer showed that in order to set up a new prosthetics department in the NHS it was necessary to offer higher than NHS rates to recruit the initial members from the open market. Once the department was established, however, new recruits could be successfully recruited internally within the NHS at lower NHS rates. Mrs Rainey, one of the later tranche of employees, asked for equal pay with the male employees who had been hired at the start-up phase. The House of Lords held the recruitment problem was a factor which justified the continued difference in pay between the original recruits and later recruits to the service. It was put in evidence that the initial offer of employment at higher rates was open to female as well as male applicants.

The House of Lords in *Rainey* was concerned to widen the s 1(3) defence beyond personal differences and to allow external grounds such as market forces to be considered because, as Lord Keith of Kinkell put it, they viewed the test under s 1(3) as essentially a causation test: was the material difference between the man and the woman's case, a difference based on sex or a difference based on some other ground?

Lord Keith of Kinkell incorporated the test of objective justification of indirect discrimination in pay under Article 119 established in *Bilka-Kaufhaus*[18] into the test of s 1(3), in part to ensure that the showing of absence of intention by the employer was not enough.[19] In addition he wanted to make it clear that the employer has the burden of convincing the court or tribunal that his grounds for an alleged discriminatory rule were not only objective but also based on a *non gender* ground, such as

16 *Methven v Cow Industrial Polymers Ltd* [1980] ICR 463, [1980] IRLR 289, CA.
17 [1987] ICR 129, [1987] IRLR 26, HL.
18 170/84: [1987] ICR 110, [1986] IRLR 317, ECJ.
19 The issue of intention had been clouded in *Jenkins* and an objective test would clearly remove it from any test of the subjective intentions of the employer.

an economic one. He could therefore accept that other objectively justified, non-gender grounds, such as administrative efficiency in *Rainey*[20], were also a valid defence under s 1(3).

The first requirement of the *Bilka* test was for the employer to produce *evidence* of a genuine business need which was itself free of discriminatory intent or effect. Thus, in *Bilka* itself, the employer's claim that its prima facie discriminatory pension policy was justified because full timers were of greater benefit to the business was rejected by the German court because of a failure to show objective evidence to support the assertion. In *Enderby*,[1] the ECJ made it plain that more was needed than the mere assertion that differences in pay between the two jobs was explained by the existence of two separate collective agreements, neither of which was internally discriminatory.[2] Moreover, in cases where the pay system is unclear or 'lacks transparency' the employer has the further burden of proof to show that the pay structure is non-discriminatory.[3] Where there are objectively verifiable economic grounds, the UK and EC courts are willing to accept them as the basis for a defence to an equal value claim.

In *Rainey*, the House of Lords indicated that economic grounds such as market forces could constitute an objective defence under s 1(3) accepting that difficulties experienced by the NHS in recruiting from within to set up its new prosthetics department in Scotland could justify its decision to pay a premium rate to attract trained prosthetists from the private sector at the set up stage and then revert to internal recruitment and internal rates for subsequent recruits when the initial shortage had been overcome. There was evidence of the shortage of trained prothetists at the earlier stage and that those jobs had been open to men and women. The economic ground was limited to its exact time period.

In *Jenkins v Kingsgate (Clothing Productions) Ltd*: 96/80[4] a group of speech therapists, a predominantly female grade, claimed equal pay for equal value with clinical psychologists and pharmacists, grades which were higher paid and predominantly male. The ECJ held that 'the state of the employment market which may lead the employer to increase the pay of a particular job in order to attract candidates, may constitute an objectively justified ground.' However, this was subject to further requirement, ie that

20 [1987] IRLR 26, ECJ.

1 [1993] IRLR 591, ECJ.

2 The objective justification test also applies to 'member states' social legislation which is indirectly discriminatory see eg *Ruzius-Wilbrink* [1989] ECR 4311; see discussion by Anderman (Ch 8) in Dine and Watt *Discrimination Law: Concepts, Limitations and Justifications* (Longman, 1996).

3 See *Handels-og Kontorfunktionaerernes Forbund i Danmark v Dansk Arbejdsgiverforening (acting for Danfoss)* [1989] IRLR 532, ECJ.

4 [1981] ECR 911, [1981] IRLR 228, ECJ.

national courts were satisfied that 'the difference in pay between the jobs in question' could be shown to be caused by 'the shortage of candidates for a job and the need to attract them by higher pay.'[5] The Court also mentioned the need for a proportionality test to be applied to the employer's economic ground.

In *Albion Shipping Agency v Arnold*[6] a woman claiming a right of equal pay with her predecessor, as she was entitled to do,[7] was countered by the employer's evidence that a sharp decrease in trading activity required lower pay. The EAT accepted the defence that the inequality was due to the changed economic climate rather than the sex of the individual.

Further, in *Benveniste v University of Southampton*[8] the Court of Appeal made the point that where the original justification for a pay difference, in that case, the financial constraints operating for the university at the time of Dr Benvenistes' appointment, disappear there is under the Act no longer a justification for a lower rate. While this at first sight might appear to raise questions about the practice of red circling, such an analogy was rejected in that case. The House of Lords has also indicated to UK courts that they can and should subject to close inspection 'economic' claims by employers which could be founded on factors which more obviously reflect historical pay inequalities between man and women. For example in *Ratcliffe v North Yorkshire County Council*[9] a local authority reduced the pay of its dinner ladies so as to bid for work in competition with outside competitors paying wages below collective bargaining levels by using local female labour. The House of Lords held that the employer was not entitled to use a market force argument to 'reduce wages below those of their male comparators'. The employer had to honour its internal commitments to equal pay under the job evaluation scheme because 'to reduce the woman's wages below those of their male comparators was the very kind of discrimination which the Equal Pay Act sought to remove'.[10]

This offers a reminder that if economic factors are not allowed to influence the application of the discrimination laws, they may nevertheless influence the outcome in other ways. Thus, as Fredman rightly points out, 'the inevitable result of a successful claim in *Ratcliffe* was to put the DSO at a competitive disadvantage and risk the loss of the contract.'[11] The only way to maintain equality of treatment between men and women in the context of a competitive tendering policy would be for the government to

5 Ibid at 595.
6 [1982] ICR 22, [1981] IRLR 525, EAT. See too *Strathclyde Regional Council v Wallace* [1996] IRLR 670, CS (financial constraints the cause of inequality)
7 See eg *Macarthys Ltd v Smith* [1979] ICR 785, [1979] IRLR 316, CA.
8 [1989] ICR 617, [1989] IRLR 122, CA. See McLean 'Discrimination as a Continuing State' [1991] ILJ 61.
9 [1995] IRLR 439, HL.
10 Ibid at 445.

restore a policy of maintaining established labour standards in competitive tendering for public contracts.

The courts have also been guided to take an extremely close look at employers' defences of separate collective bargaining structures as an objective justification for differences in pay between men and women. The courts now recognise that the employer bears responsibility for internal inequalities in pay even if caused by historic differences in bargaining power and must give an objective justification for those differences. Thus, in *Enderby*, the ECJ was insistent that the mere existence of separate collective agreements, conducted for each of the professional groups and without any discriminatory effect within each group, was not as such a sufficiently objective justification for the difference in pay between the two jobs. The court recognised that to allow the mere existence of separate agreements to preclude a prima facie finding of discrimination would be to invite the use of separate collective agreements as a device to circumvent the principle of equal pay.[12]

A second example of objective difference other than sex under s 1(3) is a difference in the overall pattern of contractual terms of complainant and comparator. In *Leverton v Clwyd County Council*[13] a Local Authority nurse claimed that her work was of equal value to clerical officers covered by the same collective agreement. On closer inspection, however, her lower weekly pay rate was due to the fact that she worked fewer hours per week and had longer holidays than her comparators.

Yet, this test can sometimes give too much discretion to employers. Thus, in *Calder v Rowntree Mackintosh Confectionery Ltd*[14] two women employed on a twilight shift, 5.30pm to 10.30pm five days a week, composed exclusively of women, received no overtime whereas men on a rotating day shift, 8am to 4pm, 4pm to midnight, alternating weekly, received shift premia. In an equal pay claim, the employer succeeded with the defence under s 1(3) that the variation in pay was genuinely due to the fact that the workers on the rotating day shift suffered a combination of physical disturbance and unsocial hours whereas the part-timers only suffered the unsocial hours. This factor rather than sex was the material difference in the two cases. Yet the Court of Appeal's acceptance of the tribunal finding seemed to underestimate the employer's obligation, as expressed by the ECJ in its *Danfoss* decision, to make its pay structures and their underpinnings in job evaluation systems sufficiently 'transparent' to be understood by employees and courts.

11 S Fredman *Women and the law* (1997, Clarendon, Oxford) at p 248.
12 See too *British Road Services v Loughran* [1997] IRLR 92, NICA.
13 [1989] ICR 33, [1989] IRLR 28, HL.

To what extent, can s 1(3) be invoked by the employer to claim that there was another term in the woman's contract which was more favourable to her than the corresponding term in the man's contract? We know that an employee can choose to compare any term of her contract with her comparator under s l(2)(c). To what extent can the compensating term argument rejected in *Hayward*[15] under s 1(2)(c) be resurrected under s 1(3)? This issue is particularly relevant to the case where the complainant and comparator are paid under different pay structures.

In *Hayward*'s case Lord Goff was prepared to imagine that Julie Hayward's better pension rights and sick pay entitlement could be a possible defence of genuine material difference in a case where men had a higher pay rate. Effectively, as Lord Goff pointed out, the difference could be attributed to separate pay structures which were not discriminatory when all terms were taken into account. However, he added the qualification that the material difference defence could not be invoked by the employer where there is direct or indirect discrimination embedded in the two relevant pay structures of the woman and her male comparator. The Lord Chancellor, Lord Mackay, was more guarded in *Hayward*. He thought that for s 1(3) to operate, it would have to be shown, at the very least, that the unfavourable character of the term in the woman's contract was in fact due to the difference in the opposite sense in the other term and that the difference was not due to the reason of sex.

In *Barber v Guardian Royal Exchange Assurance Group*,[16] the ECJ stated that the principle of equal pay must be ensured in respect of each element of remuneration and not only on the basis of a comprehensive assessment of the consideration paid to workers, without adding any qualification to the statement of principle. *Barber* was a case where the work was the same and the pay structure was the same for complainant and comparator apart from the one term. Secondly, Article 119 is concerned only to achieve equal work 'equal pay without discrimination based on sex'.

Article 119 applies the principle of equal pay for equal work to mean the elimination of all discrimination on grounds of sex with regard to all aspects and conditions of remuneration.[17] In principle, therefore, if different pay structures apply to complainant and comparator and these are not discriminatory on grounds of sex there could continue to be a compensating term defence under Article 119 as well as s 1(3).[18]

14 [1993] IRLR 212, CA.
15 *Hayward v Cammell Laird Shipbuilders Ltd* [1988] ICR 464, [1988] IRLR 257, HL.
16 C-262/88: [1990] ICR 616, [1990] IRLR 240, ECJ.
17 See Article 1 of the Equal Pay Directive 75/117/EEC.
18 See eg *Bullock v Alice Ottley School* [1993] ICR 138, [1992] IRLR 564, CA.

## The job evaluation defence

According to the scheme of the amending Act, where a job evaluation scheme is in force and it is non-discriminatory this will provide the employer with a complete defence. Under s 2A(2) work will not be regarded as of equal value if it is given different values in a job evaluation system which complies with s 1(5) and there are no reasonable grounds for determining that the evaluation was made on a discriminatory system.

Where an employer seeks to have an equal value complaint dismissed under this provision, the burden of proof lies upon him both to show that the system complied with s 1(5) and that the system was non-discriminatory.

To satisfy the requirements of s 1(5) a study must be 'analytical'. The jobs of *each* worker covered by the study must have been valued in terms of the demand made on the worker under various headings such as effort, skill, decision etc. As was pointed out by the Court of Appeal in *Bromley v H & J Quick Ltd*,[19] it is not enough that 'bench mark' jobs have been evaluated on such a basis if the jobs of the complainant and the comparators have not been.

Moreover, the Court pointed out that the onus placed on the employer by s 2A(2)(b) to show that there were no reasonable grounds for determining that the job evaluation system was discriminatory requires the employer to show the basis of the study, how it worked and what was taken into account at any stage. In practice, it will then be up to employees to point to alleged discriminatory characteristics of the scheme and the employer can give an explanation.

The test of discriminatory job evaluation systems has been elaborated in *Rummler v Dato-Druck GmbH*,[20] a case brought to the European Court of Justice on Article 1(2) of the Equal Pay Directive. In *Rummler*, the ECJ indicated that a non-discriminatory job classification system is one that not only applies the same criteria to men and women but also one which is 'not organised as a whole in such a manner that it has the practical effect of discriminating generally against workers of one sex'. In that case an employee argued that the job evaluation system discriminated on grounds of sex because it used an absolute measure of muscular effort as a criterion for job evaluation and this tended to undervalue women's jobs because of their relatively lower levels of muscular strength. The ECJ held that a job classification system was not discriminatory solely because of their relatively lower levels of muscular strength. It held that a job classification system was not discriminatory solely because one of its criteria is based

19 [1988] ICR 623, [1988] IRLR 249, CA; see also *Dibro Ltd v Hore* [1990] ICR 370, [1990] IRLR 129, EAT. See further sources in fn 7 on p 268.

20 237/85: [1986] ECR 2101, [1987] IRLR 32, ECJ.

on characteristics more commonly found among men than women. It went on to say, however, that if a job classification system is not to be discriminatory overall, it must be so designed, if the nature of the work so permits, to take into account other criteria for which female employees may show particular aptitude. For example, if a job evaluation scheme assigned a heavy weighting to physical effort and a lower weighting to manual dexterity (normally a more developed ability of women) it could be attacked on that ground. Moreover, the measurement of effort cannot be based on the average performance of workers of one sex.

## Procedure

The procedure provided by the amending regulation has proved to be a formidable obstacle to successful equal value claims. It is long and tortuous and has been accurately described by a barrister specialising in the field as 'a game of snakes and ladders with few ladders and many snakes'.[1]

The procedure for equal value cases provides two main stages before the tribunal hearing. The first, the 'sifting' stage, has become a major hurdle. The tribunal needs to decide whether or not 'it is satisfied that there are … reasonable grounds for determining that the work is of equal value' (Sch 2, s 2A(1)). This requires the claimant effectively to present a prima facie or at least an arguable case of unequal pay using her own evidence and expert witness.

To surmount this hurdle is a precondition for discovery of such matters as the job descriptions of other grades[2] as well as the tribunal's decision to require an independent expert to prepare for a report.[3] This sifting stage effectively duplicates the pre-hearing review (and deposit procedure) provided by the Employment Act 1989.

The sifting stage can also be used by employers as a more elaborate exercise to discredit an equal value claim. For tribunals may be addressed on the issue of genuine material difference before commissioning an independent expert's report. For example in *Leverton v Clwyd County Council*[4] the employer successfully raised a material factor defence at that stage, effectively turning the preliminary hearing into a final hearing.[5]

Moreover, where an employee brings an equal value claim and there is in existence a job evaluation scheme she must make an arguable case that

1 Anthony Lester at an IRST Conference April 1989.
2 See eg *Clwyd County Council v Leverton* [1985] IRLR 197, EAT.
3 Ibid.
4 Ibid.
5 Regulation 8(2E) provides that the tribunal may hear evidence and argument upon the issue of the material difference defence before it requires an expert to prepare a report.

a job evaluation was discriminatory as a precondition of a referral of the issue to an independent expert for investigation and report.

Initially this test was thought to place a burden of proof on the female applicant.[6] However, in *Bromley v H & J Quick*[7] the Court of Appeal held that the onus was on the employer where he argues that the equal value complaint should be dismissed:

(a) to show that there has been a job evaluation study which satisfied the requirements of s 1(5); and
(b) that there are no reasonable grounds for determining that the evaluation contained in the study was tainted by sex discrimination.

> 'It must follow that it is for the employer to explain how a job evaluation study worked and what was taken into account at each stage. This in turn could give the applicant an opportunity to point to particular matters as indicating or possibly indicating that the system involved direct or indirect sex discrimination. The employer then can have an opportunity to explain and the tribunal can decide at the end of the hearing whether or not there were no reasonable grounds to determine that the job evaluation system discriminates on grounds of sex'.[8]

The second stage, after the tribunal has sifted the factors under ss 2A(1) and 8(2E), is when the tribunal adjourns the hearing and requires an independent expert to prepare a report (Regulation 7A). The independent expert is expected to report back within 42 days but in fact the process is taking much longer (anywhere from three to twelve months). The evidentiary weight of the expert's recommendation is 'considerable' but it does not shift the burden of proof to the employer. Reports by the parties' experts are admissible and it is now common for one or both of the parties to commission such reports. The multiplication of expert reports can create difficulties for industrial tribunals at the hearing stage.

## THE LEGAL MECHANISMS IN THE EQUAL PAY ACT

The EPA originally provided several different procedural methods of bringing equal pay claims - yet the right of an individual to make a complaint has assumed paramount importance.

Conceptually the fact that unequal pay arises from unequal pay structures would counsel a legislative approach to equalisation of pay which takes a collective form. For example it might have been more appropriate to provide a wide ranging claim by trade unions or individuals

6 *Neil v Ford Motor Co Ltd* [1984] IRLR 339, IT.
7 [1988] ICR 623, [1988] IRLR 249, CA.
8 [1988] ICR 623, [1988] IRLR 249, CA.

against alleged discriminatory pay structures which could be submitted to arbitration by the CAC and result in collective reforms. However, the 'collective remedy' provided by the Act is so narrow in scope that it has rarely been used to correct discriminating pay structures on a collective basis. Instead, the individual equal pay claim has been used as a device to attack collective pay structures. As Szyszczak has pointed out, 'There are many disadvantages in reliance on such a legal mechanism.'[9] Nevertheless where an equal pay claim is well founded, it can have the effect of a class action. Unlike cases of sex discrimination where the individual's claims can be isolated from the collective pattern of discrimination, an individual claim can set a precedent for a group of employees in the same grade as the claimant and can even encourage other women in contiguous grades to bring analogous claims. Certain sectors of industry, in particular banking, building societies, etc, bear witness to the tendency of managers to reform whole pay structures, either in anticipation of law suits or in response to single claims. For example in the banking sector an action by one bank teller in Lloyd's Bank prompted wide scale response in Midland Bank, followed by NatWest, etc.

Nevertheless this type of legislative mechanism creates pressures upon the judiciary to be cautious in decisions establishing the regulatory line on such issues as the employer's defences. The UK amending legislation provides so many procedural obstacles that the substantive claim is difficult to achieve. It clearly needs considerable reform[10] at the same time to reduce differences in pay between men and women to any significant extent, and requires active and effective pressure on collective pay structures along with individual equal value claims. In the meantime, the freestanding claim under article 119 operates as a safety net.

9 The Equal Pay Directive and UK Law' in McCrudden (ed) *Women, Employment and European Equity Law* (1987).

10 See, eg Equal Opportunities Commission 'Equal Pay for Men and Women: Strengthening the Acts' (1990).

PART III

# Collective labour legislation

# Introduction

Collective labour relations in Britain today are highly regulated by labour legislation. Trade union organisations are subject to comprehensive legal rules and their entitlement to organise strikes and other industrial action is closely circumscribed. Closed shop agreements and arrangements are tightly restricted by law.

Employing organisations are regulated by legislation giving recognised trade unions a right to disclosure of information relating to collective bargaining, to be consulted on health and safety issues, redundancies, transfer of undertakings and certain pension decisions. Finally, individuals have both a right to trade union membership and activity and a right to non-membership.

To understand the current law of labour relations in Britain, however, one cannot concentrate solely upon the present position. For in a sense, the extensive collective labour legislation of the past is the second act of a two-act drama. The first act consists of the long period of legal non-intervention or collective laissez-faire during which collective bargaining emerged and developed with relatively little help from the law. The story of the long period of 'voluntarism' from the mid-nineteenth century to the early 1960s has been frequently told and cannot receive a detailed description here.[1] The emergence of a fully developed collective bargaining system without legal support was partly a product of a strong trade union movement which 'chose' a wide legal immunity for strikes and a narrow base of positive statutory protection for workers and trade unions in a series of political 'settlements' with governments in 1871, 1875 and 1906.[2] The trade unions' inclination towards voluntarism, however, was partly influenced by the fact that some employers and employers associations,

1 See eg Wedderburn *The Worker and the Law* (3rd edn); Davies and Freedland *Labour Legislation and Public Policy* (OUP, 1993).
2 Fox *History and Heritage* (1985) pp 131-137.

from an early stage, were prepared to establish systems of collective bargaining first at district level, later at industry-wide level and more recently at company-wide level. That there were employers antagonistic to the growth of trade unions can be seen in the landmarks of trade union history: the *Taff Vale* case,[3] the early organising experiences of the general unions[4] and the repeated pleas of a minority of TUC members at the AGM for legal support for trade union recognition.[5] Throughout the formative years of UK labour relations, however, a significant number of employers were prepared to recognise trade unions and deal with them on the basis of voluntary joint disputes procedures and collective agreements.[6]

The employers' motives for this course of action varied. In the first place, those employers and employers' associations who gave early recognition to trade unions particularly the trade unions of skilled craftsmen, were careful to preserve the right to manage in the structure of collective bargaining.[7] Collective bargaining was not based on the workshop where management decisions about working methods, the pace of work or discipline and dismissals could be brought into collective negotiations. Instead it was kept at the district level where groups of employees bargained through employers' associations to establish district wage rates while raising labour costs also had the effect of ensuring that all employees in the district competed on the basis of the same labour costs. The evolution of trade unions along occupational lines was favourable to employers because it reinforced the structure of district bargaining and divided the workforce in any one firm or workplace.[8] Moreover, the employers' acceptance of the recommendations of the Whitley Committee of 1918 for formal conciliation and negotiating machinery at industry-wide level which led to the development of industry-wide collective bargaining in the UK in a wide scale by the 1940s, occurred partly because employers saw such structures in their interests. For with formal collective bargaining focused at industry-wide level, there was little need to give formal recognition to trade unions at the workplace.[9]

Moreover, from the employer's viewpoint 'voluntarism' had the advantage of limiting the extent of legal regulation of business activity

3 See eg Clegg, Fox and Thompson *A History of British Trade Unions since 1898: Vol I 1889-1910* (1964) Ch 9.

4 See eg Saville 'Trade Unions and Free Labour' in Briggs and Saville (eds) *Essays in Labour History* (1967) p 317.

5 See TUC AGM Reports 1893-1903. Bell of the Railway Workers Union lost his motion for compulsory arbitration on several occasions.

6 See eg Burgess *The Challenge of Labour* (1980).

7 Burgess, op cit, pp 26-27, draws attention to the disciplinary effect collective bargaining had on the rank and file and the role of union leaders in settling local disputes.

8 Phelps Brown *The Growth of British Industrial Relations* (1965) p 125; *The Origins of Trade Union Power* (1986) p 111; Burgess, op cit, pp 26-27.

9 Fox *History and Heritage* (1985) pp 291-300.

and managerial decision-making. Confined to the regulation of hours of work and safety in factories, methods of payment of wages, and Wages Council legislative machinery which established minimum wages in 'sweated trades' where pay was low and collective bargaining was weak or non existent, regulatory legislation resulted in few burdens to the majority of employers. Even the Fair Wage Resolution legislation that evolved from 1891 requiring wage levels based on collective bargaining rates to be paid by all employers contracting with the government created few difficulties since all employers could bid on the basis of similar labour costs. Certainly, employers' associations took an active role in shaping the minimalist role of collective labour law: s 4 of the Trade Union Act 1871 which provided that collective agreements between trade unions and employers' associations were not legally enforceable; the Conciliation Act of 1896 which set the pattern for voluntary conciliation and the Industrial Courts Act 1919 which assured that arbitration was not legally binding were all strongly supported by employer groups.[10]

As we now know, the legacy of the voluntary system for the institutions of industrial relations included a number of features which were not thought conducive to the competitive economic conditions of the post war period: a propensity to wage inflation, restrictive practices, multi-unionism owing to the growth of 'horizontal unions' such as craft and general unions, rather than vertical unions organised along industrial lines. It also included the development of the closed shop institution as a signific component of collective bargaining systems.[11]

Whatever its flaws for public policy makers in the 1960s, however, collective bargaining continued to be seen by a majority of employers as useful for their purposes. Indeed, when the Heath Government introduced comprehensive labour legislation in 1971 it was striking to observe that few employers made use of the legal sanctions which were placed at their disposal by the legislation and many collaborated with trade unions in avoiding the full impact of the legal framework in their collective bargaining arrangements.[12]

British employers today are far more divided in their approach to trade unionism and collective bargaining. The sectors of established collective bargaining are diminishing in the face of the intensification of competition in product and service markets. Trade union membership as a percentage of the workforce is declining in response to changes in the composition of the workforce. Moreover, employers are engaged in derecognition

10 Phelps Brown *The Origins of Trade Union Power* (1986) Ch III.
11 Dunn and Gennard *The Closed Shop in British Industry* (1984).
12 See Weekes, Mellish, Dickens and Lloyd, *Industrial Relations and the Limits of Law* (1975).

policies in increasing numbers.[13] Nevertheless, a considerable core of established collective bargaining remains in many sectors of industry. Approximately half of all employees' terms and conditions are influenced by collective bargaining. About two thirds of the workforce, ie about 6.9 million individuals, are trade union members. Recent industrial relations surveys indicate that almost half of all employers who are prepared to reach an accommodation with trade unions engage in collective bargaining.

Employers prepared to reach an accommodation with trade unions vary in their approach. Studies by Purcell and Sisson,[14] and later Edwards,[15] indicate their diversity. One minority group has been identified as 'constitutionalists', such as Ford, who codify rules in collective agreements. Another related group consist of those firms which insist on 'strike free agreements' with single unions or 'single table bargaining.'[16] A majority group consists of more informal 'consulters', such as ICI and the large oil companies, in which trade unions are recognised and collective bargaining is well developed but there is no desire on the part of management to codify everything in a collective agreement. Instead there is a reliance upon procedures for consultation and disputes resolution. In both cases, however, there is some consistency of approach attempted throughout the organisation. A third group of managers, called 'standard moderns' by Purcell and Sissons are 'fire fighters', take a more ad hoc and pragmatic approach to trade unions and industrial relations altering it as circumstances change and making little real attempt to achieve consistency between different establishments of the same firm.

What all categories have in common is that they are firms in which management legitimises the unions' role in certain areas of joint decision-making because it sees this role as conducive to its own interests as measured by stability, promotion of consent, effective communication, etc. They see it in their interests to maintain an accommodation with trade unions and use the institution of collective bargaining to establish a system of joint regulation in certain areas.

On the other hand, the firms which oppose trade unions also display differences in style. One group consists of 'forceful opposition', in which directors and senior managers have virtually no contact with trade unions and are determined to use all legal means to prevent trade union membership and activity among the workforce. Grunwick was a good example. Another group consisting of US firms such as IBM, Hewlett Packard and Kodak, some Japanese subsidiaries and British firms such as Marks and Spencer, adopts a more indirect form of opposition in the form

13 See eg Clayden 'Union Derecognition' (1989) 27 BJIR 214.

14 Purcell and Simpson 'Strategies and Practice in the Management of Industrial Relations' in Bain (ed) *Industrial Relations in Britain* (1983).

15 Edwards *Managing the Factory* (1987) Ch 5.

16 Lewis 'Strike Free Deals and Pendulum Arbitration' (1990) 28 BJIR 32.

of 'sophisticated paternalism'. These companies firmly refuse to recognise trade unions and take the position that they can best look after their employees' interests but they take considerable care in recruitment, selection, training, counselling and remuneration to keep employees sufficiently happy to be unattracted to trade unions.

In recent years, however, there has been considerable evidence of employers derecognising trade unions, suggesting that this group is gaining ground.[17] The techniques used vary from outright derecognition in certain grades to creeping derecognition, in which employers make it a point over a period of time to impress upon individual employees the virtues of individual bargaining as an employee with staff status, until the majority of employees have been persuaded that collective bargaining is no longer in their interests. Furthermore, single union agreements and 'single table' bargaining are increasingly being introduced, particularly by foreign investors, suggesting a change in the attitude of employers to collective bargaining structures.[18]

Nevertheless, collective bargaining remains a method of job regulation for a significant proportion of the workforce. During the 1980s and early 1990s when employers were in a position to end collective bargaining relationships, many chose not to do so, preferring instead to restructure collective bargaining to allow greater flexibility to management. In the event, there have been changes in the way in which collective bargaining is now being conducted.

Consequently, collective labour legislation as it relates to rights of association (Ch 14), rights of information and consultation (Ch 15) and rights of industrial action (Ch 16) must still be assessed with the awareness of two sectors in the labour market. First, an established sector of ongoing and self regulating systems of collective bargaining perpetuated by mutual self-interest, and second a sector of employers who are either fiercely resistant to the introduction of trade unionism and collective bargaining or are embarked upon the enterprise of derecognising or reducing the influence of trade unions.[19]

17 See eg Clayden 'Union Derecognition' (1989) 27 BJIR 214; Taylor *The Future of the Trade Unions* (Andre Deutsch, 1994), ch2.

18 Smith & Morton 'Union Exclusion and the Decollectivisation of Industrial Relations in Contemporary' (1993) BJIR March. See eg Brown 'The Changing Role of Trade Unions in the Management of Labour' (1986) BJIR 161 at 164.

19 See eg *Associated British Ports v Palmer: Associated Newspapers Ltd v Wilson* [1995] IRLR 258, HL.

CHAPTER 15

# Rights of association

## INTRODUCTION

The rights of association underlying collective labour legislation are based on the basic political freedom of association of individuals, comparable to the freedoms of speech, assembly and religion found in the Constitutions of many countries. As combinations of labour developed in response to the more collective, late nineteenth century methods of organising work throughout Europe generally, the growing political and economic power of workers forced acceptance of the principle of freedom of trade union organisation as a legitimate expression of freedom of association, ie as the only way in which individual employees with inadequate bargaining power, pursuing their self interest, could effectively obtain a counterweight to the economic power of employers.

The legal recognition of the principle of a right to join and organise trade unions occurred in Europe in two stages. Initially, most European states removed statutory criminal prohibitions, recognising a freedom to join and organise trade unions, a freedom which meant that the state would allow workers and trade unions to use self help measures to achieve recognition by employers and defend themselves against employer resistance to trade union membership.[1]

This removal of illegality was followed by a second stage, the creation of positive legislative rights against employers.[2] The shift to positive rights required legislators at an early stage to translate the principle of freedom of association into a set of legal limits upon employers, in particular limits upon their attempts to discourage trade unions by dismissals or by other

1 Kahn Freund, O *Labour and the Law* London, Stevens (1983, 3rd edn) eds P Davies and M Freedland.

2 In the UK there was a gap of 50 years between statutory recognition of the freedom to organise and the freedom to strike. See *Kahn Freund*.

means short of dismissal. It also required them to choose the priorities to be attached to three separate tiers of freedoms embedded in the principle of freedom of association.[3]

At the base of the principle of freedom of association is the entitlement of individuals to extend their personal freedom and improve their position by organising into trade unions and dealing 'collectively' through representatives with their employer. At this point, the right can be translated into a straightforward duty placed upon employers not to interfere with this right by using their powers to dismiss or otherwise deter or penalise trade union membership or activity.

In the process of translating the basic freedom to organise into a positive right to trade union membership and activity, however, it is necessary to decide how to reconcile it with the second tier of freedom of association, the freedom of individuals to choose which union they wish to join. For as Summers has pointed out, the strengthening of one may be at the expense of another.

> 'For example, the freedom of workers to organise fulfils its function only to the extent that the union can be effective in collective bargaining, but the freedom to choose between organisations requires rival unions which may fragment workers' power in the babble of competing spokesmen.'[4]

Equally relevant to legislators is the factor that multi-union representation may result in an unstable or unworkable collective bargaining structure.

Finally, the freedom to join trade unions based upon the values of autonomy, implies a third tier freedom, the freedom not to join trade unions. Here too, the strengthening of one freedom often occurs at the expense of the other - the greater the right of the individual not to join, the less may be the effectiveness of collective action. The way these freedoms are reconciled varies from country to country.[5] There is also considerable variation within the international conventions.

## THE INTERNATIONAL STANDARDS: THE RIGHT TO MEMBERSHIP

The first two tiers of freedom of association are clearly entitled to legislative protection according to international sources, though the extent

3 Summers 'Freedom of Association and Compulsory Unionism in Sweden and the United States' 112V Pa L Rev 647 (1964).

4 Ibid.

5 Von Prondynski, F *Freedom of Association and Industrial Relations: A Comparative Study* (1987) Mansell.

of the protection differs dramatically as between the International Labour Organisation (ILO) and the European Convention of Human Rights and Fundamental Freedoms (ECHR). The ILO Convention (No 87 of 1948) Freedom of Association and Protection of the Right to Organise in Article 2 provides that, 'Workers and employers without distinction whatsoever, shall have the right to establish and . . . to join organisations of their own choosing without previous authorisation'. This right to establish independent unions was soon followed by the Convention (No 98 of 1949) on the Right to Organise and Collective Bargaining in a form which urges those adhering to the convention to provide statutory protection for workers against acts of anti-union discrimination by employers including dismissal for trade union activity and yellow dog contracts ie employment contracts conditional upon non-membership of trade unions.

The European Convention for the Protection of Human Rights and Fundamental Freedoms (ECHR) provides in Article 11 that, 'Everyone has the rights to freedom of peaceful assembly and to freedom of association with others, including the right to form and join trade unions for the protection of his interests'.

Both standards offer protection for a right to membership of a union and a union of one's choice. However, they differ markedly in the extent to which in creating statutory standards, freedom of association should be extended beyond a basic right to membership [and activity] to a right of collective representation vis à vis the employer for individual issues or even to a right of representation for the purpose of collective bargaining. The ILO depicts the right to bargain freely with employers with respect to conditions of work as an essential element of the principle of freedom of association, implying not only a right of choice of trade union membership but also representation for the purposes of collective bargaining.[6] Moreover, the ILO and the Council of Europe's Social Charter 1961, Article 6, also endorse the right to strike. The ILO convention, however, is essentially only a catalyst to States to enact legislation. Its powers of enforcement are weak, if not almost non-existent.[7] In contrast, the European Convention on Human Rights provides a basis for appeal from national legislation. However, Article 11 which protects the basic freedom as a right of employees to form and join trade unions for the

6 See Reports of Freedom of Association Committee of the Governing Body of the ILO discussed in von Prondynski, *Freedom of Association and Industrial Relations* p 90.

7 Pankert, A 'Freedom of Association' in Blanpain, R *Comparative Labour Law and Industrial Relations* (Kluwer) p 148. See too Ewing. *Britain and the ILO* (2nd ed, 1994) Ch 5; G Morris 'Freedom of Association and the Interests of the State' in Ewing, Gearty and Hepple (eds) *Human Rights and Labour Law* (1994).

protection of their interests does not specifically mention collective bargaining.[8]

In the *National Union of Belgian Police* case[9] the European Court of Human Rights held that the Belgian government's refusal to consult with the applicant union, though it consulted with other police unions, did not violate Article 11 of the Convention because:

> '... while Article 11(1) presents trade union freedom as one form of a special aspect of freedom of association, the article does not guarantee any particular treatment of trade unions, or their members, by the state such as the right to be consulted by it.'[10]

Von Prondynski suggests that this statement by the Court 'was apparently referring to consultation by the state not necessarily as an employer'. He points to the further statement of the Court that 'the members of a trade union have a right, in order to protect their interests, that the trade union should be heard'.[11]

The ECHR in the *Swedish Train Drivers* case[12] stated that freedom of association under Article 11 included the 'freedom to protect the occupational interests of trade union members' but gave no indication of the specific measures of protection which were embraced by the principle. It held that under Article 11 the appellant union did not have the right to a separate collective bargain with the government. The court was reluctant to extend the protection under Article 11 to the right to strike but it left open the possibility of a positive right to collective bargaining.[13]

It may be possible therefore in the fullness of time and with the right selection of cases, that the ECHR will be interpreted to give a right of representation as an incident of the principle of freedom of association.[14] However, it seems unlikely that a right to bargain collectively can be derived from the principle of freedom of association expressed in the Convention.

8 Further, the European Social Charter of 1961 in Part I Article 5 states 'All workers and employers shall have the right to freedom of association ... for the protection of their economic and social interests', and in Article 6 includes a purely collective right, the 'right to bargain collectively'.

9 (1975) 1 EHRR 578.

10 ECHR 27 October 1975, p 13, para 28.

11 Ibid at p 90. However, the Court also held that a government policy to reduce the number of unions was not in itself incompatible with Article 11 of the European Convention. What mattered was how the government went about implementing it.

12 (1976) 1 EHRR 617 Schmidt and Dahlström, 6 February 1976 p 11, para 36.

13 Ibid at paras 40-41.

14 See Leader, *Freedom of Association: A Study in Labour Law and Political Theory* (1992); See too Novitz 1997 ILJ 79.

## INTERNATIONAL STANDARDS: A RIGHT TO NON-MEMBERSHIP?

The concept of non-membership as an element of the right of association, though boldly asserted in the recent European Community Charter of Fundamental Rights, the 'Social Charter', is less clearly expressed in ILO and ECHR sources. Succeeding ILO conferences have proved unreceptive to efforts to expand the conventions to include protection of non-membership.[15] Article 11(1) of the European Convention on Human Rights creates the possibility of an argument that a right to non-membership is not excluded. In *Young, James and Webster v United Kingdom*[16] the Labour Government was found to be in breach of Article 11(1) because of legislation in 1976 which provided that the dismissal of three existing employees by British Rail for refusing to join a trade union after a new union membership agreement had been brought in was automatically unfair unless the refusal to join was based on religious grounds. While the judges were in agreement that, on the facts, the UK law was in breach of Article 11(1) in such a situation and that 'the negative aspect of freedom of association is necessarily complementary to... its positive aspect',[17] there was considerably less support for the proposition that an unqualified right to non-membership could be read into the Convention.[18] Further in *Gustafsson v Sweden*,[19] the ECHR held that while Article 11 contains an implicit right to refuse to join a trade union, it does not extend to a right to refuse to enter into a collected agreement.

The international conventions then leave considerable scope for individual countries to develop their own particular adaptation of the principle of freedom of association into legislation. Yet there are limits and the UK in recent years has been the target of several cases of alleged non-compliance.[20]

## THE CURRENT LEGAL FRAMEWORK FOR FREEDOM OF ASSOCIATION IN THE UK

In the UK, the current legislation relevant to the right of association is a curious amalgam of two groups of rights. First, there are the rights of trade

15 Napier, B, 'Dismissals - The New ILO Standards' 1983 ILJ 17.
16 [1981] IRLR 408, ECHR.
17 Ibid.
18 See O'Higgins P 'The Closed Shop and the European Convention on Human Rights' (1981) Human Rights Review 6; Forde M 'The "Closed Shop" case' [1982] ILJ 1; Von Prondynski, F 'Freedom of Association and the Closed Shop' [1982] Cambridge Law Journal 256.
19 [1996] 22 EHRR 409, ECHR, Novitz [1997] ILJ 79.
20 See eg *Council of Civil Service Unions v Minister for the Civil Service* [1985] IRLR 28, HL.

union membership and activity, in effect since 1974. Second, there are the rights of non-membership introduced in 1980 and considerably strengthened in the Employment Act 1990.

## THE RIGHTS TO TRADE UNION MEMBERSHIP AND ACTIVITY

The positive rights of trade union membership and activity are a late addition to UK collective labour law. Prior to 1971, there were no rights of trade union association membership and activity. Trade union members had only a freedom of membership and activity in the sense of an immunity against criminal liability. Apart from the two war time periods, there were few legal constraints upon employers' decisions to blacklist, dismiss or discriminate in other ways against workers because of their trade union membership and activity. In 1968, the Donovan Commission, as part of a more comprehensive set of recommendations for the reform and extension of collective bargaining, suggested that the step should be taken to introduce more positive protection of the right to organise as well as a statutory union recognition procedure.

The Donovan Commission viewed the issue of freedom of association in ILO terms as related essentially to trade union recognition and the extension of collective bargaining (para 219). However, rather than recommending a type of legal framework which gave comprehensive legal protection to such rights, it recommended specific protection against unfair dismissal for trade union membership and activities and some legal limits on the use of 'yellow dog' contracts (para 540).

The first statute to provide a right of free association of workers in independent trade unions was the short-lived Industrial Relations Act 1971. This Act recognised 'the principle' of free association of workers in independent trade unions . . . so organised as to be representative, responsible and effective bodies for regulating relations between employers and workers. It gave every worker the right to be a member of the registered trade union of his or her choice and to take part in its activities at an appropriate time. Finally it also provided a right to dissociate, ie 'not to be a member of any or a particular organisation of workers whether registered or not'.

Most trade union rights in the Act, however, were predicated upon trade union registration, a status which was boycotted by TUC unions, distorting the experience of a positive right to organise during the period.

When a Labour Government was returned to power in 1974, and immediately repealed the Industrial Relations Act, it produced legislation to give positive rights to trade union membership and activity as part of an array of legislation to support collective bargaining. Instead of fashioning a comprehensive legal framework for trade union organisational rights it chose to enact three specific statutory rights for individual employees: a right to trade union membership, a right to trade union activity and a right to time off to engage in trade union activities. These 'rights', as amended by the Employment Act 1990, continue to provide the basis of protection for the first two tiers of the principle of freedom of association, freedom to join trade unions and freedom of choice of trade unions. Yet they have also been qualified to strike a balance between workers' rights to protection and managerial interests in running a business.

In terms of legislative techniques, this latter qualification of the legal right is explicit only in the case of the right to time off to engage in trade union activities which must be 'reasonable' in the circumstances. In the case of the other two rights, the legislation takes the form of a strict prohibition. Nevertheless, as we shall see, a balance is struck in the course of judicial interpretation.

The positive right of association in the UK consists, first of the right of employees[1] regardless of length of continuous service to be or to become 'a member of an independent trade union'.[2] This right is protected against dismissal (TULR(C)A, s 152(1)(a),[3] discriminatory action short of dismissal (TULR(C)A, s 146(1)(a)) and a refusal to offer employment on such grounds (TULR(C)A, s 137).

Secondly there is the 'right to take part or to propose to take part at any appropriate time in the activities of an independent trade union'. This right is protected against dismissal (TULR(C)A, s 152(1)(b))[3] and discriminatory action short of dismissal (TULR(C)A, s 146(1)(b)).[4]

Protection against action short of dismissal taken by the employer for the purpose of preventing or deterring the employee from or penalising the employee for being or seeking to become a member of an independent trade union or taking part in its activities can in principle apply to a wide range of measures, such as refusal to promote,[5] to pay increments, or to

1 See Ch 6.

2 An independent trade union is defined in TULR(C)A, s 5 as one that is neither 'under the domination or control of' nor 'liable to interference' tending towards such control by an employer or employer groups arising out of the provision of financial or material support or by any other means'. See von Prondynski *Freedom of Association and Industrial Relations* (1987) p 43. See *Government Communications Staff Federation v Certification Officer* [1993] IRLR 260.

3 See eg *Bass Taverns Ltd v Burgess* [1995] IRLR 596, CA. A dismissal for trade union membership is automatically unfair and an employee so dismissed is given right to a remedy of interim relief pending a decision of the industrial tribunal.

4 But past trade union activities as a ground for refusing employment can sometimes be viewed as a refusal on grounds of trade union membership under s 137. See eg *Harrison v Kent County Council* [1995] ICR 434, EAT.

5 See *Gallacher v Department of Transport* [1994] IRLR 231, CA (subject to adequate proof).

confer benefits given to other employees who are not members of a union.[6] The remedy in such cases of action short of dismissal is solely compensation including expenses and loss of benefit (TULR(C)A, s 149). However, compensation has been held to include an amount which takes into account 'injury to the individual other than injury to his pocket'.[7]

Protection against dismissal for union membership or activities under s 152 takes the form of a strict prohibition. It is an automatically unfair dismissal for 'an inadmissible reason' without any further reasonableness test. The burden of proof is normally on employees.[8]

The remedies for dismissal for trade union membership and activity include an order to pay compensation at an enhanced level in which the basic award must amount to 'not less than' £2,770 (s 156) and workers who apply for reinstatement or re-engagement are entitled to receive a 'special award' of £13,775 to £26,800 (ss 157-158) with the minimum increased to £20,600 where an order for reinstatement or re-engagement has been made and the employer fails to comply with it (s 158).

Finally, for employees who claim that they have been dismissed for reasons of trade union membership or activities TULR(C)A, ss 161-6 provide a special remedy of interim relief, ie a revival of the employees contract of employment if it has been terminated or its continuation, if still in force.

Since 1990, employees have legal protection against a refusal of employment on the grounds of trade union membership. Under TULR(C)A, s 137(1) 'refusal of employment'[9] is defined widely not only to consist of a refusal or deliberate omission to offer the job but also to include a refusal or deliberate omission to entertain or process an application or enquiry (s 137(5)(a)); causing the applicant to withdraw or cease to apply or enquire and making an offer of employment the terms of which are such that no reasonable employer who wished to fill the post would offer (s 137(5)(b) and (d)).

The protection also extends beyond a situation where the employer refuses to hire an individual for trade union membership in general to a

6 See *Associated Newspapers Ltd v Wilson; Associated British Ports v Palmer* [1995] IRLR 258, HL. TULR(C)A, s 146 as amended by TURER 1993 (see discussion at p 267).

7 *Brassington v Cauldon Wholesale Ltd* [1977] IRLR 479 at 483; see also *Cheall v Vauxhall Motors Ltd* [1979] IRLR 253.

8 See eg *O'Dea v ISC Chemicals Ltd* [1995] IRLR 599, CA; *Smith v Hayle Town Council* [1978] ICR 996, [1978] IRLR 413, CA; however, where the employee is qualified to complain of unfair dismissal under s 57(3) the employer has an onus of proving the reason for dismissal. See eg *Maund v Penwith District Council* [1984] ICR 143, [1984] IRLR 24, CA; *Shannon v Michelin (Belfast) Ltd* [1981] IRLR 505, CA.

9 See Townshend Smith 'Refusal of Membership on grounds of Trade Union Membership or Non Membership: The Employment Act 1990' 1991 ILJ 102.

refusal to hire a person because he or she is not a member of a particular union (s 143(3)) or one of a number of particular unions.

This rule does not only strike at the pre-entry closed shop;[10] it would also apply to an employer who attempts to protect settled collective bargaining arrangements with a limited number of recognised trade unions. Hence, where job applicants are members of a trade union which is not approved under Bridlington Principles, they cannot lawfully be obstructed for that reason in their application for employment.[11]

## RIGHTS TO TRADE UNION MEMBERSHIP

The first right to consider is that of an individual who wishes to join or form a trade union. The classic case has been that of an individual or a small group of employees who have joined a trade union and who are subjected to deterrent measures from an employer who views them as an unwelcome bridgehead of trade unionism in the workplace. In such cases of employer opposition to trade unionism, ss 137, 146 and 152 of TULR(C)A apply to regulate cases of dismissal or alleged deterrent measures short of dismissal for union membership, such as a policy of not promoting union members, or considering them for pay increments, etc.

To understand the precise scope of the protection we must first ask how wide is the right to trade union membership as such. Does it extend to a mere right to hold a membership card, or are there essential features , certain incidents of trade union membership which could be regarded as integral elements of the right of trade union membership?

With the enactment in 1990 of a right not to be refused employment for reasons of trade union *membership*, however, this issue becomes more important.[12] It could also be relevant to a definition of rights under Article 11 of the ECHR.[13] For example in *Discount Tobacco and Confectionery Ltd v Armitage*[14] in which an employee was dismissed after asking a union official to intervene on her behalf to write to the employer to clarify and settle the terms and conditions of employment, an employer attempted to argue that this was a dismissal for trade union activity as opposed to trade union membership. The EAT held that the tribunal's decision that the employee had been dismissed for trade union membership, ie resorting to

10 See discussion below, p 308.

11 For the right for officials, including shop stewards and members of recognised trade unions to reasonable time off to engage in trade union activities - see TULR(C)A, s 168. See p 306.

12 Cf *Taylor v Butler Machine Tool Co Ltd* [1976] IRLR 113, EAT.

13 See discussion in previous section.

14 [1990] IRLR 15, EAT. Cf *Fitzpatrick v British Railways Board* [1990] ICR 674 holding that only activities with the current employer were protected.

help from the trade union official was not an error of law. It rejected the employer's argument that a distinction could be drawn between 'membership' and taking up the union's services, because the latter were an important, if not primary, incident of trade union membership as well as an outward and visible manifestation of trade union membership. Moreover, in *Harrison v Kent County Council*,[15] the EAT accepted that the industrial tribunal could conclude that a person refused employment for past trade union activism was refused employment for membership under s 137(1).

These decisions however must be read in the light of the House of Lords statements in *Associated Newspapers v Wilson; Associated British Parts Ltd v Palmer*[16] to the effect that while *Discount Tobacco* may have been correct on its facts, there was no justification for equating membership rights with rights to use essential trade union services. Yet in *Speciality Care v Pachela*[17] the EAT held that it was open to an industrial tribunal to hold that a dismissal for engaging the assistance of the trade union in a protest over a change in hours was a dismissal for trade union membership under s 152(1)(a).[18]

Where an applicant is rejected on the basis of extensive trade union activities with a prior employer, there can come a point where the decision is held to be predominantly because of the prior activities rather than the prior membership.[19] Section 137 of TULR(C)A contains no language requiring that the reason for dismissal must be wholly or mainly membership as opposed to trade union activities. However, the omission of the latter ground in the section will be used in its interpretation. Moreover, not all trade union activities will be viewed by judges as part and parcel of union membership such as making use of the services of a union official.[20] One incident of membership that should receive protection under s 137 is previous experience as a shop steward. The fact that an individual formally held union office itself is clearly an incident of

15 [1995] ICR 434, EAT.
16 [1995] IRLR 258, HL.
17 [1996] IRLR 248, EAT.
18 Cf *City of Birmingham District Council v Beyer* a union activist dismissed for giving a false name and references when his real identity was discovered after a short period of employment. The court held that union activities prior to employment were not protected. Could he have been more successful with a claim that his dismissal was essentially for the incidents of union membership in his past employment? [1978] 1 All ER 910, [1977] IRLR 211, EAT; Von Prondynski *Freedom of Association and Industrial Relations, A Comparative Study* p 74, suggests that this could be the case; Simpson B 'The Employment Act 1990 in Context' [1991] MLR 418 at 419 suggests that the 1990 Act would not have made a difference in the case of a blacklist for trade union activities. See discussion by Townshend-Smith (1991) ILJ 102 at 107.
19 Ibid; Cf *Fitzpatrick v British Railways Board* [1990] ICR 674.
20 See *Wilson* and *Palmer* [1995] IRLR 258, HL.

membership. It might be possible for employers to argue that a shop steward can be refused employment because of certain unlawful activities with a previous employer, but union office as such should be prima facie protected.[1]

To what extent is the right of representation for the purposes of collective bargaining an incident of trade union membership? In *Wilson v Associated Newspapers* the Court of Appeal held that an industrial tribunal was entitled to find that an employer who offers a larger pay increase to employees who switched to personal contracts instead of collectively agreed terms and conditions was doing this for the purpose of deterring employees from, or penalising employees for, trade union membership since the abandonment of union representation would eventually cause the union 'to wither on the vine.' This amounted to a reading of the right of membership in s 146 as much more than merely membership as such. The House of Lords in *Wilson* and *Palmer* reversed, holding that the employer's failure to offer pay increases to those refusing individual contracts amounted to an 'omission' and was not 'action' in the meaning of s 146.[2]

In reaction to the Court of Appeal, however, the government had meanwhile enacted, in TURER 1993, a rather unusual legislative constraint upon the tribunal's exercise of its discretion to make a finding of fact as to the employer's purpose. TULR(C)A, s 148(3), now provides that if there is (a) evidence that the employer's purpose was to further a change in his relationship with all or any class of his employees as well as (b) penalising or deterring trade union membership, then the tribunal must take the former reason as the employer's purpose unless it considers that the action was such as no reasonable employer would take as having been for the purpose of (a).This statutory provision can allow anti-union conduct cloaked in a reorganisational guise. It also is a singularly inappropriate use of legislative power to force tribunals to make decisions against the grain of their own finding of fact.

The rights to trade union membership in ss 137, 146 and 153 of TULR(C)A extend to the second tier of freedom of association, the choice of a particular trade union. These provisions all offer protection to individuals for being, or proposing or seeking to become 'a member of

1 Townshend Smith draws attention to the link between s 168 of TULR(C)A time off provisions (op cit fn 7) and the legitimate activities of officials. He also rather less convincingly argues that strike action cannot be said to be an activity inherent in membership and protected under s 152. This ignores the residual protection for striking employees of s 238; which while now greatly reduced, nevertheless, in principle, contains some protection against the victimisation of striking employees: see Ch 16.

2 [1995] IRLR 258, HL.

*an* independent trade union' (italics added). It is true that s 146(1)(c) unlike s 146(1)(a) talks of a non-membership 'of any trade union or of a particular trade union …'. However, in *Ridgway and Fairbrother v National Coal Board*,[3] when the Coal Board attempted to justify its payment of higher rates of pay in collieries where the newly recognised UDM could establish majority membership as compared to the pay in NUM pits, by arguing that s 146(1)(a) applied only to any union whatsoever and not to any particular union, it was not successful. The Court of Appeal held that s 146(1)(a) covers a case where an employer attempts to prevent an employee from being a member of a particular trade union as well as one where the purpose is to prevent him from being a member of any trade union whatsoever. Lord Justice May indicated that one important reason for so holding was that, despite the absence of the specific phrase in s 146(1)(a), 'I find it a much more acceptable concept that an employee should be, or become a member of a trade union of his own choice rather than one of his employer's choice which he may be compelled to join'.[4]

In the event, these sections offer protection against an employer who attempts to prevent an employee from being a member of, and being represented by, a trade union, either where the employer had already recognised another trade union, or where the employee has been found by the TUC Disputes Committee to be properly a member of a different union already recognised by the employer.[5]

However, there are limits to the scope of these protections. Employers have some right to confer certain benefits upon the members of trade unions which they have recognised which do not extend to employees who are members of another union. In *Carlson v Post Office*[6] where members of a trade union not recognised by the employer were refused comparable rights to a licence to park on the employer's premises, Slynn J suggested that to establish a breach of s 146(1), there must be a finding 'that the purpose of the action taken is to penalise an individual for membership of a particular union'.

A further factor is the effect on the individual employee. Under s 146(1) an employee has the right not to have action short of dismissal taken *against him as an individual* by his employer for the purpose of preventing him from being a member of an independent trade union (emphasis added). This phrase has been held to require that the discriminatory action taken by the employer must affect the employee personally and not merely as a

3 [1986] IRLR 379, EAT, para 9.
4 [1987] IRLR 80 at 86.
5 See eg *Cheall v Vauxhall Motors Ltd* [1979] IRLR 253; *Carlson v Post Office* [1981] ICR 343, [1981] IRLR 158.
6 [1981] ICR 343, [1981] IRLR 158, EAT. See now *Wilson* and *Palmer* [1995] IRLR 258, HL and TULR(C)A, s 148(3), as amended.

member of a trade union which has been discriminated against.[7] The inclusion of these words was in response to the House of Lords decision in *Post Office v Union of Post Office Workers*[8] in which the Law Lords held that while 'discrimination against a man's trade union generally affects him personally', there must be a distinction between small and negligible prejudice on the one hand and substantial and necessary effects on the other. In *Ridgway and Fairbrother v National Coal Board*[9] in which the NCB paid a higher rate in collieries where the UDM had a majority membership, the Court held that the action taken by the employer, though against the trade union, - lower wage rates - could also be regarded as taken against individuals, because of the loss of money in their pay packets. Similarly, in *Carlson v Post Office*[10] the refusal of a parking licence to members of a non recognised union was clearly against individuals as well as against the trade union organisation. Moreover, in *Wilson v Associated Newspapers*[11] the Court of Appeal held that the granting of a pay rise to those who signed new personal contracts and the witholding of that pay rise from those who did not was action taken against employees as individuals under s 137.

Judicial recognition of the nexus between the individual and trade union membership and activity has not always been so forthcoming under s 152. For example, in *Carrington v Therm A-Stor Ltd*,[12] management decided to dismiss twenty employees in response to a request by a trade union for recognition. Most but not all of those dismissed were trade union members. The Court of Appeal found that the provisions of the Act did not extend to reprisals against the trade union. To be caught by s 152, it was necessary for the dismissals to occur because of the particular employee's union membership or activities. Counsel for the trade unionists had attempted to argue that s 152 should be construed in such a way as to recognise its 'collective dimension', ie that individual rights to union membership and activity were in their nature collective and that if the employees were members of a wider group and the reason for the dismissals was the activities of that group it followed that the reason for their dismissal was their union membership or activities, albeit with others.

The Court held, however, that such a decision went beyond the limits of purposive construction. The section, as drafted, was concerned solely with the dismissal of an employee and what he or she had done. It was not concerned with an employer's reactions to a trade union's activities, but

7 *National Coal Board v Ridgway and Fairbrother* [1987] IRLR 80, CA.
8 [1974] ICR 378, [1974] IRLR 22, HL.
9 Ibid at 94.
10 [1981] ICR 343, [1981] IRLR 158, EAT.
11 [1993] IRLR 336, but see now n 13 supra.
12 [1983] 1 All ER 796, [1983] IRLR 78, CA.

with his reaction to an individual employee's activities in a trade union context.

The Employment Appeal Tribunal had stated that such a construction, if given to the section, would render it inoperable in many instances where it must have been intended to apply. The Court of Appeal indicated that it could see that such dismissal could discourage trade union membership and would give the unions a justifiable grievance. Nevertheless it thought that effect could only be given to the intentions of Parliament as expressed in the statute, applying the normal canons of construction for resolving ambiguities or any lack of clarity; for a more purposive approach could easily lead to a misreading of Parliamentary intention.

Under other legal systems there has been a clearer connection established between individual rights to join trade unions, and the group right to engage, in meaningful collective activity.

In the USA, for example, the National Labor Relations Act combines its prohibitions of employer conduct with a statement of employee rights in s 7:

> 'Employees shall have the right to self organisation to form join or assist labor organisations to bargain collectively through representatives of their own choosing and to engage in other concerted activities for the purpose of collective bargaining or other mutual aid or protection.'

NLRA, s 8(a)(1) then makes it an unfair labour practice for employers to interfere with, restrain or coerce employees in the exercise of their rights guaranteed in section 7. Moreover this generally unfair labour practice is then reinforced by two specific prohibitions placed upon employers - not to dominate or interfere with the running of a trade union (s 8(a)(2)) or to encourage or discourage membership in any labour organisation by discrimination in regard to hire or tenure of employment or any term or condition of employment (s 8(a)(3)).

Finally if employers are found to have violated these prohibitions the National Labor Relations Board can serve the employer with cease and desist and reinstatement orders backed up by penalties of fine and imprisonment, including a court order to reinstate the dismissed employee. This legislative formulation of the right to organise has resulted in a clearer understanding by US judges that the policy of the legislation is to protect employees from the 'anti-union animus' of employers. Under such a legislative framework, dismissals of the *Therm-A-Stor* type are determined by the intent of the employer to discourage union activity rather than the more individualistic test applied under the UK legislation.

Under TULR(C)A, s 146, as amended by TURER, in contrast, there is the risk that the anti-union motive of the employer will be disregarded in the interpretation given by industrial tribunals to the right to trade union membership and activity.

## RIGHTS TO PARTICIPATE IN TRADE UNION ACTIVITY

The right to take part in trade union activities includes protection against dismissal (s 152) and discriminatory action short of dismissal (s 146). These legal protections extend to a basic range of organisational activities, including those of a small group of employees attempting to organise in order to have representation rights and possibly recognition by the employer as well as the activities of recognised unions. However, these protections are qualified both in the legislation and by judicial interpretation.

First, as with membership, the dismissal of an employee for taking part in the activities of an independent trade union at the appropriate time, is automatically unfair, and an employee so dismissed is given a right upon application to an industrial tribunal to a remedy of interim relief pending a decision by the industrial tribunal on the fairness of the dismissal (ss 161-166). Secondly, an employee has the right as an individual not to be penalised for, or deterred or prevented from trade union activities by action short of dismissal taken against him by his employer.

Protection is available as long as the activity is connected with the more institutional aspects of trade union organisational activity, such as taking part in trade union meetings,[13] shop stewards' activity, discussion of trade union matters,[14] attempts to recruit a fellow employee,[15] consulting a shop steward or full-time trade union representative[16] or attempting to form a workplace union.[17]

In *Chant v Aquaboats Ltd*[18] however, an employee who was not a shop steward acted as an informal spokesman for a group of employees raising a grievance with management and organising a petition. Even though he had the petition vetted by his union office, his activities were held not to be the activities of a trade union. In the circumstances, the fact that he was a spokesman and happened to be a trade unionist was not enough.

Secondly, the right not to be dismissed or penalised for participation in trade union activities, unlike the right of trade union membership, is restricted by the requirement that the activities must occur at an 'appropriate time'. This requirement balances the interests of management with the protection. 'Appropriate time' has been defined in part as 'outside

13 *Miller v Rafique* [1975] IRLR 70, IT.

14 *British Airways Engine Overhaul Ltd v Francis* [1981] ICR 278, [1981] IRLR 9, EAT.

15 *Brennan v Ellward (Lancs) Ltd* [1976] IRLR 378, EAT.

16 *Lyon and Scherk v St James Press Ltd* [1976] ICR 413, [1976] IRLR 215, EAT.

17 *Dixon and Shaw v West Ella Developments Ltd* [1978] ICR 856, [1978] IRLR 151, EAT.

18 [1978] 3 All ER 102, [1978] ICR 643, EAT. But see *Dixon and Shaw v West Ella Developments Ltd* [1978] ICR 856, [1978] IRLR 151, EAT.

working hours',[19] eg lunch hours, dining breaks, or just before starting work and just after quitting time.[20] Further, it has been held that s 152(2) also provides that the activities may occur during working hours if they occur with the agreement or consent of the employer.[1] Any trade union activity during work hours, without consent, for example a sudden stoppage of work for the purpose of consulting a trade union official is not a trade union activity at the appropriate time.[2] The employer's consent needs to be specific. For example in *Robb v Leon Motor Services Ltd*[3] the EAT held that a general commitment by the employer in the written statement permitting him to take part in trade union activities 'at the appropriate time' was too vague to give him consent to carry out shop steward activities during working hours where the union was not recognised and there was no agreement on union activities during working hours. However, an employer's consent may be implied as well as expressed.[4] For example, in *Zucker v Astrid Jewels Ltd*[5] the EAT upheld a tribunal's decision that an employee had the implied consent of the employer to talk to other employees about trade union issues during working hours where chat generally was allowed between employees because the work process was not disrupted. Yet as the Court of Appeal made clear in *Marley Tile Co Ltd v Shaw*,[6] although consent can be implied, industrial tribunals could not infer consent from the silence of a manager when he said nothing in response to an announcement of an unaccredited shop steward that he would be calling a meeting during working hours. Once an employer has given his consent, however, he may not be completely free to withdraw it at will. For example, in the case of a meeting with no fixed duration an employer's order to return to work may not automatically be regarded as a 'revocation' of consent within the meaning of s 152(1)(b), even though the employer may be entitled after a time to say 'Well, enough's enough - we want you to go back to work'.[7] An employer's consent to an employee's entitlement to time off to attend regular trade union meetings may become a term of the employee's contract of employment.

Finally, taking part in a strike or other form of industrial action, even if official, may not be protected trade union activity under ss 146 or 152(1) despite being in layman's terms the very essence of trade union activities.

19 Section 146 and 152.
20 See *Post Office v Union of Post Office Workers* [1974] 1 All ER 229, [1974] ICR 378, HL.
1 S 152.
2 See *Brennan v Ellward (Lancs) Ltd* [1976] IRLR 378, EAT.
3 [1978] ICR 506, [1978] IRLR 26, EAT.
4 See *Marley Tile Co Ltd v Shaw* [1980] ICR 72, [1980] IRLR 25, CA.
5 [1978] ICR 1088, [1978] IRLR 385, EAT.
6 [1980] ICR 72, [1980] IRLR 25, CA.
7 See eg *PJ Mirors Ltd v Speck* [1977] EAT 378/76.

The Act has been interpreted to provide that s 238, which withdraws tribunal discretion in certain cases of dismissal for industrial action, overrides s 152 which protects trade union activities. Hence it was possible for the EAT to say in *Drew v St Edmundsbury Borough Council*[8] that taking part in industrial action does not constitute taking part in the activities of an independent trade union within the meaning of s 152. On the other hand, the planning of industrial action can fall into the category of taking part in trade union activities.[9] It is only when employees are selectively dismissed or selectively re-engaged and s 238 does not apply to preclude tribunal jurisdiction that the question of s 152(1) may come into play, along with the unfair dismissal protection of s 98(4).[10]

The current legal framework also accommodates a limited right of freedom of choice of trade union for the purpose of trade union activity. In *Post Office v Union of Post Office Workers and Crouch*[11] the House of Lords held that employees were entitled to take part in the organisation and recruitment activities of a trade union on the premises of an employer even though another trade union had been recognised by the employer as the sole representative of employees in that employee grade. This right was qualified by the requirement that 'it did not cause substantial inconvenience to their employer or to fellow workers who are not members of their trade union' but it meant that, in *Crouch*'s case, employees could post notices on notice boards, and meet on the employer's premises at times when, in accordance with their contracts of employment, they were not actually working.

In *Carter v Wiltshire County Council*[12] in reliance upon this qualification, an employer was held to be justified in refusing a request by an independent union, other than the one it recognised, to hold a meeting in the Social Club at its Fire Station after work.

Moreover, in *Carlson v Post Office*,[13] Slynn J drew attention to the need for a finding 'that the purpose of the action taken is to penalise an individual for membership of a particular union'.

In either case, whether the qualification is one of the need to show evidence of the employer's intent to penalise or merely to inconvenience the employee, the right to membership in and the related activities of a rival trade union is heavily qualified by judicial interpretation striking a balance between two values: employee rights and managerial interests.

8 [1980] IRLR 459, EAT. See further Ch 17.

9 See eg *Britool Ltd v Roberts* [1993] IRLR 481, EAT.

10 See Ch 17.

11 [1974] ICR 378, [1974] IRLR 22, HL.

12 [1979] IRLR 331, IT.

13 [1981] ICR 343, EAT. See now *Wilson* and *Palmer* as to purpose. See too TULR(C)A s 148(3).

## TIME OFF WORK FOR TRADE UNION DUTIES

In marked contrast to the basic protections against anti-trade union discrimination by employers, section 168(1) of TULR(C)A entitles employees who are officials[14] of an independent recognised trade union to have reasonable time off with pay[15] to carry out any duties, as such an official, which are concerned with either negotiations with the employer related to collective bargaining matters for which the trade union has been recognised (s 168(1)(a)) or the performance of trade union functions agreed with the employer (s 168(1)(b)) and to receive training in issues of industrial relations relevant to his duties concerned with the collective bargaining matters in s 168(1). This right is subject to the test by industrial tribunals that the time off must be reasonable in the circumstances. In *Ministry of Defence v Crook*,[16] the EAT indicated that the test to be applied by industrial tribunals should be a range of reasonable employer responses similar to that under the unfair dismissals legislation: s 98(4). These provisions are to be read in the light of the ACAS Code of Practice on Time Off for Trade Union Duties and Activities.[17]

Embedded in the reasonableness test of s 168(1) are in fact two sub tests. First, is the subject for which time off is claimed a fit one under the section? For example, were the duties of the official concerned with negotiations with the employer related to matters of collective bargaining, for which the trade union was recognised: (s 168(1)(a)). Alternatively, were these duties of the official concerned with the performance of trade union functions agreed with the employer: s 168(1)(b).[18] Secondly, if so, is it reasonable in all the circumstances to give time off taking into account, for example, the amount of time off requested,[19] time off received on previous occasions,[20] and whether the issue was already covered by collective agreement?[1]

The first test was changed quite radically by the requirement in the Employment Act 1990 that the right to time off in s 168 must be limited

14 Officials include union officers and shop stewards elected and appointed under the rules.
15 Pay is the amount which he normally would have received had he worked during the period of time off. See eg *Beecham Group Ltd v Beal (No 2)* [1983] IRLR 317; *Thomas Scott & Sons (Bakers) Ltd v Allen* [1983] IRLR 329, CA; *Hairsine v Kingston upon Hull City Council* [1992] IRLR 211, EAT. See too Fitzpatrick (1983) ILJ 258.
16 [1982] IRLR 488.
17 See SI 1991 No 968.
18 See eg *London Ambulance Service v Charlton* [1992] IRLR 510.
19 *Depledge v Pye Telecommunications Ltd* [1981] ICR 82, [1980] IRLR 390.
20 Cf *Wignall v British Gas Corpn* [1984] ICR 716, [1984] IRLR 493, EAT.
1 *Depledge v Pye Telecommunication* [1981] ICR 82, [1980] IRLR 390. See too *Hairsine v Kingston upon Hull City Council* [1992] IRLR 211, EAT.

to matters in respect of which the trade union is, in fact, recognised.[2] Prior to 1990, as long as a union was recognised by an employer to some extent, it was possible for officials to obtain paid time off for matters concerned with industrial relations more generally. For example in *Beal v Beecham Group Ltd*[3] the Court of Appeal held that union representatives could be given paid time off to attend a national trade union advisory meeting to co-ordinate the next pay claim, since 'duties concerned with industrial relations' were not limited to the immediate process of collective bargaining but extended to 'preparatory and explanatory work by officials'. Moreover in *Young v Carr Fasteners Ltd*,[4] an official was allowed paid time off to attend a course on participation schemes despite the absence of participation in the employer's scheme, since it was likely that the issue would arise in future negotiations.

The Court of Appeal in *Beal's* case also approved the decision by the EAT in *Sood v GEC Elliott Process Automation*[5] in which Slynn, J stated that the test of an official's duties should not be limited by the precise term of the recognition. It could include for example taking 'part in the planning of strategy and in discussing with other workers who are at the time negotiating with their employers, so long as the latter employers are associated with a particular trade union official's own employers.' However that was under the 'old' law! Under the 'new' law there must be a finding that the duties were related to or connected with a collective bargaining matter with the employer (and no longer associated employer) and that there was recognition by that employer for that particular matter. However, once this nexus is established, the new law is more relaxed about the number of duties which may qualify: s 168 refers to 'any duties'.[6]

The Code of Practice clearly indicates that the purpose of the section is to extend the rights of trade union representatives at work place level within a framework agreed between management and trade union. Nevertheless, it promotes the idea that managers should give shop stewards facilities including office space and that employers should allow paid time off for a wide range of trade union sponsored training. As well as a wide range of trade union duties including collective bargaining with management, feedback to employees being represented, grievance

2 See, eg, *London Ambulance Service v Charlton* [1992] IRLR 510; *British Bakeries (Northern) Ltd v Adlington* [1989] ICR 438, [1989] IRLR 218, CA; *Ashley v Ministry of Defence* [1984] ICR 298, [1984] IRLR 57, EAT. See also Deakin 'Equality Under a Market Order: The Employment Act 1990' 19 ILJ 1, 16-17.

3 [1982] ICR 460, [1982] IRLR 192, CA; see too *Young v Carr Fasteners Ltd* [1979] ICR 844, [1979] IRLR 420, EAT.

4 [1979] IRLR 420, EAT.

5 [1980] ICR 1, [1979] IRLR 416, EAT.

6 *London Ambulance Service v Charlton* [1992] ICR 773, [1992] IRLR 510, EAT. This may weaken the proximate relevance test in *Adlington* and *Ashley*.

handling, representation at industrial tribunals and meetings with other officials on issues relevant to the employer. The Code has been rewritten before in the light of s 168.

Finally, under s 170 employees are entitled to reasonable time off during working hours to take part in the activities of an independent trade union of which they are members and which is recognised by the employer as representative for their category of employee. The Code indicates that the right to time off should extend widely to representation both inside the firm and on outside bodies and emergency meetings including those to consider industrial action which affects them. The Code clearly excludes participation in industrial action as an activity for which time off is allowed.[7]

At a less legalistic level, it may be observed that the statutory time off provisions, combined with the shop steward's facilities policy enunciated in the Code, coincided with a period of considerable expansion of part-time workplace representatives as well as full-time convenors or chief shop stewards. There was some evidence that this increase, and in particular the increase in shop steward training was stimulated by legislation, but it was also consistent with the general increase in trade union membership in the 1975-1979 period. Certainly since the late 1970s there has been a decline in the overall numbers of shop stewards.

The effect of these statutory rights for individual trade unionists, it has been suggested, has been less to increase the spread of trade unions than to deepen 'union participation in workshops where union recognition had been conceded many years earlier.'[8]

## THE RIGHT TO DISSOCIATE AND THE CLOSED SHOP

The right to dissociate currently embodied in UK legislation has been introduced in recent years as part of a wider legislative programme designed to promote individualism at the expense of established collective structures. It goes beyond a recognition that embedded in the concept of freedom of association is the freedom not to associate; it calls into question the legitimacy of trade unions as collectivities enhancing the freedom of their members as individuals by the use of collective institutions.

This perspective views trade unions as labour monopolies, a source of market restraint using collective bargaining to impose union rates instead of the more competitive market rates and threatening individual freedom

7 ACAS Code of Practice No 3; Time Off for Trade Unions Duties and Activities.
8 Bain and Price 'Union Growth: Dimensions, Determinants and Destiny' in Bain G (ed) *Industrial Relations in Britain* (1983); see also Daniel and Milward 'Workplace Industrial Relations in Britain' [1983] 37-39, 142-144.

through the institution of the closed shop. Hayek has argued that trade unions should be curbed of their coercive powers because they have 'now become the open enemies of the ideal of freedom of association by which they once gained the sympathy of the true Liberals . . .'.[9] As Von Prondynski has perceptively pointed out however 'Hayek's concern with trade unions, and in particular with trade union security arrangements has in the end less to do with individual freedom than with economic policy.'[10]

For Hayek's view is one that leads to a policy that the law should be used not to encourage collective bargaining but 'to eliminate the labour market monopoly power' of trade unions and reduce the power of trade unions to raise union wages. This view influenced the Conservative Government's policy of dismantling many legal supports for collective bargaining since 1979, including statutory recognition and legislative props for collectively agreed wage rates.[11]

A legal right to dissociate is of relatively recent vintage in the UK. In the Industrial Relations Act 1971 the rights of association and dissociation were treated as co-existent. Section 5(1) of the Act provided: (a) a right to be a member of such trade union as he may choose; and (b) a right not to be a member of a trade union at all.

In TULRA 1974, however, the right to dissociate was intentionally omitted because the Act was concerned to provide a broad basis of legal support for the closed shop .

There were three features of the legal structure created by the 1974 Act, as amended in 1976, which promoted trade union membership and the closed shop institution. First, it created a presumption that, provided the trade union had negotiated a closed shop agreement in an approved form (a union membership agreement or UMA), a dismissal for non-membership would be automatically fair unless the reason for non-membership was based on religious grounds: EPCA s 58(3). This helped to create the conditions for the growth of post-entry closed shops.[12]

Secondly, industrial action to support a closed shop and union membership received statutory immunity. A primary strike or the threat of a primary strike to obtain a closed shop was covered by the immunity of TULRA, s 13. Moreover, industrial action for such a purpose against a secondary employer was also protected, a fact which led to attempts to compel closed shops along with trade union recognition in the graphics sector of the printing and advertising industry.[13]

9 *The Times*, 10 October 1978.
10 Von Prondynski, op cit, p 231.
11 See discussion in Ch 2.
12 See eg Dunn, S and Gennard, J *The Closed Shop in British Industry* (1984) Chs 4 and 5.
13 See eg Report of Inquiry into Certain Trade Union Recruitment Activities (Leggat Committee) 1979 Cmnd 7706.

Thirdly, as we have seen, the Employment Protection Act 1975 created a positive right to associate in the form of individual employee protections: including in particular a right not to be dismissed or otherwise penalised for trade union membership and activity.

The legal strategy pursued by the Conservative government from 1980-1996 was progressively to remove the legal props to the closed shop built into the unfair dismissals legislation of the 1974-1976 period, whilst gradually developing a legal right of employees not to be a trade union member even where there is no closed shop.

The Conservative government's concern with the freedom of the individual caught in a collective setting had long preoccupied them with the closed shop institution as it had evolved in Britain. The decision of the European Court of Human Rights in the *James*[14] case confirmed their view that the legal regime provided by TULRA 1974, as amended in 1976, was a violation of the individual's basic human right not to join a trade union. Moreover, the Government considered that closed shops operated to strengthen trade unions' ability to engage in industrial action and thereby enhanced their power vis-à-vis employers.

The Employment Act 1980 began the step by step process of reversing the presumption of fairness of dismissals in a closed shop setting by providing that in all closed shop agreements whether existing or new, it was automatically unfair to dismiss an employee for non-membership inter alia where the employee had resigned from or refused to join a trade union because he objected on grounds of conscience or other deeply held personal conviction to being a member of any trade union.

That Act also introduced the requirement of a secret ballot for all new closed shop agreements or arrangements.[15] Moreover, it gave employees or prospective employees in a closed shop situation a right not to be unreasonably excluded or expelled from membership in a trade union where membership was necessary to obtain employment (ss 4, 5). It also made any 'union labour only' term or condition in commercial contracts void (TULR(C)A, s 144) and removed statutory immunity under what is now s 219 of TULR(C)A for any industrial action taken to induce or

14 *Young, James and Webster v United Kingdom* [1981] IRLR 408, ECHR; Forde 'The Closed Shop Case' [1982] 11 ILJ 1.

15 Dismissal for non-membership would be automatically unfair unless the union or unions had obtained a majority of 80% of the group of employees covered by the agreement in favour of the closed shop in a secret ballot. It also provided for a Code of Practice on Closed Shop agreements and arrangements, issued by the Secretary of State for Employment with quasi-legal rules for ballots. The Employment Act 1982 went a step further by providing that all dismissals in any closed shop situation were presumed unfair unless a secret ballot resulting in an affirmative vote of 80% of those voting or 85% of those eligible to vote had been conducted within five years of the dismissal.

support such a term (TULR(C)A, s 222). Finally, it articulated for the first time a positive right to employees not to join trade unions, albeit with a limited scope, by providing that outside legitimate closed shops any dismissal for non-membership in a trade union was automatically unfair (now TULR(C)A, s 152) and any penalty for non-membership short of dismissal was unlawful (now TULR(C)A, s 146).

The Employment Act 1982 set out a scheme to provide compensation from state funds for employees who were dismissed for non-membership between 1974 and 1980 as long as they could claim unfair dismissal under the rules of the 1980 Act (Sch 1).[16]

In the Employment Act 1988 the Conservative government, brushing aside closed shop ballots,[17] took the step of creating an unqualified right not to be unfairly dismissed[18] or penalised by action short of dismissal because of non-membership of[19] (refusal to join or resignation from) a trade union, whether or not a closed shop was in existence at the workplace, and had received an overwhelming majority vote from the workforce in support.

These measures to encourage individuals to dissociate from collective action were reinforced by new remedies and institutions provided in the various acts. In the 1980 Act, the principle had been established that in cases of dismissals for non-membership in a closed shop context, the minimum compensation would be enhanced by a special award providing today a minimum of £13,775 and a maximum of £27,500.[20] In the 1982 Act the remedy of interim relief was extended to the dismissed non-unionist to allow him to apply to continue the contract in existence until the tribunal hearing.[1] Moreover, under the two Acts, either an employee who was dismissed in a 'closed shop situation' or the employer could insist upon making the trade union or trade unionist a party to the unfair dismissal action as long as it could be shown that the trade union or individual had exerted pressure on the employer to obtain the dismissal. The 1988 Act established a new institution, the Commissioner for the Rights of Trade Union Members (CROTUM), to help individuals to bring cases against trade unions.

In the 1990 Act, the process of creating obstacles for union security arrangements was taken one stage further by making it unlawful to

16 See Ewing and Rees 'Closed Shop Dismissals 1974-80: A Study of the Retroactive Compensation Scheme' [1983] ILJ 148.
17 EA 1988, s 11.
18 TULR(C)A, s 152(1)(c).
19 TULR(C)A, s 146(1)(c).
20 TULR(C)A, s 158(1). In a case where reinstatement or re-engagement is ordered and not complied with the minimum special award rises to £20,600 (s 158(2)).
1 TULR(C)A, ss 161-3.

discriminate against non-union members in the hiring process. TULR(C)A, s 137 now provides that it is unlawful inter alia to refuse a person employment:

(a) because . . . he is not a member of a trade union; or
(b) because he is unwilling to accept a requirement—
  (i) to take steps to become or cease to be, or to remain or not to become, a member of a trade union; or
  (ii) to make payments or suffer deductions in the event of his not being a member of a trade union.

This protection applies to a refusal to be a member of a particular trade union as well as all trade unions.[2]

The main purpose of this part of the section is to provide further legal weapons to stop the practice of the pre-entry closed shop. It complements s 174, TULR(C)A, as amended by TURER 1993, which provides protection against unreasonable expulsions and exclusions from trade unions in cases inter alia where membership is necessary to obtain employment[3] and s 3 of the EA 1988 which gives a trade union member a general right not to be unjustifiably disciplined by his union.[4] It also complements the common law rights of trade union members vis-à-vis trade union organisations.[5]

The statute defines a refusal of employment in wider terms than the protection for trade union membership. Thus where an employer makes an offer conditional upon trade union membership and the employee rejects it for that reason, this is deemed to be a refusal of employment by the employer.[6] In addition, deliberately omitting to entertain and process an application or inquiry (s 137(5)(a)); and causing an applicant to withdraw or cease to pursue an application (s 137(5(b)); deliberately omitting to offer employment of the description applied for (s 137(5)(d)); and offers withdrawn, or which the employer causes the applicant not to accept (s 137(5)(e)); are all deemed to be refusals of employment under the section.

2 Under s 137(4) if there is an arrangement or practice whereby employment is offered only to individuals approved or put forward by a trade union and the trade union only puts forward individuals who are union members, a person who is not a member and is refused employment under such a scheme 'shall be taken to have been refused employment because he is not a member of a trade union' and hence entitled to the protection of s 137(1).

3 See s 14 of TURER 1993, amending ss 174-177 of TULR(C)A. See discussion in Smith and Wood *Industrial Law* (4th edn, 1990) pp 471-476; Simpson 'Individualism vs Collectivism: an Evaluation of s 14 of TURER 1993' (1993) ILJ 181.

4 See eg *NACODS v Gluchowski* [1996] IRLR 252, EAT.

5 Ibid, pp 461-470. Wedderburn (Lord) *The Worker and the Law* (3rd edn, 1981).

6 TULR(C)A, s 137(6).

Moreover, certain actions by employers are deemed to be refusals of employment for non-membership: eg adverts or notices which indicate, or which might reasonably be understood as indicating, that a job is open only to union members, give rise to a conclusive presumption that a non-member who is refused that job has been refused because of non-membership;[7] as well, a refusal of employment in pursuance of a labour supply arrangement or practice by a trade union(s) because of non-membership.[8] Furthermore the Act makes it unlawful for employment agencies to refuse to provide their services to job seekers who are not union members.[9]

This change in the legal framework surrounding the closed shop will mean that individuals who are discriminated against will have increased legal protection available to them. The Act provides for enforcement by individual complaint to an industrial tribunal[10] with a joinder procedure to allow anyone exerting pressure on the employer to be joined in the action and pay compensation.[11] The main remedy is compensation up to a maximum compensatory award for unfair dismissal, but the tribunal is also empowered to recommend practicable action to obviate or reduce the adverse effects of discriminatory conduct and a failure to comply without justification with the recommendation would result in increased compensation (s 140).

Even before these changes in the law, the pre-entry closed shop institution itself was on the decline owing to other factors - the decline in industries where it was concentrated and the impact of technology in craft based sectors. Lord McCarthy has estimated that the number of employees in such arrangements in 1990 was no more than 150,000.[12]

In post entry union shop arrangements the new legal rules will mean that employers will be careful of what they say in interviews but will not necessarily welcome non-union employees. On the other hand, they are unlikely to be willing to dismiss non-union employees given the legal penalties even with the probable trade union liability. In some instances this may lead to a tacit acceptance of non-unionists continuing to work alongside unionists where the workforce and the union grudgingly accept the arrangement. In other cases, the net effect of the legislation may be to produce transfers[13] or paid resignations rather than dismissals in such situations.

7 TULR(C)A, s 137(3).
8 TULR(C)A, s 137(4).
9 TULR(C)A, s 138.
10 TULR(C)A, ss 139-41.
11 TULR(C)A, s 142.
12 HL Deb, vol 521, 10 July 1990.
13 See eg the facts in *Courtaulds Northern Spinning Ltd v Sibson* [1988] ICR 451, [1988] IRLR 305, CA (now appealed to ECHR).

CHAPTER 16

# Legal support for trade unions and collective bargaining and employee representation

## POSITIVE RIGHTS TO RECOGNITION

Legal support for trade union recognition was introduced quite late in Britain. Even as late as the 1960s the TUC[1] could argue that 'trade unions in Britain have succeeded through their own efforts in strengthening their organisation and in obtaining recognition, not relying on the assistance of government through legislation'. However, by that time, changes in the labour market away from manual to non-manual employment and the decrease in employment in industries with high trade union densities indicated that the historical base for trade unionism in the private sector was eroding.

In 1968 the Donovan Commission's suggested reform of labour law also included a recommendation for a statutory union recognition procedure as a useful means of support for trade unions and collective bargaining in the face of declining trade union membership.[2] These recommendations made no attempt to place upon UK employers a direct legal duty to recognise and bargain with a trade union, enforced by contempt of court orders, along American lines. Instead, they emphasised the virtues of voluntary settlement based on conciliation or mediation, with a penalty consisting of an unilaterally imposed arbitration award requiring the employer to pay wage rates and other terms which reflected union rates.

This approach was adopted, in a modified way, in the Industrial Relations Act but the experience under that Act, as mentioned, was heavily distorted by the TUC unions' unwillingness to 'register' and obtain the benefits of positive legal rights.[3]

1 Evidence to the Royal Commission on Trade Unions and Employers' Associations London (HMSO, 1986).
2 Royal Commission on Trade Unions and Employers' Associations; para. 224.
3 See *Industrial Relations and the Limits of the Law.*

The 1975 Act included provisions that enabled an independent trade union which was refused recognition for the purpose of collective bargaining to obtain legal support along the lines recommended by the Donovan Commission.[4] Under these provisions (which were repealed by the Conservative Government's Employment Act 1980), a union could make a complaint to ACAS about an employer's refusal to recognise an independent union and ACAS was required first to conciliate and then investigate the extent of employee support for recognition. Following the investigation it was, if it saw fit, empowered to make a recommendation that the employer bargain with the union.[5] That is, to take such steps to carry on negotiations as might reasonably be expected to be taken by an employer ready and willing to carry out the recommendation (EPA, s 15(2)).

The employer's duty to bargain under the 1975 Act was therefore little more than a procedural obligation requiring the employer to engage in discussions with the trade union over the relevant subject but not requiring any substantive concession.[6] A failure to bargain was not penalised by a court order backed up by contempt powers, but only by an arbitration award by the Central Arbitration Committee against an employer who refused to comply with an order to recognise to give an improvement in pay or other terms of employment to individual employees who were the subject of the recognition claim.

As long as employers cooperated in an ACAS inquiry it was possible for ACAS to determine not only the extent of trade union membership among employees but also the extent of trade union support, ie whether they would join a trade union if that union were recognised by the employer to negotiate on their behalf. Moreover, ACAS had the discretion to decide what percentage of support called for a recommendation of recognition for collective bargaining purposes and whether a lower level of support called for representation rights.

If an employer refused to comply with an ACAS recommendation for recognition and the matter, after further conciliation attempts by ACAS, was referred to the Central Arbitration Committee, the CAC could only impose an award of an increase on levels of remuneration and other terms and conditions of employment. In practice, the CAC viewed its role as providing a 'substitute for a hard bargain which recognition had it been granted would have provided'.[7] It was not prepared to make an award of recognition as such since that could not readily be converted into a term

4 EPA, ss 11-16.

5 The recommendation could consist of a general recommendation to bargain or a recommendation to bargain over 'further issues' where the union was already recognised. In the event, claims for further recognition were more.

6 Anderman *Employment Protection: A New Legal Framework* (Butterworths, 1976) pp 3-4.

7 Award 78/808.

of employees' contracts. Nor did it make an effort to penalise recalcitrant employers by awarding exemplary levels of pay hours and holidays.

Hence the statutory procedure, as such, created few legal disincentives to firms who were prepared to pay union rates and who were determined to protect their managerial autonomy from trade union influence.

The weakness of the sanction did not prevent the judiciary viewing the procedure in draconian terms. The legal supports for trade union recognition were 'an interference with individual liberty' and required safeguards against abuse. Some of the weaknesses of the statutory procedure and particularly the remedy for non compliance were due to the Labour Government's unwillingness to take a more forthright view of the uses of legislation to support trade union recognition. It was ambivalent about the use of the law to promote voluntary collective bargaining because of the possible impact of the legislation upon collective bargaining along lines similar to the American experience with the duty to bargain in good faith.[8]

It was said initially by Lord Wedderburn that the lack of an enforceable right to be recognised was 'not too high a price to be paid for the maintenance of what will still be fundamentally a voluntary system of collective labour relations'.[9] However, even the relatively weak UK recognition laws produced a form of legal regulation which impinged upon the voluntary system. Judicial decisions about whether staff associations were 'independent trade unions' produced results which were sharply at variance with trade union views.[10]

Secondly, although the determination of the boundaries of bargaining groups by ACAS were often guided by a concern to maintain existing arrangements with companies and industry as much as possible, the courts were not always willing to accept ACAS's judgment particularly where it refused to recommend recognition to a union with majority support in a specific grade of employee.[11]

In *UKAPE v ACAS*[12] Lord Denning considered that ACAS should give greater weight to the rights of individual trade unionists to a representative of their choice following the principle of freedom of association under Article 11 of the ECHR. Eventually, when the decision was set aside by the House of Lords, Lord Scarman stated that the Convention did not support the proposition that 'every trade union which can show it has

8 See Wedderburn *The Worker and the Law* (1976) p 183.
9 Wedderburn: 'The Employment Protection Act 1975: Collective Dimensions' [1976] 39 MLR 169 at 183.
10 See eg *Squibb UK Staff Association v Certification Officer* [1978] ICR 115, [1977] IRLR 355, EAT.
11 The policy was eventually upheld by House of Lords: *UKAPE v ACAS* [1980] ICR 201, [1980] IRLR 124.
12 [1980] IRLR 124.

members employed by a particular company has a right to recognition for the purposes of collective bargaining'. However, this decision came rather late in the period.

Another feature of the decisions in the 1975-9 period was the limited form of recognition allowed under the s 11 recommendation. The union could only be recognised for the purposes of collective bargaining ie 'for the purpose of negotiating related to or connected with the collective bargaining issues set out in TULRA, s 29(1)'.

There was no recognition of trade union representation rights short of collective bargaining such as a right of representation for the purpose of presenting grievances or disciplinary appeals.

Thirdly, when ACAS judgments were subject to judicial review of the criteria applied to recognition questions, particularly those involving inter-union disputes, the results created trade union concern about the compatibility of legal machinery with their own disputes procedure for resolving inter-union jurisdictional disputes, the so-called Bridlington Procedures.[13] Wedderburn's revised opinion was:

> 'The movement has been disillusioned by the operation of some of 'its' laws and has realised afresh the limitations that inevitably fall upon trade unions who trust in the regulation of industrial relations by the law.'[14]

At the same time, any evaluation of the experience of the statutory recognition procedure, 1975-80, must also take into account the enormous growth in trade union membership that occurred during the same period. It has been estimated that trade union membership rose from 8 to 12 million workers, reaching 60% of the total workforce. Although union recognition obtained under the statutory procedure only accounted for 65,000 employees, it would be wrong to conclude that the compulsory recognition procedure had only a marginal impact. In the first place, the considerable successes achieved by voluntary conciliation under s 2 of the 1975 Act exceeded those of the compulsory procedure and could not be guaranteed to have occurred in the absence of a statutory procedure. Moreover, the tendency of a statutory recognition procedure to create a climate of opinion encouraging the voluntary recognition of trade unions cannot be entirely discounted, even if it was also true that much of the growth in trade union membership during this period occurred in the public sector.

Furthermore Dickens and Bain make the point that once the statutory procedure was perceptibly weakened by judicial decisions 'revealing to employers that they could successfully obstruct ACAS and avoid a recognition recommendation and the CAC had shown that employers

13 *EMA v ACAS (No 2)* [1980] 1 All ER 896, [1980] 1 WLR 302; see also R Simpson *'Judicial Control of ACAS'* (1979) 8 ILJ 160.

14 13 Israel Law Rev p 457.

ultimately could not be forced to recognise unions', there was a decline in voluntary recognition.[15]

Finally, the repeal of EPA, s 11 did not occur in isolation. It must be seen in the context of other measures designed to control the expansion of recognition by self help measures. For example, under s 186 of TULR(C)A any trade union recognition, negotiation or consultation clauses in a contract for the supply of goods or services are void and under s 187 it is actionable to refuse to contract with or accept tenders from an employer on the grounds that he does not recognise a particular trade union. Moreover, under s 144 a union membership requirement in a contract for goods and services is void and under s 145 a refusal to deal with suppliers of goods and services on union membership grounds is prohibited. In addition, s 225 removes the statutory protection for industrial action in s 219 in the case of any pressure to impose a trade union recognition requirement. And, s 222 removes s 219 protection in the case of industrial action to enforce union membership. Finally, TULR(C)A, s 224 places severe limits upon secondary action, a traditional prop to recognition for some trade unions.[16]

## THE STATUTORY RIGHTS OF RECOGNISED TRADE UNIONS

The repeal of the statutory recognition procedure in 1979 did not dramatically affect the statutory trade union rights to disclosure of information,[17] consultations over redundancies,[18] transfers of the undertaking,[19] health and safety[20] and pensions[1] as well as the right to time off for trade union duties[2] and the right to appoint safety representatives.[3] For while all these rights presuppose that a trade union has been recognised by the employer for the purposes of collective bargaining, it is not necessary for the recognition to have been granted under the statutory procedure.

15 'A Duty to Bargain: Union Recognition and Information Disclosure' in Lewis (ed) *Labour Law in Britain* p 80.

16 Note that the Labour Government has now proposed reintroducing a legal procedure for trade unions to obtain recognition. See '*Farness at Work*' (Cmd 3968, 1988: See Appendix below, Annex I).

17 TULR(C)A, ss 181-5. But see the special rules relating to recognition for disclosure purposes discussed on p 288.

18 TULR(C)A, ss 188-192.

19 Transfer of Undertaking (Protection of Employment) Regulations 1981, regs 10 and 11.

20 Health and Safety at Work etc Act 1974, s 2.

1 Social Security Pensions Act 1975, s 61.

2 TULR(C)A, ss 168-173. Discussed in Ch 14. The scope of the right to time off for trade union duties was narrowed in 1990: see discussion at p 273.

3 Health and Safety at Work etc Act 1974, s 2(4).

What is required, however, under the legislation is at the very least[4] that the trade union must be found as a matter of fact to be recognised by the employer in relation to the descriptions of workers for the purposes of collective bargaining.[5]

This poses few problems in the case of established relationships. Normally, recognition of the trade union(s) is expressed in a collective agreement in return for a promise by the trade union(s) not to organise industrial action until the disputes procedure is exhausted and on occasion express recognition by the union of management's rights.[6] However, recognition can also be implied from established relationships. For example, in *Joshua Wilson & Bros Ltd v USDAW*[7] despite the employer's assertion to the contrary there was clear and unequivocal evidence of recognition based on his actions. The employer had adopted the rates of pay of the trade association and had allowed the union to publicise Joint Industrial Council wage increases. The union could collect subscriptions on company premises, and had been consulted on job allocations, security and disciplinary matters.

In contentious cases, the criteria applied by the judiciary to the test of recognition is whether in fact the employer has agreed to recognition. For example in *NUGSAT v Albury Bros Ltd*[8] the Court of Appeal stressed that the 'attitude of the employer was particularly important'. An act of recognition moreover, was 'such an important matter involving such serious consequences for both sides . . . that it should not be held to be established unless the evidence is clear'. In that case the employer's membership in the trade association was not enough; nor was its payment of trade association rates or discussions with a union official over a union member's wages. A more positive acknowledgement by the employer was required.[9]

In *USDAW v Sketchley Ltd*[10] the EAT confirmed moreover, that the statutory test of recognition required there to be recognition for the purposes of negotiation over terms and conditions. Representational rights in grievance procedures, acceptance of the appointment of shop stewards and allowing them to collect dues were not sufficient to satisfy the statutory definition.

4 In some cases, eg disclosure of information, there is a further requirement of recognition in respect of specific matters. See *R v Central Arbitration Committee, ex p BTP Dioxide Ltd*, discussed on p 321. See also time off for union duties p 306.
5 TULR(C)A, s 178(3), 'Collective bargaining' is now defined as meaning negotiations relating to or connected with one of the matters specified in s 178(2) of TULR(C)A.
6 See discussions in Ch 5.
7 [1977] ICR 530.
8 [1979] ICR 84, [1978] IRLR 504, CA; applied in *Cleveland County Council v Springett* [1985] IRLR 131, EAT.
9 Ibid.
10 [1978] IRLR 120, EAT; see too *NUTGW v Charles Ingram & Co Ltd* [1977] ICR 530, [1977] IRLR 147.

In that case, the employer had responded to a threat of a strike over redundancy by agreeing in a memorandum to give the union advance notice of any discussion over redundancy at branch level and to concede that premium redundancy payments as well as voluntary redundancy could be discussed. The EAT was willing to remit the issue to the industrial tribunal to decide whether the memorandum was a bargain with the trade union and that therefore the union could be viewed as statutorily recognised for the purposes of consultation rights over redundancy. In the public sector, where employers have had an obligation effectively to recognise appropriate trade unions, employers retain considerable discretion to decide which unions are appropriate.[11]

These cases indicate that the employer continues to have considerable control both over the fact of recognition generally and as to the specific matters for which trade union recognition has been granted. As we shall see however employers now have many statutory obligations to inform and consult elected representatives of employees whether or not they are recognised trade unions.[12] One remaining statutory right solely available to recognised trade unions is the right to disclosure of information for the purposes of collective bargaining.

## DISCLOSURE OF INFORMATION

Section 181 of TULR(C)A requires employers to disclose information in connection with collective bargaining rather than to provide employees more generally with financial information about the firm as called for under proposed EC Directives.

The original legislative plan, as in the Industrial Relations Act 1971, was to require employers to give out both types of information. Thus the 1971 Act required firms of more than 350 employees to issue financial statements to all employees as well as to disclose information for collective bargaining purposes. Today, the rudiments of a legislative employee information policy can be found in s 1 of the Employment Act 1982 which requires the Board of Directors of companies of 250 employees or more to include in their annual report a statement of the information given to, and consultation carried out with, employees (and their representatives) during the previous year. Moreover, companies are required to give employees the information contained in the annual report to shareholders.

11 See eg *R v Post Office, ex p ASTMS* [1981] 1 All ER 139, [1981] ICR 76, CA; *R v British Coal Corpn, ex p UDM* [1988] ICR 36. See Fredman and Morris *The State as Employer: Labour Law in the Public Services* (Mansell, London, 1989).

12 See eg TULR(C)A, s 188.

The provisions of the 1992 Act, however, are limited to the disclosure of information to trade unions, with the ostensible aim of enhancing and extending collective bargaining. These provisions are complemented by a Code of Practice issued by ACAS which operates as a guide to interpretation and suggests quite a wide range of information which might be disclosed.[13]

One reason why the legislation was retained since 1979 is that it is not simply an advantage for trade unions in the bargaining process. It is also useful to prompt employers to present information in such a way as to produce more realistic demands by trade unions by convincing them to take into greater account the economic problems of the firm.[14]

Indeed, the Act specifically provides that employers do not have to provide original documents, or even copies of original documents, but are entitled to prepare information in a special form to be disclosed to trade unions.[15] This entitlement is a virtual invitation to the sophisticated presentation.

Under the Act, the employer's duty at first sight seems wide. A recognised, independent trade union is entitled to all information relating to the employer's undertaking (or an associated employer's undertaking) as is in his possession which applies to any stage of collective bargaining. However, the statutory right is hedged with many qualifications. In the first place not only must the trade union be recognised for the purposes of collective bargaining for negotiations; it must also be recognised specifically to bargain on any 'matter' for which it seeks information.[16] Further, to succeed, the union must show that the disclosure will be in accordance with good industrial relations practice and that without such information it will be impeded to a material extent in engaging in collective bargaining.[17]

Furthermore, even if the information meets these tests, an employer can refuse to divulge it if it has been communicated in confidence or is otherwise confidential or its release would cause substantial injury to the undertaking, or be damaging to national security.[18]

Moreover, the remedy for a failure or refusal to disclose is weak. Against a recalcitrant employer, a trade union has only the legal sanction of

13 Disclosure of Information to Trade Unions for Collective Bargaining Purposes ACAS Code of Practice (1977). See Gospel 'Disclosure of Information to Trade Unions' (1976) 5 ILJ 221; Gospel and Williams 'Disclosure of Information the CAC approach' [1981] ILJ 10.

14 Dickens, L 'What are Companies Disclosing for the 1980s' Personnel Management 1980 April 28.

15 TULR(C)A, s 182.

16 Section 181(2). *R v Central Arbitration Committee, ex p BTP Tioxide* [1981] ICR 843, [1982] IRLR 60; see also eg [1980] 215 IRLR 8.

17 *Civil Service Union v Central Arbitration Committee* [1980] IRLR 274, QB.

18 TULR(C)A, s 182(1).

submitting a claim to the Central Arbitration Committee (CAC) for an arbitration award against the employer, taking the form of an improvement in the terms and conditions of the contract of individual employees. There is no possibility of a court order compelling the employer actually to disclose the relevant information.

That said, this might be too legalistic a reading of the statute. The statutory provisions may have an indirect effect upon managerial practice encouraging voluntary disclosure of information more generally[19] and specifically when a complaint is brought.[20]

Nevertheless, the signal sent by the UK statute to managers is different in kind from that suggested in the EC draft directives. The emphasis in the Vredling Directive,[1] the Fifth Directive, the European Company Statute and now Draft European Works Council Directive,[2] is upon continuous information along a wider front.

For example, in the Vredling Directive it was stipulated that every six months the dominant undertakings should disclose to representatives of employees of subsidiaries through the management of these subsidiaries information specifically on the following:

(a) structure and manning;
(b) the economic and financial situation;
(c) situation and probable development of the business, production and sales;
(d) employment situation and probable trends;
(e) production and investment programmes;
(f) rationalisation plans;
(g) manufacturing and working methods, particularly new working methods;
(h) all procedures and plans liable to have a substantial effect on employees' interests.

In the European Company Statute and the Fifth Directive, if workers are not actually elected as part of the supervisory board of a company then a body representing workers would have specific legal rights to receive regular reports on the progress of the company's business and be informed

19 See discussion in Dickens and Bain 'A Duty to Bargain: Union Recognition and Information Disclosure' in Lewis (ed) *Labour Law in Britain* p 80 at p 100.

20 Dickens and Bain indicate that a 'majority of cases are in fact disposed of without a hearing and the CAC's reports show two-thirds of all cases withdrawn between 1977 and 1983 as resulting in full or partial closure'(p 100).

1 Council Directive on Procedures for informing and consulting the Employees of Undertakings with complex structures in particular Transnational Undertakings, 24th October 1980, OJ 1980 0297/3 (Vredling); Docksey 'Information and Consultation of Employees' [1986] MLR 28.

2 The European Works Councils Directive 94/95/EC discussed in final section of this chapter. See Hall 'Beyond the EC Works Council Directive' [1992] BJIR 547.

and consulted prior to all meetings of the board (or of the supervisory part of a two-tier board) receiving all the information concerning the agenda of each meeting.

The main reason for the difference of approach is that the EC directives are more concerned with information as an integral feature of consultation and participation rather than collective bargaining and it is to that feature that we shall return in the next section.

## COLLECTIVE CONSULTATION OVER REDUNDANCIES

In addition to being regulated by the redundancy payments legislation and the unfair redundancy dismissals provisions, employers are required to consult with recognised trade unions as well as to notify the government in advance of redundancies. Enacted as part of the Social Contract programme of legislation, but now ss 188-92 of TULR(C)A, these provisions are essentially an implementation of the EC's Directive on Collective Redundancies. They have since been supplemented by the Transfer of Undertakings (Protection of Employment) Regulations 1981 which implements the EC Acquired Rights Directive.[3]

Under s 188 of TULR(C)A an employer who proposes[4] to make 20 or more employees redundant at any one 'establishment'[5] has an obligation to inform and consult about such a decision either with employee representatives elected by such employees with a trade union which has been recognised for collective bargaining for those grades of employee.[6] The consultation must begin 'in good time'. But if an employer[7] proposes

3 The EC Directive on the Approximation of the Laws of the Member States Relating to Collective Redundancies (OJ 1975, L48/29). The EC Directive on Safeguarding Employees' Rights in the Event of Transfers of Undertakings (OJ 1977, L61/26). See McMullen *Business Transfers and Employee Rights* (1992, 2nd edn).

4 See *APAC Kirvin Ltd* [1978] IRLR 318 (proposes requires the employer to have 'formed some view' about numbers, timing and method at 320). The EC Directive say 'contemplates' which suggests that consultation should begin before a view is formed. Cf *R v British Coal Corpn and Secretary of State for Trade and Industry, ex p Vardy* [1993] IRLR 104, HC; but see contra *Griffin v South West Water Services Ltd* [1995] IRLR 15, HC.

5 An 'establishment' can encompass more than one site (see eg *Clarks of Hove Ltd v Bakers Union* [1978] IRLR 366, CA) or be a single company within a group (see eg *Rockfon A/S v Nielsen* [1996] IRLR 168, ECJ.

6 Under s 188 in its current form, the employer may choose between the two. This option could soon be removed by legislation implementing the proposals in 'Fairness at Work'.

7 These provisions apply to each employer separately. Associated employers cannot be aggregated see *E Green & Son (Castings) Ltd v ASTMS* [1984] ICR 352, [1984] IRLR 135, EAT. Cf approach taken to associated companies in the proposed European Works Councils Directive. Nielsen and Szyszczak *The Social Dimension of the European Community* (1991) pp 171-177.

to dismiss as redundant 100 or more employees at an establishment[8] in a 90-day period, then consultation must begin 90 days before the first dismissal takes effect. If an employer proposes to dismiss as redundant 20 or more employees, then consultation must begin at least 30 days before the first of those dismissals take effect.

At first sight, the statutory rights appear to be extensive. The information that s 188 requires the employer to disclose in writing to representatives for the purpose of consultation before a redundancy decision is taken[9] includes the reasons for the redundancy proposal, the numbers and descriptions of employees whom it is proposed to dismiss as redundant, the total number of employees of any such description employed by the employer at the establishment in question, the proposed method of selecting the employees who may be dismissed, and the proposed method of carrying out the dismissals, with due regard to any agreed procedure, including the period over which the dismissals are to take effect and the proposed method of calculating the amount of any redundancy payment to employees who may be dismissed.

As the EAT pointed out in *Sovereign Distribution Services Ltd v TGWU*,[10] the object of the statutory duty to consult is to provide the (only) 'opportunity for employees through their recognised trade unions to be able to seek to influence the redundant decision and to put forward other ideas and other considerations, not only as to the overall decisions but also as to the individuals who should be made redundant and other aspects which may be material.'

Moreover, as the EAT put it in *Spillers-French (Holdings) Ltd v USDAW*:[11]

> 'The consultation may result in new ideas being ventilated which avoid the redundancy situations altogether. Equally it may lead to a lesser number of persons being made redundant than was originally thought necessary. Or it may be that alternative work can be found during the period of consultation.'

Furthermore, as the EAT stated in *NUT v Avon CC* [1978] IRLR 58 the consultation must be genuine and not a sham and occur for example after dismissal notices have been issued. Furthermore, a reasonable time must be allowed for such an exchange.[12]

The actual obligation of the employer to consult with trade union representatives, however, is essentially procedural in effect. Originally, it

8 An establishment is a particular place, building etc. See eg *Barratt Developments (Bradford) Ltd v UCATT* [1978] ICR 319, [1977] IRLR 403, EAT.
9 See *Re Hartlebury Printers Ltd* [1993] 1 All ER 470, [1992] IRLR 516: *Hough v Leyland DAF Ltd* [1991] IRLR 194, EAT.
10 [1990] ICR 31, [1989] IRLR 334, EAT.
11 [1980] ICR 31 at 37.
12 *E Green & Son (Castings) Ltd v ASTMS* [1984] IRLR 135.

consisted of little more than an obligation to discuss. Thus, according to s 188(5) of TULR(C)A, the employer need only consider any representations made by the representatives, reply to them, and state his reasons if he rejects any of those representations. TURER 1993 s 34 deleted this requirement and replaced it with a more focused duty to consult not only about the information disclosed in s 188(4) but also about ways of (a) avoiding the dismissals; (b) reducing the numbers of employees to be dismissed; and (c) mitigating the consequences of the dismissals. Moreover, under the 1993 amendment, the consultation must be undertaken with a view to reaching agreement with the representatives.

The statute gives the employer a defence where there are 'special circumstances which render it not reasonably practicable' (s 188(7)) for him to comply with any of the statutory requirements. In such a case, an employer must show that he or she took all such steps towards compliance with the requirement as are reasonably practicable in those circumstances. The courts have applied the special circumstances test with some degree of rigour. Thus, a sudden decision to cease trading after a long period of financial difficulty could not be viewed as special circumstances excusing the company from their duty to inform and consult. It required 'something out of the ordinary run of events',[13] sudden financial disasters - such as insolvency due to a withdrawal of a prospective purchaser and a bank calling in a receiver,[14] or a failure to procure a government loan[15] - have been held to be special circumstances justifying no consultation by the employer. The 1993 Act added to this exception the limit that 'where the decision leading to the proposed dismissals is that of a person controlling the employer, a failure of that person to provide information shall not amount to special circumstances under s 188(7).'[16]

Where an employer fails to meet his obligation to inform and consult in good time, the relevant employee representatives may enforce their rights by making a complaint to an industrial tribunal. The remedy, however, consists either of a declaration (rarely sought) or of financial compensation which the employer must pay to individual employees who have lost the opportunity of being represented in the requisite consultation process. The employee representatives cannot obtain a court order compelling the employer to comply with its statutory duties towards them.

The amount of compensation is provided in the form of a protective award (s 189(3)), consisting of a week's pay for every week in a 'protected period', that is, a period determined by the tribunal to be just and equitable

13 *Clarks of Hove Ltd v Bakers' Union* [1979] 1 All ER 152, [1978] IRLR 366, CA.
14 *USDAW v Leancut Bacon Ltd* [1981] IRLR 295, EAT.
15 *Hamish Armour (Receiver of Barry Staines Ltd) v ASTMS* [1979] IRLR 24, EAT.
16 See *GMB v Rankin and Harrison* [1992] IRLR 514, EAT (in which shedding employees to make a business more attractive was not a special circumstance).

in all the circumstances having regard to the employer's default (s 189(4)). Hence while it is up to the employee representatives to initiate a complaint, it is left to the individual employee to enforce the penalty for the employer's failure to comply by presenting a complaint to an industrial tribunal (s 190).

The maximum amount of the award varies with the required consultation period, which in turn is related to the number of workers involved. Thus in the case of a collective dismissal of over a 100 employees in a 90 day period, the maximum protective award consists of 90 days' pay. In the case of redundancies of over 20 employees, the maximum award is 30 days' pay. Subject to the maxima, the courts have tended to assess the protective period in terms of compensation rather than penalty, ie the loss to employees of the wages which they would have obtained during a period of proper consultation rather than the severity of the employer's failure to consult. As the EAT put it in *Talke Fashions Ltd v Amalgamated Society of Textile Workers and Kindred Trades*:[17] 'the seriousness of the default ought to be considered in its relationship to the employees and not in its relationship to the trade union representative who has not been consulted'. In *Spillers-French (Holdings) Ltd v USDAW*,[18] however, after the EAT concluded from the authorities that the purpose of the statute was to compensate the individual employee in the event of the default of the employer, it went on to define the key element in the assessment of compensation as 'not the loss or potential loss of actual remuneration during the relevant period by the particular employee [but rather] the loss of days of consultation which have occurred'.[19] Slynn J added that the Tribunal would also have to 'consider how serious was the breach on the part of the employer?'

Thus, where an employer, as in *Sovereign Distribution Services Ltd v TGWU*,[20] informs the trade unions on the same day as employees were given notice of dismissal, and fails to provide the written information required by s 188(4) and where the only meeting held was one called by the trade union, it was well within the industrial tribunal's discretion to treat the employer's breach as substantial and make a protective award close to the upper limit, because it had been clear that there had been virtually no consultation in the sense of meaningful consultation. The tribunal could take a sliding scale approach but it must not be a penal approach on the employer.[1]

17 [1977] ICR 833, [1977] IRLR 309, EAT.

18 [1980] ICR 31, [1979] IRLR 339.

19 Ibid at 342. See too *GKN Sankey Ltd v NSMM* [1980] IRLR 8, EAT.

20 [1990] ICR 31, [1989] IRLR 334, EAT; see also *TGWU v Ledbury Preserves (1928) Ltd* [1986] ICR 492, [1986] IRLR 492, EAT in which Gibson J suggested that this in itself may be an indication that consultation had not taken place.

1 [1990] ICR 31, [1989] IRLR 334 at 337, EAT.

Where an employer attempts to buy out employees' legal rights to consultation by paying them the full protective award in cash and avoiding the actual consultation process there appears to be some recourse for unions or employees under the statute. In *Vosper Thornycroft (UK) Ltd v TGWU*[2] employers made 304 shipbuilding employees redundant without prior consultation with the trade unions by giving each dismissed employee a payment of 13 weeks' pay, ie 91 days to cover their liability of a maximum protective award of 90 days. In effect, the employer was making use of the right to set off, under s 190(3), any payment made to the employee by way of damages for breach of contract against the employer's liability for a protective award. Now under TURER that entitlement to set off has been deleted from the statute. In the event, employees will now be entitled to pay during the notice period in addition to the protective award (s 34).

One further complication facing employers who are planning a redundancy on such a basis is the relationship between their obligation to consult under s 188 and their obligation to provide notice of termination of employees under ERA, s 86. In principle an employer who issues notices of termination during the process of consultation is not consulting over proposed redundancies but presenting the trade union and employees with a fait accompli.[3] In practice, however, as long as the notices of dismissal have not actually expired during the minimum period for the consultation process, it is possible for employers to fit some of the period of notice of dismissal within the period of consultation.[4]

Finally, the protective award is not viewed as the equivalent of a requirement that the employer actually retain the employee in employment for a protected period, on the analogy of interim relief in cases of dismissal for trade union membership and activity or non-membership. Instead of providing for actual earnings to be paid during the period, the award is measured by the employee's pay for normal working hours, a formula which excludes non-compulsory overtime.

In addition to the obligation to consult recognised trade unions, employers are required to notify the Secretary of State when they propose to dismiss 20 or more employees for redundancy (s 193). Periods of advance notification correspond to the same periods as those set out for consultation with employee representatives. A failure to meet this statutory duty is punishable by a fine of up to level 5 on the standard scale (currently £5,000) (s 194). The idea behind these provisions is to put the Department of Trade and Industry in a position to help to place redundant employees in new jobs or in government retraining courses. Yet this recognition of a

2 [1988] ICR 270, [1988] IRLR 232, EAT.
3 *GMWU (MATSA) v British Uralite Ltd* [1979] IRLR 413, IT. See Bourn *Redundancy Law and Practice* (1983) Butterworths.
4 *Bourn*, p 57.

public interest in redundancies is relatively modest. Unlike other countries, employers are required only to notify, not to obtain the consent of public authorities, before making large scale redundancies.[5] The changes to s 193 introduced by the 1993 Act will widen the employer's duty in two respects. The definition of dismissals for redundancy extends to other forms of reorganisations which result in dismissal[6] and the employer cannot rely on a decision taken by a 'parent' company as a special circumstance justifying its failure to comply with its statutory obligation.[7]

It is difficult to judge the effect of the redundancy consultation provisions as a platform for trade union influence in managerial decisions concerning redundancies.

Collective consultation by trade unions may in fact set the stage for collective bargaining over redundancies. For in the UK, unlike other countries with a peace obligation barring strikes in such cases,[8] trade unions may lawfully organise industrial action in support of their position over redundancies as long as it does not involve secondary action and is properly balloted.

Of course, the reality is often different. Redundancies often occur in a period of recession and at a time when the demand for a firm's products is low. These conditions undermine the union's bargaining strength and make it more difficult for it to use the process of consultation as a stepping stone to bargaining for substantive changes to the management proposals for redundancies. Moreover, management often take the occasion of the legal process of consultation to engage in a separate but related process of appealing directly to the workforce as a whole by informing them about the economic 'facts of life' facing the company and the need to make cuts in order to survive. Consultation with unions and employee represenatives have become part of the process by which a modern firm now 'manages' redundancy.[9] Nevertheless, while the legal provisions are not a direct prop to collective bargaining, they do require employers to engage in a process of discussion with and listen to the merits of the arguments by employee representatives about a proposed management decision as well as the possibilities of modifying that decision.

However, even if consultation legislation has been strengthened in these ways, it remains capable of injecting an element of joint regulation only

5 Davies and Freedland *Labour Law Text and Materials* (2nd edn, 1984) at p 249.

6 'In this chapter references to dismissal as redundant are references to dismissal for a reason not related to the individual concerned or for a number of reasons all of which are not so related': TULR(C)A s 195(1) as amended by TURER, s 34.

7 TULR(C)A, s 193(7) as amended by TURER, s 34.

8 See eg Germany, Sweden.

9 See J Gennard 'Great Britain' in E Yemin (ed) *Workforce Reductions in Undertakings* (1982) p 136. Levie, Gregory and Lorentzen (eds) *Fighting Closures* (1984) pp 202-203; Daniel, W W *The United Kingdom in Managing Workforce Reduction: An International Survey* (1985) p 79.

in respect of the *effects* of investment decisions taken at higher levels of management. It is significant, for example, that even in Germany, which has a system of co-determination in this field, the works council participates in the creation of a 'social plan' to provide benefits for employees who are affected by the redundancy decisions.[10]

## INFORMATION AND COLLECTIVE CONSULTATION OVER TRANSFERS OF AN UNDERTAKING

### Information and consultation over transfers of undertakings

Accompanying the rights of information and consultation over redundancies are the rights to information and consultation over transfers of undertakings, contained in the Transfer of Undertaking Regulations[11] which implement the Acquired Rights Directive (77/187).

In any case of a transfer of an undertaking, employers have an obligation to inform and consult appropriate representatives of the employees affected.[12] The employer must give the representatives the following information long enough in advance to enable proper consultation to take place:

(a) that the relevant transfer is to take place, the time and the reasons for it;
(b) the legal, economic and social implications for the affected employees;
(c) the measures envisaged to be taken in relation to those employees in connection with the transfer; and
(d) if the employer is the transferor, the measures which the transferee envisages he will be taking.[13]

As with the collective redundancy provisions, the 1995 amendments widen the category of appropriate representatives to include employee representatives directly elected, either solely for this purpose or, if elected for another purpose, appropriate for this purpose, such as a works council. They also give the employer the choice to consult either employee representatives or trade union representatives.[14]

10 See Weiss 'Germany' in Blanpain *International Encyclopaedia for Labour Law and Industrial Relations*.

11 See Ch 11.

12 'Affected employees' are any employees of either employer who may be affected by the transfer or measures taken in connection with it: Reg 10(1).

13 Regulation 10(2)

14 This choice is to be curbed if the Labour governments proposed amendments in 'Fairness at Work' are enacted.

In the case of consultations prior to transfers, however, there is a more explicit difference in consultation rights over the management investment decision to transfer the undertaking and the consequences for employees of that decision. Thus, the employer has a duty only to *inform* authorised representatives sufficiently long enough before the decision to transfer to enable consultations to take place in respect of 'the fact,' the time of the transfer, and not 'proposals' for a transfer.[15] In contrast, in the case of measures which either the transferor or the transferee employer envisages will be taken which may affect the employees of either employer, the relevant employer has a duty to *consult with a view to reaching agreement* over the measures to be taken with the affected employees, and in the process of consultation must consider any representations and reply to them giving any reasons for rejection.[16]

This formal difference in the duties of employers has to be seen in context. Employers can always insist upon a strict division between information rights and consultation rights during consultations over the consequences of the transfer. Yet, if the social power of employees is sufficient, consultations convened to discuss the consequences of a transfer decision can on occasion be widened to include issues relating to the decision itself.

At the same time, the penalties for non-observance of the legal obligations are not very great. Where an employer fails to comply with any of its information or consultation obligations, a complaint may be made by the recognised trade unions, employee representatives or any affected employees but the maximum compensation is four weeks' pay for each employee.[17]

## Information and collective consultation and European Works Councils

The characteristic feature of the rights of employee representatives in relation to redundancies and transfers is that even when they amount to influence over the employer's decision, their focus is upon the effects of specific investment decisions by employers. They offer little guarantee that such consultations can take place in the context of the ongoing investment decisions taken at higher levels of management. It is with this

15 See eg Hepple (1982) ILJ at 38.

16 Regulation 10 (5) and (6). Under Reg 10(7) if there are special circumstances which make it not reasonably practicable for an employer to perform a duty imposed upon him by the information and consultation rights, he must take all such steps as are reasonably practicable.

17 Regulaiton 11. As with the redundancy consultation provisions, there are protections against victimisation of employee representatives and time of rights to consult with affected employees.

in mind that EU social policy has long included efforts to combine the Labour Law Directives with other directives designed to provide employee representatives with information and consultation rights in respect of the wider strategic investment decisions of management. In the European Commission's 'Communication on Worker Information and Consultation,'[18] and in the Davignon Report,[19] the creation of works councils at the national level have been proposed. These proposals are meant to fill a vacuum in EU social policy created by the prior enactment of the European Works Council Directive.[20]

An important feature of a policy of providing information and consultation rights over strategic corporate decisions is the need to create a legal structure that deals effectively with the transnationalisation of corporate structures. Attempts have been made to provide information and consultation rights in groups of companies with establishments in two or more states since the 1970s. The European Company Statute provides for a number of models of company-wide consultation at EC level, but this statute has still not obtained unanimous support within the Council of Ministers.[1] The second effort consisted of proposals for wider information and consultation rights in the Vredling Directive, which would have given consultative or collective bargaining organisations at national level a bridge to the headquarters of transnational firms. Again this was unable to command unanimous support at the highest level. However, in 1994, the EC finally enacted a right of employee representatives to be informed and consulted in the form of a European Works Council Directive.

The Directive is designed not so much to harmonise national legislation as to create certain European-wide structures of information and consultation with employees at the Community-wide level where there was a noticeable gap to fill due to the increasing transnationalisation of corporate structures. Thus, the Directive creates a requirement for either a European works council or a Community-wide structure of information and consultation in all 'Community-scale enterprises,'[2] leaving to member states the responsibility to determine the method of employee representation to the European Works Council. This was perhaps inevitable given the division between works councils and collective bargaining models of worker representation at plant and company level in the different member states.

18 COM (95) 547 Final 14 November 1995.

19 Published May 1997, DGV.

20 See eg *Wedderburn* supra.

1 A working party set up in 1998 has produced a new amended proposal for a Regulation on the Statute for a European Company (SE) 6633/88 DG C II.

2 The directive defines this as an enterprise which includes within its control firms with a thousand employees within the 15 member states and at least 150 employees in two EC countries.

While clearly concerned with the social issues of ensuring greater democracy at work, and the need to contribute to social cohesion in the face of the inevitable economic restructuring entailed in the creation of a single market, the Directive was also based on the view that it would contribute to the improved productivity and competitiveness of European industry. Many of the most successful companies in Europe in a wide number of industrial sectors had already put in place voluntary information and consultation schemes at the group level offering a prototype for a European Works Council. In France, Thomson Electronics, BSN, Bull, Pechiney, Elf Aquitane, St Gobain and Rhone Poulenc, in Switzerland, Nestle and in Germany, Allianz, Volkswagen and Mercedes Benz, all provided models for legislation.

While the European Works Council Directive promotes legally based information and consultation at the Community wide level it gives little direct support for collective bargaining at that level. It remains agnostic about the issue whether the worker representatives at national level are trade union representatives or works councillors[3]

## Elements of the Directive

The Directive provides that there shall be a European Works Council, or information and consultation procedure in every 'community scale enterprise,' paid for by the employer and held at the EC headquarters.[4] The Directive adopts the unusual method of stipulating a default legislative procedure and then allows two options for the parties to negotiate their

3 In the group level works councils which existed before the Directive was enacted, the favoured institution was a joint management-employee representative committee, meeting annually shortly after the annual shareholders meeting, to receive and discuss information about corporate strategy, finance and employment. Provision was made for further ad hoc meetings in a number of companies. At least five group councils provided that unions could either participate directly on such councils or could designate particular employee representatives.

4 The Directive requires such enterprises, wherever their actual headquarters may be, to have a headquarters in the EC, at least for the purpose of meeting their obligations under the Directive. This means that companies with headquarters outside the relevant countries in the EC will have to nominate a representative company as its EC headquarters or, failing that, the headquarters of that enterprise will be deemed to be subsidiary in the member state with the largest number of employees in the EC. Moreover, to resolve any issues of conflicts of law, the law of the member state where the EC headquarters of the enterprise is located will be the law generally applicable to all subsidiaries and employees in all member states. Only in the case of the rules for protection of worker representatives, secrecy and confidentiality, and the rules for choosing worker representatives will the relevant law be that of the member state in which the subsidiary is located.

own procedure in the shadow of the requirements of the fall back statutory provisions.

One option, available only until the Directive is actually implemented in national legislation, is for employers to negotiate renewable agreements creating their own form of information and consultation arrangement. The second option, available once the Directive has been enacted into national law, consists of management negotiations with employee representatives to set up a transnational information and consultation procedure. Management may choose to take the initiative themselves or they may wait until they receive a request in writing from their employees or their representatives ( at least 100 employees in at least two states) in which case they must respond by establishing a Special Negotiating Body, consisting of three to seventeen employee representatives, covering each of the member states in which the company has operations. The representatives can have the support of experts, including economists or accountants and must reach agreement within three years either to establish a European Works Council or a procedure for informing and consulting employees.

If an enterprise fails to conclude an agreement with its worker representatives in any of the forms above, then the third option, the 'default procedure' provided in the Annex, must come into effect. This stipulates that there should be 3-30 employee representatives from all member states selected to form a Select Committee. This Committee will meet yearly with central management, starting with a written report by management on the progress of the business, including developments in the structure of the business, its economic and financial situation, the probable development of the business in terms of its production and sales, the situation and probable development of employment and investment and any substantial changes concerning organisation, introduction of new working methods or production processes, transfers of production, mergers, cutbacks or closures of firms, plants or departments and collective redundancies. Moreover, where exceptional circumstances affect employees to a considerable extent, such as in relocations, closures, large-scale layoffs, there is a right to be informed and consulted.

## The EWC and information and consultation

The net effect of all three options therefore is to require at least annual information and consultation with employee representatives and the managers at the European level over matters of corporate strategy as well as matters which more immediately affect the workforce. While the French company councils established before the Directive emphasised the information aspect of the process, in their meetings to discuss information about corporate strategy, finance and employment, the Directive lays greater stress upon the consultation aspect . In its default provisions, the Directive requires formal consultation on any exceptional circumstance affecting the employees' interests to a considerable extent , such as relocations, closures and layoffs. It requires that the employee representatives shall have the right to meet, at its request, the central management or any other decision-making body of management at the Community-wide level, at which any representatives from the affected establishments or companies on the EWC will be entitled to participate. This will thus create possibilities for European-wide consultations to feed into national consultations over collective redundancies and transfers of undertakings. In addition, the Directive requires worker representatives to be informed and consulted on the basis of an annual report by central management on the progress of the business at the Community-wide level whether it is one company or a group of companies. The required items on the agenda are as follows:

- the structure, economic and financial situation
- the probable direction of the business and of production and sales
- the situation and probable trend of employment, investments
- substantial changes concerning organisation
- introduction of new working methods or production processes
- transfers of production, mergers, cutbacks or closures whether full or partial and collective redundancies

This array of information is protected by obligations of confidentiality outside the Council but will, among employee councillors, allow a steady build-up of information about the strategic development of the firm over a period of years. Moreover, the works councillors will have access to experts of their choice to help them in consultations.

At this stage it is difficult to evaluate precisely what effect the legislative change will have. It could lead to an infusion of ideas from worker representatives into strategic company management at the European level and this could be viewed as improving the management of transnational companies in the EC as well as partially meeting employee desires for consultation prior to management decisions.

The effect of the legislation on the process of collective bargaining is even more difficult to predict. Although the statute does not go beyond requiring consultation and stops well short of promoting bargaining, it does create the conditions for greater co-operation between worker representatives from the different member states who work for the same multinational. At least 30 employees of each of the estimated 1300 MNCs operating in the EC will have an opportunity to meet regularly, confer over issues of common policy and perhaps create a fertile basis from which transnational bargaining can evolve. On the other hand, differences of language, culture and national economic and industrial relations conditions could conspire to maintain rivalries and resistance to such co-operation. It may be that the appropriate conditions for transnational co-operation in collective bargaining will not be established until the single market begins to produce more obvious cases of companies making active use of differences in pay rates and labour costs in different member states.

CHAPTER 17

# Management decisions and industrial action

## INTRODUCTION

One of the main social constraints upon managerial decisions is the capacity of employees collectively to withdraw their labour and thereby cause economic loss to a firm. Industrial action, whether in the form of an all out strike or a go slow, work to rule or overtime ban, can have sufficient adverse economic effects upon a firm to convince management to modify their original position on an issue.

For employees, industrial action, or the credible threat of industrial action, is a factual power which is, in a sense, the counterpart of managerial prerogative, the factual power of management to put into effect unilaterally changes in working arrangements. In the UK it is used not only to underpin set piece negotiations over wages and hours - the 'conflicts of interest' mentioned in the European Community Social Charter. It is also used as a sanction which is 'a kind of self help for employees which the law, and often an agreed grievance procedure, is too slow to supplant'.[1]

Thus, whilst much industrial action is directed towards support for pay claims and other 'economic' issues in formal collective bargaining, a not inconsiderable amount arises from workplace relationships and is addressed to reversing or modifying unpopular managerial decisions,[2] including disciplinary and dismissal decisions, alleged breaking of agreements or procedural arrangements, custom and practice imposing changes in working arrangements without consultation, etc.

As a social process, industrial action has both a collective and an individual dimension. It is a collective activity in the sense that it almost

1 Hepple and Kahn Freund *Laws Against Strikes* p 8.

2 See Edwards 'The Pattern of Collective Action' in Bain *The System of Industrial Relations* p 233.

always requires a group of employees acting in concert to achieve the desired impact. While there are occasional examples of spontaneous industrial action, most forms of industrial action, whether 'unofficial' or 'official', require organisation and leadership.[3]

At the same time, industrial action requires individuals, as individuals, to implement a collective decision to withdraw labour. If employees strike they lose their pay, and the amount of strike pay they receive, if any, can be quite small in comparison to their regular pay. A strike, moreover, can require participation in picketing as well as a loss of pay. Industrial action short of a strike, can involve direct confrontation with supervisors as well as a loss of pay.

Legislation provides the ground rules for the exercise of the power to take industrial action by a technique similar to its approach to the factual power of management. It first confers legitimacy upon the pre-existing factual power and then sets limits to its exercise.

In the case of industrial action, the legitimacy consists of a mix of legal 'freedoms' and 'rights'. The freedom to strike, in the case of individual workers, consists of the freedom to withdraw labour without committing a crime. In the case of trade union organisations, and leaders and organisers of industrial action, it consists of the ability to organise industrial action without incurring criminal liability. Both the 'freedom' to organise and to take part in industrial action were established in 1875.[4]

A 'right' to strike in contrast consists of a limit placed upon the powers of the employer to act in response to industrial action, either to bring an action for damages or an injunction, or to take self-help measures such as stopping pay or dismissals.

By establishing a 'right' to strike, legislators have accepted the principle that to a certain extent industrial action can be justified, despite its costs in terms of loss of production to the striking firm, its employees, customers and suppliers and possibly the public.[5] This is so partly because to some extent the right to strike is understood as a safeguard against the imbalance of power between individual employee and employer, and that it provides a necessary underpinning to collective bargaining. It has long been

3 Batstone, Ferner and Terry *The Social Organisation of Strikes,* Basil Blackwell. 'Official action', before it received a formal legal definition in the 1982 and 1990 Employment Acts, meant industrial action approved by the trade union executive committee. 'Unofficial action' meant any action not so approved, led by the officials of the union - shop stewards - or workplace leaders who had no official position in the trade union.

4 Conspiracy and Protection of Property Act 1875.

5 A right to strike is accepted as an essential and legitimate means for workers to use to promote their economic interests by ILO Committee of Exports and in the European Community Social Charter of 1989. See discussion in Deakin and Morris *Labour Law* (2nd ed) Ch 11; See Ben Israel *International Labour Standards*: *The Case of Freedom to Strike* (1994), Kluwer.

recognised that without a credible threat of damaging industrial action there is little assurance that management will be willing to engage in meaningful negotiation with trade union representatives over disputed issues of management decision-making. And meaningful collective bargaining has been accepted albeit, grudgingly at times, as a necessary method of determining wage levels in a decentralised way as well as the basis of a measure of industrial democracy in working life.

The right to strike and, in certain cases, the freedom[6] have long been qualified by the requirement that the industrial action must be taken 'in contemplation of furtherance of a legitimate trade dispute', that is to say a dispute about matters which broadly relate to the collective bargaining process. This qualification has had the effect of placing industrial action taken in protest against government action, or otherwise for 'political' motives, outside the range of lawful industrial action in the UK.[7] It also confines lawful industrial action to a range of collective bargaining issues which do not directly question business investment decisions.

Even if the collective bargaining justification has been widely accepted as the basis of the right to strike, quite fundamentally different views have been held about where the line should be drawn between lawful and unlawful industrial action to pursue collective bargaining objectives.

Labour legislation in the UK has historically veered between two rather different views of the legitimacy of industrial action. On the one hand, a 'wide' view, most recently expressed in the Trade Union Labour Relations Act 1974,[8] allowed secondary action, sympathetic action and action taken for a wide variety of motives. A 'narrow' view contained in the Industrial Relations Act 1971 and developed in the Employment Acts 1980, 1982, 1988 and 1990 as well as the Trade Union Act 1984 and TURER 1993 prohibits almost all forms of secondary and sympathetic industrial action, hoping to confine it to disputes arising from particular employment units and limits the scope of legitimate motives for industrial action.[9]

While legislation has veered periodically between these two views of the scope for legitimate industrial action, it has fairly consistently[10] defined the scope of the 'right to strike' in the form of a set of statutory immunities

6 Conspiracy and Protection of Property Act 1875.

7 See eg *National Sailors' and Firemen's Union of Great Britain and Ireland v Reed* [1926] Ch 536 (General Strike); *Sherard v AUEW* [1973] IRLR 188, CA (dispute between TUC and Government); *Express Newspapers v Keys* [1980] IRLR 247 (day of action).

8 As amended in 1976. This view arguably resurrected the view of the Trade Disputes Act 1906.

9 See eg Averbach *Legislating for Conflict* (Clarendon Press, Oxford, 1990); Davies and Freedland *Labour Legislation and Public Policy* (Clarendon Press, Oxford, 1993); Ewing *The Right to Strike* (Clarendon Press, Oxford, 1991).

10 Apart from the Industrial Relations Act 1971.

or 'protections'[11] from tort liabilities. Instead of providing that 'all employees have the right to strike in defence of their interests, subject to the following limitations', legislation offers an 'immunity' or 'protection' to individual organisers and leaders and trade unions against specific economic torts such as inducement of breach of contract, interference with commercial relations and conspiracy to injure. Though these are 'immunities' in form, they are 'rights' in substance because they preclude the employer from taking legal action for damages or an injunction against those individuals or trade unions who commit the tort. However, one consequence of this form is that the immunities apply only to the liability of the leaders and organisers of industrial action and, historically, to the trade union organisation itself. They do not protect individual workers from any illegality attaching to participation in industrial action, since the basic illegality committed by employees taking part in industrial action is not a tort,[12] but a breach of their employment contracts.[13]

In the event, employees taking part in industrial action remain vulnerable to the employer's self-help disciplinary measures such as withholding pay and dismissals, even if the organisation of industrial action is otherwise lawful by virtue of the statutory immunity.[14] Moreover, the breach of contract can be a potential 'unlawful means' in the economic torts which make the organisation of industrial action unlawful, such as for example, inducement of breach of contract.

## A PARTICIPATION IN INDUSTRIAL ACTION BY EMPLOYEES

Given that they have no right to participate in industrial action, employees are left only with a basic freedom to strike recognised since 1875 when the repeal of the Employers and Workmen Act removed the statutory basis for criminal penalties for individuals participating in most strikes.[15]

Prior to 1867, 'desertion of one's master', or withdrawing one's labour in breach of contract, was a crime punishable by imprisonment. Even after 1867, with the repeal of the Master and Servant Act, employees could be imprisoned for 'aggravated misconduct' and employees could be ordered to specifically perform their contract, ie to go back to work. An average

11 See eg TULR(C)A, s 219. Since 1992 the vocabulary has changed. The statutory immunities are now called 'protections' and qualified by 'exclusions from protection'.
12 See *National Coal Board v Galley* [1958] 1 All ER 91, [1958] 1 WLR 16, CA.
13 See eg *Simmons v Hoover Ltd* [1977] QB 284, [1977] ICR 61, EAT
14 See discussion, Part B.
15 Some criminal liabilities were retained in the Conspiracy and Protection of Property Act 1875 and potential criminal liabilities remained for certain types of picketing. But after 1895 for most workers to strike was no longer a crime, apart from the two wartime periods.

of 10,000 prosecutions of workmen took place each year[16] in England and Wales during the 1850s and 1860s and early 1870s. Criminal legal proceedings in the 19th century were used tactically by employers as a response to industrial action. After causing striking employees to be arrested, employers would offer a return to work as an alternative to imprisonment.

After 1875, with participation in industrial action no longer a crime in most cases, employers were forced to rely on civil measures. It soon became clear that there were certain defined limits to the capacity of the civil courts to provide help in dealing directly with employees who withdrew their labour. Employers retained the capacity to use self-help measures such as dismissing striking employees and bringing in replacements. They could also bring civil actions against the leaders and organisers of industrial action if not after 1906. However, they could not ask the civil courts for an injunction directed against employees en masse to return to work or to stay at work.

In the late 19th century the equity courts had begun to develop the doctrine that in the case of a contract for personal services there could be no remedy of specific performance . Initially, the judiciary were reluctant to make such orders because they required constant supervision. By 1890, however, the courts were prepared to recognise explicitly that to compel persons to work against their will was a form of involuntary servitude. As Fry LJ put it in *De Francesco v Barnum*,[17] contracts of service should not be turned into 'contracts of slavery'.

This rule of equity jurisdiction is now codified in TULR(C)A 1992, s 236 which states that:

> 'No court shall whether by way of -
> (a) an order for specific performance or specific implement of a contract of employment, or
> (b) an injunction or interdict restraining a breach or threatened breach of such a contract,
> compel an employee to do any work or attend at any place for the doing of any work.'

This inhibition upon the judicial enforcement process vis-à-vis the individual is the legal foundation of employees' factual power to take industrial action: ie an inhibition upon the capacity of the legal process directly to secure a collective return to work. Courts may have the power to order the leaders of a strike or a trade union organisation to end their authorisation of industrial action but they cannot actually order employees en masse to return to work.

16 D Simon 'Master and Servant' in J Saville *Democracy and the Labour Movement* London 1954, p 160.

17 (1890) 45 Ch D 430 at 438.

In many cases, as Hepple and Kahn Freund have argued,[18] it is possible to achieve an end to a strike indirectly by sanctions against the leaders and organisers of strikes or by denying tax refunds, unemployment benefit, or social security payments to families. Nevertheless it is equally important to recognise that these measures are indirect. In the last resort, if employees have the will and the resources, and the circumstances are right they have the power to remain out of work and affect the employer's profit position even if their leaders and trade union organisations are subject to a court order. A good example of this was offered by the case of *Ford Motor Co Ltd v AEF*[19] when on the day the union was ordered to call off the strike the numbers of striking employees increased from about 3,000 to almost 4,500. Similarly, in the seamen's strike of 1988, even though the NUS called off the action at Dover on 4th February, 1988, in the face of proceedings for contempt and was on the 11th February fined £7,500 for contempt, 2,300 P & O seafarers remained on strike for six weeks until they were dismissed.[20]

That experience also dramatically illustrates the limits of the freedom to take part in strikes. For although the scope of the freedom is unqualified, applying whatever the employees' reasons for leaving work or taking industrial action, it is secured only against the Court's exercise of its powers of specific performance. It does not preclude employers from responding to industrial action by dismissing employees, and finding replacements[1] (or stopping pay when employees take industrial action short of a strike).[2]

Nevertheless, this limitation of the legal process is a factor that employers must take into account in their calculations. If the numbers participating in industrial action are sufficiently large, and employers intend, as most do, to retain their existing workforces , then they must find a means of convincing employees to return to work as opposed to expecting that a particular legal sanction will inevitably coerce them to return to work. In fact, in many, if not most, cases of industrial action or threatened industrial action, managers tend to take an industrial relations approach and negotiate over the issues which prompted the industrial action in the first place. Moreover, in the current conditions on the labour market, management may choose to view employee dissatisfaction as a symptom of a problem to be solved. With the product market viewed as requiring a high quality of work performance, employer attitudes towards the workforce have been tempered by the realisation that loyalty and commitment are economically important.

18 Laws against strikes, Fabian Pamphlet, 1972, p 8.
19 [1969] 2 QB 303, [1969] 2 All ER 481.
20 Auerbach 'Injunction Procedure in the Seafarers Dispute' [1988] 17 ILJ 227.
1 See the *News International* case discussed on p 367.
2 See eg *Wiluszynski v London Borough of Tower Hamlets* [1988] IRLR 154 (discussed next section).

On the other hand, there are cases where managers may decide that negotiation or responsiveness are not likely to produce the desired results, either because they wish to derecognise the union or because they disagree in principle with the trade union position and have no wish to compromise or because they think that resort to legal action may have a particular effect on the trade union's negotiating position. In such cases, employers may resort to two possible courses of legal action. They may decide to bring an action for damages in order to obtain an injunction against the leaders and organisers of industrial action, and the trade union organisation itself, if they can make a case that the industrial action falls outside the scope of the statutory protections. Alternatively, employers may decide to deal directly with employees participating in industrial action - using self-help measures such as stopping pay or dismissals.

Let us look at the relevant law affecting each of these courses of action.

## EMPLOYER SELF-HELP MEASURES, THE EMPLOYMENT CONTRACT AND INDUSTRIAL ACTION

At common law, virtually all forms of industrial action are treated alike, as a breach of employment contracts by employees. A strike is regarded as a serious breach, or repudiation, of the contract because the employee has disregarded an essential condition of the contract of service - the performance of work.[3] Industrial action short of a strike is also a breach[4] though its seriousness will vary with the tactic used. In the case of strikes, pay is almost always not paid and employees may be dismissed or replaced. In the cases of industrial action short of a strike a stoppage of pay is a commonly used sanction by employers, even in sectors of established collective bargaining.

### Industrial action short of a strike

Industrial action short of a strike can consist of a go slow, a work to rule, a ban on overtime or even 'working without enthusiasm'. These actions are in breach of the contract of employment whenever they result in a failure to discharge a material part of the employees' contractual duties.[5] Yet, as we have seen, the contractual duties of employees are not always clearly defined. They are sometimes expanded by the addition of implied terms. For example, a refusal to work 'voluntary' overtime is generally

3 *Simmons v Hoover Ltd* [1977] QB 284, [1977] ICR 61, EAT.
4 See eg *Wiluszynski v London Borough of Tower Hamlets* [1988] IRLR 154.
5 Ibid.

not a breach of contract because it does not consist of a refusal to perform a contractual task.[6]

In *ASLEF (No 2)*,[7] however, a 'work to rule', although consisting of a strict observance of the employer's own rules, was held to be a breach of an implied term that 'within the terms of the contract the employee must serve the employer faithfully with a view to promoting those commercial interests for which he is employed'. Lord Denning considered it to be a breach because of the wilful disruption and obstruction of 'the employer as he goes about his business' hinting at motive as well as effect.[8] The duty of faithful service was expanded in *British Telecom plc v Ticehurst*[9] to include a case where a manager refused to sign an undertaking that she would no longer participate in industrial action in the form of a withdrawal of good will. Lord Justice Ralph Gibson indicated that there is a breach of the implied term of faithful service when the employee does an act or omits to do an act which is within her contractual discretion but she exercises that discretion in order to disrupt the employer's business.

Further, in *Cresswell v Board of Inland Revenue*,[10] a group of tax officers of the Inland Revenue who refused to cooperate with the introduction of a new computerised system of administering PAYE were told that they were to be in a breach of an implied obligation to adapt themselves to new methods and techniques in the course of their employment.

Once an industrial action has been established as a breach of contract, employers have considerable disciplinary powers. Even if the employment contract does not expressly provide that the employer may suspend his obligation to pay wages, employers can stop pay until the industrial action short of a strike has ended.[11]

In *Sim v Rotherham Metropolitan Borough Council*,[12] Scott J had suggested certain limits to the employer's right to deduct pay in response to 'partial' industrial action. He held that the employer's entitlement in the case of such partial performance was to set off against the claim for wages any claim for damages consisting of the loss incurred by him as a result of the employee's failure to work fully in accordance with his

6 *Power Packing Casemakers v Faust* [1983] QB 471, [1983] ICR 292, CA, but see *Camden Exhibition and Display Ltd v Lynott* [1966] 1 QB 555, [1965] 3 All ER 28, CA.

7 *Secretary of State for Employment v ASLEF (No 2)* [1972] 2 QB 455, [1972] ICR 19, CA.

8 Ibid; see too *Solihull Metropolitan Borough v NUT* [1985] IRLR 211.

9 [1992] ICR 383, [1992] IRLR 219, CA.

10 [1984] 2 All ER 713, [1984] ICR 508.

11 See eg *British Telecom plc v Ticehurst* [1992] ICR 383, [1992] IRLR 219, CA. In principle, the employer can also sue the employee for breach of contract but the scope for damage is limited: see eg *NCB v Galley* [1958] 1 All ER 91.

12 [1987] Ch 216, [1986] ICR 897.

contract. This view, which was consistent with general contract law,[13] would have meant that an employer would have had to present proof of loss incurred as a result of the industrial action as a precondition to an entitlement to set-off.[14]

However, in *Miles v Wakefield Metropolitan District Council*[15] the House of Lords held that an employer is entitled to make deductions from an employee's wages for that part of the work not done even while retaining him in employment. *Miles* was a case where a superintendent registrar of births, marriages and deaths took industrial action by refusing to conduct weddings on Saturdays, though he was willing to perform all his other duties on that day. The employer insisted on performance of his full range of duties and instructed him not to attend for work at all on Saturday unless he was prepared to work normally. When Miles refused to comply, the employer deducted a day's pay.

The Law Lords' decision firmly in favour of the employer was partly a procedural decision that in an employee's action for breach of contract, the employee has the initial burden of proving that he worked or was ready and willing to render the services required by the contract. Underlying this procedural point was the substantive point that in a contract of employment, wages and work go together and wages are remuneration which must be earned. If a worker declines to work, then an employer need not pay. As the Law Lords put it, 'where an employee absents himself from work voluntarily, the question was not whether the employer had a right to withhold wages for the period but rather is the employee entitled to sue for and recover from his employer in respect of a period during which he has made it perfectly clear that he is not ready and willing to perform his own contractual obligations'.[16] This decision marked the end of the line of the argument in *Sim* that the employer's only entitlement to withhold pay while the contract was in existence was limited to an action for damages for breach of contract.

In *Miles*, the Law Lords had appeared to give some encouragement to the principle of partial payment in cases of go slows or incomplete performance of work. Lords Brightman and Templeman thought that the employee would be entitled to recover on a quantum meruit basis and Lord Oliver said only that an employer had no right to deduct 'self assessed damages'. Lord Bridge expressed doubts about the principle of quantum meruit and Lord Brandon reserved his opinion.[17]

13 See discussion in *Shrubsall* [1989] ILJ 241.
14 See eg *Jakeman v South West Thames Regional Health Authority* [1990] IRLR 62.
15 [1987] AC 539, [1987] IRLR 193, HL.
16 Ibid.
17 Ibid.

Moreover, in *Bond v CAV Ltd*,[18] there was a suggestion that where an employer accepted work done, to some extent, he may be viewed as 'waiving' his entitlement to deduct. Thus in *Bond*, workers who refused to work on special machines but were otherwise allowed to work normally, were successful in obtaining full contractual remuneration from employers because the employees were ready and willing to work the normal contract and this work was accepted by the employer.

In *Wiluszynski v London Borough of Tower Hamlets*,[19] however, the Court of Appeal carefully limited the type of case where there could be partial payment based on quantum meruit or waiver. Wiluszynski was an estates officer who, following union instructions, took 'limited industrial action' in the form of a 'boycott' of enquiries from council members, a small part of his contractual duties. The Council responded by warning him that unless he performed his full range of duties, he would not be paid. A later letter sent to him stated that any limited work done would be regarded as unauthorised and voluntary, not undertaken for remuneration. During the five weeks of the action, Wiluszysnki attended work and when the action ended he cleared up the backlog of member enquiries in 2-3 hours. During these weeks no salary was paid by the employer and Wiluszynski brought an action to recover full salary, claiming substantial performance and waiver by the employer of the right not to pay.

The Court of Appeal, reversing Davies J in the High Court, held, following *Miles*, that where an employee indicates that for an indefinite period he will not be performing a material part of his contractual service, the employer is entitled in response to decline in advance to accept the preferred partial performance. There was no waiver in allowing the employee to continue to work; the employer in such a case had no duty of physical ejection. As long as no other positive act was done by the employer which was inconsistent with the position of refusing to accept incomplete performance; such as active supervision of the limited performance, the mere fact of benefit received from the work which the employee insisted on doing, would not be sufficient to amount to a waiver or estoppel.

If *Wiluszynski* may have limited the scope for partial payment based on quantum meruit, it did not extinguish it altogether. Where an employer 'accepts' incomplete performance there will be liability for a reasonable proportion of the remuneration either on quantum meruit grounds[20] or on the grounds of a substituted contract.[1]

18 [1983] IRLR 360.

19 [1988] IRLR 154, CA.

20 *Miles v Wakefield Metropolitan District Council* [1987] ICR 368, [1987] IRLR 193, HL.

1 See eg *Bond v CAV Ltd* [1983] IRLR 360; see Shrubsall [1989] ILJ 241.

For example, in *Royle v Trafford Borough Council*,[2] a case where a teacher acting under union instructions refused to accept five extra pupils in addition to his normal quota of thirty one, the employer's deduction of full pay for the six months was held to be not justified since he had in effect waived the 'imperfect performance'. Given the employer's own account of the imperfect performance, the court itself proposed a 'just' deduction of 5/36th of the employee's salary during the period.

Nevertheless, the case law provides the employer with considerable discretion to respond to industrial action by a refusal to pay contractual remuneration. If employees engage in industrial action short of a strike consisting of partial performance of the contract, ie refusing to discharge a material part of their contractual duties, and employers make it unequivocally clear that this is unacceptable, they can withhold all payment while such industrial action continues,[3] in effect 'locking out' employees defensively. The one exception to this is where the industrial action consists of refusing to carry out duties in circumstances of danger which was serious and imminent and which they could not reasonably have been expected to avert.[4]

Employers have been able to take the concept of 'defensive lockout' a step further than merely withholding payment for work not being done fully and refusing to employ workers unless they agree not to join in industrial action in progress. In *Chappell v Times Newspapers Ltd*[5] employers were held entitled to withhold pay from employers who refused to give an undertaking that they would not, if called upon, join in a rotating selectional form of industrial action. However, where an employer without contractual justification - say because employees refuse to accept a contractual variation - suspends payment to employees who are otherwise ready and willing to perform their full range of contractual duties, in effect an *offensive* lockout, employees could bring an action for damages for breach of contract either for the failure to pay wages during the relevant period or for the pay owed during the period of notice of termination.[6]

2 [1984] IRLR 184.

3 *Wiluszynski v Tower Hamlets London Borough Council* [1989] ICR 493, [1989] IRLR 259, CA. Moreover, such a deduction is an exception to the protections of the Wages Act. See *Sunderland Polytechnic v Evans* [1993] ICR 392, [1993] IRLR 196 discussed in Chapter 4.

4 ERA 1996, s 100(1)(d) and (e).

5 *Chappell v Times Newspapers Ltd* [1975] 2 All ER 233, [1975] ICR 145, CA. See too *British Telecommunications plc* v *Ticehurst* [1992] ICR 383, [1992] IRLR 219, CA.

6 Moreover, this action might also be a 'lockout' for the purposes of s 238 of the TULR(C)A, and be subject to the law of unfair dismissals.

### Strikes and the contract of employment

In the case of strikes, the breach of contract is regarded as repudiatory because it is a breach of an essential condition of the contract. This legal view of strikes is at odds with the reality that in most cases both parties fully accept that employment will continue once the industrial action is ended, but a doctrine of the strike as a suspension of the employment contract has not evolved at common law. In *Morgan v Fry*[7] Lord Denning was prepared to recognise that in the modern law of trade disputes a right could be implied into contracts that 'upon due strike notice, the contract is suspended during the strike and revives again when the strike is over'. In *Simmons v Hoover Ltd*,[8] however, Phillips J rejected this reason, stating that it would require legislation to establish a principle of suspension in English law. In *Boxfoldia Ltd v NGA*,[9] moreover, it was made clear that a notice of industrial action was not enough to avert a breach. To do that, it was necessary for employees to give notice of termination of contract. Today, s 180 of TULR(C)A places limits upon the incorporation of the peace obligation in the collective agreement into the contract of employment, but this simply removes an alternative basis for repudiation. There has been no legislative provision to the effect that a strike is no more than a suspension of the contract, such as is found in the law of many European countries.[10]

## STATUTORY EMPLOYMENT PROTECTION AND INDUSTRIAL ACTION

In *Simmons v Hoover Ltd*[11] one reason given by Phillips J for rejecting an implied right of suspension was that the statutory employment protections such as unfair dismissal, redundancy payments and continuity of service operate on the assumption that participation in strikes is repudiatory conduct and then graft on special rules to apply.

It is true that statute law has made provision since 1965 to ensure that where an employee is away from work because he or she is taking part in a strike, or has been locked out, the week during which the employee is away from work will not destroy continuity of service even if it does not

7 [1968] 2 QB 710, [1968] 3 All ER 452, CA.
8 [1977] QB 284, [1977] ICR 61, EAT.
9 [1988] ICR 752, [1988] IRLR 383.
10 See Wedderburn 'The Right to Strike' in *Employment Rights in Britain and Europe* (1991) Lawrence and Wishart.
11 [1977] QB 284, [1977] ICR 61, EAT.

count towards total service.[12] However, whilst this may protect continuity for the purposes of notice of termination, redundancy payment or unfair dismissal as well as other employment protections, it offers no assurance that the substance of those statutory protections will apply. As we shall see, employees who participate in industrial action may be dismissed by their employer without statutory notice or pay in lieu, a redundancy payment or the possibility of claiming unfair dismissal.

## Industrial action and redundancy payments

Where employees are dismissed for participating in industrial action in response to an announcement of redundancies but prior to receiving formal statutory notice of termination of contract for the redundancy, they lose their entitlement to a redundancy payment. This is true, even if a redundancy was widely known to be in preparation, because a 'collective' notice of redundancy had been issued to the trade union and the strike was in protest against the redundancy decisions.[13] Only during the employee's obligatory notice of termination under ERA, s 86 does the statute provide some protection. Though the employer may still dismiss the employee for misconduct (engaging in a strike),[14] the employee's redundancy payment can be preserved by the industrial tribunal.[15] Prior to the statutory notice period, the common law view of industrial action as repudiatory has been incorporated into the definition of the scope of the statutory protection.[16]

The omission of a statutory assurance that redundancy payments are preserved when dismissals occur in a strike called over the issue of redundancy can lead to an unscrupulous employer provoking a strike prior to a redundancy to avoid redundancy payments. It also adds to the pressures upon workers not to take industrial action in protest against redundancy. Managers have been known to warn employees of this fact as part of a programme to 'manage' redundancies.

12 See ERA 1996, s 216. Anderman *Law of Unfair Dismissal* (1985, 2nd edn) pp 24-25.

13 See eg *Simmons v Hoover Ltd* [1977] QB 284, [1977] ICR 61, EAT.

14 ERA, s 140.

15 ERA, s 143 (time lost owing to strike can be deducted).

16 Participation in industrial action can also result in the loss of a guarantee payment ERA, s 29(3), protection against deductions from wages under Part II of the ERA (ERA, s 14(5)). Moreover, entitlement to state benefits will be lessened: Jobseekers Act 1995, s 14.

## Industrial action and unfair dismissal protection

One might have thought that the unfair dismissals law would have provided protection for employees claiming that their dismissals for taking part in lawfully organised official industrial action were unfair.[17] Instead, TULR(C)A, s 238 provides only that employees who are *selectively* dismissed for taking part in official industrial action can claim that the dismissal is unfair. As long as an employer dismisses all employees who are participating in official industrial action at the time when any striking employee is dismissed, the statute gives an 'immunity' to the employer from unfair dismissal claims by providing that 'industrial tribunals shall not determine whether a dismissal is fair or unfair' in such cases.

Section 238 requires the employer to establish first of all that at the date of dismissal:

> '(1) the complainant was taking part in a strike or other industrial action.'

At this stage what is examined is what the employee was actually doing and not the employee's motives behind their action.[18] The test is not the subjective test of the employer's reason under s 98(4); it is the objective test of whether in fact the employee was taking part in industrial action.[19]

In its 1974 form, this section required the employer to show as well:

> '(2) That none of the employees who were taking part in the action ('relevant employees') were retained or were offered re-engagement after the strikes.'

This second requirement, which produced much litigation,[20] was considerably eased by the 1982 Employment Act. 'Relevant employees', ie those employees who were grouped with the complaining employee for the purpose of the non-selectivity requirement, were greatly reduced in scope to those who were striking *at the time of the employee's dismissal* and those who were employed *at the employee's own establishment*. Moreover, a significant exception to the non-selectivity principle was introduced by allowing reinstatement of one or more of such employees after three months without jeopardising the employer's immunity from a claim for unfair dismissal.

The purpose of the 1982 Act was to reduce the legal constraints placed upon the power to dismiss in response to industrial action contained in

17 The current Labour Government are proposing to change the law of unfair dismissals to provide such a right: see 'Fairness at Work' para 4.22.

18 *Coates v Modern Methods and Materials Ltd* [1983] QB 192, [1982] ICR 763, EAT.

19 *Manifold Industries Ltd v Sims* [1991] ICR 504, [1991] IRLR 242, EAT; followed in *Jenkins v P&O European Ferries (Dover) Ltd* [1991] ICR 652, EAT; *Bolton Roadways Ltd v Edwards* [1987] IRLR 392, EAT; but see *McKenzie v Crosville Motor Services Ltd* [1990] ICR 172, [1989] IRLR 516, EAT.

20 See Anderman *Law of Unfair Dismissal* (2nd edn) Ch 11.

the 1974 Act. Its premise was that employers should have more than merely a reserve power to dismiss an entire workforce,[1] they should also be able to use the threat of dismissal to prompt a return to work. Hence by providing that 'relevant employees' were only those on strike at the time of dismissal, s 238 created the basis for employers to dismiss all employees who remained out after a number of employees originally on strike had been 'persuaded' to return. Moreover, by providing that 'relevant employees' were only those at the employee's own establishment, it also gave the employer the freedom to deal separately with the workforces in each plant taking part in industrial action. They could dismiss selectively as between establishments but not within establishments. Finally the 1982 Act allowed employers to re-hire selectively among dismissed strikers after a three month period, thus further eroding the principle of non-selectivity contained in the 1974 Act. These changes, criticised as a 'recipe for victimisation', were not the final reform of this section.[2]

## Dismissals and unofficial strikes

In the 1990 Act a new element was added to the employer's 'immunity' against a complaint for unfair dismissal for dismissing employees for taking part in industrial action. Section 237 of TULR(C)A now provides that an employee will have no right to complain of unfair dismissal, 'if at the time of dismissal he was taking part in an unofficial strike or other unofficial industrial action'[3] as long as some or all of the striking employees are union members. This withdrawal of the right to complain of unfair dismissal will clearly help to deter unofficial strikes by allowing employers to respond to such action by dismissing either unofficial leaders or participants selectively, without waiting for three months, though its stated motive was to preclude the possibility that organisers of unofficial action could be successful in an unfair dismissal case.[4] Moreover, if an employer dismisses one or more employees under this section, any industrial action taken in response to such a dismissal or in the belief that such a dismissal has occurred will lose its statutory immunity even if otherwise lawful (TULR(C)A, s 223).

1 The premise of the 1974 Act was that while employers should be able to dismiss all employees in extremis without a tribunal determination of the merits of the dispute, any victimisation or selective dismissals in the context of industrial action should be tested for reasonableness by industrial tribunals.

2 See Wallington 'The Employment Act 1982: section 9 - A Recipe for Victimisation' [1983] MLR 310.

3 The removal of the right to complain is not the same as removal of tribunal jurisdiction. Unofficial strikers may still be relevant employees for the purpose of s 238. See Simpson, B 'The Employment Act 1990 in Context' [1991] MLR 418 at 436.

4 'Unofficial Action and the Law' Cm 821 London HMSO 1989 para 3.7.

Section 237 defines industrial action as 'unofficial' in respect of an employee unless the employee is: (a) a member of a trade union which 'authorised' or 'endorsed' the action in accordance with s 20(2) of TULR(C)A; (b) not a union member but others participating in the action are members of a union which has authorised or endorsed the action; or (c) none of the participants in the industrial action are union members.

The question of when industrial action is unofficial is explicitly made a question of fact for the tribunal to decide by reference to the facts at the time of the dismissal (s 237(4)). However, the issue of whether a trade union has authorised or endorsed the industrial action will be determined by reference to rules of trade union responsibility for industrial action set out in s 20(2) of TULR(C)A. (See part B). If a trade union decides to repudiate industrial action in accordance with that section, the Act provides a breathing space of at least one full working day for unofficial strikers to reconsider their position (s 237(4)) before they will be vulnerable to selective dismissal. In such a situation the trade union also has at least one full working day within which it may decide to make the strike official by holding a ballot and obtaining protection under s 219.

The legislation as it is formulated today has been shaped into a wide discretion to employers to dismiss employees in response to strikes or other forms of industrial action. Moreover, it is legally possible for employers to dismiss an entire workforce for taking part in industrial action which was provoked by the employer in the first instance, and replace them with permanent replacements. This is quite rare in the case of firms with large workforces, although it is not unheard of. Wapping was a notable example.[5] However, where the numbers of employees out on strike are small, such a step is more conceivable for employers, particularly as part of a campaign to resist trade union recognition.

Naturally if employers consider that it is in their interests that they have to impose selective dismissals of strikers in the context of a continuing relationship, s 237 removes the constraint of an unfair dismissal action. However, it is not always realistic for employers involved in ongoing collective bargaining relationships to make use of selective dismissals. Although s 223 of TULR(C)A removes the statutory protection under s 219 from any industrial action if the reason for it is the fact or belief that the employer has selectively dismissed unofficial strikers, employers cannot disregard the potential for such dismissals to damage relationships with the remaining body of employees and undermine a personnel and human resource management policy aimed at building up trust and confidence in its workforce in a highly competitive commercial climate.

5 See Ewing and Napier 'The Wapping Dispute and Labour Law' (1986) Camb LJ 285.

## B THE 'RIGHT TO STRIKE' AND THE TRADE UNION IMMUNITIES

The extensive legislative regulation of industrial action introduced by the Conservative Government in the Employment Acts 1980, 1982, 1988 and 1990, as well as the Trade Union Act 1984 and TURER 1993 has transformed the substance of the trade union immunities.[6] It has sharply restricted the scope of lawful industrial action, introduced the requirement of secret ballots and provided a wide basis for trade union responsibility for industrial action of officials and members. However, it has accomplished all this by drawing upon the pre-existing legal structures of the common law liabilities for industrial action, which have been in place since the late 19th century, and the statutory trade union immunities, which were enacted originally in 1906 and which were an integral part of the Trade Union and Labour Relations Act enacted during the period of the Social Contract.

In a legal action by an employer[7] or other interested individual[8] in response to industrial action the current legal framework requires four basic issues to be decided:

(i) Does the industrial action in question give an employer a cause of action in tort at common law?
(ii) If so, does s 219[9] of TULR(C)A provide protection from that tort liability?
(iii) Has the cause of action been restored because the protection has been removed by anything in ss 222-235?
(iv) What is the extent of the liability of trade union organisation for the acts of officials and members as defined by ss 20 and 21 of TULR(C)A?

Consequently, to understand the law of industrial action today it is necessary to take something of an archaeological approach - taking into account the contribution of each period to the current legal structure.

6 See Auerbach *Legislating for Conflict* (Clarendon, Oxford, 1992).

7 *Merkur Island Shipping Corpn v Laughton* [1983] ICR 490, [1983] IRLR 218, HL, before 1993 other plaintiffs were possible, but not likely. See eg *Falconer v ASLEF and NUR* [1986] IRLR 331.

8 Since 1993 s 22 of TURER has inserted s 235A-C into TULR(C)A which gave individuals a right to bring an action in the High Court for unlawful industrial action against trade union organisations and organisers with assistance from a new Commissioner for Protection Against Unlawful Industrial Action.

9 Or in rare cases s 220.

## THE COMMON LAW RESPONSE TO TRADE UNION ACTIVITY AND THE EARLY STATUTORY IMMUNITIES

In the nineteenth century the immediate and instinctive response of the courts to the use of industrial action by trade unions was to view it as a criminal conspiracy to injure. After the Conspiracy, and Protection of the Property Act 1875 directly removed criminal liability by providing a specific statutory immunity for criminal conspiracy, as long as it was in contemplation and furtherance of a trade dispute,[10] the courts resorted to 'civil conspiracy', 'inducement to breach of employment contracts', and 'interference with trade', all of which outflanked the 1875 Act by making the organisation and leadership of strikes unlawful as torts or civil wrongs.

The judges viewed strikes as 'civil conspiracies' in the first place because of their purpose to inflict economic harm and because there was no justification. In 1892 the House of Lords was prepared to say that a group of businessmen who banded together for the purpose of keeping competing ship owners out of the shipping trade could 'justify' such action because their predominant purpose was to compete, and any injury done to a rival ship owner by excluding him from the field was only incidental to that purpose.[11] At this time, however, the judiciary would not accept that the trade union's main purpose in organising industrial action was that of furthering the interests of their members by, say, improving wage prospects, and that the consequential injury to others was only incidental to that purpose. To the judges, the essence of the tort was the *agreement intentionally* to commit economic harm even if no unlawful means were used. This tort was called *simple conspiracy* or *conspiracy to injure*.[12] The same act if done by an *individual* which caused and was intended to cause economic harm, was not tortious.[13] It was to require another 40 years before the judges could accept unequivocally that industrial action taken for the purpose of promoting trade union interests in collective bargaining, and using no unlawful means, could be justified even if the by-product was economic harm to the employer or third parties.[14]

10 Conspiracy and Protection of Property Act 1875. See also Trade Union Act 1871, s 2 - this Act also gave an immunity against restraint of trade.
11 *Mogul SS Co Ltd v McGregor, Gow & Co* [1892] AC 25, HL.
12 *Quinn v Leathem* [1901] AC 495, HL. See too *Lonrho v Shell Petroleum Co Ltd (No 2)* [1982] AC 173, HL.
13 *Allen v Flood* [1898] AC 1, HL.
14 *Crofter Hand Woven Harris Tweed Co Ltd v Veitch* [1942] AC 435, [1942] 1 All ER 142, HL; see also *Reynolds v Shipping Federation Ltd* [1924] 1 Ch 28.

## Interfering with employer's business and inducement to breach of employment contracts

Moreover, in addition to viewing industrial action as taken for an unlawful purpose, the judiciary also found that it involved the use of unlawful means. Industrial action was a tortious *interference* with the employer's business.[15] Furthermore, the act of calling or organising a strike itself amounted to an *unlawful inducement to employees to break their contracts of employment.* The employees' participation in the strike was a breach of their employment contracts and the organisers approach to the employees to take industrial action 'induced', ie caused this breach.[16]

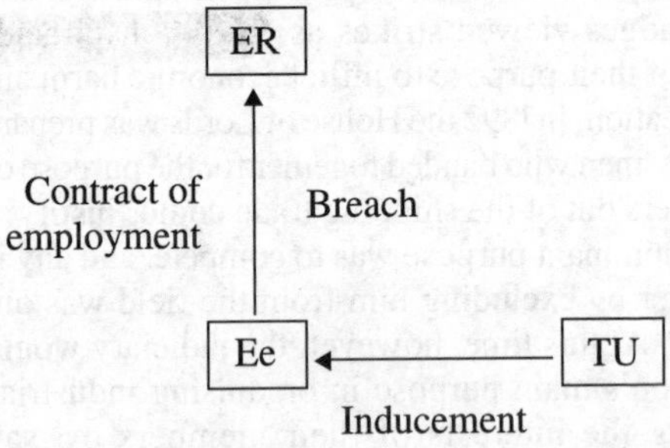


Significantly these torts applied to all industrial action without regard to the underlying industrial dispute which gave rise to it. In the case of inducement to breach of contract and interference there could be no defence of justification because the essence of the tort was the use of unlawful means.

In addition to creating these torts, the courts also found trade union organisations liable for the industrial action taken by a section of their membership. In *Taff Vale*[17] the House of Lords held that the trade union, although an unincorporated association, could be sued in tort and its entire funds, not excluding the funds set aside for its members' welfare benefits, could be subject to attachment to enforce any judgment.

In 1906, the trade unions were able to obtain from the successful Liberal Government a series of immunities against the specific torts created by the judges in the period between 1875 and 1906. The Trade Disputes Act

15 *Allen v Flood* [1898] AC 1, HL

16 *Taff Vale Rly Co v ASRS* [1901] AC 426, HL.

17 [1901] AC 426, HL. For a good historical discussion of the effect of the *Taff Vale* judgment see Clegg, Fox and Thompson *A History of British Trade Unions Since 1889* Vol 1, 1889-1910 (1964). See also Saville, J 'Trade Unions and Free Labour: The Background to the Taff Vale Decision' in *Essays in Labour History.*

1906 provided that 'it shall not be actionable' for individuals to commit the specific torts of conspiracy to injure, inducement of breach of employment contracts or interference with employers' business, etc. Those immunities were qualified by the 'golden formula' derived from the 1875 Act, that to be lawful the acts must be taken 'in contemplation or furtherance of a trade dispute'. The Act also provided a general immunity for the trade union's vicarious liability for the acts of their officials in organising industrial action. Section 4 provided that 'trade unions shall not be liable in tort'. There was no qualification based on the trade dispute formula. There was simply a general immunity for the trade union organisation and, hence its funds, against the possibility of an action for damages.

The enactment of the blanket immunity for trade unions in the 1906 Act as part of the political settlement between the trade unions, the Labour Party and the Liberal Government, was portrayed in Conservative circles then and since as arrogant - creating a privilege which placed the trade unions above the law rather than a mere immunity.

At the time the strategic consideration for the trade unions was to obtain relief from the effects of the *Taff Vale* decision which had created the risk that a trade union's funds could be depleted by damages actions by employers arising out of a single strike by a section of the membership. By establishing the principle in statute law that trade union organisations were not liable in tort, moreover, the union funds could be insulated from any further judicial attempts to outflank the specific immunities spelt out in the 1906 Act.

Section 4 of the 1906 Act, finally, ensured that the 'right to strike' would be unaccompanied by the burden of any corresponding legal responsibilities. For in 1871, 1875 and again in 1906 an alternative form of legal framework providing positive rights could be obtained only at the cost of a statutory definition of trade union responsibility for industrial action which went beyond the union's proposals to limit responsibility to industrial action expressly authorised by the union executive.[18]

This legal framework, which created a structure of trade union immunities which lasted through to 1970, has been described as 'abstentionist' in nature, or as a legislative policy of 'collective laissez-faire'. Yet these labels mislead as well as instruct. For the law intervened to regulate industrial action in other ways.

Under the law of picketing, for example, the police had a residual discretion to preserve public order which overrode the narrow 'right to

18 In 1903 the trade unions were prepared to accept a limited form of trade union responsibility for industrial action, ie industrial action endorsed by a majority vote of their executive. But this formula was rejected by the Conservative government at the time. See Clegg, Fox and Thompson, op cit, pp 321-322.

picket' in s 5 of the 1906 Act.[19] The Emergency Powers Act 1920, amended in 1964, gave the government the power to declare a state of emergency where strikes or any other events interfered with 'the supply and distribution of food, water, fuel or light or with the means of locomotion' and by order in council direct the use of troops 'to secure the potentials of life for the community'.[20] The Conspiracy and Protection of Property Act 1875 imposed special criminal liabilities upon strikers in the Gas, Water and, at a later date the Electricity Supply industry.[1] Moreover, specific legislation provided and continues to provide that the Police, the Armed Forces, Merchant Seamen and Post Office Workers could all commit criminal offences if they took industrial action.[2] Finally, the 1906 Act, as we have seen, did nothing to neutralise the breach of contract of employees who took part in a strike, leaving employees vulnerable to dismissal by the employer for participation in industrial action.

The immunities created in the 1906 Act survived for more than sixty years. Though modified by the arrangements during the two world wars and temporarily reshaped on the statute books by a law introduced by the Conservative Government after the General Strike, they were reinstated in the post-war period.[3]

By the early 1960s, however, the social acceptance of non-interventionism began to break down as high employment levels brought a shift in the market power of labour. During this period, judicial acceptance of trade unions and collective bargaining was eroded by the widespread concern with shop stewards and trade union power. It became clear, once again, that a legal framework based on specific statutory immunities against torts was a precarious form of protection for trade unionists. In three major cases the courts created new forms of tort liability for industrial action which were not specifically mentioned in the 1906 Act, making more widely available the 'labour injunction' and damages

19 Section 5 (as indeed s 15 of TULRA 1974) makes only peaceful attendance lawful. It does not extend to a right to stop a driver for the purpose of peaceful persuasion. *Broome v DPP* [1974] AC 587, [1974] ICR 84, HL. The police may avoid an anticipated breach of the peace and limit the number of pickets *(Piddington v Bates* [1960] 3 All ER 660, *Kavanagh v Hiscock* [1974] QB 600, [1974] 2 All ER 177) and use road blocks to prevent pickets reaching the picket line. *Moss v McLachlan* [1985] IRLR 76; see also *R v Mansfield Justices, ex p Sharkey* [1985] QB 613, [1984] IRLR 496. Moreover attempts to seal off entry by tactical placement of pickets (*Tynan v Balmer* [1967] 1 QB 91, [1966] 2 All ER 133) or mass picketing (*Thomas v NUM (South Wales Area)* [1986] Ch 20, [1985] IRLR 136) are outside the scope of the immunity. See Kahn, Lewis, Livock and Wiles, *Picketing: Industrial Disputes, Tactics and the Law* (1983). Today, there is a Code of Practice on Picketing and a Public Order Act 1986.

20 Morris, G 'Strikes in Essential Services' Mansell [1986] Chs 3, 4. Morris, G 'Industrial Action in Essential Services: The New Law' (1991) ILJ 89.

1 Ibid.

2 Ibid.

3 See Wedderburn, K W W (Lord) *The Worker and the Law* (3rd edn, Penguin).

as an employer response to industrial action. The new torts concentrated on the use of unlawful means, since judicial development of the tort of conspiracy had brought in the defence of justification where employees had a genuine trade union reason for their action.[4]

## INTIMIDATION

In *Rookes v Barnard*[5] a demand by a trade union official and a shop steward combined with a threat to strike if the demand was not met was viewed as a threat by an employee (the shop steward) to commit an unlawful act, ie to break his contract of employment.[6] This was the tort of intimidation. The transaction was also viewed as a conspiracy to commit an unlawful act by the full-time official together with the shop steward and other employees.

This meant that virtually all communication which contained a threat, whether explicit or veiled, was unlawful at common law, allowing the employer to take out an injunction against the shop steward and full-time trade union official. Moreover, the effect of this tort was to make almost all primary industrial action unlawful whatever its underlying reason since some indication in advance had to be given to the employer and this could be viewed as a threat. The Labour government's immediate response to this judicial development was to enact the Trade Disputes Act 1965 to make the threat to commit an unlawful act or a conspiracy to commit an unlawful

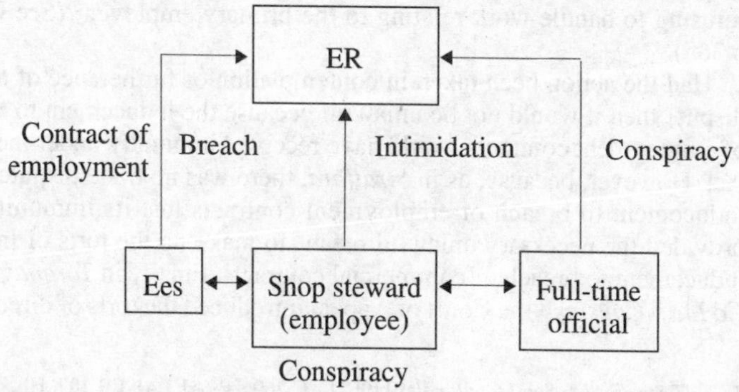


4 See eg *Crofter Hand Woven Harris Tweed Co Ltd v Veitch* [1942] AC 435, [1942] 1 All ER 142; *Sorrell v Smith* [1925] AC 700, HL; and *Reynolds v Shipping Federation Ltd* [1924] 1 Ch 28.

5 [1964] AC 1129, [1964] 1 All ER 367, HL.

6 The breach of contract in *Rookes* consisted of the breach of the no-strike clause in the collective agreement as incorporated in the employee's contract. The point, a contentious one, had been conceded by defendant's counsel.

act not actionable where that unlawful act was a breach of a contract of employment.

## INDUCEMENT TO BREACH OF COMMERCIAL CONTRACT AND SECONDARY INDUSTRIAL ACTION

The judicial activism of the late 1960s also resulted in the creation of new torts which developed the category of unlawful means to make secondary industrial action unlawful. In *Stratford v Lindley*[7] the House of Lords held that the approach by a strike organiser to a secondary employer could be viewed as the tort of *direct* inducement to breach of a commercial contract which was not protected by the 1906 Act, because the Act gave immunity only to the inducement of breach of the employment contract between the employer and employees. There also had to be evidence of 'pressure, persuasion or procuration' ie that the breach had in fact been induced. The new tort presupposed that the inducement was intentional and that it was taken with the knowledge of the contract term which would be broken.[8] (see Figure p 365).

Moreover, where the action was not taken in contemplation or furtherance of a trade dispute, the courts could also find a new tort of *indirectly* inducing a breach of commercial contracts by unlawful means. The organiser of the industrial action indirectly procures the breach of the commercial contract by approaching the employees of the secondary employer and inducing them to break their contracts of employment by refusing to handle work relating to the primary employer.[9] (See Figure p 365).

Had the action been taken in contemplation or furtherance of a trade dispute then it would not be unlawful because the inducement to breach of employment contracts would have received immunity under the 1906 Act. However, because, as in *Stratford*, there was no trade dispute,[10] the inducement to breach of employment contracts lost its immunity and provided the necessary unlawful means to make up the torts of indirect inducement to breach of commercial contracts. Finally in *Torquay Hotel Co Ltd v Cousins*[11] the Court of Appeal introduced the torts of direct (and

7 *JT Stratford & Son Ltd v Lindley* [1965] AC 269, [1964] 3 All ER 102, HL.

8 Ibid.

9 *DC Thomson & Co Ltd v Deakin* [1952] Ch 646, [1952] 2 All ER 361, CA. The distinction between direct and indirect was also underlined in *Middlebrook Mushrooms*; fn 17 below.

10 Ibid.

11 [1969] 2 Ch 106, CA. See now *Middlebrook Mushrooms Ltd v TGWU* [1993] ICR 612, [1993] IRLR 232, CA, where giving leaflets to customers was held not to be an interference with contractual relations because the latter were hypothetical.

indirect) interference with the performance of commercial contracts, which could apply where technically there was no breach of the commercial contract because a 'labour difficulties' clause excused the breach.

The Labour government chose not to deal with these new torts affecting secondary action by immediate legislation and instead appointed a Royal Commission to study Trade Unions and Employers Associations, the Donovan Commission. The Donovan Report contained a diagnosis of the causes of industrial conflict and a prescription for its cure. It diagnosed the causes of industrial conflict as the decline of the effectiveness of collective bargaining institutions at the national, or industry-wide level, to provide regulation at workshop level, and the demonstrable inadequacies of the institutional machinery of workshop collective bargaining that had emerged in the post-war period. Workshop bargaining, with its autonomy, informality and fragmentation, the Report argued, could be reformed into a more orderly institution by an extension of official trade union activity and formal collective agreements and procedures to the workshop level. It recommended an increase in formal written agreements at plant and company level and the revision of the rule books or constitutions of trade unions to include a description of the powers and functions of shop stewards.

The Donovan Report stressed that the necessary reforms ought to be effected by voluntary means rather than compelled by law. It also discussed legal reforms but these were viewed as marginal to the main thrust of the Commission's recommendations. However, neither the Conservative opposition nor the Labour government of the day were prepared to rely on a voluntaristic approach to the reform of industrial relations.

In the 1968-70 period the Labour government attempted to introduce legal restrictions on industrial action in the form of a conciliation pause and strike ballots. In 1971-1974 the Conservative government attempted to introduce a comprehensive system of legal regulation of collective bargaining. Both were ineffective in achieving their aims. The proposals for legislation contained in the Labour government's White Paper ('In Place of Strife' 1969) were withdrawn in return for a solemn and binding undertaking by the TUC that it would take certain steps to help resolve certain unconstitutional and unofficial strikes. The Conservative government's legislation, the Industrial Relations Act 1971, was ultimately repealed by the Labour government when it returned to office in 1974, but long before its repeal it had demonstrated its inability to achieve its objective of applying a viable new legal framework of law to British collective bargaining, and 'had virtually been placed in suspended animation because the potential repercussions of bringing actions were too risky for most possible litigants'. During this period British trade unions and work groups (with the acquiescence and in some cases the support of employers) quite dramatically demonstrated a capacity to resist by industrial means Parliamentary efforts to bring collective bargaining within the web of legislative regulation.

What was particularly noticeable about the 1971-74 experience was the support given by employers to the pattern of resistance to the legislation.[12] In the first place, during that period it was quite obvious that many employers did not generally see it as in their immediate interests to make use of the new and wide legal restriction on strikes. Labour injunctions during the period were relatively infrequent. Moreover, in many cases employers actively cooperated in preventing the legal restrictions from reaching the workplace. For example, the 1971 Act's attempt to make collective agreements legally enforceable by creating a statutory prescription in favour of legal enforceability of collective agreements met with the response that virtually every agreement concluded after the Act became law included a provision that it was not to be legally enforceable.[13]

When a Labour government was returned to power in 1974 the Industrial Relations Act was repealed almost in its entirety; only its unfair dismissal provisions were retained. The Labour government chose to revert to a revised form of statutory immunities for industrial action.

## THE TRADE UNION IMMUNITIES IN THE 1974 ACT

The 1974 Act, as amended by the 1976 Act, set itself the task of creating wide immunities to the leaders and organisers of strikes and other industrial action as well as to the trade union organisations themselves. First, the immunity enjoyed by trade union organisations against tort liability for industrial action was restored in full. The Labour Government rejected the Donovan Commission argument that this should be limited by the golden formula.

Many of the 1974 Act's specific tort immunities for industrial action survive to this day in the form of TULR(C)A, s 219. Thus s 219(1)(a) provides that an act done by a person in contemplation or furtherance of a trade dispute shall not be actionable in tort on the grounds that it induces any other person to break a contract. This applies to any contract whether a commercial or employment contract and it applies to direct as well as indirect inducement.

Section 219(1)(a) also provides a protection for the tort of interference with the performance of contract. It states that an act is not to be actionable

12 Weekes, Mellish, Dickens and Lloyd *Industrial Relations and the Limits of the Law* (1975).

13 Weekes, Mellish, Dickens and Lloyd *Industrial Relations and the Limits of the Law* (1975).

in tort on the grounds only that it interferes or induces another person to interfere with the performance of a contract. This protection extends to direct and indirect interference with any contracts and thereby gives statutory protection from the tort in *Torquay Hotel.*

These protections can also apply, as long as the act is in contemplation or furtherance of a trade dispute, to prevent inducement to breach of contract or interference from being the requisite 'unlawful means' used in the commission of any tort, not mentioned in TULR(C)A: for example, in the case of such new torts as inducement to breach of statutory duty[14] or interference with the trade or business of another person.[15] Since inducement and influence are not actionable, they are not actionable even by someone other than the immediate target of the act.[16]

These immunities, however, cannot apply to any new torts created by the judiciary which are not specifically mentioned in s 219, for example, inducement of breach of statutory duty or hindering its performance[17] or interference with the trade or business of another person by the doing of an unlawful act.[18]

Thirdly s 219(2) provides a statutory immunity for conspiracy to injure, if one is still needed after *Crofter's* case. It states that a combination to do an act in contemplation of a trade dispute shall not be actionable in tort if the act is one which, if done without any such agreement or combination, would not be actionable in tort. This also ensures that the tort of conspiracy to commit an unlawful act is restricted to cases where the acts done are themselves tortious. The section also creates an immunity for conspiracies to break contracts of employment - the *Rookes* tort - since breach of contract is not a tort.

The effect of these provisions as they stood until 1980 was to provide an extremely wide immunity. Primary industrial action was protected by the immunities in the forerunner of s 219(1) against conspiracies, interference, intimidation of, and inducement to, breach of employment contracts, but not inducement of breach of statutory duty which affected primary action in essential services.[19] Secondary industrial action was

14 See eg *Meade v London Borough of Haringey* [1979] 2 All ER 1016, [1979] ICR 494, CA; *Barretts & Baird (Wholesale) Ltd v IPCS* [1987] IRLR 3.

15 See eg *Merkur Island Shipping Corpn v Laughton* [1983] 2 AC 570, [1983] 2 All ER 189, HL.

16 See eg *Hadmor Productions Ltd v Hamilton* [1983] 1 AC 191, [1982] IRLR 102, HL.

17 See eg *Meade v London Borough of Haringey* and *Barretts & Baird (Wholesale) Ltd v IPCS* (see note 14, ante).

18 *Merkur Island Shipping Corpn v Laughton* [1983] 2 AC 570, [1983] IRLR 218, HL; on the other hand in essential services an 'intent to injure' can make a non-actionable breach of a statutory duty unlawful means for the purpose of such a tort, *Associated British Ports v TGWU* [1989] IRLR 305 at 314, 316, CA. See Morris G 'Industrial Action in Essential Services: The New Law' [1991] ILJ 89 at 95.

19 See Morris, G op cit.

protected by the immunities specifically set out in that provision against torts in connection with commercial contracts and sympathetic action was protected by the concept of immunity for action in furtherance of a trade dispute. In the event, the main limit on lawful industrial action was the definition of trade dispute, itself quite wide.

The width of the 1974-1976 statutory immunities made the judiciary distinctly uneasy. The Court of Appeal attempted drastically to narrow the immunities for secondary action 'in contemplation or furtherance of a trade dispute' by creating limitations on the meaning of 'in furtherance' of a trade dispute. In a trilogy of cases, however, the House of Lords restored the full width of the immunities for secondary action.[20] There was some evidence of judicial sensitivity to the policy behind the 1974-1976 Act. Lord Scarman indicated that he was relieved that the judges would not have to sit like 'some back seat driver in trade disputes' and that the policy of the 1974-1976 Act was to put 'the law . . . back to what Parliament had intended when it enacted the Act of 1906 - but stronger and clearer than it was then'.[1]

Yet the other Law Lords were careful to indicate quite explicitly to the Conservative government, now once again in power and preparing new labour legislation, that they were disquieted by the scope of the immunities contained in the 1974-1976 Acts.[2] Lord Diplock said that he regarded the extended immunities as 'intrinsically repugnant'. Lord Keith saw trade unionists as 'privileged persons' able to bring about disastrous consequences with legal impunity'.[3] The Conservative government, having held their fire on the issue of law regulating secondary action pending the results of the *Duport Steels Ltd* case, were soon to respond to these views.

## THE REDUCTION OF THE STATUTORY IMMUNITIES BY THE CONSERVATIVE GOVERNMENT 1980-1993

To Conservative thinking, the statutory immunities against torts committed in contemplation or furtherance of a trade dispute ('the golden formula') were the bastion of trade union power against employers, since they provided the legal foundation for industrial action to underpin collective bargaining. The Trade Union and Labour Relations Acts 1974 and 1976, it was thought, created a 'permissive' legal framework, one which allowed excessive secondary action, excessive support for closed shops, and excessive freedom for strikes taken with mixed collective bargaining and

20 *NWL Ltd v Woods* [1979] 3 All ER 614, [1979] ICR 867; *Express Newspapers Ltd v McShane* [1980] ICR 42; *Duport Steels Ltd v Sirs* [1980] ICR 161.
1 *NWL Ltd v Woods* [1979] 3 All ER 614, [1979] ICR 867 at 886.
2 *Duport Steels Ltd v Sirs* [1980] ICR 161 at 177.
3 Ibid at 188.

'political' motives. Moreover, the reinstatement of a blanket immunity for trade union organisations for the tortious acts of their officials or members in the context of industrial action in TULRA was a prime target for reform.

To reduce the scope of trade union power in this sphere, the government introduced three major changes to the legal framework to industrial action all designed to restrict the immunities: (i) the trade union immunities were narrowed; (ii) trade unions were given legal responsibility for industrial action; and (iii) secret ballots were required before all official action.

## (i) Narrowing the immunities

The scope of the statutory immunities was narrowed to compress legitimate industrial action into a narrow band of 'primary' action, making unlawful most forms of industrial action by workers directed against employers other than their own managers at their own workplace. As the government stated in 1980:

> '. . . objective of the policy . . . is quite specific. It is this; workers are to be permitted the self help of lawful industrial action only within their own employment unit. That is the rule on which the market is to work . . . '

In pursuit of this objective the government took three main steps:[4] (a) it narrowed the scope of lawful picketing, (b) it reduced the scope for secondary industrial action, and (c) it narrowed the definition of a lawful 'trade dispute'.

### *(a) Narrowing the immunities and picketing*

The 1980 and 1982 Acts substantially reduced the basic statutory immunity for picketing, in s 220 of TULR(C)A, to attendance by employees (or certain ex-employees)[5] at or near their own place of work, or attendance by trade union representatives of those workers, 'for the purpose of peacefully obtaining or communicating information or peacefully persuading any person to work or abstain from working'.

The immunity for picketing before 1980 had already been interpreted to confer no more than an immunity from the criminal law for 'attendance for the purpose of communication' and peaceful persuasion and did not extend to a right to impede access to work by employees or delivery

4 It also removed statutory immunity from the following: s 223 action taken because of dismissal for taking unofficial action; s 222 action taken to enforce trade union membership; s 225 pressure to impose a union recognition requirement.

5 In which case they can only picket their former place of work.

vehicles for such purposes.[6] Moreover, attendance had to be at or near the place of work and not on the premises.[7] If picketing, 'working in' or 'sitting in' takes place on the employers premises, s 220 offers no protection against a civil action, eg an injunction for trespass. The Secretary of State's Code on Picketing, which has to be taken into account by the criminal as well as the civil courts, requires that pickets and their organisations 'ensure that in general the number of pickets does not exceed six at any entrance to a workplace' and that 'frequently a smaller number will be appropriate (para 31).[8]

To this limited immunity the 1980 Act introduced the further limitation that it would only apply to workers attending at or near *their own place of work*, unless the worker was a 'mobile' worker, ie without a fixed place of work.[9]

For the ordinary employee, therefore, after the 1980 Act:

> '. . . lawful picketing . . . does not enable a picket to attend lawfully at an entrance to or exit from any place of work which is not his own, even if those who work there are employed by the same employer or covered by the same collective bargaining arrangements.' (Picketing Code of Practice)

The net effect of this change was to require that any lawful picketing at other premises of an employer involved in a dispute had to be done by individuals employed at those premises.[10] Although picketing is subject to regulation by the police in accordance with the law of public order, the main method of enforcing the rule established by a narrowed s 220 is an injunction by employers; in other words the statutory framework now offered employers a credible civil law option when faced by such picketing.

### *(b) Narrowing the immunities and 'secondary' industrial action*

The Employments Act 1980 and 1990 have also removed the protection for most forms of secondary industrial action. Under s 224 of TULR(C)A secondary action is defined as occurring where a person: '(a) induces another to break a contract of employment or interferes or induces another to interfere with its performance, or (b) threatens that a contract of employment under which he or another is employed will be broken or its

6 *Broome v DPP* [1974] AC 587, [1974] ICR 84, HL; *Kavanagh v Hiscock* [1974] QB 600, [1974] 2 All ER 177.

7 See eg *Rayware Ltd v TGWU* [1989] ICR 457, [1989] IRLR 134, CA.

8 See eg *Thomas v NUM (South Wales Area)* [1986] Ch 20, [1985] ICR 886; *News Group Newspapers Ltd v SOGAT '82 (No 2)* [1987] ICR 181, [1986] IRLR 337. See generally Lewis 'Picketing' in Lewis (ed) *Labour Law in Britain* (1986) pp 195-221.

9 In such a case the employee could picket 'at any premises of his employer from which he works or his work is administered'.

10 TULR(C)A, s 219(3) removes statutory immunity from all acts done in the course of picketing unless in accordance with s 220.

performance interfered with, or that he will induce another to break a contract of employment or to interfere with its performance, *if the employer under the contract of employment is not a party to the dispute*'.

An inducement of breach of employment contract under this section consists of an approach by an individual trade union organiser to the employees of the secondary employer to organise either a strike or a boycott by such employees directed against the commercial contractual relationship between the two employers.

A threat of breach of employment contract, etc under s 224 in such circumstances involves a direct approach to the secondary employer by the trade union organiser designed to disrupt the commercial relationship between the two employers.

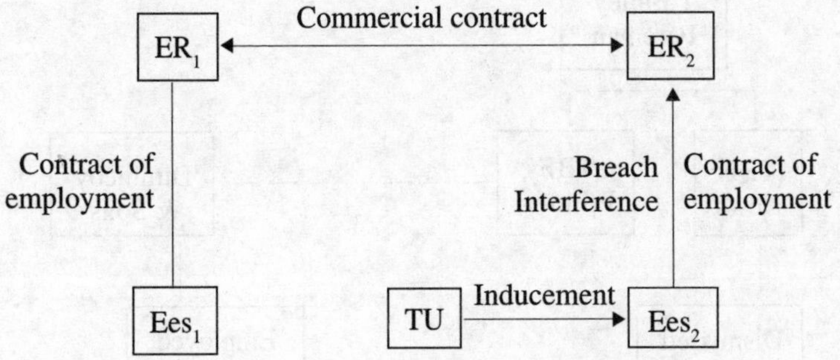


Where such secondary action results in the breach of or interference with commercial contracts, or threatens to do so, then the basic protection of s 219 is withdrawn.

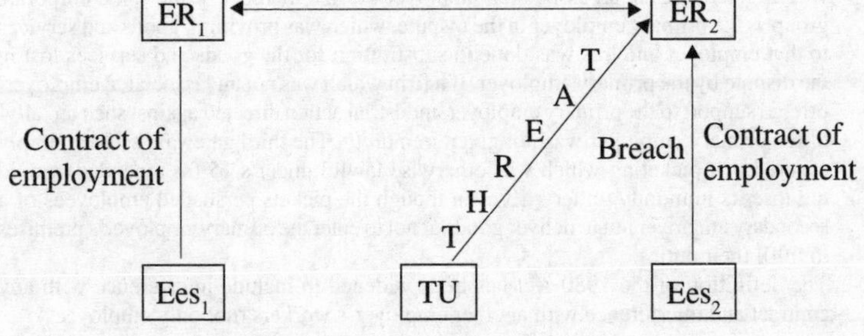

Since 1990,[11] all secondary action[12] has been unlawful, apart from lawful primary picketing which has a secondary effect. Section 224 of the 1993 Act now provides that:

> 'An act is not protected if one of the facts relied on for the purpose of establishing liability is that there has been secondary action which is not lawful picketing.'

Moreover, s 224(4) makes it clear that, for the purposes of secondary action, an 'employer is not to be treated as party to a dispute between another employer and workers of that employer; and where more than one employer is in dispute with his workers, the dispute between each employer

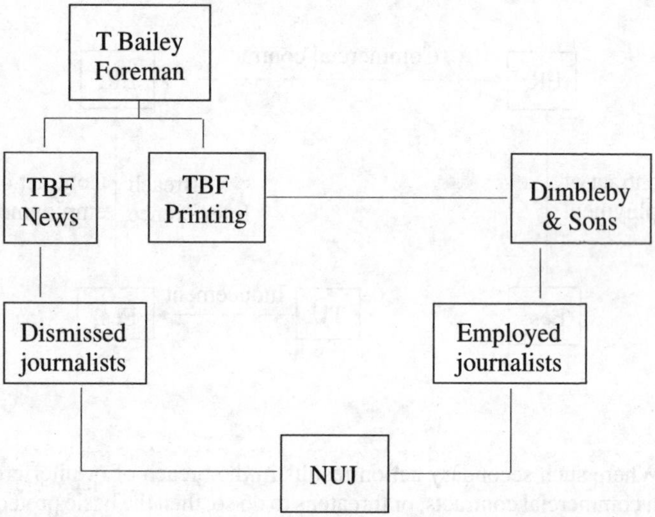


11 In the Employment Act 1980 there were three 'gateways' or exceptions which allowed immunity to be retained. The first contractor-gateway, s 17(3), applied to a case where the secondary action was directed against an employer who has a current, commercial contract with the primary employer, ie the party to the trade dispute. The second gateway, the 'associated employer' exception, applied only where the union's action was directed against an associated employer of, ie a member of the same corporate group as the primary employer in the dispute, which was providing goods and services to that employer and this was done in substitution for the goods and services lost in the dispute by the primary employer. If a firm which was not an 'associated employer' offered support to the primary employer, industrial action directed against such an 'ally' of the primary employer was not given immunity. The third gateway, s 17(5) simply ensured that picketing which was otherwise lawful under s 15 (as amended) would not lose its immunity under s 13 even though the pickets persuaded employees of a secondary employer not to deliver goods or not to enter the primary employer's premises to fulfil their duties.

12 The definition of the 1980 Act has been widened to include interference with any contract and interference with another employer's workers (not only employees).

and his workers is to be treated as a separate dispute'. This effectively endorses the decision in *Dimbleby & Sons Ltd v National Union of Journalists*,[13] in which the House of Lords held that where a firm had created a corporate structure dividing the enterprise into separate subsidiaries, each subsidiary was to be treated as a separate employer for the purpose of regulating secondary action. In *Dimbleby* a group of journalists working for Dimbleby & Sons refused to supply copy to their employer because of its printing contract with TBF (Printers) Ltd. This action was taken in furtherance of an NUJ dispute with TBF Ltd in Nottingham. In fact T Bailey Foreman was a holding company consisting of a newspaper group, TBF Ltd, with whom the journalists had their dispute, and TBF (Printers) Ltd, with whom Dimbleby and Sons had their printing contract.

The House of Lords held that the trade dispute was with TBF Ltd, the newspaper company, but the action was directed towards the commercial contract between an entirely different company, TBF (Printers) Ltd, and Dimbleby and Sons and hence it was secondary action. The House of Lords was unwilling to lift the 'corporate veil'.

The cumulative effect of the narrowing of the immunities for 'secondary' action, therefore, is not merely to deprive almost all secondary action of lawful status. It also places companies in a position to determine for themselves what is or is not lawful action. They may structure their corporate group to include 'buffer' companies to limit the entitlement of trade unions to organise legitimate industrial action against different operations of the same enterprise. They may then resort to legal action - an injunction or an action for damages - to ensure that the unlawful industrial action is curbed.

This approach figured prominently in the preparation of Rupert Murdoch's organisation, News International, for the shift of its operations from Fleet Street to Wapping.[14] News Corporation, through its subsidiary in the UK, News International, published *The Times* and the *Sunday Times* through Times Newspapers (TN) and the *News of the World* and the *Sun* through The News Group (NG). News International arranged its distribution of papers through a separate company News International Distribution (NID), its supplies through News International Supplies (NIS) and its advertising through News International Advertising (NIA). When the newspaper publishing companies, TN and NG, sacked their NGA and SOGAT print workers and moved production to Wapping, the industrial action taken to disrupt contracts made by NID, NIS and NIA was outside the first gateway of the 1980 Act, s 17(3), because the employers with

13 [1984] 1 All ER 751, [1984] ICR 386.
14 See eg Ewing and Napier 'The Wapping Dispute and Labour Law' [1986] Cambridge Law Journal 285; see also Wedderburn *The Worker and the Law* (2nd edn) pp 604-605.

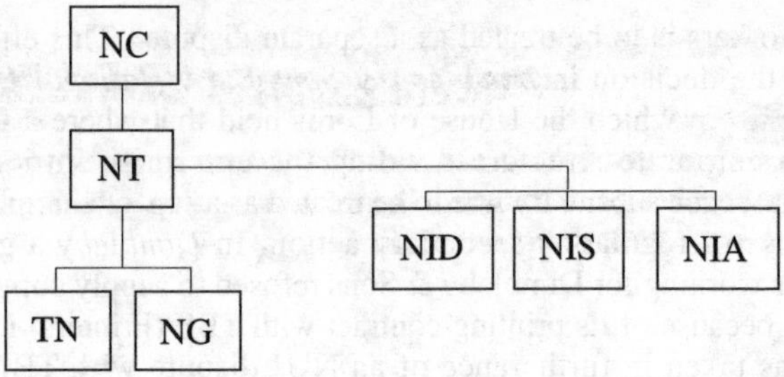


whom the print workers were in dispute, TN and NG, had no contracts with the distributors, suppliers and advertisers (many of whom employed SOGAT or NGA workers). These employers had subsisting commercial contracts only with News International.[15]

In the USA, where two employers form an alliance for the purpose of defeating industrial action, the relevant trade unions are entitled to treat the 'ally' as if he were a primary employer.[16] In EC Countries where there is 'sufficient community of interest' trade unions may engage in certain limited forms of sympathetic action.[17] In such countries, the corporate veil is not sacrosanct in the context of industrial action.

### *(c) Narrowing the definition of a lawful trade dispute*

The Employment Act 1982 took the process of narrowing the boundaries of lawful industrial action a step further by redefining the golden formula - in particular the scope of a 'trade dispute'.[18]

Ever since the 1875 Act, the dividing line between lawful and unlawful action has been the golden formula - 'in contemplation or furtherance of a trade dispute'. A 'trade dispute' was defined quite widely, first in the 1906 Act and later in s 29(1) of TULRA as consisting of a dispute between 'employers and workmen or between workmen and workmen' which was connected with one of the following:

(a) terms and conditions of work or physical conditions;
(b) engagement, non-engagement, termination or suspension;
(c) allocation of work;
(d) matters of discipline;
(e) union membership or non-membership;

15 Under the 1992 Act, the gateways no longer exist and companies continue to enjoy considerable discretion to draw the line between lawful and unlawful action.
16 See eg US National Labor Relations Act, s 8(b)(iii).
17 Aaron, *Industrial Conflict - A Comparative Legal Survey* (1972).
18 See Simpson, B 'A Not So Golden Formula' [1983] 46 MLR 463.

(f) facilities for trade union officials;
(g) machinery for negotiation or consultation and including union recognition for representation.

Today, the issues listed in s 244(1) of TULR(C)A as falling within the definition of a trade dispute remain the same but the scope for lawful trade disputes has been narrowed by the Employment Acts in three other important respects.

In the first place, the basis for 'sympathetic' action has been narrowed by defining a trade dispute as a dispute between workers and their employer wholly or mainly related to one of the issues listed.

## 'Workers and their employer': the parties to the dispute

The effect of narrowing the phrase to 'workers and their employer' was both to narrow the category of legitimate parties to the dispute and the scope of legitimate issue for dispute. The wide definition of parties in the original version of s 29(1) included workers who were not employed by the employer[19] and the trade union itself.[20] Hence it extended to demarcation and jurisdictional disputes as well as cases where the trade union did not have members in the employer's firm. Today, the only legitimate party on the workers' side are workers employed (or formerly employed)[1] by the employer.[2]

## The matter in dispute

Moreover, after 1982, the dispute between workers and their employer itself had to be one genuinely concerning their employment.

For example, in *Dimbleby & Sons Ltd v NUJ*,[3] the House of Lords found that the refusal by employees to provide copy to their employer because of his contract with another non-union printing firm which had dismissed journalists who had taken industrial action was not a dispute 'as to the terms of their employment' because inter alia the allocation of work between workers or groups of workers in s 218(c) related only to allocation

19 TULRA, s 29(6).
20 TULRA, s 29(4), now repealed.
1 Former employees who were dismissed in connection with the dispute TULR(C)A, s 244(5).
2 TULR(C)A, s 244.
3 [1984] 1 All ER 751, [1984] ICR 386, HL.

of work among workers employed by their own employer not the allocation of work to employees in another firm.

Furthermore, any sympathetic action taken in response to matters occurring abroad can be the subject of a trade dispute only where the individuals who were taking the industrial action were themselves affected in respect of a listed matter in their employment.[4]

## The motive for the industrial action: 'wholly or mainly'

Secondly, the range of disputes between workers and their own employer, which were given immunity in the golden formula, was greatly narrowed by changes in the test of motive. Under the 1906 and 1974 Acts the dispute had to be 'connected with' a listed employment or collective bargaining matter.

The dividing line between lawful and unlawful industrial action was determined by whether a dispute was genuinely taken for a listed purpose even if other motives such as personal or political motives were present in the minds of those organising and participating in the industrial action. This was assured by the statutory phrase 'connected with'. As long as a dispute was 'connected with' a listed object, it would receive immunity even if it were not the predominant motive for the dispute. For example, in *Duport Steels Ltd v Sirs*,[5] Lord Diplock made the point that even if one of the purposes of industrial action was to 'coerce the government', in this case to pay more to workers on strike in the public sector, provided the strike was 'connected with' or furthered the pay claims, it was protected. It might be possible in a particular case to find that the non industrial motive was the exclusive motive, or that it so excluded the industrial motive that the latter was a sham or pretext.[6] However, even if the non industrial motive was the predominant motive, the industrial action would receive immunity under the 1974-1976 Act as long as the dispute was genuinely connected with a listed industrial issue.[7]

In the 1982 Act, the Conservative government reintroduced a 'predominant' motive test by replacing 'connected with' by the requirement that the dispute relate 'wholly or mainly' to one or more of the listed industrial issues. The effect of this change was to place judges in the position once again (TULR(C)A, s 244(1)) of determining which of two

4 TULR(C)A, s 244(3); compare the 'Flags of Convenience' cases, eg *NWL v Woods* [1979] 3 All ER 614, [1979] ICR 867, HL.

5 [1980] 1 All ER 529, [1980] ICR 161, HL.

6 Remark by Lord Scarman in *NWL Ltd v Woods* [1979] 3 All ER 614, [1979] ICR 867, HL; see too Lord Cross's remark in *Universe Tankships Inc of Monrovia v ITWF* [1982] ICR 262, [1982] IRLR 200.

7 *NWL v Woods* [1979] 3 All ER 614, [1979] IRLR 478, HL.

motives was the predominant motive and which the ancillary motive. For example in *Mercury Communications Ltd v Scott-Garner*[8] the refusal of trade unionists to connect Mercury to British Telecommunications lines because in their view it represented a threat to their jobs, was held as not to be the 'predominant purpose' of the dispute. Rather the dispute was part of a campaign against the government policy of ending the BT monopoly. And in *Wandsworth London Borough Council v National Association of Schoolmasters etc*[9] the Court of Appeal was prepared to accept that the *main* purpose of the proposed boycott of the tests associated with the National Curriculum was the workload it imposed, ie its effects on terms and conditions of union members rather than objections to the policy itself.

Trade unions cannot convert a non industrial dispute into an industrial dispute by simply couching it in the form of a contractual demand. In *BBC v Hearn*[10] the Court of Appeal hinted that such a tactic might be possible. However, in *Universe Tankships*,[11] Lord Cross warned that 'a dispute which in reality has no connection with terms and conditions of employment' cannot be turned into one by trade unions insisting that the employer incorporate a particular term in the employee's contract.

## 'In contemplation or furtherance'

The third element of the golden formula was that the action taken had to be either in contemplation or furtherance of a trade dispute. If in contemplation the dispute must be impending or likely to occur, if in furtherance the dispute must be in existence and the act done in the course of it and for the purpose of promoting the interests of a party to it.[12] Otherwise there were few inhibitions in the statutory phrase. In the late 1970s the Court of Appeal attempted to curb the wide scope of 'furtherance' by bringing in a remoteness test (ie no tertiary action) and a requirement that the action must be capable of furthering the dispute or achieving the objective.[13] However, the House of Lords rejected the objective test of 'furtherance', accepting that the statutory test was 'honesty of purpose' of the striking employees rather than 'reasonableness' or 'expediency'. Moreover, Lord Denning's attempt to read in a remoteness limitation to 'furtherance' was rejected by the Law Lords because there was no such restriction expressed in the statute.

8 [1984] ICR 74, [1983] IRLR 494, CA.
9 [1993] IRLR 344, CA.
10 [1977] ICR 685, [1977] IRLR 273, CA.
11 [1983] 1 AC 366, [1982] IRLR 200, HL.
12 *Conway v Wade* [1909] AC 506, HL.
13 See eg *Express Newspapers Ltd v McShane* [1979] 2 All ER 360, [1979] IRLR 79, CA.

Section 244 leaves these decisions in place as regards furtherance. However, the definition of permissible secondary industrial action in s 224 of TULR(C)A incorporates the substance of the restrictions to in furtherance introduced by the Court of Appeal. The net effect of the narrowing of the definition of trade disputes together with s 224 has been to place employers and others[14] in a position to take legal action against most forms of non-primary industrial action.

## (ii) Trade union liability for industrial action and the new remedies for employers

The Employment Act 1982 fundamentally altered the nature of the legal framework for labour relations by making trade union organisations liable for the acts of their officials who authorised or endorsed industrial action outside the scope of the now narrowed statutory immunities. In the Trade Disputes Act 1906, and again in the Trade Union and Labour Relations Act 1974, British trade unions had obtained a blanket statutory immunity for tort liability. The immunity was not limited to torts committed in the course of a trade dispute; the statutes stated that trade unions were not to be liable in tort. When the Labour government restored the blanket immunity in 1974, it ignored the recommendation of the Donovan Commission that its scope should be reduced to cover only those acts committed in contemplation or furtherance of a trade dispute. The original purpose of the immunity was to prevent a trade union's funds from being exhausted by a successful legal action arising out of only one strike, the fate that befell the trade union in the *Taff Vale* case of 1901.[15] The fact that the organisational immunity went beyond the scope of the statutory immunity enjoyed by individual union members or officials who organised industrial action, however, had led it to be viewed as a 'special privilege' in Conservative circles.

By introducing in the 1982 Act the principle of trade union accountability for industrial action it 'authorised' or 'endorsed' (TULR(C)A, s 20); the Conservative government could claim at an ideological level to be removing the special privileges and bringing the trade unions within the 'rule of law'. At a more pragmatic level, however, the 1982 Act's provisions meant that employers would have a defendant against whom their legal sanctions could be far more effective. This was only partly true of the remedy of damages which could be brought by an employer against a trade union. The 1982 Act was carefully designed to avoid the appearance of resurrecting the excesses of the *Taff Vale* judgment.

14 See ss 235A, B and C inserted by s 22 of the 1993 Act. See p 352 above.
15 [1901] AC 426, HL.

It provided that where an employer brought an action for damages against a trade union the amount of damages that could be obtained in any one proceeding was limited by the size of the union's membership (for a union with a membership of over one million the maximum amount of damages was set at £250,000); and damages and costs could not be recovered from the provident funds of the unions (TULR(C)A, s 22).

The more dramatic addition to the employer's armory of legal remedies provided by the 1982 Act was an injunction directly against the trade union organisation to end its 'authorisation' or 'endorsement' of industrial action. Before 1982, employers could only obtain injunctions against the individual union officials or unofficial leaders who organised industrial action, and hence the main mode of enforcement of a contempt of a court action for disobeying injunctions was a fine, ultimately enforceable by imprisonment for a failure to pay. This created something of a 'martyr's charter' under the Industrial Relations Act as the 'Pentonville Five' case of 1973 demonstrated.[16] Under the 1982 Act, however, once the trade union organisation can be made a defendant, the labour injunction can be enforced by a fine followed by sequestration of the union funds which involves a freezing of the assets of the union to ensure that the fine is paid, and the potential for enormous costs to be added to the fine itself.[17] Indeed, according to the court rules, judges have a discretion directly to sequester the funds of the union as a primary method of obtaining compliance with the injunction. Furthermore, the amount of the fine, or the amount of the costs of sequestration payable by the union is not affected by the statutory limits on damages. By shifting the emphasis on enforcement from imprisonment of individuals to remedies directed against the funds of trade union organisations, the Act provides the employer with a far more effective legal sanction.[18]

It does not automatically result in an end to the industrial action. For if the workforce feels sufficiently strongly about an issue they can remain on strike unofficially, ie without trade union support. But where the industrial action is in fact propped up either financially through strike pay, or organisationally, owing to the leadership of the trade union organisation, an injunction could produce an end to the industrial action or a catalyst for further negotiation with the trade union.

16 See Weekes, Mellish, Dickens and Lloyd *Industrial Relations and the Limits of the Law* p 197. A shift to claims for damages against trade union organisations under the 1971 Act was announced in the *Heatons* case, see p 375, note 5, infra.

17 See O'Regan 'Contempt of Court and the Enforcement of Labour Injunctions' (1991) MLR 385.

18 See Evans 'The Use of Injunctions in Labour Disputes' (1987) BJIR 419.

## Injunction procedure

Finally, the procedure for obtaining an interlocutory injunction itself presents few obstacles to employers. An injunction can be obtained by an employer on an ex parte basis, ie without the defendant appearing, if the case is sufficiently urgent.[19] Otherwise an inter parties hearing, based almost entirely on affidavit evidence, can be procured within a few days.

In theory, an interlocutory injunction is meant only to freeze the positions, ie restore the status quo prior to the strike, pending the full trial on the issue of damage. In practice, however, the interim measure is the only one the employer usually wants because of the way it provides relief from the effects of the strike.

To obtain an interlocutory injunction, employers must first establish that they have 'a serious question to be tried'.[20] As long as they make no mistakes as to the issues of law which are relevant, all employers have to do is to present sufficient evidence that there is a triable issue.[1] Then they must convince the court that they will suffer more irreparable damage from a continuance of the industrial action than the defendant will suffer if an injunction is granted.

This second step, the so-called 'balance of convenience' test, almost always results in a finding in favour of the employers because they are always able to demonstrate tangible financial loss as long as the industrial action continues, whereas it is rare to find judicial appreciation of the fact that a temporary halt to a strike will often mean that it is permanently ended.[2] Moreover, it is always open to employers to argue that with the maximum limits to damage for any one proceeding in s 22 of the 1992 Act, there is no assurance of full recovery of loss at a full trial.

Employers, therefore, can make use of their ready access to this legal sanction in negotiations with trade unions. They can decide when to apply for a hearing, a writ and when to serve the summons. They can also decide whether or not to ask the court to enforce the injunction against a trade union which is in contempt, for the courts will not enforce their own order unless the breach is brought to their attention.[3] Once that step is taken,

19 TULR(C)A, s 221 requires in ex parte proceedings that reasonable steps taken in respect of notice of the application and opportunity for defendant to be heard.

20 *American Cyanamid Co v Ethicon* [1975] AC 396, HL, reduced the earlier requirement of a strong prima facie case to the less onerous test of an arguable case. The attempt in TULRA, s 17(2), to ensure that the likelihood of an immunity defence at the trial should decisively influence the interlocutory proceeding foundered on its loose drafting. All it required was that judges 'shall have regard to' this factor.

1 *Middlebrook Mushrooms Ltd v TGWU* [1993] ICR 612, [1993] IRLR 232, CA.

2 See eg *Union Traffic Ltd v TGWU* [1989] ICR 98, [1989] IRLR 127, HC.

3 See eg *Clarke v Chadburn* [1985] 1 All ER 211, [1984] IRLR 350, para 13. *Mirror Group Newspapers v Harrison* (7 November 1986, unreported).

however, the employer loses the element of control. The issue moves from the realm of private law to public law; the court, or its appointed sequestrator, decides the means to be used to enforce the court order.[4]

## Official and unofficial action

The Employment Act 1982 also contained a provision establishing the dividing line between official and unofficial industrial action. Under the EA 1982, s 15(2) (now s 20(1) of TULR(C)A), a union is liable for the acts originally authorised or subsequently endorsed by a 'responsible person' of the trade union, eg the executive committee; the president or general secretary; employed officials such as full time officers and committees to whom they reported.

Since the *Heatons* case in 1972, however, the courts could find that industrial action had been impliedly authorised or endorsed by the trade union organisation.[5] Against the background of this legal precedent, the 1982 Act provided an elaborate set of rules to determine whether the trade union had effectively repudiated unofficial industrial action. Thus, according to the 1982 Act, unless the union rules explicitly prohibited the authorisation or endorsement of industrial action by any individual official, to avoid liability a union's executive committee, or its president or general secretary had to publicly repudiate 'unofficial' industrial action 'as soon as reasonably practicable', notify its organisers without delay and in writing - and avoid behaving in a manner which was inconsistent with its purported repudiation.[6] These rules placed considerable pressure on trade unions to take elaborate steps to distance themselves from any unofficial industrial action which is not likely to receive trade union endorsement.

In the 1990 Act the Conservative government decided to act on the view that 'unofficial action was subject to fewer constraints than official action'. Unofficial action could retain the statutory immunities without a secret ballot. Moreover, the organisers of unofficial action, unlike trade unions, were difficult to identify and not likely to have sufficient assets to sue.[7]

The Act extends the liability of trade unions for unofficial industrial action in three respects. It widens the categories of individuals who can authorise or endorse industrial action on the unions' behalf. Thus s 20(2) of TULR(C)A now provides that a trade union's responsibility for

4 See eg O'Regan 'Contempt of Court and the Enforcement of Labour Injunctions [1991] MLR 385; see also Lightman 'A Trade Union in Chains: Scargill Unbound' [1987] Current L Prob 25.

5 *Heatons Transport (St Helens) Ltd v TGWU* [1972] ICR 308, [1972] IRLR 25, HL; see Hepple, B 'Union Responsibility for Shop Stewards' [1972] ILJ 197.

6 EA 1982, s 15(2).

7 Unofficial Action and the Law, Cm 821 London HMSO 1989.

industrial action will follow from any act authorised or endorsed by any person empowered by the rules to do, authorise or endorse acts of the kind in question; the principal executive committee or the president or general secretary; or by any other committee of the union (including any group of persons constituted in accordance with union rules) and any other official of the union (whether employed by it or not), ie including lay officials such as shop stewards. An official shall also be taken to have authorised or endorsed any action that is done, authorised or endorsed by any group set up wholly or partly to co-ordinate industrial action, of which he or she is a member.[8]

Simpson sums up this extension of trade union liability in the following terms:

> 'A trade union is thus made responsible not only for the acts of joint shop stewards' committees which include one of its officials. It could also become liable for acts by any member of an informal work group if the group includes one of the union officials . . . The extent of vicarious liability that this imposes on unions is much greater than that under the notion of authority deriving from the bottom as well as the top in the *Heatons* case in 1972.'

Secondly, under s 20(4) of TULR(C)A, authorisation or endorsement of industrial action by the president, general secretary, principal executive committee or any other union committee or official will make the union responsible for industrial action, *regardless of anything in the union rules*, or any other contract or rule of law; the union's rule book definition of responsibility will no longer prevent liability. The only exception to authorisation or endorsement under s 29(2) is repudiation by the union under s 21.

Under s 21 of TULR(C)A, a trade union can repudiate unofficial action and avoid liability for the actions of union committees and officials (as newly defined) only if the principal executive committee, the president or general secretary repudiates them 'as soon as reasonably practicable' after 'learning of any of them' and then only by giving 'written notice of the repudiation to the committee or official in question without delay' and by 'doing its best to give individual written notice of the fact and date of repudiation, without delay - (i) to every member of the union who the union has reason to believe is taking part, or might otherwise take part, in industrial action as a result of the act, and (ii) to the employer of every such member' (s 21(2)).

The notice to individual members, moreover, must contain the following statement: 'Your union has repudiated any call (or calls) for industrial action to which this notice relates and you will give no support to unofficial industrial action taken in response to it (or them). If you are dismissed

8 Section 20(3)(b).

while taking unofficial industrial action, you will have no right to complain of unfair dismissal' (s 21(3)). Furthermore, if any time after a purported repudiation the executive, president or general secretary of a union behaves 'in a manner . . . inconsistent with the purported repudiation' the act is no longer treated as repudiated (s 21(5)).[9]

In summary, the amendments to the law of unfair dismissal and unofficial strikes when combined with the 1990 extension of the criteria for trade union repudiation of unofficial industrial action puts trade unions to a stark choice. They must decide either to repudiate industrial action which they have no intention of making official knowing that in such a case their members will be vulnerable to selective dismissals or they must make a strike official and ensure that a ballot is held to avoid an injunction or an action for damages. The Act reinforces the pressures for centralised decision-making by trade unions in respect of support for industrial action which were created by the 1982 Act. It also ensures that participants in unofficial industrial action will be both isolated from any official support and vulnerable to the sanctions of selective dismissal. This will clearly discourage and deter unofficial action but will not extinguish it altogether particularly when recessionary conditions are replaced by conditions with healthier order books. It effectively reduces the number of occasions when full time officials will help to resolve industrial conflict by working with workplace groups once unofficial industrial action has taken place. The deterrent effect of this legal framework also has a less obvious industrial relations cost.

## (iii) The new conditions for statutory protection: strike ballots

The third major legislative step taken by the Conservative government was to introduce to the narrowed statutory protection for industrial action the further qualification that all 'official' action had to receive prior authorisation from the membership in a secret ballot. Section 226(1) of TULR(C)A provides that the protections of s 219 are withdrawn if the union calling or endorsing the industrial action did not receive a majority vote in favour of the action in a secret ballot held in accordance with the Act.[10]

9 Under s 21(6) these officials must also confirm in writing that industrial action is repudiated should any request be received within six months of a purported repudiation from a secondary employer or other person who had not been served notice of repudiation in writing.

10 See Hutton, 'Solving the Strike Problem: Part II of the Trade Union Act 1984' [1984] ILJ 212.

The first requirement under s 227 is that 'all those members . . . who it is reasonable at the time of the ballot for the unions to believe will be called upon' to participate 'in the strike or other industrial action . . .' must be balloted and no others.[11] Secondly, normally there should be a separate ballet of employees at each workplace. Whenever the union ballots employees in more than one workplace, it must provide a separate ballot and obtain a majority vote in each workplace, unless the workplaces have common conditions of employment or occupational descriptions in which case they may be aggregated.[12]

The vote must be by a postal ballot.[13] The voting paper, moreover, must contain a question (however framed) which requires an answer 'yes' or 'no' whether the voter is prepared to take part in a strike or industrial action short of a strike.[14] The ballot paper must also include a statement, not otherwise qualified or commented on, that 'If you take part in a strike or other industrial action, you may be in breach of your contract of employment' (s 229). It must also specify who is authorised to call industrial action if the ballot is successful (s 230).

A ballot is required before a trade union either 'authorises' or 'endorses' industrial action. Section 20(2)-(4) applies to determine whether or not a call for industrial action has been so authorised or endorsed. Consequently, to avoid liability for unballoted, unofficial, action under the 1984 Act, trade unions must make strenuous efforts to repudiate it following the rules of s 21 of TULR(C)A.[15]

Where a trade union decides to make an unofficial strike official it must first take formal steps to repudiate the unofficial strike, which include the requirements that the trade union give written notice to individual members stressing lack of support for the industrial action and the lack of a right to complain of unfair dismissal before holding the secret ballot, if it wishes the balloted action to be lawful.[16] The trade union cannot authorise or endorse a 'call' for industrial action before the date of the ballot.

Finally as soon as is reasonably practicable after the ballot is held, the trade union must take such steps as are reasonably necessary to inform persons entitled to vote and the employer[17] of the number of votes cast in

11 Section 227; *London Underground v RMT* [1995] IRLR 636, CA; cf *Monsanto plc v TGWU* [1987] 1 All ER 358, [1986] IRLR 406, CA; *RJB Mining UK Ltd v NUM* [1997] IRLR 621, QB.

12 Section 228; see McKendrick 'The Rights of Trade Union Members - Part I of the Employment Act 1988' [1988] ILJ 141 at 145-147.

13 See TULR(C)A 1992, s 230.

14 If both possibilities are contemplated they must be voted upon separately on the ballot. See eg *West Midland Travel Ltd v TGWU* [1994] IRLR 578.

15 See previous section, p 376.

16 See TULR(C)A, s 233(3)(a).

17 See TULR(C)A 1992, s 231A.

the ballot, the number of yes votes, the number of no votes and the number of spoiled voting papers[18].

First, all employers must be given notice of a ballot and its contents and those employees reasonably believed to be entitled to vote seven days before the ballot is held; second, a specimen ballot paper must be provided to employers not later than three days before the ballot is held (s 226A); third, the ballot must be subject to independent scrutiny by a 'scrutineer' with a report prepared on the ballot and sent to the union and any relevant third parties who ask for one (s 226B); fourth, if the ballot is successful, the union must give at least seven days' written notice to employers of any industrial action to be taken including which employees will take part in such action and when and whether their participation will be continuous or discontinuous and when industrial action is intended to begin.[19] The balloted industrial action must take place within four weeks of the ballot.[20] The call for industrial action can only be made by a person or descriptions of persons specified on the ballot paper.[1]

Finally to avoid a claim brought by a union member under s 62, the ballot must also meet three sets of statutory conditions: TULR(C)A, s 227, s 229, and s 233. The statutory balloting provisions as they now stand ensure a degree of legal complexity which adds to the range of issues which judges can already fasten upon to find a strike ballot unlawful if they choose to do so.[2] In this they will be aided by the Code of Practice on Ballots before Industrial Action which came into effect in April 1990 and which provides a detailed guideline on how ballots should be conducted.[3] One amendment in the 1990 Act, however, appears to reduce the effect of a legal impediment to successful strike ballots.

Under s 234(2) of TULR(C)A, where a court order restraining a trade union from calling industrial action is set aside the union is now able to apply to a court forthwith to obtain an order that the period of 'restraint' shall not count towards the four week period, as long as the application is

18 TULR(C)A 1992, s 231.
19 See TULR(C)A, s 234A.
20 Section 234.
1 Section 233.
2 For examples of such instances see *Shipping Co Uniform Inc v International Transport Workers' Federation* [1985] ICR 245; *London Underground Ltd v NUR* [1989] IRLR 341; *Blue Circle Cement Ltd v TGWU* (7 July 1989, unreported) ; see Simpson [1989] ILJ 234; for examples of counter instances see: *British Railways Board v NUR* [1989] ICR 678, CA; *Monsanto plc v TGWU* [1987] ICR 269, CA; *Post Office v UCW* [1990] ICR 258, CA; Auerbach [1990] ILJ 120.
3 The Code of Practice was authorised by the EA 1988. For an analysis of its drafts and final form see Simpson [1990] ILJ 293; see also McCarthy Hendy and Wedderburn 'Ballots on Industrial Action: The Draft Code of Practice' [1989] IER.

made before eight weeks from the date of the ballot.[4] The court's discretion to make such an order is curtailed where it considers that the result of the ballot no longer represents the views of those who voted in it or an event is likely to occur as a result of which the vote would be against industrial action if another ballot were held: s 234(4). Nevertheless, s 234(2) accepts in principle the need not to reballot after an injunction is lifted on appeal.

The 1984 Act as a whole was portrayed as a means of promoting democracy within trade union organisations. It provides that in the field of strikes, as well as elections of union officials, and political funds, decisions should be taken by direct voting by the membership in secret ballots. This, it was argued, would help to restore the unions to their members. Yet, curiously in view of this aim, the 1984 Act provided in the case of strike ballots that only the employer against whom the industrial action was taken could bring an injunction or action for damages to enforce the legal condition of the strike ballot.[5] It was not until the 1988 Act that employees who were in the group deprived of a strike ballot were given a right to bring an action in the High Court against trade unions for industrial action not balloted in accordance with the Act.[6]

## Trade unions and individual members

A clear priority for individual rights in the collective setting is evident in the new rights of trade union members consolidated in Part I of Chapter V of TULR(C)A. Section 62 gives individual trade union members a right to enjoin trade union officials who attempt to organise industrial action without a ballot. Section 63 gives union members a right not to be denied access to courts by any rule in the union rule book or court practice of insisting on exhaustion of remedies. Section 64 creates a new legal right for individuals who have at any time been members of a trade union, not to be 'unjustifiably disciplined'. Section 64(2) lists prohibited forms of discipline.[7] Section 65 provides that any such disciplinary action taken or

4 See eg the contrary experience in *Associated British Ports v TGWU* [1989] ICR 557, CA and HL noted Simpson [1989] ILJ 234; *Barretts & Baird (Wholesale) Ltd v IPCS* [1987] IRLR 3; see Simpson [1987] MLR 506 at 507.

5 It also raised the possibility that, with the immunity of TULRA, s 13 removed, customers and other contracts of the primary employer could bring an action in tort against the trade union. Cf *Falconer v ASLEF and NUR* [1986] IRLR 331, Cty Ct.

6 See McKendrick 'The Rights of Trade Union Members - Part I of the Employment Act 1988' 1988 ILJ 141. Of course trade union members could bring an action at common law where the union rule book contained rules requiring ballots before industrial action. See eg Ewing 'The Strike, the Courts and the Rule Book' [1985] ILJ 160.

7 S 64(2) including expulsion, fines or reinbursements of strike pay or depriving access to any other benefit of membership, or if another union is advised or encouraged not to accept him as a member.

threatened to be taken by a trade union against a member because of his or her opposition to or failure to take part in or support a strike or other industrial action (s 65(2)(a) and (b)) is unlawful and subject to a special compensatory award (s 67)[8]. Section 65(2)(c) also provides similar protection for trade union members who are disciplined for 'whistleblowing' or bringing a proceeding against their union officials for certain alleged breaches of union rules or laws[9]. Under TURER 1993 five more types of conduct are added to the list in s 65(2) of conduct for which individuals may not be disciplined: including not agreeing to a check off (s 65(2)(f)) changing unions or refusing to join a union (g) or working with non-members or for an employer who hires non-members (h) & (i).[10] Section 68, as amended by TURER 1993[11], introduces new limits to 'check off', or union subscription deduction arrangements, such that they must be authorised by the worker in writing to the employer every three years. Section 69 provides that every member shall have a right to terminate membership in a trade union whether or not such a right is contained in the union rule book. Finally, it created a new institution, the Commissioner for the Rights of Trade Union Members (CROTUM), to arrange and finance legal advice and representation in litigation by members to enforce a wide range of statutory rights or claims of a breach or threatened breach of union rules.[12]

These measures make plain the Conservative Government's concern with the coercion of individuals by collective action in many forms. Section 65(2) goes so far as to suggest a rejection of the legitimacy of majority rule within a collective workforce, for it allows a worker to take part in a ballot for industrial action and then disregard the results of the majority. Its agenda is to create a 'fundamental right not' to strike. As the CBI and EEF have pointed out, this provision tends to undermine the stability of existing industrial relations arrangements. It may be an example of a labour legislative policy which has sacrificed the usual concern with managerial efficiency upon the altar of an ideological commitment to the freedom of the individual; alternatively it may be viewed as an attempt further to undermine the economic effects of collective action.

8 See discussion in Leader, S 'The European Convention on Human Rights, the Employment Act 1988 and the Right to Refuse to Strike' [1991] ILJ 39.

9 TULR(C)A s 109(1)(a)-(b) See discussion by Simpson [1991] MLR at pp 425-426.

10 See TURER, s 16.

11 See TURER, s 15.

12 See TULR(C)A, ss 109-114.

## CONCLUSIONS

More than a decade of labour legislation has effectively imposed upon trade unions a comprehensive web of legal regulation directed at industrial action. In marked contrast to the experience of the 1971-1974 period, the new legislative rules have become 'living law'.

Employers, after the 1982 Act, have made use of their legal sanctions against trade union organisations, in particular the remedy of the labour injunction. This has been used primarily against strikes called without secret ballots (almost two-thirds), but also against secondary action, and unlawful picketing.[13] The attractions of injunctive relief to employers were enhanced by the courts' exercise of discretion in enforcing orders for contempts of court by fines and sequestration.[14]

Compliance with court orders has been substantial but not complete. Evans's investigations found that injunctions resulted in an immediate lifting of the industrial action or withdrawal of official support in three-quarters of the cases studied; unionists ignored injunctions in almost more than one-quarter of the cases.[15] The availability of the new remedy and the demonstrable willingness of employers to make use of it has clearly had a deterrent effect.

The evidence for this consists of the way there has been a steady increase in the use of ballots before industrial action and the extent to which unions have introduced changes in their rule books to adopt the balloting requirement. Moreover, trade unions have centralised the formal authority to endorse strikes. Finally, there is empirical evidence that secondary action and secondary picketing have declined.

At the same time, the new legal rules and remedies have also been used as part of the negotiation process by both sides. In the early cases employers dealt with the failure to ballot in particular by raising the legal stick of an application for an injunction and then dropping the legal action once a settlement has been reached.

However, the overwhelming majority of strike ballots have been held without legal intervention and in 1989 84% resulted in a vote in favour of industrial action. Trade unions have also discovered that once favourable strike ballots have been secured, they can operate as a lever to extract employer concessions without industrial action. Ballots are fast becoming a permanent part of negotiation processes.[16]

13 Evans 'The Use of Injunctions in Labour Disputes' (1987) BJIR 419. See eg *London Underground Ltd v NUR* [1989] IRLR 341; *London Underground Ltd v NUR (No 2)* [1989] IRLR 343; *Blue Circle v TGWU* (7 July 1989, unreported); *Associated British Ports v TGWU* [1989] ICR 557, CA and HL.

14 See O'Regan 'Contempt of Court and the Enforcement of Labour Injunctions' (1991) MLR 385.

15 Evans 'The Use of Injunctions in Labour Disputes' (1987) BJIR 419.

With collective labour relations now placed under a system of comprehensive legal control, it has become fashionable to describe them as 'juridified' in the sense that they are closely intertwined with legal norms and that legal processes of dispute resolution replace disruptive social processes of dispute resolution such as industrial action. Along with employers, employees and trade unions are making increasing use of legal action as a device to resolve industrial disputes.[17] Yet what has been the impact of this phase of juridification? In its current phase, legislation clearly places obstacles in the way of trade unions recruiting in new areas and increasing trade union membership. In particular, the narrowing of trade union immunities has created difficulty for unions to make use of secondary industrial pressure and unofficial action to support trade union recognition demands. Moreover, it reinforces and encourages employer policies of derecognition and decollectivisation. However, it has not extinguished bargaining power in established trade union sectors, where workforces are not dependent upon secondary action. As the effect of the 1979-1981 depression began to wear off and the British economy improved its performance in the late 1980s, the bargaining power of trade unions in key collective bargaining sectors was sufficient to raise wage levels once again. Restrictive labour laws are not an assurance of restricted economic power of unionised employees.

Moreover, while the scale of collective bargaining in the 1990s is under threat owing to the changing attitudes of employers who are increasingly 'reconsidering the centrality and significance of collective bargaining arrangements with their organisation',[18] it is still the case that more than 60% of the workforce are covered by collective agreements.

Furthermore, the Labour Government now proposes to give a measure of legal support to trade unions in 'Fairness at Work'.

Consequently, it would be a mistake for the student or practitioner of labour law to assume that the subject can be understood by reference solely to its legal sources: legislation and the caselaw. An understanding of the inter-relationship between law, collective bargaining and industrial relations remains a *sine qua non* for the effective understanding of labour law.

16 ACAS, Annual Report, 1987. Cf Brown and Wadhwami 'Impact of Industrial Relations Laws on the Economy Nat'l Inst Econ Rev' Feb (1990).

17 See eg ACAS, Annual Report, 1992.

18 ACAS, Annual Report, 1992 p 19; see too Smith and Morton 'Union Exclusion and the Decollectivisation of Industrial Relations in Contemporary Britain' (1993) BJIR, March.

APPENDIX

# Fairness at Work (Cm 3968)

## ANNEX I A STATUTORY PROCEDURE FOR TRADE UNION RECOGNITION

### The procedure for obtaining recognition

(i) An independent trade union, or group of two or more independent unions acting jointly, which wishes to be recognised in a business with more than 20 employees will submit a formal request to the employer, in writing, specifying the group of employees on behalf of whom it is seeking recognition ('the bargaining unit'). (For simplicity the following description refers to a single union, but such references should be read as covering two or more unions acting jointly.) Employers will remain free to recognise voluntarily unions which do not hold a certificate of independence, and existing recognition of such unions can continue, but non-independent unions may not invoke the statutory procedure to obtain recognition.

(ii) The employer will have 14 days from the receipt of the request to respond; if the employer agrees to the request then the formal procedure will be closed; if the employer, while not accepting the request, for example because he does not agree that the group of employees proposed by the union is an appropriate bargaining unit, is willing to negotiate with the union, then the employer and union will have at least 28 days in which to try to reach an agreement. If both parties consent, they may invite ACAS to assist them in reaching an agreement. They may continue to negotiate for as long as both sides are willing.

(iii) If the employer does not respond to the union request within 14 days, or if he rejects it and refuses to negotiate, the union may, at the end of that period, make an immediate application for the Central Arbitration Committee:

a. to determine whether the bargaining unit proposed by the union is appropriate, and if not, to specify what would be an appropriate bargaining unit; and/or

b. to determine whether the union has the support of a majority of the employees in the appropriate bargaining unit.

The CAC, having received an eligible application, will first examine whether there is prima facie evidence that the union enjoys a reasonable level of support such as to make it likely that there could be a majority in favour of union recognition in the bargaining unit. Evidence of reasonable support might take the form of membership records or a petition signed by a sufficient number of employees. The employer too may submit evidence. If the CAC is not satisfied that the union has sufficient support, it will not proceed with the application. In consultation with interested parties, the Government will draw up guidance for the CAC on how reasonable support should be defined.

(iv) A union may also make an application for the CAC to determine either or both of the above questions if the employer and union have been unable to agree on one or both issues and at least 28 days have elapsed since the employer first responded to the union's request. However, the CAC will not entertain an application if, within 14 days of responding to the union's request, the employer proposed, without conditions, that the parties seek the assistance of ACAS but the union refused. Nor will the CAC entertain an application if it has evidence that another trade union is already recognised in respect of some or all of the employees concerned. In the event that two or more unions separately make applications with reasonable support in respect of the same group or overlapping groups of employees, the CAC will cease all work on those applications.

As indicated above, two or more unions may combine to seek joint recognition in respect of a group of employees, and may, if necessary, submit a joint application to the CAC. Where competing or overlapping applications have been made, they may be withdrawn, whereupon a single union or two or more acting jointly may recommence the procedure for recognition by making a single request for recognition. The TUC may attempt to resolve disputes between its affiliates but this will not be part of the statutory procedure.

(v) Where the CAC decides to proceed with an application, it will first try to broker an agreement between the employer and union, allowing up to 28 days for this stage; if at the end of that period the employer and union remain at odds over whether the bargaining unit proposed by the union is appropriate, the CAC will, normally within seven days, determine the appropriate bargaining unit(s). In doing so, the CAC should take particular account of the bargaining unit's compatibility with the need for effective management, as well as:

- the views of the employer and of the union;
- any existing national or local bargaining arrangements;
- the desirability as a general rule of avoiding small, fragmented bargaining units within an undertaking;
- the characteristics of the employees in the bargaining group proposed by the union and of any other of the employer's employees whom the CAC consider relevant; and
- the location of employees.

The CAC may decide that the appropriate bargaining unit is that proposed by the union, a group proposed by the employer, or a different group identified by the CAC (which might be the whole of the employer's workforce or any smaller group).

If the CAC decides on a different bargaining unit to that proposed by the union, it will be able to reject any application if the union cannot show a reasonable level of support for recognition in that unit (see (iii) above). The union itself may feel it has no chance of success in a ballot, and should therefore be able to withdraw its application at any time. Equally, if the employer drops his objections to the union application, the parties should be able to reach an agreed settlement and discontinue the procedure at any time.

(vi) Once the bargaining unit has been agreed, or decided by the CAC, the employer may accept that the union enjoys the support of a majority of the workforce. In this case the CAC will issue a declaration that the union is recognised for the bargaining unit in question. The CAC will also issue a declaration if it is satisfied, having examined carefully suitable evidence from the union and, if it wishes, from the employer, that more than 50% of the bargaining unit are members of the union seeking recognition. Otherwise the CAC will arrange for a secret ballot of the bargaining unit to be conducted by an independent body which is qualified to act as a scrutineer in industrial action ballots. The ballot will normally be carried out within 21 days of the determination of the bargaining unit. During that period, the employer will grant the union reasonable access to the employees to be balloted. The Government is minded to ask ACAS to draw up a statutory Code of Practice to help employers and unions understand what reasonable access means in practice. Employees who campaign for or against recognition or union membership will be protected against dismissal or action short of dismissal. If the scrutineer is satisfied, for example after consulting the employer and the union, that there is no risk of improper interference, the ballot may be conducted at the workplace. Otherwise it will be a postal ballot with voting papers sent to employees' home addresses. The employer will be under a legal duty to co-operate with both the body conducting the ballot and the trade union, to provide both with the names and, if the ballot is postal, addresses of the employees to be balloted. As far as is reasonably practicable, every member of the bargaining unit agreed or decided by the CAC will be entitled and able to vote, but nobody else. The cost of the ballot will be shared equally between the employer and the union.

(vii) The body conducting the ballot will notify the result to the CAC, the employer and the union. The CAC will issue a declaration that the union is to be recognised for the bargaining unit agreed or decided by the CAC provided that a majority of those voting and at least 40% of those eligible to vote have supported recognition, Otherwise it will issue a declaration that the union is not recognised.

## The consequences of recognition

(vii) Where a union has achieved recognition through this procedure (because the employer has agreed to recognition - see step (ii) above, or following the involvement of ACAS and/or the CAC), the employer and the union must try to reach a procedure agreement to give effect to recognition and set out how they will conduct collective bargaining. If both parties consent, they may invite ACAS to assist them. Such an agreement may, if the parties wish and so indicate in the agreement, be legally binding (as is the case under the existing law), and could then be enforced through the courts.

However, if, after three months from the date of the employer's agreement to recognition or the CAC declaration, as the case may be, no agreement has been reached, the union may apply to the CAC to have a default procedure agreement applied (though again negotiations can be extended if both sides agree). The CAC will first try to broker an agreement between the employer and the union. If at the end of a period which it considers reasonable in the circumstances the CAC has been unable to reach an agreement with the parties, it may impose a collective bargaining procedure which will be legally binding on both parties. The procedure will be based on a model laid down in legislation and drawn up with the advice of ACAS, with such amendments as the CAC considers desirable in the specific circumstances. It will provide for collective bargaining to cover pay, hours and holidays as a minimum. There are conflicting views on whether training should also be included. The Government would welcome responses on this point. The parties may add other items if they wish.

The terms of agreements resulting from collective bargaining are normally incorporated into individual employees' contracts either explicitly or by custom and practice and thus set the minimum terms and conditions for all employees in the bargaining unit. Under the existing law an employer and employee can agree different terms if they wish. Since the current law allows flexibility and works well, the Government sees no reason to change it.

## Enforcement

(ix) Since the procedure will be legally binding, by way of a deemed contract between employer and union, either party will be able to apply to a court if it believes the other is in breach of the procedure. A court could make an order for specific performance. Failure to comply with such an order could be a contempt of court.

(x) An independent union or an employer may also apply to the CAC in order to have the default procedure applied if it considers that the other party is not honouring the terms of a recognition agreement which is not legally binding, whether negotiated before the procedure came into force, outside this procedure or following a CAC recognition declaration. On receipt of such an application the CAC will notify the employer and allow the parties one month to try to reach an agreement. If they fail to do so, the CAC will impose a legally binding collective bargaining procedure in the same way as in the second paragraph of (viii).

## Derecognition

(xi) There will be a broadly similar procedure for resolving disputes where an employer seeks to derecognise a union because he believes the majority of the bargaining unit no longer supports recognition. The Government invites views on how and in what circumstances this procedure should apply.

## Renewed applications for recognition or derecognition

(xii) Where a union has unsuccessfully applied for recognition for a group of employees, the CAC will not entertain a new application by that union for recognition in respect of the same or substantially the same group within a period of three years from the date of the declaration on the first application. Similarly, the CAC will not entertain an application for derecognition within three years of either a recognition declaration or an unsuccessful request for derecognition.

## Changing the bargaining unit

(xiii) There may be circumstances, eg following business restructuring, take-over, divestment, merger of unions, where it is appropriate for the bargaining unit to be changed. The law will need to make allowance for this. If, following a change in circumstances which affects the relevance of the bargaining unit, the employer and the union are unable to agree on whether the bargaining unit for which the union is recognised should change, either may apply to the CAC for a fresh determination of the bargaining unit. If the CAC determines that the bargaining unit should include employees who were not previously part of it, the employer may seek to invoke the derecognition procedure, in which case the normal procedure will apply. In all other circumstances the existing recognition arrangements will apply to the new bargaining unit subject to any modifications agreed between the employer and the union or judged appropriate by the CAC where it has applied a default procedure.

# ANNEX II SUMMARY OF PROPOSALS AND ISSUES FOR CONSULTATION

## New Rights for Individuals

The Government **proposes** to:

1. reduce the qualifying period for protection against unfair dismissal to one year (paragraph 3.10)
2. abolish the maximum limit on awards for unfair dismissal (paragraph 3.5)
3. introduce legislation to index-link limits on statutory awards and payments, subject to a maximum rate (paragraph 3.8)

and the Government **invites views** on:

4. whether the limits on additional and special awards should be retained, or tribunals should be able to award aggravated damages (paragraph 3.7)
5. its options for changing the law which allows employees with fixed term contracts to waive their right to unfair dismissal and statutory redundancy payments (paragraph 3.13)
6. whether further action should be taken to address the potential abuse of zero hours contracts and, if so, how to take this forward without undermining labour market flexibility (paragraph 3.16)
7. whether legislation should be introduced to extend the coverage of some or all existing employment rights by regulation to all those who work for another person (paragraph 3.18)

## Collective Rights

The Government **proposes** to:

8. enable employees to have a trade union recognised by their employer where the majority of the relevant workforce wishes it. Statutory procedures for both recognition and derecognition will be introduced (paragraph 4.11)
9. change the law in line with its belief that in general those dismissed for taking part in lawfully organised official industrial action should have the right to complain to a tribunal of unfair dismissal (paragraph 4.22)
10. make it unlawful to discriminate by omission on grounds of trade union membership, non-membership or activities (paragraph 4.25)
11. prohibit blacklisting of trade unionists (paragraph 4.25)
12. amend the law on industrial action ballots and notice to make clear that, while the union's notice to the employer should still identify as accurately as reasonably practicable the group or category of employees concerned, it need not give names (paragraph 4.27)
13. create a legal right for employees to be accompanied by a fellow employee or trade union representative of their choice during grievance and disciplinary procedures (paragraph 4.29)
14. abolish the CROTUM and CPAUIA and give new powers to the Certification Officer to hear complaints involving most aspects of the law where CROTUM is currently empowered to provide assistance (paragraph 4.31)
15. make funds available to contribute to the training of managers and employee representatives in order to assist and develop partnerships at work (paragraph 2.7)

and the Government **invites views** on:

16. whether training should be among the matters automatically covered by an award of trade union recognition (paragraph 4.18)
17. how a procedure for derecognition should work (paragraph 4.18)
18. how protection against dismissal for those taking part in lawfully organised industrial action should be implemented (paragraph 4.23)
19. how to simplify the law and Code of Practice on industrial action ballots and notice (paragraph 4.26)

## Family-Friendly Policies

The Government **proposes** to:

20. extend maternity leave to 18 weeks, to align it with maternity pay (paragraph 5.14)

21. give employees rights to extended maternity absence and to parental leave after one year's service (paragraph 5.19)
22. provide for the contract of employment to continue during the whole period of maternity or parental leave, unless it is expressly terminated by either party, by dismissal or resignation (paragraph 5.21)
23. provide similar rights for employees to return to their jobs after parental leave as currently apply after maternity absence (paragraph 5.22)
24. provide three months' parental leave for adoptive parents (paragraph 5.23)
25. provide a right to reasonable time off for family emergencies, which will apply to all employees regardless of length of service (paragraph 5.28)
26. ensure that employees are protected against dismissal or detriment if they exercise their rights to parental leave and time off for urgent family reasons (paragraph 5.29)

and **invites views** on:

27. simplifying notice of maternity leave (paragraph 5.17)
28. its options for framing legislation to comply with the Parental Leave Directive (paragraph 5.16)
29. the particular difficulties small firms might face in complying with the Directive on parental leave (paragraph 5.26)

# Index